Lecture Notes in Computer Science 1781

Edited by G. Goos, J. Hartmanis and J. van Leeuwen

Springer
Berlin
Heidelberg
New York
Barcelona
Hong Kong
London
Milan
Paris
Singapore
Tokyo

David A. Watt (Ed.)

Compiler Construction

9th International Conference, CC 2000
Held as Part of the Joint European Conferences
on Theory and Practice of Software, ETAPS 2000
Berlin, Germany, March 25 - April 2, 2000
Proceedings

Springer

Series Editors

Gerhard Goos, Karlsruhe University, Germany
Juris Hartmanis, Cornell University, NY, USA
Jan van Leeuwen, Utrecht University, The Netherlands

Volume Editor

David A. Watt
University of Glasgow
Department of Computing Science
Glasgow G12 8QQ, Scotland
E-mail: daw@dcs.gla.ac.uk

Cataloging-in-Publication Data applied for

Die Deutsche Bibliothek - CIP-Einheitsaufnahme

Compiler construction : 9th international conference ; proceedings /
CC 2000, held as part of the Joint European Conferences on Theory and
Practice of Software, ETAPS 2000, Berlin, Germany, March 25 - April 2,
2000 / David A. Watt (ed.). - Berlin ; Heidelberg ; New York ;
Barcelona ; Hong Kong ; London ; Milan ; Paris ; Singapore ; Tokyo :
Springer, 2000
    (Lecture notes in computer science ; Vol. 1781)
    ISBN 3-540-67263-X

CR Subject Classification (1991): D.3.4, D.3.1, F.4.2, D.2.6, I.2.2

ISSN 0302-9743
ISBN 3-540-67263-X Springer-Verlag Berlin Heidelberg New York

Springer-Verlag is a company in the BertelsmannSpringer publishing group.
© Springer-Verlag Berlin Heidelberg 2000

Typesetting: Camera-ready by author, data conversion by DA-TeX Gerd Blumenstein
Printed on acid-free paper   SPIN 10719928   06/3142 5 4 3 2 1 0

Foreword

ETAPS 2000 was the third instance of the European Joint Conferences on Theory and Practice of Software. ETAPS is an annual federated conference that was established in 1998 by combining a number of existing and new conferences. This year it comprised five conferences (FOSSACS, FASE, ESOP, CC, TACAS), five satellite workshops (CBS, CMCS, CoFI, GRATRA, INT), seven invited lectures, a panel discussion, and ten tutorials.

The events that comprise ETAPS address various aspects of the system development process, including specification, design, implementation, analysis, and improvement. The languages, methodologies, and tools which support these activities are all well within its scope. Different blends of theory and practice are represented, with an inclination towards theory with a practical motivation on one hand and soundly-based practice on the other. Many of the issues involved in software design apply to systems in general, including hardware systems, and the emphasis on software is not intended to be exclusive.

ETAPS is a loose confederation in which each event retains its own identity, with a separate program committee and independent proceedings. Its format is open-ended, allowing it to grow and evolve as time goes by. Contributed talks and system demonstrations are in synchronized parallel sessions, with invited lectures in plenary sessions. Two of the invited lectures are reserved for "unifying" talks on topics of interest to the whole range of ETAPS attendees. The aim of cramming all this activity into a single one-week meeting is to create a strong magnet for academic and industrial researchers working on topics within its scope, giving them the opportunity to learn about research in related areas, and thereby to foster new and existing links between work in areas that were formerly addressed in separate meetings. The program of ETAPS 2000 included a public business meeting where participants had the opportunity to learn about the present and future organization of ETAPS and to express their opinions about what is bad, what is good, and what might be improved.

ETAPS 2000 was hosted by the Technical University of Berlin and was efficiently organized by the following team:

Bernd Mahr (General Chair)
Hartmut Ehrig (Program Coordination)
Peter Pepper (Organization)
Stefan Jähnichen (Finances)
Radu Popescu-Zeletin (Industrial Relations)

with the assistance of BWO Marketing Service GmbH. The publicity was superbly handled by Doris Fähndrich of the TU Berlin with assistance from the ETAPS publicity chair, Andreas Podelski. Overall planning for ETAPS conferences is the responsibility of the ETAPS steering committee, whose current membership is:

Egidio Astesiano (Genova), Jan Bergstra (Amsterdam), Pierpaolo Degano (Pisa), Hartmut Ehrig (Berlin), José Fiadeiro (Lisbon), Marie-Claude Gaudel (Paris), Susanne Graf (Grenoble), Furio Honsell (Udine), Heinrich Hußmann (Dresden), Stefan Jähnichen (Berlin), Paul Klint (Amsterdam), Tom Maibaum (London), Tiziana Margaria (Dortmund), Ugo Montanari (Pisa), Hanne Riis Nielson (Aarhus), Fernando Orejas (Barcelona), Andreas Podelski (Saarbrücken), David Sands (Göteborg), Don Sannella (Edinburgh), Gert Smolka (Saarbrücken), Bernhard Steffen (Dortmund), Wolfgang Thomas (Aachen), Jerzy Tiuryn (Warsaw), David Watt (Glasgow), Reinhard Wilhelm (Saarbrücken)

ETAPS 2000 received generous sponsorship from:

the Institute for Communication and Software Technology of TU Berlin
the European Association for Programming Languages and Systems
the European Association for Theoretical Computer Science
the European Association for Software Development Science
the "High-Level Scientific Conferences" component of the European
  Commission's Fifth Framework Programme

I would like to express my sincere gratitude to all of these people and organizations, the program committee members of the ETAPS conferences, the organizers of the satellite events, the speakers themselves, and finally Springer-Verlag for agreeing to publish the ETAPS proceedings.

January 2000   Donald Sannella
                                    ETAPS Steering Committee Chairman

Preface

The International Conference in Compiler Construction (CC) is a forum for presentation and discussion of recent developments in language processors and language design. It emphasizes practical methods and tools. CC 2000 was the ninth conference in the series.

The CC conference originated as a series of workshops organized since 1986 by Günter Riedewald in East Germany. In 1992 the series was relaunched by Uwe Kastens in Paderborn. It was highly appropriate that the first CC conference of the new millennium should take place in Berlin, newly restored as the capital city of reunified Germany.

The CC conference, originally biennial, federated to ETAPS in 1998 and became annual. Despite that major change, the number of submissions and the number of accepted papers have remained stable. The program committee received 46 submissions for CC 2000, from which eighteen high-quality papers were selected for presentation. These papers are included in these proceedings.

The invited speaker at CC 2000 was Reinhard Wilhelm, whose talk was entitled *Shape Analysis*. A paper based on the invited talk opens these proceedings.

The work of the CC 2000 program committee was conducted entirely by electronic means. This made it practicable for all program committee members to participate fully in discussions of individual papers, to re-read papers, and in some cases to provide extra reviews. I believe that the quality of the paper selection process benefited greatly from this mode of working.

I am glad to acknowledge the hard work and friendly cooperation of all my colleagues on the program committee. I also wish to thank the much larger number of additional reviewers who helped us to read and evaluate the submitted papers. As a first-time program chair I have particular reason to appreciate the support and advice of the ETAPS chair, Don Sannella, and of the CC steering committee. Finally, I wish to thank all the authors of submitted papers for their continued interest, without which the CC conference could not thrive.

January 2000   David Watt

CC Steering Committee

Peter Fritzson (Sweden)   Kai Koskimies (Finland)
Tibor Gyimothi (Hungary)   David Watt (UK)
Stefan Jähnichen (Germany)   Reinhard Wilhelm (Germany)
Uwe Kastens (Germany)

CC 2000 Program Committee

Rudolf Eigenman (USA)
Christine Eisenbeis (France)
Christian Ferdinand (Germany)
Guang Gao (USA)
Görel Hedin (Sweden)
Olivier Michel (France)
Simon Peyton Jones (UK)
Lawrence Rauchwerger (USA)

Mooly Sagiv (Israel)
Helmut Seidl (Germany)
Martin Simons (Germany)
Chau-Wen Tseng (USA)
Bruce Watson (South Africa)
David Watt (UK, chair)
Hans Zima (Austria)

CC 2000 Reviewers

Gagan Agrawal
José Nelson Amaral
Brian Armstrong
Denis Barthou
Siegfried Benkner
Peter Brezany
Manuel Chakravarty
Jong-Deok Choi
Philippe Clauss
Albert Cohen
Jean-François Collard
Graham Collins
Charles Consel
Aino Cornils
Ron Cytron
Franck Delaplace
Nurit Dor
Étienne Duris
Daniel Étiemble
Paul Feautrier
Ines Fey
Cedric Fournet
Jean-Louis Giavitto
Manish Gupta
David Hanson
Paul Havlak
Chung-Hsing Hsu
François Irigoin
Anders Ive

Alin Jula
Daniel Kaestner
Richard Kennell
Christoph Kessler
Seon Wook Kim
Torsten Klein
Marc Langenbach
James Larus
Erwin Laure
Daniel Lavery
Jaejin Lee
Xavier Leroy
Tal Lev-Ami
Wei Li
Eva Magnusson
Florian Martin
Wellington Martins
Éduard Mehofer
Oege de Moor
Rishiyur Nikhil
Anders Nilsson
Rinetskey Noam
Preeti Ranjan Panda
Sven Panne
Insung Park
Michael Parkes
Jonas Persson
Patrik Persson
Wolf Pfannenstiel

Sara Porat
Jan Prins
James Riely
Martin Rinard
Sven Robertz
Erven Rohou
Bernhard Scholz
Ran Shaham
Viera Sipkova
Anthony Sloane
V.C. Sreedhar
Arthur Stoutchinin
Doaitse Swierstra
Clemens Szyperski
Olivier Temam
Alexandre Tessier
Henrik Theiling
Stephan Thesing
François Thomasset
Michael Voss
Philip Wadler
David Wakeling
Reinhard Wilhelm
Eran Yahav
Hongbo Yang
Pen-Chung Yew
Hao Yu
Chihong Zhang
Wolf Zimmermann

Table of Contents

Shape Analysis

Reinhard Wilhelm[1], Mooly Sagiv[2], and Thomas Reps[3]

[1] Fachbereich Informatik,
Universität des Saarlandes
[2] Department of Computer Science,
Tel-Aviv University
[3] Computer Science Department,
University of Wisconsin at Madison

Abstract. A shape-analysis algorithm statically analyzes a program to determine information about the heap-allocated data structures that the program manipulates. The results can be used to understand or verify programs. They also contain information valuable for debugging, compile-time garbage collection, instruction scheduling, and parallelization.

1 Introduction

Pointers and anonymous objects stored in the heap seem to be the dark corner of imperative programming languages. There are only a few treatments of the semantics of pointers. Most semantic descriptions of imperative programming languages even assume the nonexistence of pointers, since otherwise the semantics of an assignment statement becomes much more complex. The reason is that an assignment through a pointer variable or pointer component may have far reaching side-effects.

These far reaching side-effects also make program dependence analysis harder, since they make it difficult to compute the aliasing relationships among different pointer expressions in a program. Having less precise program dependence information decreases the opportunities for automatic parallelization and for instruction scheduling.

The usage of pointers is error prone. Dereferencing NULL pointers and accessing previously deallocated storage are two common programming mistakes. The usage of pointers in programs is thus an obstacle for program understanding, debugging, and optimization. These activities need answers to many questions about the structure of the heap contents and the pointer variables pointing into the heap.

Shape analysis is a generic term denoting static program-analysis techniques attempting to determine properties of the heap contents relevant for the applications mentioned above.

1.1 Structure of the Paper

The structure of the paper is as follows: In Section 2, a number of questions about the contents of the heap are listed. Subsection 2.1 presents a program that will

A. Watt (Ed.): CC/ETAPS 2000, LNCS 1781, pp. 1–17, 2000.

be used as a running example, a program that destructively reverses a singly linked list. Subsection 2.2 shows how shape analysis would answer the questions about the heap contents produced by this program. Section 3 then introduces a parametric shape analysis along the lines of [23], which provides for a generative way to design and implement shape-analysis algorithms. The "shape semantics" plus some additional properties that individual storage elements may or may not possess are specified in logic, and the shape-analysis algorithm is automatically generated from such a specification. Throughout the paper, abstraction functions and transfer functions are given intuitively, by means of examples. Section 4 presents experience obtained via an implementation done in Java. Section 5 briefly discusses related work. Section 6 presents some conclusions.

2   Questions About the Heap Contents

Shape analysis has a somewhat constrained view of programs. It is not interested in numerical or string values that programs compute, but exclusively in the linked structures they build in the heap and in the pointers into the heap from the stack, from global memory, or from cells in the heap. We will therefore use the term *execution state* to mean the set of cells in the heap and their connectivity by pointer components of heap cells and the values of pointer variables in the store.

Among the questions about execution states that we might wish to pose at points in a program are:

NULL-pointers: May a pointer variable or a pointer component of a heap cell contain NULL? This is valuable debugging information at the entry of a statement attempting to dereference this pointer.

May-Alias: May two pointer expressions reference the same heap cell? The absence of may-aliasing can be used for improving program dependence information [3,20].

Must-Alias: Will two pointer expressions always denote the same heap cell? This may be used to predict a cache hit or to trigger a prefetch.

Sharing: May a heap cell be shared?[1] There are many uses for such information. Explicit deallocation of a shared node may leave the storage manager in an inconsistent state (e.g., if the heap cell is deallocated twice – by calls on the deallocator at each predecessor). A nonshared cell may be explicitly deallocated when the last pointer to it ceases to exist. This again is valuable for debugging.

Reachability: Is a heap cell reachable from a specific variable or from any pointer variable? Unreachable cells are certainly garbage.

Disjointness: Will two data structures pointed to by two distinct pointer variables ever have common elements? Disjoint data structures may be processed in parallel by different processors and may be stored in different memories [8].

---

[1]   Later on in the paper the term "shared" means "heap-shared" i.e., pointed to by two or more pointer components of heap cells. Sharing due to two pointer variables or one pointer variable and one heap cell component pointing to the same heap cell is also deducible from the results of shape analysis.

Cyclicity: May a heap cell be part of a cycle? If not, garbage collection could be done by reference counting.

Shape: What will be the "shape" of (some part of) the heap contents? Shapes (or, more precisely, shape descriptors) characterize data structures. A shape descriptor could indicate whether the heap contains a singly linked list, potentially with/definitely without a cycle, a doubly linked list, a binary tree, etc. Many of the properties listed above are ingredients of shape analyses, e.g., sharing, cyclicity, reachability, disjointness.

Shape analysis can be understood as an extended type analysis; its results can be used as an aid in program understanding, debugging [6], and verification.

2.1 An Example: Destructive Reverse

The following program, `reverse`, is used as a running example. It destructively reverses a list pointed to by `x` into one pointed to by `y`.

```
/* reverse.c */
#include "list.h"
List reverse(List x) {
    List y, t;
    y = NULL;
    while (x != NULL) {
        t = y;
        y = x;
        x = x->n;
        y->n = NULL;
        y->n = t;
    }
    return y;
}
```

It assumes the declaration of a `List` data type

```
/* list.h */
typedef struct node {
    struct node *n;
    int data;
} *List
```

The control flow graph of `reverse` is reproduced in Fig. 1. The program points are labeled for ease of reference. The body of the loop does the following: Pointer variable `t` holds on to the current y-list (n_3), while `y`

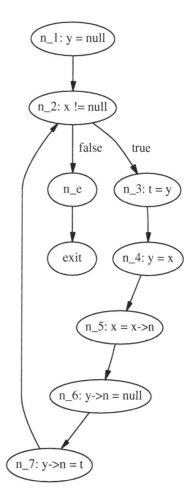

Fig. 1. Flow graph of a list-reversal program

grabs the head of the current x-list (n_4). x is then moved to the tail of the current x-list (n_5). y->n is first nulllified (n_6) and then made to connect the new head to the old y-list (n_7) [2].

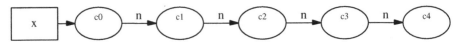

Fig. 2. An input list for reverse

The workings of reverse is exemplified on the input list shown in Fig. 2. Table 1 shows the execution state after n_3 during the first four iterations of the loop.

Let us assume that the input to this program will be a non-empty acyclic singly linked list made up of unshared elements like the one shown in Fig. 2. Some correct answers to the questions listed in Section 2 would be:

after n_3:
  - x and y point to acyclic singly linked lists; the y-list may be empty,
  - t and y are may- and must-aliases or both point to NULL.
  - x never points to NULL,
  - the lists to which x and y point are disjoint,
  - no list element is heap-shared.

after n_4: x and y are must-aliases, and therefore also may-aliases.

after n_5: x and y are not may-aliases, and therefore not must-aliases. (Note that this would not be the case if the initial x-list contained a cycle).

everywhere: there are no garbage cells.

2.2   Answers as Given by Shape Analysis

Shape analysis will be started under the aforementioned assumption that the input to the program will be a non-empty acyclic singly linked list. This is expressed by the so-called shape graphs shown in Fig. 3.

Shape analysis of reverse will produce information for each program point about the lists that can arise there. For program point n_3, the results would be given as the shape graphs shown in Fig. 4.

These graphs should be interpreted as follows:

  - A rectangular box containing the name p represents pointer variable p. The pointer variables of program reverse, namely x, y, and t, appear boxed in the shape graphs in Figures 3 and 4.

---

[2] Splitting this assignment into two steps is done to simplify the definition of the semantics.

Table 1. The first four iterations of the loop in **reverse** after n_3

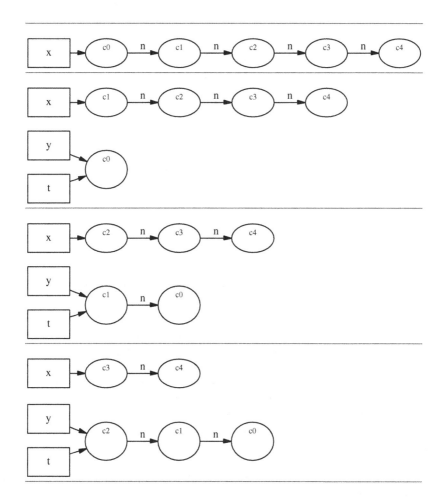

- Ovals stand for abstract locations. A solid oval stands for an abstract location
  that represents exactly one heap cell. In Fig. 3(b), the oval u represents the
  one cell of an input list of length 1.
  A dotted oval box stands for an abstract location that may represent one
  or more heap cells; in Fig. 3(a) the dotted oval u represents the cells in the
  tail of the input list. In the example input list shown in Fig. 2, these are the
  cells $c1, c2, c3$, and $c4$.
- A solid edge labeled c between abstract locations m and m' represents the
  fact that the c-component of the heap cell represented by m will point to
  the heap cell represented by m'. Fig. 4(e) indicates that the n-component of
  the heap cell represented by u will point to the heap cell represented by $u0$.

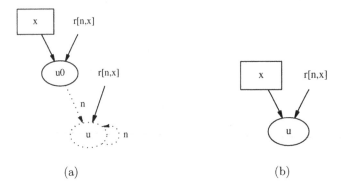

(a)   (b)

Fig. 3. A description of the input to **reverse**. (a) represents acyclic lists of length at least 2, (b) lists of length 1.

This edge represents the n-component of $c1$ pointing to $c0$ in the third figure in Table 1.

- A dotted edge labeled c between abstract locations m and m' tells us that the c-component of one of the heap cells represented by m may point to one of the heap cells represented by m'. In the case when m and m' are the same abstract location, this edge may or may not represent a cycle. In Fig. 4(d), the dotted self-cycle on location $m0$ represents n-components of heap cells represented by $m0$ possibly pointing to other heap cells represented by $m0$. Additional information about non-heap-sharing (see below) implies that, in this case, the dotted self-cycle does not represent a cycle in the heap.

  Fig. 4(d) represents the execution state of the second figure in Table 1. The dotted location $m0$ represents the heap cells $c2, c3, c4$; the dotted n-back-edge represents the two pointers from $c2$ to $c3$ and from $c3$ to $c4$, respectively.

- Other solid edges to an abstract location m represent properties that are definitely possesed by the heap cells represented by m. For example, a solid edge from a pointer variable p to m represents the fact that p will point to the heap cell represented by m, i.e., this heap cell will have the property "pointed-to-by-p". Another property in the example is "reachable-from-x-through-n", denoted in the graph by **r[n,x]**. It means that the heap cells represented by the corresponding abstract location are (transitively) reachable from pointer variable **x** through n-components.

  Solid ovals could be viewed as abstract locations having the property "uniquely representing", later on called "not-summarized".

- A dotted edge from a property to an abstract location indicates that the heap cells represented by that location may or may not have that property.

- The absence of an edge from a property to an abstract location m means that the heap cells represented by m definitely do not have this property.

  In Fig. 4(a), the absence of an edge from **y** to the location $u0$ means that **y** will definitely not point to the cell represented by $u0$. The absence of a

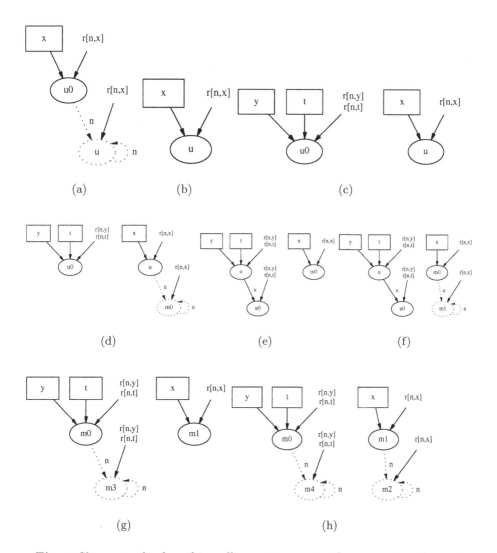

Fig. 4. Shape graphs describing all execution states that can arise after n_3

pointer variable p in a shape graph means that in the stores represented by this graph p points to NULL.

In the analysis of **reverse**, a very important heap cell property is **is** which means "is (heap-)shared". It does not show up in any of the graphs in Fig. 4, signifying that no heap cell is be shared in any of the execution states that can arise after n_3.

In summary, the shape graphs portray information of three kinds:

solid meaning "always holds" for properties (including "uniquely representing"),
absent meaning "never holds" for properties, and
dotted meaning "don't know" for properties (including "uniquely representing"),

In the following, "always holds" and "never holds" will be called *definite*
values of properties, while "don't know" will be called the *indefinite* value.

Each shape graph produced at some program point describes execution states
that could occur when execution reaches that program point. The set of all
graphs produced at some program point describes (a superset of) all the execution states that can occur whenever execution reaches that program point.

With this interpretation in mind, all the claims about the properties of the
heap contents after n_3 can be checked by verifying that they hold on all of the
graphs shown in Fig. 4.

3   Shape Analysis

The example program `reverse` works for lists of arbitrary lengths. However,
as was described in the preceding section (at least for one program point), the
description of the lists occurring during execution is finite: there are 8 graphs
describing all x- and y-lists arising after n_3. This is a general requirement for
shape analysis. While the data structures that a program builds or manipulates
are in general of unbounded size, their shape descriptor has to have a *bounded
size*.

This representation of the heap contents has to be *conservative* in the sense
that whoever asks for properties of the heap contents—e.g., a compiler, a debugger, or a program understanding system—receives a reliable answer. The claim
that "pointer variable p or pointer component p->c never has the value NULL at
this program point" may only be made if indeed this is the case for all executions
of the program and all program paths leading to the program point. It may still
be the case that in no program execution p (resp. p->c) will be NULL at this
point, but that the analysis will be unable to derive this information. In the field
of program analysis, we say that program analysis is allowed to (only) "err on
the safe side."

In short, shape analysis computes for a given program and each point in the
program:

a finite, conservative representation of the heap-allocated data structures
that could arise when a path to this program point is executed.

3.1   Summarization

The constraint that we must work with a bounded representation implies a loss
of information about the heap contents. Size information, such as the lengths of

lists or the depths of trees, will in general be lost. However, structural information may also get lost due to the chosen representation. Thus, there is a part of
the execution state (or some of its properties) that is exactly represented, and
some part of the execution state (or some of its properties) that is only approxi-
matively represented. The process leading to the latter is called *summarization*.
Summarization intuitively means the following:

- Some heap cells will "lose their identity", i.e., will be represented together
  with other heap cells by one abstract location.
- The connectivity among those jointly represented heap cells will be represented conservatively, i.e., each pointer in the heap will be represented, but
  several such pointers (or the absence of such pointers) may be represented
  jointly.
- Properties of these heap cells will also be represented conservatively. This
  means the following:
  - a property that holds for all (for none of the) summarized cells will be
    found to hold (not to hold) for their summary location,
  - a property that holds for some but not all of the summarized cells will
    have the value "don't know" for the summary location.

As will be seen in Subsection 3.5, one of the main problems is how to extract
an abstract location from a summary location when (in a concrete execution
of the program) a pointer is advanced to one of the heap cells represented by
this summary location. This process will be called "materializing a new abstract
location out of a summary location".

3.2   Static Program Analysis

Shape analysis is a *static program analysis* technique. It can thus be couched in
terms of the theory of *Abstract Interpretation*, cf. [4,17]. The most important
ingredient of any static program analysis is an *abstraction function*. The abstraction function relates two worlds: in the case of shape analysis, the *concrete
world* of program execution states and the *abstract world* of shape graphs. It
maps an execution state to its bounded, conservative representation. The abstraction function does what is described as summarization above.

The *concrete semantics* of the programming language is given by a set of
functions f_{st} for each statement st of the language. They describe the effect
of the statements on an execution state. The *abstract semantics* describes the
effect of the statements on the representation of execution states. It is given in
the form of an *abstract transfer function* $f_{st}^{\#}$ for each statement st. Applying $f_{st}^{\#}$
will be called *abstractly executing st*.

3.3   Parametric Shape Analysis

"Shape analysis" is a generic term standing for a whole class of algorithms of
different power and complexity trying to answer questions about structures in

the heap. In our setting, a particular shape-analysis algorithm is determined by a set of properties that heap cells may have (and whose values will be tracked by the shape-analysis algorithm).

First, there are the *core properties*, e.g., the "pointed-to-by-p"-property for each program pointer variable p and the property "connected-through-c", which pairs of heap cells (l_1, l_2) possess if the c-component of l_1 points to l_2. These properties are part of any pointer semantics. The core properties in the particular shape analysis of the `reverse` program are "pointed-to-by-x", denoted just by x, "pointed-to-by-y", denoted by y, and "pointed-to-by-t", denoted by t, and "connected-through-n" denoted by n.

Further properties are called *instrumentation properties* [23]. They are determined by what the analysis is meant to observe. They are expressed in terms of the core properties. Our example analysis should find out properties of programs manipulating acyclic singly linked lists. Sharing properties are important to detect acyclicity. Reachability properties from specific pointer variables are important to keep disjoint sublists summarized separately when a pointer moves through a list.

Therefore, the instrumentation properties in our example analysis are "is-heap-shared", denoted by is, "reachable-from-x-through-n", denoted by r[n,x], "reachable-from-y-through-n", denoted by r[n,y], and "reachable-from-t-through-n", denoted by r[n,t]. A property existing in every shape analysis is "not-summarized".

3.4   Abstraction Functions

The abstraction function of a particular shape analysis is determined by a subset of the set of all properties, the so-called *abstraction properties*.[3] The principle is that heap cells that have the same definite values for the abstraction properties are summarized to the same abstract location. Thus, if we view the set of abstraction properties as our means of observing the contents of the heap, the heap cells summarized by one summary location have no observable difference.

In Fig. 3(a), all the cells in the tail of an input list of length at least two are summarized by the abstract location u, since they all have the property r[n,x] and do not have the properties x, y, t, r[n,y], r[n,t], is. The abstract location $u0$ represents exactly the first cell of the input list. It has the properties x and r[n,x] and none of the other properties.

3.5   Analyzing a Statement

An abstract semantics of the pointer statements available in the language has to be specified in some formalism. It describes how the core and the instrumentation properties change when a statement is executed.

The most complex statement involving pointers is the one that moves a pointer along a pointer component. In the `reverse` program there is one such statement, n_5: x=x->n. Its semantics will be described by means of an example.

---

[3] [23] uses only unary properties.

The shape graph in Fig. 5(a) describes some of the lists that can arise before program point n_5.

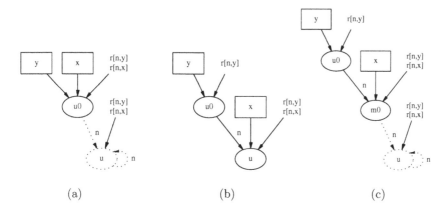

Fig. 5. (a): A shape graph that arises before n_5; (b) and (c): the two shape graphs resulting from (abstractly) executing x=x->n on shape graph (a).

At n_5 the statement x=x->n is (abstractly) executed. One candidate result might be the shape graph in which x has moved along the indefinite edge labeled n to point to the abstract location u. However, this would not be an acceptable shape graph, since it is not in the image of the abstraction function. To see this, note that a summarized abstract location representing one or more heap cells cannot have the definite property "pointed-to-by-x". The semantics of C (as well as of other languages with pointers) implies that any pointer variable or pointer component can only point to at most one cell at any one time. Hence, only two cases are possible: (i) x points to NULL, or (ii) x points to exactly one cell.

A better approach to creating the shape graph that results from (abstractly) executing x=x->n is to do a case analysis of the reasons why u's "not-summarized" property and the two n-edges are indefinite.

- The first case assumes that a definite n-edge exists starting at u0, and that u represents exactly one heap cell. What about the indefinite trivial cycle labeled n on u? The absence of an is-edge to u indicates that the cell represented by u is not shared. Thus, the back-edge from u to u in Fig. 5(a) cannot represent a concrete back pointer, since there is already one solid edge to u representing a concrete pointer. Hence, the indefinite back-edge from u to u has to be eliminated. The abstract execution of the statement x=x->n results in the graph shown in Fig. 5(b).
- The second case also assumes that a definite n-edge exists starting at u0. However, we now assume that u represents more than one heap cell. A new definite abstract location, called m0, is then "materialized" out of u. It represents the first of the cells in the tail of the x/y-list. The definite edge starting

at $u0$ is made to point to it. The argumentation about a potential back-edge to it is the same as in the first case: the newly materialized location does not have the property is and thus cannot be the target of a back-edge. The execution of the statement x=x->n results in the graph shown in Fig. 5(c).

– A third case would have the indefinite n-edge representing the absence of a pointer from the cell represented by $u0$ to any of the cells represented by u. However, this is incompatible with the fact that the r[n,x] and r[n,y] properties of u have the (definite) value 1. Hence, this case is impossible.

The less powerful a shape analysis is, the more information about the heap contents will in general be summarized. Most shape-analysis algorithms are exponential or even doubly exponential in some parameters derived from the program and some parameters determined by the set of properties to be observed.

4   Implementation and Experience

The three-valued-logics approach described in this paper has been implemented in the TVLA-engine (Three-Valued Logic Analysis) by Tal Lev-Ami at Tel-Aviv University [16]. This prototype implementation in Java is good for experimenting with analysis designs. Small examples like reverse can be analyzed in a few seconds on a Pentium 166 MHz PC. Bigger examples, e.g., Mobile Ambients [18], may take several hours.

A surprising experience was the following: Although one expects that a more precise analysis is more costly in terms of time and space, this is not necessarily true in three-valued logic based analyses: A more precise analysis may create fewer unneeded structures and thus run faster. For instance, Lev-Ami analyzed a program to sort the elements of a linked list. When a list-merge function was analyzed without reachability properties, the analysis created tens of thousands of graphs such that the machine ran out of space. Adding reachability properties reduced the number of graphs to 327 and the analysis time to 8 seconds.

A number of issues need to be addressed for the TVLA-engine to become a useful tool for large programs.

5   Related Work

Only a very brief account of related work can be given in this paper. A more detailed treatment is given in [22].

5.1   Types and Allocation Sites

One of the earliest properties of heap cells used for abstraction has been the point in the program at which the cells were allocated, i.e., their *allocation site* [12,2,24,1,19]. Cells allocated at different program points would never be represented jointly by one node. The motivation behind this approach was that "nodes allocated in different places probably are going to be treated differently, while all nodes allocated at a given place will probably be updated similarly" [2].

This is sometimes true and sometimes not true. For example, allocation-site information fails to keep abstract locations separate when all cells of a data structure are allocated at the same program point.

The methods described above use additional information such as sharing or heap reference counts to improve the precision of the results.

Types have also been used to partition the set of heap cells. In a typed language, a typed pointer may only point to cells of the appropriate type. They could be used if nothing else is available. However, they will lead only to very coarse representations because often all cells of a data structure have the same type.

Both allocation-site information and type information induce a static partition on the heap. This is in contrast with the approach described above, which induces a dynamic partition on the heap.

5.2 Pointer Variables

[25,21,22] used only the "pointed-to-by-p" properties to define the abstraction function. Additional information such as non-sharing information was used to improve precision. The algorithm given in [21,22] was the first to achieve *strong nullification* and *strong update* of pointer values for statements that modified pointer values. This means, the algorithm could delete or overwrite existing pointers in a conservative way. As a result it was able to materialize new nodes out of summary nodes as described in Section 3.5.

For efficiency reasons, the method presented in [21,22] (as well as the methods described in [12,15,14,2,24]) merged all the information available at a program point into one shape graph. This made the semantics hard to understand and implied a loss in precision. A more precise variant of this method (which is also easier to understand) is described in [17]. It uses sets of shape graphs at each program point.

5.3 k-Bounded Approaches

Another approach to represent unbounded structures in a bounded fashion is to choose a constant k and to represent everything "within a diameter k" precisely and to summarize heap cells outside of this diameter. Applied to our problem of shape analysis, this would mean representing lists precisely up to a length of k, trees up to a depth of k, and general graphs up to a diameter of k, and then summarizing the rest of the data structure. The approach of [11] corresponds to using the "reachable-from-p-via-access-path-α"-property with $|\alpha| \leq k$.

The Jones-Muchnick formulation has two drawbacks:

– The analysis yields poor results for programs that manipulate cons-cells beyond the k-horizon. For example, for the list-reversal program **reverse**, little useful information is obtained. The analysis algorithm must model

what happens when the program is applied to lists of lengths greater than k. However, the tail of such a list is treated conservatively, i.e., as an arbitrary, and possibly cyclic, data structure.
- The analysis may be extremely costly because the number of possible shape-graphs is doubly exponential in k.

In addition to Jones and Muchnick's work, k-limiting has also been used in a number of subsequent papers (e.g., [10]).

5.4   Methods Not Based on Shape Graphs

There are also several algorithms for finding may-alias information for pointer variables that are not based on shape-graphs. The most sophisticated ones are those of Landi and Ryder [13] and Deutsch [5]. For certain programs that manipulate lists, Deutsch's algorithm offers a way of representing the exact (infinite set of) may aliases in a compact way.

A different approach was taken by Hendren and Nicolau, who designed an algorithm that handles only acyclic data structures [9,7].

6   Conclusions

We conclude with a few general observations.

6.1   A Parametric Framework for Shape Analysis

The method that has been surveyed in this paper provides the basis for a *parametric* framework for shape analysis. Such a framework has two parts: (i) a language for specifying various properties that a heap cell may or may not possess, and how these properties are affected by the execution of the different kinds of statements in the programming language, and (ii) a method for generating a shape-analysis algorithm from such a description. The first is an issue having to do with *specification*; the specified set of properties determines the characteristics of the data-structure elements that the static analysis can distinguish. The second is an issue of how to generate an appropriate algorithm from the specification. The ideal is to have a fully automatic method—a yacc for shape analysis, so to speak: The "designer" of a shape-analysis algorithm supplies *only* the specification, and the shape-analysis algorithm is created automatically from this specification. The TVLA system discussed in Section 4 implements such a parametric framework.

Different instantiations of the framework create analyses that use different classes of shape graphs, and hence are prepared to identify different classes of store properties that hold at the different points in a program. Different classes of shape graphs may be needed, depending on the kinds of linked data structures used in a program and on the link-rearrangement operations performed by the program's statements. (In general, an instantiation of the framework will handle every program, but may produce conservative results due to the use of a class of shape graphs that does not make appropriate distinctions.) The essence of the particular shape-analysis methods discussed in Section 5 can be captured via different instantiations of the framework.

The instantiation of the analysis framework described in Subsection 3.3 is sufficiently powerful to successfully analyze the **reverse** program, which works on singly linked lists. It would also produce precise information on many other programs that deal with singly linked lists. However, it would fail on programs that operate on doubly linked lists, since the **is**-property would hold on all but the first and the last elements of such lists. An instantiation for doubly linked lists would need the following two properties:

forward-backward-pairing: If the forward-pointer of a heap cell $c1$ points to a heap cell $c2$, then the backward-pointer of $c2$ must point to $c1$.

backward-forward-pairing: If the backward-pointer of a heap cell $c1$ points to a heap cell $c2$, then the forward-pointer of $c2$ must point to $c1$.

Different versions of doubly linked lists would need some additional properties for the first and last elements, e.g., requiring that the "unused" pointer has the value NULL.

6.2   Biased Versus Unbiased Static Program Analysis

Many of the classical dataflow-analysis algorithms use bit vectors to represent the characteristic functions of set-valued dataflow values. This corresponds to a logical interpretation (in the abstract semantics) that uses two values. It is *definite* on one of the bit values and *conservative* on the other. That is, either "false" means "false" and "true" means "may be true/may be false, or "true" means "true" and "false" means "may be true/may be false". Many other static-analysis algorithms have a similar character.

Conventional wisdom holds that static analysis must inherently have such a one-sided bias. However, the material developed in [23] shows that while *indefiniteness* is inherent (i.e., a static analysis is unable, in general, to give a definite answer), one-sidedness is not: By basing the abstract semantics on 3-valued logic, definite truth and definite falseness can both be tracked, with the third value capturing indefiniteness.

This outlook provides some insight into the true nature of the values that arise in other static analyses:

– A one-sided analysis that is precise with respect to "false" and conservative with respect to "true" is really a 3-valued analysis over false, true, and "don't know" that conflates true and don't know (and uses "true" in place of don't know).

– Likewise, an analysis that is precise with respect to "true" and conservative with respect to "false" is really a 3-valued analysis over false, true, and "don't know" that conflates false and don't know (and uses "false" in place of don't know).

In contrast, the shape-analysis work has shown how to create analyses that are unbiased: They are precise with respect to both false and true, and use a separate "don't know" value to capture indefiniteness.

Acknowledgements

Tal Lev-Ami carried out the implementation of TVLA. One instantiation of TVLA was used to analyze the example program and generate the figures used in the paper. Hanne Riis Nielson provided very helpful comments.

References

1. U. Assmann and M. Weinhardt. Interprocedural heap analysis for parallelizing imperative programs. In W. K. Giloi, S. Jähnichen, and B. D. Shriver, editors, *Programming Models For Massively Parallel Computers*, pages 74–82, Washington, DC, September 1993. IEEE Press. 12

2. D.R. Chase, M. Wegman, and F. Zadeck. Analysis of pointers and structures. In *SIGPLAN Conf. on Prog. Lang. Design and Impl.*, pages 296–310, New York, NY, 1990. ACM Press. 12, 13

3. F. Corbera, R. Asenjo, and E.L. Zapata. New shape analysis techniques for automatic parallelization of C code. In *International Computing Symposium*, 1999. 2

4. P. Cousot and R. Cousot. Abstract interpretation: A unified lattice model for static analysis of programs by construction of approximation of fixed points. In *Symp. on Princ. of Prog. Lang.*, pages 238–252, New York, NY, 1977. ACM Press. 9

5. A. Deutsch. Interprocedural may-alias analysis for pointers: Beyond k-limiting. In *SIGPLAN Conf. on Prog. Lang. Design and Impl.*, pages 230–241, New York, NY, 1994. ACM Press. 14

6. N. Dor, M. Rodeh, and M. Sagiv. Detecting memory errors via static pointer analysis. In *Proceedings of the ACM SIGPLAN-SIGSOFT Workshop on Program Analysis for Software Tools and Engineering (PASTE'98)*, pages 27–34, June 1998. Available at "http://www.math.tau.ac.il/~ nurr/paste98.ps.gz". 3

7. L. Hendren. *Parallelizing Programs with Recursive Data Structures*. PhD thesis, Cornell Univ., Ithaca, NY, Jan 1990. 14

8. L. Hendren, J. Hummel, and A. Nicolau. Abstractions for recursive pointer data structures: Improving the analysis and the transformation of imperative programs. In *SIGPLAN Conf. on Prog. Lang. Design and Impl.*, pages 249–260, New York, NY, June 1992. ACM Press. 2

9. L. Hendren and A. Nicolau. Parallelizing programs with recursive data structures. *IEEE Trans. on Par. and Dist. Syst.*, 1(1):35–47, January 1990. 14

10. S. Horwitz, P. Pfeiffer, and T. Reps. Dependence analysis for pointer variables. In *SIGPLAN Conf. on Prog. Lang. Design and Impl.*, pages 28–40, New York, NY, 1989. ACM Press. 14

11. N.D. Jones and S.S. Muchnick. Flow analysis and optimization of Lisp-like structures. In S.S. Muchnick and N.D. Jones, editors, *Program Flow Analysis: Theory and Applications*, chapter 4, pages 102–131. Prentice-Hall, Englewood Cliffs, NJ, 1981. 13

12. N.D. Jones and S.S. Muchnick. A flexible approach to interprocedural data flow analysis and programs with recursive data structures. In *Symp. on Princ. of Prog. Lang.*, pages 66–74, New York, NY, 1982. ACM Press. 12, 13

13. W. Landi and B.G. Ryder. Pointer induced aliasing: A problem classification. In *Symp. on Princ. of Prog. Lang.*, pages 93–103, New York, NY, January 1991. ACM Press. 14

14. J.R. Larus. *Restructuring Symbolic Programs for Concurrent Execution on Multi-processors.* PhD thesis, Univ. of Calif., Berkeley, CA, May 1989. 13

15. J.R. Larus and P.N. Hilfinger. Detecting conflicts between structure accesses. In *SIGPLAN Conf. on Prog. Lang. Design and Impl.*, pages 21–34, New York, NY, 1988. ACM Press. 13

16. T. Lev-Ami. TVLA: A framework for Kleene based static analysis. Master's thesis, 2000. 12

17. F. Nielson, H. Riis Nielson, and C. Hankin. *Principles of Program Analysis.* Springer Verlag, 1999. 9, 13

18. F. Nielson, H. Riis Nielson, and M. Sagiv. A Kleene analysis of mobile ambients. In *Proceedings of ESOP'2000*, 2000. 12

19. J. Plevyak, A.A. Chien, and V. Karamcheti. Analysis of dynamic structures for efficient parallel execution. In U. Banerjee, D. Gelernter, A. Nicolau, and D. Padua, editors, *Languages and Compilers for Parallel Computing*, volume 768 of *Lec. Notes in Comp. Sci.*, pages 37–57, Portland, OR, August 1993. Springer-Verlag. 12

20. J.L. Ross and M. Sagiv. Building a bridge between pointer aliases and program dependences. In *Proceedings of the 1998 European Symposium On Programming*, pages 221–235, March 1998. Available at "http://www.math.tau.ac.il/~ sagiv". 2

21. M. Sagiv, T. Reps, and R. Wilhelm. Solving shape-analysis problems in languages with destructive updating. In *Symp. on Princ. of Prog. Lang.*, New York, NY, January 1996. ACM Press. 13

22. M. Sagiv, T. Reps, and R. Wilhelm. Solving shape-analysis problems in languages with destructive updating. *Trans. on Prog. Lang. and Syst.*, 20(1):1–50, January 1998. 12, 13

23. M. Sagiv, T. Reps, and R. Wilhelm. Parametric shape analysis via 3-valued logic. In *Symp. on Princ. of Prog. Lang.*, 1999. Available at "http://www.cs.wisc.edu/wpis/papers/popl99.ps". 2, 10, 15

24. J. Stransky. A lattice for abstract interpretation of dynamic (Lisp-like) structures. *Inf. and Comp.*, 101(1):70–102, Nov. 1992. 12, 13

25. E. Y.-B. Wang. *Analysis of Recursive Types in an Imperative Language.* PhD thesis, Univ. of Calif., Berkeley, CA, 1994. 13

Optimizing Java Bytecode Using the Soot Framework: Is It Feasible?

Raja Vallée-Rai, Etienne Gagnon, Laurie Hendren, Patrick Lam,
Patrice Pominville, and Vijay Sundaresan

Sable Research Group, School of Computer Science
McGill University
{rvalleerai,gagnon,hendren,plam,patrice}@sable.mcgill.ca
vijaysun@ca.ibm.com

Abstract. This paper presents Soot, a framework for optimizing
Java[TM] bytecode. The framework is implemented in Java and supports
three intermediate representations for representing Java bytecode: Baf,
a streamlined representation of Java's stack-based bytecode; Jimple, a
typed three-address intermediate representation suitable for optimization; and Grimp, an aggregated version of Jimple.
Our approach to class file optimization is to first convert the stack-based
bytecode into Jimple, a three-address form more amenable to traditional
program optimization, and then convert the optimized Jimple back to
bytecode.
In order to demonstrate that our approach is feasible, we present experimental results showing the effects of processing class files through
our framework. In particular, we study the techniques necessary to effectively translate Jimple back to bytecode, without losing performance.
Finally, we demonstrate that class file optimization can be quite effective by showing the results of some basic optimizations using our framework. Our experiments were done on ten benchmarks, including seven
SPECjvm98 benchmarks, and were executed on five different Java virtual
machine implementations.

1   Introduction

Java provides many attractive features such as platform independence, execution safety, garbage collection and object orientation. These features facilitate
application development but are expensive to support; applications written in
Java are often much slower than their counterparts written in C or C++. To
use these features without having to pay a great performance penalty, sophisticated optimizations and runtime systems are required. For example, Just-In-
Time compilers[1], adaptive compilers such as Hotspot[TM] and Way-Ahead-Of-
Time Java compilers[18,17] are three approaches used to improve performance.

Our approach is to statically optimize Java bytecode. There are several
reasons for optimizing at the bytecode level. Firstly, the optimized bytecode
can then be executed using any standard Java Virtual Machine (JVM) implementation (interpreter, JIT, adaptive), or it could be used as the input to a

A. Watt (Ed.): CC/ETAPS 2000, LNCS 1781, pp. 18–34, 2000.

bytecode→C or bytecode→native-code compiler. Thus, the overall performance improvement is due to both our static bytecode optimization, and the optimizations and sophisticated runtime systems used in the virtual machines executing the optimized bytecode. Secondly, many different compilers for a variety of languages (Ada, Scheme, Fortran, Eiffel, etc.) now produce Java bytecode as their target code. Thus, our optimization techniques can be applied as a backend to all of these compilers.

The goal of our work is to develop tools that simplify the task of optimizing Java bytecode, and to demonstrate that significant optimization can be achieved using these tools. Thus, we have developed the Soot[20] framework which provides a set of intermediate representations and a set of Java APIs for optimizing Java bytecode directly. Since our framework is written in Java, and provides a set of clean APIs, it should be portable and easy to build upon.

Early in our work we found that optimizing stack-based bytecode directly was, in general, too difficult. Thus, our framework consists of three intermediate representations, two of which are stackless representations. *Baf* is a streamlined representation of the stack-based bytecode, whereas *Jimple* and *Grimp* are more standard, stackless intermediate representations. Jimple is a three-address representation, where each instruction is simple, and each variable has a type. It is ideal for implementing standard compiler analyses and transformations. Grimp is similar to Jimple, but has aggregated expressions. Grimp is useful for decompilation, and as a means to generate efficient bytecode from Jimple.

In order to optimize bytecode we first convert bytecode to Jimple (the three-address representation), analyze and optimize the Jimple code, and then convert the optimized Jimple back to bytecode. In this paper we focus on the techniques used to translate from Jimple to efficient bytecode, and we give two alternative approaches to this translation.

Our framework is designed so that many different analyses could be implemented, above and beyond those carried out by `javac` or a JIT. A typical transformation might be removing redundant field accesses, or inlining. For these sorts of optimizations, improvements at the Jimple level correspond directly to improvements in final bytecode produced.

We have performed substantial experimental studies to validate our approach. Our first results show that we can indeed go through the cycle, bytecode to Jimple and back to bytecode, without losing any performance. This means that any optimizations made in Jimple will likely also result in optimizations in the final bytecode. Our second set of results show the effect of optimizing class files using method inlining and a set of simple intraprocedural optimizations. These results show that we can achieve performance gains over a variety of Java Virtual Machines.

In summary, our contributions in this paper are: (1) three intermediate representations which provide a general-purpose framework for bytecode optimizations, and (2) a comprehensive set of results obtained by applying our framework to a set of real Java applications.

The rest of the paper is organized as follows. Section 2 gives an overview of the framework and the intermediate representations. Section 3 describes two alternative approaches to translating Jimple back to bytecode. Section 4 presents and discusses our experimental results. Section 5 discusses related work and Section 6 covers the conclusions and future work.

2   Framework Overview

The Soot framework has been designed to simplify the process of developing new optimizations for Java bytecode. Figure 1 shows the overall structure of the framework. As indicated at the top of the figure, many different compilers can be used to generate the class files. The large box labeled SOOT demonstrates that the framework takes the original class files as input, and produces optimized class files as output. Finally, as shown at the bottom of the figure, these optimized class files can then be used as input to Java interpreters, Just-In-Time (JIT) compilers, adaptive execution engines like Hotspot™, and Ahead-of-Time compilers such as the High Performance Compiler for Java (HPCJ)™ or TowerJ™.

The internal structure of Soot is indicated inside the large box in Figure 1. Shaded components correspond to modules that we have designed/implemented and each component is discussed in the following subsections.

2.1   Jimplify

The first phase is to *jimplify* the input class files, that is, to convert class files to the Jimple three-address representation. We convert to a three-address representation because optimizing stack code directly is awkward for several reasons. First, the stack implicitly participates in every computation; there are effectively two types of variables, the implicit stack variables and explicit local variables. Second, the expressions are not explicit, and must be located on the stack[25]. For example, a simple instruction such as add can have its operands separated by an arbitrary number of stack instructions, and even by basic block boundaries. Another difficulty is the untyped nature of the stack and of the local variables in the bytecode, as this does not allow analyses to make use of the declared type of variables. A fourth problem is the jsr bytecode. The jsr bytecode is difficult to handle because it is essentially a interprocedural feature which is inserted into a traditionally intraprocedural context.

We produce Jimple from bytecode by first processing the bytecode from the input class files and representing it in an internal format.[1] During this translation jsr instructions are eliminated by inline expansion of code. After producing the internal form of bytecode, the translation to Jimple code proceeds as follows:

1. *Produce naive 3-address code*: Map every stack variable to a local variable, by determining the stack height at every instruction. Then map each instruction which acts implicitly on the stack variables to a 3-address code statement

---

[1] We currently use a tool called Coffi to achieve this translation.

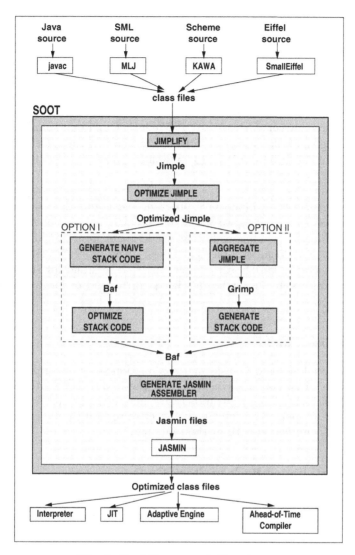

Fig. 1. Soot Framework Structure

which refers to the local variables explicitly. For example, if the current stack height is 3, then the instruction `iadd` would be translated to the Jimple statement `$i2 = $i2 + $i3`. This is a standard technique and is also used in other systems [18,17].

2. *Type the local variables*: The resulting Jimple code may be untypable because a local variable may be used with two different types in different contexts. Thus, we split the uses and definitions of local variables according to webs[16]. This produces, in almost all cases, Jimple code whose local vari-

ables can be given a primitive, class, or interface type.[2] To do this, we invoke an algorithm described in [9]. The complete solution to this typing problem is NP-complete, but in practice simple polynomial algorithms suffice. Although splitting the local variables in this step produces many local variables, the resulting Jimple code tends to be easier to analyze because it inherits some of the disambiguation benefits of SSA form[5].

3. *Clean up the code*: Jimple code must now be compacted because step 1 produced extremely verbose code[18,17]. We have found that simple aggregation (collapsing single def/use pairs) followed by copy propagation/elimination of stack variables to be sufficient to eliminate almost all redundant stack variables.

Figure 2(a) shows an input Java program and Figure 2(b) shows the bytecode generated by `javac` as we would represent it in our Baf representation. Figure 2(c) shows the Jimple code that would result from jimplifying the bytecode. Note that all local variables have been given types. Variables beginning with $ correspond to variables that were inserted to stand for stack locations, whereas variables that do not begin with $ correspond to local variables from the bytecode.

2.2   Optimize Jimple

Most of the analyses and transformations developed by our group, as well as other research groups, are implemented using the Jimple representation. We have currently implemented many intraprocedural and interprocedural optimizations. In this paper we focus on studying the effect of several simple intraprocedural techniques in conjunction with method inlining.

2.3   Convert Jimple Back to Stack Code

Producing bytecode naively from Jimple code produces highly inefficient code. Even the best JIT that we tested can not make up for this inefficiency. And it is very important that we do not introduce inefficiencies at this point that would negate the optimizations performed on Jimple.

We have investigated two alternatives for producing stack code, labeled Option I and Option II in Figure 1. These two options are discussed in more detail in Section 3, and they are experimentally validated in Section 4.

2.4   Generate Jasmin Assembler

After converting Jimple to Baf stack code, the final phase is to generate Jasmin [11] assembler files from the internal Baf representation. Since Baf is a relatively direct encoding of the Java bytecode, this phase is quite simple.

---

[2] Other cases must be handled by introducing type casts and/or introducing extra copy statements.

```
Object[] a;
int x;

public void f(int i, int c)
{ g(x *= 10);
  while(i * 2 < 10)
    { a[i++] = new Object();
    }
}
```

(a) Original Java Source

```
.method public f(II)V
    aload_0
    aload_0
    dup
    getfield A/x I
    bipush 10
    imul
    dup_x1
    putfield A/x I
    invokevirtual A/g(I)V
    goto Label1

Label0:
    aload_0
    getfield A/a [Ljava/lang/Object;
    iload_1
    iinc 1 1
    new java/lang/Object
    dup
    invokenonvirtual
        java/lang/Object/<init>()V
    aastore

Label1:
    iload_1
    iconst_2
    imul
    bipush 10
    if_icmplt Label0

    return
```

(b) Bytecode

```
public void f(int, int)
{
    Example this;
    int i, c, $i0, $i1, $i2, $i3;
    java.lang.Object[] $r1;
    java.lang.Object $r2;

    this := @this;
    i := @parameter0;
    c := @parameter1;
X:$i0 = this.x;
X:$i1 = $i0 * 10;
    this.x = $i1;
    this.g($i1);
    goto label1;

label0:
Y:$r1 = this.a;
    $i2 = i;
    i = i + 1;
    $r2 = new java.lang.Object;
    specialinvoke $r2.<init>();
Y:$r1[$i2] = $r2;

label1:
Z:$i3 = i * 2;
Z:if $i3 < 10 goto label0;

    return;
}
```

(c) Jimple

Fig. 2. Translating bytecode to Jimple

3   Transformations

After optimizing Jimple code, it is necessary to translate back to efficient Java bytecode. Figure 3(a) illustrates the bytecode produced by a naive translation from Jimple.[3] Note that this naive code has many redundant store and load instructions reflecting the fact that Jimple computation results are stored to local variables, while stack-based bytecode can use the stack to store many intermediate computations.

---

[3] Note that our Baf representation closely mirrors Java bytecode. However, we do streamline the representation somewhat and preserve the variable names as much as possible.

3.1   Option I: **Produce Naive Baf and Optimize**

The main idea behind Baf optimizations is to identify and eliminate redundant store/load computations. Figure 3(b) shows the results of applying the Baf optimizations on the naive code given in Figure 3(a).

The optimizations currently in use are all performed on discrete basic blocks within a method. Inter-block optimizations that cross block boundaries have also been implemented, but to date these have not yielded any appreciable speedups on the runtime and are not described here. In the following discussion it is assumed that all instructions belong to the same basic block.

In practice, the majority of the redundant store and load instructions present in naive Baf code belong to one of the following code patterns:

store/load (sl pair) : a store instruction followed by a load instruction referring to the same local variable with no other uses. Both the store and load instructions can be eliminated, and the value will simply remain on the stack.

store/load/load (sll triple) : a store instruction followed by 2 load instructions, all referring to the same local variable with no other uses. The 3 instructions can be eliminated and a dup instruction introduced. The dup instruction replaces the second load by duplicating the value left on the stack after eliminating the store and the first load.

We can observe these patterns occurring in Figure 3(a) where labels A, B, C and E each identify distinct sl pairs, and where labels D and G identify sll triples.

To optimize a Baf method our algorithm performs a fixed point iteration over its basic blocks identifying and reducing these patterns whenever possible. By reducing, we mean eliminating an sl pair or replacing an sll triple to a dup instruction.

Reducing a pattern is trivial when all its instructions directly follow each other in the instruction stream. For example, the sl pairs at labels A and E in Figure 3(a) are trivial ones. However, often the store and load instructions are far apart (like at labels B and C.) To identify pairs of statements to reduce, we must determine the effect on the stack of the intervening bytecode. These bytecodes are called the *interleaving sequences*.

We compute two pieces of information as a means to analyse interleaving sequences and their effects/dependencies on the stack. The net effect on the stack height after executing a sequence of bytecode is referred to as the *net stack height variation* or *nshv*. The minimum stack height variation attained while executing a sequence of bytecode is referred to as the *minimum stack height variation* or *mshv*. A sequence of instructions having both $nshv = 0$ and $mshv = 0$ is referred to as a *level sequence*.

If interleaving sequences are level sequences, then the target patterns can be reduced directly. This is because one can just leave the value on the stack, execute the interleaving instructions, and then use the value that was left on the stack. This is the case for the sl pair labeled B, and later the sl pair labeled C, once B has been reduced. Finally, the sll triple D can be reduced, once both B and C have been reduced. In general, however, many such interleaving sequences will not be level and no reductions will be possible without some reordering of the block's bytecode.

```
public void f(int, int)
{ word this, i, c, $i2, $r2;

  this := @this: Example;
  i := @parameter0: int;
  c := @parameter1: int;
  load.r this;
  fieldget <Example: int x>;
A:store.i c;
A:load.i c;
  push 10;
  mul.i;
G:store.i c;
F:load.r this;
G:load.i c;
  fieldput <Example: int x>;
F:load.r this;
G:load.i c;
  virtualinvoke
     <Example: void g(int)>;
  goto label1;

label0:
  load.r this;
  fieldget
  <Example: java.lang.Object[] a>;
B:store.r c;
  load.i i;
C:store.i $i2;
  inc.i i 1;
  new java.lang.Object;
D:store.r $r2;
D:load.r $r2;
  specialinvoke
  <java.lang.Object: void <init>()>;
B:load.r c;
C:load.i $i2;
D:load.r $r2;
  arraywrite.r;

label1:
  load.i i;
  push 2;
  mul.i;
E:store.i $r2;
E:load.i $r2;
  push 10;
  ifcmplt.i label0;

  return;
}
```

(a) naive Baf generated from Jimple

```
public void f(int, int)
{ word this, i, c;

  this := @this: Example;
  i := @parameter0: int;
  c := @parameter1: int;
  load.r this;
F:load.r this;
F:load.r this;
  fieldget <Example: int x>;
  push 10;
  mul.i;
G:store.i c;
G:load.i c;
  fieldput <Example: int x>;
G:load.i c;
  virtualinvoke
     <Example: void g(int)>;
  goto label1;

label0:
  load.r this;
  fieldget
   <Example: java.lang.Object[] a>;
  load.i i;
  inc.i i 1;
  new java.lang.Object;
D:dup1.r;
  specialinvoke
  <java.lang.Object: void <init>()>;
  arraywrite.r;

label1:
  load.i i;
  push 2;
  mul.i;
  push 10;
  ifcmplt.i label0;

  return;
}
```

(b) optimized Baf

Fig. 3. Optimizing Baf

If an interleaving sequence has $nshv > 1$ for a sll triple or $nshv > 0$ for a sl pair, then our algorithm will try to lower the $nshv$ value by relocating a bytecode having a positive $nshv$ to an earlier location in the block. This is illustrated by the movement of instructions labeled by F in Figures 3(a) and 3(b) in an attempt to reduce the pattern identified by G. Another strategy used when $nshv < 0$ is to move level subsequence ending with the pattern's store instruction past the interleaving sequence. Of course, this can only be done if no data dependencies are violated.

Applying these heuristics produces optimized Baf code which becomes Java bytecode and is extremely similar to the original bytecode. We observe that except for two minor differences, the optimized Baf code in Figure 3(b) is the same as the original bytecode found in Figure 2(b). The differences are: (1) the second load labeled by F is not converted to a dup; and (2) the pattern identified by G is not reduced to a dup_x1 instruction. We have actually implemented these patterns, but our experimental results did not justify enabling these extra transformations. In fact, introducing bytecodes such as dup_x1 often yields non-standard, albeit legal, bytecode sequences that increase execution time and cause many JIT compilers to fail.

3.2   Option II: **Build Grimp and Traverse**

In this section, we describe the second route for translating Jimple into byte-code. The compiler javac is able to produce efficient bytecode because it has the structured tree representation of the original program, and the stack based nature of the bytecode is particularly well suited for code generation from trees[2]. Essentially, this phase attempts to recover the original structured tree representation, by building Grimp, an aggregated form of Jimple, and then producing stack code by standard tree traversal techniques.

Grimp is essentially Jimple but the expressions are trees of arbitrary depth. Figure 4(a) shows the Grimp version of the Jimple program in Figure 2(c).

Aggregation of bytecode The basic algorithm for aggregation is as follows. We consider pairs *(def, use)* in extended basic blocks, where *def* is an assignment statement with sole use *use*, and *use* has the unique definition *def*. We inspect the path between *def* and *use*, to determine if *def* can be safely moved into *use*. This means checking for dependencies and not moving across exception boundaries. We perform this algorithm iteratively, and the pairs are considered in reverse pseudo-topological order to cascade the optimizations as efficiently as possible. Examples of these aggregation opportunities are shown in figure 2(c) at the labels X, Y and Z. X and Z are trivial cases because their aggregation pairs are adjacent, but the pair at Y are a few statements apart. Thus before producing the aggregated code in 4(a) the interleaving statements must be checked for writes to this.a.

Peephole optimizations In some cases, Grimp cannot concisely express Java idioms. For example, the increment operation in a[i++] = new Object(); cannot be expressed, because Grimp only allows a definition to occur as the left-hand

```
public void f(int, int)
{ word this, i, c, $i2;

  this := @this: Example;
  i := @parameter0: int;
  c := @parameter1: int;
  load.r this;
  fieldget <Example: int x>;
  push 10;
  mul.i;
  store.i c;
  load.r this;
  load.i c;
  fieldput <Example: int x>;
  load.r this;
  load.i c;
  virtualinvoke
      <Example: void g(int)>;
  goto label1;

label0:
  load.r this;
  fieldget
    <Example: java.lang.Object[] a>;
  load.i i;
  inc.i i 1;
  new java.lang.Object;
  dup1.r
  specialinvoke
      <java.lang.Object: void <init>()>;
  arraywrite.r;

label1:
  load.i i;
  push 2;
  mul.i
  push 10;
  ifcmplt.i label0;

  return;
}
```

```
public void f(int, int)
{
  Example this;
  int i, c, $i1, $i2;

  this := @this;
  i := @parameter0;
  c := @parameter1;
X:$i1 = this.x * 10;
  this.x = $i1;
  this.g($i1);
  goto label1;

label0:
  $i2 = i;
  i = i + 1;
Y:this.a[$i2] =
      new java.lang.Object();

label1:
Z:if i * 2 < 10 goto label0;

  return;
}
```

(a) Grimp   (b) Baf generated from Grimp

Fig. 4. Generating Baf from Grimp

side of an assignment statement, not as a side effect.[4] To remedy this problem, we use some peephole optimizations in the code generator for Grimp.

For example, for the increment case, we search for Grimp patterns of the form:

```
s1:    local = <lvalue>;
s2:    <lvalue> = local/<lvalue> + 1;
s3:    use(local)
```

and we ensure that the local defined in s_1 has exactly two uses, and that the uses in s_2, s_3 have exactly one definition. Given this situation, we emit code for only s_3. However, during the generation of code for s_3, when local is to

---

[4] This design decision was made to simplify analyses on Grimp.

be emitted, we also emit code to duplicate `local` on the stack, and increment
`<lvalue>`. An example of this pattern occurs just after `Label0` in Figure 4(a).

This approach produces reasonably efficient bytecode. In some situations the
peephole patterns fail and the complete original structure is not recovered. In
these cases, the Baf approach usually performs better. See the section 4 for more
details.

4   Experimental Results

Here we present the results of two experiments. The first experiment, discussed
in Section 4.3, validates that we can pass class files through the framework,
without optimizing the Jimple code, and produce class files that have the same
performance as the original ones. In particular, this shows that our methods
of converting from Jimple to stack-based bytecode are acceptable. The second
experiment, discussed in Section 4.4, shows the effect of applying method inlining
on Jimple code and demonstrates that optimizing Java bytecode is feasible and
desirable.

4.1   Methodology

All experiments were performed on dual 400Mhz Pentium II[TM] machines. Two
operating systems were used, Debian GNU/Linux (kernel 2.2.8) and Windows
NT 4.0 (service pack 5). Under GNU/Linux we ran experiments using three
different configurations of the Blackdown Linux JDK1.2, pre-release version 2.[5]
The configurations were: interpreter, Sun JIT, and a public beta version of Bor-
land's JIT[6]. Under Windows NT, two different configurations of Sun's JDK1.2.2
were used: the JIT, and HotSpot (version 1.0.1)

Execution times were measured by running the benchmarks ten times, dis-
carding the best and worst runs, and averaging the remaining eight. All executions were verified for correctness by comparing the output to the expected
output.

4.2   Benchmarks and Baseline Times

The benchmarks used consist of seven of the eight standard benchmarks from the
SPECjvm98[7] suite, plus three additional applications from our collection. See
figure 5. We discarded the *mtrt* benchmark from our set because it is essentially
the same benchmark as *raytrace*. The *soot-c* benchmark is based on an older
version of Soot, and is interesting because it is heavily object oriented, *schroeder-
s* is an audio editing program which manipulates sound files, and *jpat-p* is a
protein analysis tool.

Figure 5 also gives basic characteristics such as size, and running times on
the five platforms. All of these benchmarks are real world applications that are

---

[5] http://www.blackdown.org

[6] http://www.borland.com

[7] http://www.spec.org/

reasonably sized, and they all have non-trivial execution times. We used the Linux interpreter as the base time, and all the fractional execution times are with respect to this base.

Benchmarks for which a dash is given for the running time indicates that the benchmark failed validity checks. In all these cases, the virtual machine is to blame as the programs run correctly with the interpreter with the verifier explicitly turned on. Arithmetic averages and standard deviations are also given, and these automatically exclude those running times which are not valid.

For this set of benchmarks, we can draw the following observations. The Linux JIT is about twice as fast as the interpreter but it varies widely depending on the benchmark. For example, with *compress* it is more than six times faster, but for a benchmark like *schroeder-s* it is only 56% faster. The NT virtual machines also tend to be twice as fast as the Linux JIT. Furthermore, the performance of the HotSpot performance engine seems to be, on average, not that different from the standard Sun JIT. Perhaps this is because the benchmarks are not long running server side applications (i.e. not the kinds of applications for which HotSpot was designed).

4.3   Straight through Soot

Figure 6 compares the effect of processing applications with Soot with Baf and Grimp, without performing any optimizations. Fractional execution times are given, and these are with respect to the original execution time of the benchmark for a given platform. The ideal result is 1.00. This means that the same performance is obtained as the original application. For *javac* the ratio is .98 which indicates that *javac*'s execution time has been reduced by 2%. *raytrace* has a ratio of 1.02 which indicates that it was made slightly slower; its execution time has been increased by 2%. The ideal arithmetic averages for these tables is 1.00 because we are trying to simply reproduce the program as is. The ideal standard deviation is 0 which would indicate that the transformation is having a consistent effect, and the results do not deviate from 1.00.

On average, using Baf tends to reproduce the original execution time. Its average is lower than Grimp's, and the standard deviation is lower as well. For the faster virtual machines (the ones on NT), this difference disappears. The main disadvantage of Grimp is that it can produce a noticeable slowdown for benchmarks like *compress* which have tight loops on Java statements containing side effects, which it does not always catch.

Both techniques have similar running times, but implementing Grimp and its aggregation is conceptually simpler. In terms of code generation for Java virtual machines, we believe that if one is interested in generating code for slow VMs, then the Baf-like approach is best. For fast VMs, or if one desires a simpler compiler implementation, then Grimp is more suitable.

We have also measured the size of the bytecode before and after processing with Soot. The sizes are very similar, with the code after processing sometimes slightly larger, and sometimes slightly smaller. For the seven SPECjvm benchmarks the total bytecode size was 0.5% larger after processing with Soot. This is not a significant increase in size.

4.4 Optimization via Inlining

We have investigated the feasibility of optimizing Java bytecode with Soot by implementing method inlining. Although inlining is a whole program optimization, Soot is also suitable for optimizations applicable to partial programs. Our approach to inlining is simple. We build an invoke graph using class hierarchy analysis[8] and inline method calls whenever they resolve to one method. Our inliner is a bottom-up inliner, and attempts to inline all call sites subject to the following restrictions: 1) the method to be inlined must contain less than 20 Jimple statements, 2) no method may contain more than 5000 Jimple statements, and 3) no method may have its size increased more than by a factor of 3.

After inlining, the following traditional intraprocedural optimizations are performed to maximize the benefit from inlining: copy propagation, constant propagation and folding, conditional and unconditional branch folding, dead assignment elimination and unreachable code elimination. These are described in [2].

Figure 7 gives the result of performing this optimization. The numbers presented are fractional execution times with respect to the original execution time of the benchmark for a given platform. For the Linux virtual machines, we obtain a significant improvement in speed. In particular, for the Linux Sun JIT, the average ratio is .92 which indicates that the average running time is reduced by 8%. For raytrace, the results are quite significant, as we obtain a ratio of .62, a reduction of 38%.

For the virtual machines under NT, the average is 1.00 or 1.01, but a number of benchmarks experience a significant improvement. One benchmark, *javac* under the Sun JIT, experiences significant degradation. However, under the same JIT, *raytrace* yields a ratio of .89, and under HotSpot, *javac*, *jack* and *mpegaudio* yield some improvements. Given that HotSpot itself performs dynamic inlining, this indicates that our static inlining heuristics sometimes capture opportunities that HotSpot does not. Our heuristics for inlining were also tuned for the Linux VMs, and future experimentation could produce values which are better suited for the NT virtual machines.

These results are highly encouraging as they strongly suggest that a significant amount of improvement can be achieved by performing aggressive optimizations which are not performed by the virtual machines.

5 Related Work

Related work falls into five different categories:

Java bytecode optimizers: There are only two Java tools of which we are aware that perform significant optimizations on bytecode and produce new class files: Cream[3] and Jax[23]. Cream performs optimizations such as loop invariant removal and common sub-expression elimination using a simple side effect analysis. Only extremely small speed-ups (1% to 3%) are reported, however. The main goal of Jax is application compression where, for example, unused methods and fields are removed, and the class hierarchy is

	# Jimple Stmts	Linux Sun Int. (secs)	Linux Sun JIT	Linux Bor. JIT	NT Sun JIT	NT Sun Hot.
compress	7322	440.30	.15	.14	**.06**	.07
db	7293	259.09	.56	.58	.26	**.14**
jack	16792	151.39	.43	.32	**.15**	.16
javac	31054	137.78	.52	.42	**.24**	.33
jess	17488	109.75	.45	.32	.21	**.12**
jpat-p	1622	47.94	1.01	.96	.90	**.80**
mpegaudio	19585	368.10	.15	-	**.07**	.10
raytrace	10037	121.99	.45	.23	.16	**.12**
schroeder-s	9713	48.51	.64	.62	.19	**.12**
soot-c	42107	85.69	.58	.45	**.29**	.53
average			.49	.45	.25	.25
std. dev.			.23	.23	.23	.23

Fig. 5. Benchmarks and their characteristics.

	Baf					Grimp				
		Linux		NT			Linux		NT	
	Sun Int.	Sun JIT	Bor. JIT	Sun JIT	Sun Hot.	Sun Int.	Sun JIT	Bor. JIT	Sun JIT	Sun Hot.
compress	1.01	1.00	.99	.99	1.00	1.07	1.02	1.04	1.00	1.01
db	.99	1.01	1.00	1.00	1.00	1.01	1.05	1.01	1.01	1.02
jack	1.00	1.00	1.00	-	1.00	1.01	.99	1.00	-	1.00
javac	1.00	.98	1.00	1.00	.97	.99	1.03	1.00	1.00	.95
jess	1.02	1.01	1.04	.99	1.01	1.01	1.02	1.04	.97	1.00
jpat-p	1.00	.99	1.00	1.00	1.00	.99	1.01	1.01	1.00	1.00
mpegaudio	1.05	1.00	-	-	1.00	1.03	1.00	-	-	1.01
raytrace	1.00	1.02	1.00	.99	1.00	1.01	1.00	.99	.99	1.00
schroeder-s	.97	1.01	-	1.03	1.01	.98	.99	-	1.03	1.00
soot-c	.99	1.00	1.02	.99	1.03	1.00	1.01	1.00	1.01	1.01
average	1.00	1.00	1.01	1.00	1.00	1.01	1.01	1.01	1.00	1.00
std. dev.	.02	.01	.01	.01	.01	.02	.02	.02	.02	.02

Fig. 6. The effect of processing classfiles with Soot using Baf or Grimp, without optimization.

compressed. They also are interested in speed optimizations, but at this time their current published speed up results are extremely limited.

Bytecode manipulation tools: There are a number of Java tools which provide frameworks for manipulating bytecode: JTrek[13], Joie[4], Bit[14] and JavaClass[12]. These tools are constrained to manipulating Java bytecode in their original form, however. They do not provide convenient intermediate representations such as Baf, Jimple or Grimp for performing analyses or transformations.

	Linux			NT	
	Sun Int.	Sun JIT	Bor. JIT	Sun JIT	Sun Hot.
compress	1.01	.78	1.00	1.01	.99
db	.99	1.01	1.00	1.00	1.00
jack	1.00	.98	.99	-	.97
javac	.97	.96	.97	1.11	.93
jess	.93	.93	1.01	.99	1.00
jpat-p	.99	.99	1.00	1.00	1.00
mpegaudio	1.04	.96	-	-	.97
raytrace	.76	.62	.74	.89	1.01
schroeder-s	.97	1.00	.97	1.02	1.06
soot-c	.94	.94	.96	1.03	1.05
average	.96	.92	.96	1.01	1.00
std. dev.	.07	.12	.08	.06	.04

Fig. 7. The effect of inlining with class hierarchy analysis.

Java application packagers: There are a number of tools to package Java applications, such as Jax[23], DashO-Pro[6] and SourceGuard[21]. Application packaging consists of code compression and/or code obfuscation. Although we have not yet applied Soot to this application area, we have plans to implement this functionality as well.

Java native compilers: The tools in this category take Java applications and compile them to native executables. These are related because they all are forced to build 3-address code intermediate representations, and some perform significant optimizations. The simplest of these is Toba[18] which produces unoptimized C code and relies on GCC to produce the native code. Slightly more sophisticated, Harissa[17] also produces C code but performs some method devirtualization and inlining first. The most sophisticated systems are Vortex[7] and Marmot[10]. Vortex is a native compiler for Cecil, C++ and Java, and contains a complete set of optimizations. Marmot is also a complete Java optimization compiler and is SSA based. There are also numerous commercial Java native compilers, such as the IBM (R) High Performance Compiler for Java, Tower Technology's TowerJ[24], and SuperCede[22], but they have very little published information.

Stack code optimization: Some research has been previously done in the field of optimizing stack code. The work presented in [15] is related but optimizes the stack code based on the assumption that stack operations are cheaper than manipulating locals. This is clearly not the case for the Java Virtual Machines we are interested in. On the other hand, some closely related work has been done on optimizing naive Java bytecode code at University of Maryland[19]. Their technique is similar, but they present results for only toy benchmarks.

6   Conclusions and Future Work

We have presented Soot, a framework for optimizing Java bytecode. Soot consists of three intermediate representations (Baf, Jimple & Grimp), transformations between these IRs, and a set of optimizations on these intermediate representations.

In this paper we have given an overview of the structure of Soot, concentrating on the mechanisms for translating Java stack-based bytecode to our typed three-address representation Jimple, and the translation of Jimple back to bytecode. Jimple was designed to make the implementation of compiler analyses and transformations simple. Our experimental results show that we can perform the conversions without losing performance, and so we can effectively optimize at the Jimple level. We demonstrated the effectiveness of a set of intraprocedural transformations and inlining on five different Java Virtual Machine implementations.

We are encouraged by our results so far, and we have found that the Soot APIs have been effective for a variety of tasks including the optimizations presented in this paper.

We, and other research groups, are actively engaged in further work on Soot on many fronts. Our group is currently focusing on new techniques for virtual method resolution, pointer analyses, side-effect analyses, and various transformations that can take advantage of accurate side-effect analysis.

Acknowledgements

This research was supported by IBM's Centre for Advanced Studies (CAS), NSERC and FCAR.

References

1. Ali-Reza Adl-Tabatabai, Michal Cierniak, Guei-Yuan Lueh, Vishesh M. Parikh, and James M. Stichnoth. Fast and effective code generation in a just-in-time Java compiler. *ACM SIGPLAN Notices*, 33(5):280–290, May 1998. 18
2. Alfred V. Aho, Ravi Sethi, and Jeffrey D. Ullman. *Compilers Principles, Techniques and Tools*. Addison-Wesley, 1986. 26, 30
3. Lars R. Clausen. A Java bytecode optimizer using side-effect analysis. *Concurrency: Practice & Experience*, 9(11):1031–1045, November 1997. 30
4. Geoff A. Cohen, Jeffrey S. Chase, and David L. Kaminsky. Automatic program transformation with JOIE. In *Proceedings of the USENIX 1998 Annual Technical Conference*, pages 167–178, Berkeley, USA, June 15–19 1998. USENIX Association. 31
5. Ron Cytron, Jeanne Ferrante, Barry K. Rosen, Mark K. Wegman, and F. Kenneth Zadeck. An efficient method of computing static single assignment form. In *16th Annual ACM Symposium on Principles of Programming Languages*, pages 25–35, 1989. 22
6. DashOPro. http://www.preemptive.com/products.html. 32

7. Jeffrey Dean, Greg DeFouw, David Grove, Vassily Litvinov, and Craig Chambers. VORTEX: An optimizing compiler for object-oriented languages. In *Proceedings OOPSLA '96 Conference on Object-Oriented Programming Systems, Languages, and Applications*, volume 31 of *ACM SIGPLAN Notices*, pages 83–100. ACM, October 1996. 32

8. Jeffrey Dean, David Grove, and Craig Chambers. Optimization of object-oriented programs using static class hierarchy analysis. In Walter G. Olthoff, editor, *ECOOP'95—Object-Oriented Programming, 9th European Conference*, volume 952 of *Lecture Notes in Computer Science*, pages 77–101, Åarhus, Denmark, 7–11 August 1995. Springer. 30

9. Étienne Gagnon and Laurie Hendren. Intra-procedural Inference of Static Types for Java Bytecode. Sable Technical Report 1999-1, Sable Research Group, McGill University, March 1999. 22

10. Robert Fitzgerald, Todd B. Knoblock, Erik Ruf, Bjarne Steensgaard, and David Tarditi. Marmot: an Optimizing Compiler for Java. Microsoft technical report, Microsoft Research, October 1998. 32

11. Jasmin: A Java Assembler Interface. http://www.cat.nyu.edu/meyer/jasmin/. 22

12. JavaClass. http://www.inf.fu-berlin.de/ dahm/JavaClass/ . 31

13. Compaq JTrek. http://www.digital.com/java/download/jtrek . 31

14. Han Bok Lee and Benjamin G. Zorn. A Tool for Instrumenting Java Bytecodes. In *The USENIX Symposium on Internet Technologies and Systems*, pages 73–82, 1997. 31

15. Martin Maierhofer and M. Anton Ertl. Local stack allocation. In Kai Koskimies, editor, *Compiler Construction (CC'98)*, pages 189–203, Lisbon, 1998. Springer LNCS 1383. 32

16. Steven S. Muchnick. *Advanced Compiler Design and Implementation*. Morgan Kaufmann, 1997. 21

17. Gilles Muller, Bárbara Moura, Fabrice Bellard, and Charles Consel. Harissa: A flexible and efficient Java environment mixing bytecode and compiled code. In *Proceedings of the 3rd Conference on Object-Oriented Technologies and Systems*, pages 1–20, Berkeley, June 16–20 1997. Usenix Association. 18, 21, 22, 32

18. Todd A. Proebsting, Gregg Townsend, Patrick Bridges, John H. Hartman, Tim Newsham, and Scott A. Watterson. Toba: Java for applications: A way ahead of time (WAT) compiler. In *Proceedings of the 3rd Conference on Object-Oriented Technologies and Systems*, pages 41–54, Berkeley, June 16–20 1997. Usenix Association. 18, 21, 22, 32

19. Tatiana Shpeisman and Mustafa Tikir. Generating Efficient Stack Code for Java. Technical report, University of Maryland, 1999. 32

20. Soot - a Java Optimization Framework. http://www.sable.mcgill.ca/soot/. 19

21. 4thpass SourceGuard. http://www.4thpass.com/sourceguard/. 32

22. SuperCede, Inc. SuperCede for Java. http://www.supercede.com/. 32

23. Frank Tip, Chris Laffra, Peter F. Sweeney, and David Streeter. Practical Experience with an Application Extractor for Java . IBM Research Report RC 21451, IBM Research, 1999. 30, 32

24. Tower Technology. Tower J. http://www.twr.com/. 32

25. Raja Vallée-Rai and Laurie J. Hendren. Jimple: Simplifying Java Bytecode for Analyses and Transformations. Sable Technical Report 1998-4, Sable Research Group, McGill University, July 1998. 20

Pipelined Java Virtual Machine Interpreters

Jan Hoogerbrugge and Lex Augusteijn

Philips Research Laboratories,
Prof. Holstlaan 4, 5656 AA Eindhoven, The Netherlands
{jan.hoogerbrugge,lex.augusteijn}@philips.com

Abstract. The performance of a Java Virtual Machine (JVM) interpreter running on a very long instruction word (VLIW) processor can be
improved by means of pipelining. While one bytecode is in its execute
stage, the next bytecode is in its decode stage, and the next bytecode
is in its fetch stage. The paper describes how we implemented threading and pipelining by rewriting the source code of the interpreter and
several modifications in the compiler. Experiments for evaluating the effectiveness of pipelining are described. Pipelining improves the execution
speed of a threaded interpreter by 19.4% in terms of instruction count
and 14.4% in terms of cycle count. Most of the simple bytecodes, like
additions and multiplications, execute in four cycles. This number corresponds to the branch latency of our target VLIW processor. Thus most
of the code of the interpreter is executed in branch delay slots.

1 Introduction

One of the most important properties of the Java Platform is its ability to
support mobile code, i.e., code that runs on a large variety of machines, often
transfered over a network [1]. This is realized by an object file format called *class
files* which contains machine instructions called *bytecodes* for a virtual machine
called Java Virtual Machine (JVM). JVM is designed so that it can be efficiently
implemented on a large variety of platforms. JVM can be implemented directly in
hardware as a JVM processor [2], by means of a software interpreter, or by means
of a just-in-time compiler [3,4] which compiles bytecodes to native machine code
just before the code is executed and caches it for future execution.

A JVM processor can potentially provide excellent execution speed performance, but they usually cannot execute other software that has to run on the
system such as video and audio decoders. Such software would have to be ported
to the JVM processor.

A software interpreter is usually slow, about 5-20 times slower than native
code, but it is portable and has low memory requirements for both code and
data.

A just-in-time compiler could approach the execution speed of optimized native code but has high memory requirements. A just-in-time compiler will be
larger than an interpreter, and require RAM to store generated native code. A
just-in-time compiler is also more complex to develop, and is not portable. Furthermore, just-in-time compilation requires an investment in compilation time

A. Watt (Ed.): CC/ETAPS 2000, LNCS 1781, pp. 35–49, 2000.

which will only be profitable when the code is executed repeatedly. A comparison between JVM processors, interpreters, and just-in-time compilers for JVM can be found in [5].

In this paper we describe a JVM interpreter for the Philips TriMedia very long instruction word (VLIW) media processor, which is targeted for embedded systems in consumer products [6,7]. For these products a dedicated JVM processor, unable to perform media processing, will not be cost-effective. Furthermore, the memory requirements of a just-in-time compiler are expected to be too high, especially for VLIWs, which require instruction scheduling and have a low native code density. That is why we have opted JVM interpreter for TriMedia.

State-of-the-art compiler technology is not able to sufficiently exploit instruction-level parallelism (ILP) in a JVM interpreter. All steps required to execute a bytecode – fetch, decode, and execute – are dependent on each other, which results in low ILP. Although there is little ILP within a bytecode, there is much more ILP between successive bytecodes. Exploiting this implies pipelined execution of the interpreter, a well-known technique employed in all performance-oriented processors. Although software pipelining [8] has been well-known for many years, the algorithms developed for it are not able to pipeline the complex, irreducible [9] control flow structure of an interpreter. In this paper we will show how we managed to pipeline a JVM interpreter with modest compiler support.

This paper is organized as follows. Section 2 provides background information on JVM and TriMedia. Section 3 describes pipelining and how we implemented it. Section 4 describes the experiments we conducted. Section 5 discusses related work. Finally, section 6 ends the paper with conclusions.

2   Background

In this section we give a brief description of JVM and TriMedia, necessary to understand the remainder of the paper.

2.1   Overview of JVM

The Java Virtual Machine is a stack-based architecture, which means that all common instructions such as additions and multiplications get their operands from the evaluation stack and put their result on the evaluation stack. An array of local variables is available for fast accessible storage of temporary scalar data. Load and store instructions move data between the evaluation stack and the local variables. The memory of the JVM consists of a heap for dynamic storage of objects and arrays. Instructions are available for allocation of objects and arrays, and for accessing and modifying them. Various kinds of control flow instructions are available for conditional branching and method invocation.

Whereas real machines have relatively simple instructions, JVM has both simple as well as several very complex instructions. Examples of the latter are instructions for memory allocation, thread synchronization, table jumps, and method invocation.

The instructions of JVM are called bytecodes. A bytecode consists of a one-byte opcode followed by zero or more operands. Each operand consists of one or more bytes. This structure, unlike the structure of a real processor, makes JVM easy to implement by a software interpreter.

2.2   The TriMedia VLIW Media Processor

The TriMedia VLIW media processor[1] is a five-issue VLIW processor with an operation set and peripherals optimized for the processing of audio, video, and graphics. 28 functional units are available; among which are 2 load/store units, 3 jump units, 5 ALUs, and 4 floating point units. Each instruction holds up to five operations that can be issued to a subset of the 28 functional units under certain combination restrictions. All functional units are connected to a central register file of 128 32-bit registers. The processor has no interlocks and stalls in cache misses. TriMedia has a 16 kbyte data cache and a 32 kbyte instruction cache.

All multi-cycle functional units, except the divide functional unit, are fully pipelined. The load/store units have a latency of three cycles, and the jump units have a latency of four cycles. A jump latency of four cycles means that three delayed instructions are executed before a jump operation becomes effective. Fifteen operations can be scheduled in these three delayed instructions and another four operations can be scheduled in parallel with the jump operation. For more information on TriMedia the reader is referred to [6,7].

3   Pipelined Interpreters

A JVM interpreter is a complex piece of software, usually written in (ANSI) C. In our case, we used both the freely available Kaffee [10] and Sun Microsystems' Personal Java [11] for the application of our pipelining techniques. In fact, these techniques are generally applicable to all types of interpreters, and not just to JVM interpreters.

We assume that an interpreter is written in C and has the following structure:

```
bytecode bc;              /* Current bytecode */
bytecode *pb;             /* Bytecode pointer */

for (;;) {
  bc = *pb;               /* Fetch */
  switch (bc) {           /* Decode */
    case ADD:
      ... = ... + ...     /* Execute bytecode */
```

---

[1] Whenever we mention TriMedia in this paper, the reader should read TriMedia TM1000 or TM1100. Future generations may have a different architecture.

```
            pb += 1;          /* Increment bytecode pointer */
            break;
        ...                   /* Other cases */
    }
}
```

An optimizing C compiler will implement the switch statement by a table jump including a range check to test whether the value is in the range of the table. Assuming that the last case of the switch is the default one, this gives a control-flow graph as shown in figure 1a for such an interpreter.

3.1   Threaded Interpreters

An indirect threaded[2] interpreter [12,13], is an interpreter with which the code to implement a bytecode jumps directly to the code to implement the next byte to be executed, rather than to a shared join point. So each bytecode performs a table jump to its successor. Such a threaded interpreter exhibits the control flow shown in figure 1c.

We have modified the TriMedia C/C++ compiler so that it can transform the control flow graph of figure 1a into that of figure 1c. This transformation comprises of two steps.

Removal of the range check. If the switch expression is of type unsigned char and the number of cases is large enough (≥ 128), the switch statement is made complete by adding the missing cases and removing the default case. This results in a 256-entry jump table and the elimination of the range check. The resulting control flow graph is shown in figure 1b.

Code duplication. The switch block S in the control flow graph of figure 1b and the join block J are duplicated for each of the 256 cases. This effectively yields the threaded interpreter. The compiler is instructed by pragmas at the end of each switch case where to perform this code duplication. As the blocks involved contain only a jump (for J) (which disappears) and two loads and a table jump (for S), the resulting increase in code size is limited. Note that the 256 jumps to J disappear.

Another way to create a threaded interpreter is to use first-class labels, as found in GNU C. In this method, each block ends with a computed goto to the next block. However, first-class labels are not part of ANSI C and are not supported by the TriMedia compiler.

The control flow graph of a threaded interpreter as shown in figure 1c is irreducible [9]. This means that there is no single loop header and control flow edges cannot be partitioned into forward and backward edges such that the forward edges form an acyclic graph and heads of backward edges dominate their tails. The authors are not aware of software pipelining algorithms that can handle irreducible control flow graphs. Therefore, we have developed our own technique for pipelining threaded interpreters.

---

[2] In the remainder of the paper we will speak about a threaded interpreter whenever we mean an indirect threaded interpreter.

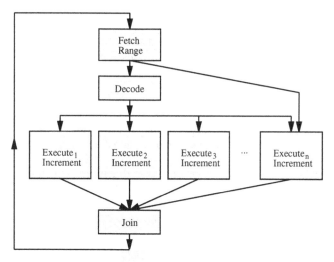

(a) Control flow graph of a table–jump–based interpreter

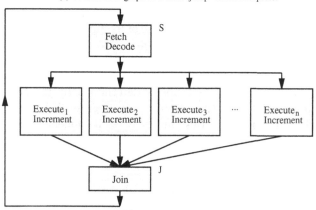

(b) Control flow graph after range check removal

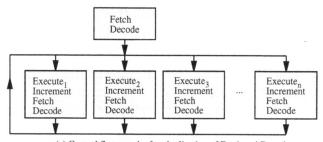

(c) Control flow graph after duplication of Fetch and Decode

Fig. 1: Control flow graphs of bytecode interpreters

3.2   Pipelined Interpreters

In the threaded interpreter shown in figure 1c the $execute_i$ and the increment/fetch/decode (IFD) parts are usually independent, because the increment value of the bytecode pointer is a constant for most bytecodes, jumps being the exception. The IFD part is expressed in pseudo C as:

```
pb += n;        /* Increment */
bc = *pb;       /* Fetch next bytecode */
t = table[bc];  /* Fetch target address from jump table */
goto t;         /* Jump to next bytecode */
```

This consists of a sequence of two loads and a jump, which can be executed parallel to the execute part of the bytecode itself on a VLIW processor like the TriMedia. For many simple bytecodes, the latency is determined by the IFD part. Therefore, a key issue in the speeding up of an interpreter on a VLIW is the decrease of this latency. The solution is to pipeline the two loads, i.e. *pb and table[bc], and the jump. The first of these loads is under the control of the programmer, so we obtain its pipelining by restructuring the source of the interpreter. The second load is compiler-generated from the switch statement. We have modified the compiler to take care of its pipelining. Without pipelining, the latency of the IFD part is $2*load+jump = 2*3+4 = 10$ cycles on a TriMedia.

The pipelining can also be explained by means of the following diagrams. Figure 2a shows the sequential execution of bytecodes. The figure illustrates that the execution time of a bytecode is determined by the IFD part, which is executed in parallel with the execute part. Figure 2b shows the pipelined execution. The pipeline comprises three stages: increment/fetch, decode, and execute/jump. While bytecode i is in its execute/jump stage, bytecode $i+1$ is in its decode stage, and bytecode $i+2$ is in its fetch stage.

Pipelining the Bytecode Fetch The bytecode fetch is pipelined by fetching bytecodes in advance and keeping these prefetched bytecodes in local variables which will be allocated to machine registers. Because the pipeline has to be two stages deep (we need to pipeline two loads), the bytecode must be fetched far enough in advance. Because bytecode instructions are of variable length, several bytes may need to be fetched in advance. The majority of the bytecodes have a length of at most three bytes. Since the bytes must be fetched two bytecode executions in advance, we decided to fetch a total of $2*3 = 6$ bytes in advance. We depict them by b1 through b6.

The pipelined interpreter code looks like this, for an instruction length of two bytes.

```
pb += 2;        /* Increment */
bc = b2;        /* Fetch next bytecode */
b1 = b3; b2 = b4; b3 = b5; b4 = b6; b5 = pb[5]; b6 = pb[6];
t = table[bc];  /* Fetch target address from jump table */
goto t;         /* Jump to next bytecode */
```

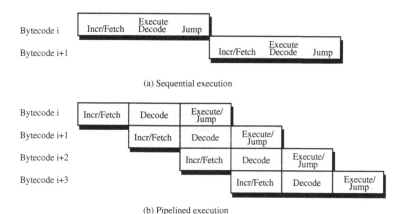

(a) Sequential execution

(b) Pipelined execution

Fig. 2: Sequential vs. pipelined bytecode interpretation. In the sequential case
(figure 2a), the operations of the IFD part are dependent on each other
while the IFD part can be executed in parallel with the execute part.
Figure 2a illustrates this.

The result of this pipelining is that the decode load (of the jump target) is
no longer dependent on any bytecode fetch. The latency of the IFD part is thus
reduced to *load+jump = 7* cycles on a TriMedia.

Pipelining Decode Load Recall that the decode load of the branch target
table[bc] is compiler-generated. The compiler can move this load from each
of the bytecode blocks into each of its predecessors. Since they are each others'
predecessors, each bytecode block gets 256 of these decode loads. Fortunately,
they are all equal apart from a difference in the instruction length **n**. So, for
each value of **n**, a version is copied to each predecessor block. In practice, this is
limited to 3 versions. This corresponds to the speculated decoding of bytecodes
due to the variable instruction length.

The result in pseudo C looks like this:

```
pb += 2;          /* Increment */
bc = b2;          /* Fetch next bytecode */
b1 = b3; b2 = b4; b3 = b5; b4 = b6; b5 = pb[5]; b6 = pb[6];
t  = t2;
t1 = table[b1];   /* Fetch target address 1 from jump table */
t2 = table[b2];   /* Fetch target address 2 from jump table */
t3 = table[b3];   /* Fetch target address 3 from jump table */
goto t;           /* Jump to next bytecode */
```

This code can be optimized by combining the shifting of the bytecodes with
the table loads, so that they can be shifted too. To this end, the compiler per-

forms an extensive analysis to prove that `t1` always equals `table[b1]`, etc. It then transforms the code as follows:

```
pb += 2;            /* Increment */
bc = b2;            /* Fetch next bytecode */
b1 = b3; b2 = b4; b3 = b5; b4 = b6; b5 = pb[5]; b6 = pb[6];
t  = t2;
t1 = t3;            /* Shift target address 1 */
t2 = table[b2];     /* Fetch target address 2 from jump table */
t3 = table[b3];     /* Fetch target address 3 from jump table */
goto t;             /* Jump to next bytecode */
```

The net result of this pipelining process is that, on a VLIW, a simple bytecode can start with a jump to its successor, and perform its actual computation in parallel with the jump. This reduces the minimum latency of a bytecode on a TriMedia to 4 cycles, the value of the branch delay.

Pipelining also increases the required number of registers to store the variables, and increases the code size of the interpreter loop. For TriMedia, the interpreter loop uses fewer than 20 registers and 30 kbyte of code. Recall that TriMedia has 128 registers and a 32 kbyte instruction cache.

3.3   Stack Caching

After pipelining, the execution time of the control flow part (IFD) of a bytecode is reduced from the sum of the latencies of two loads and a jump to the maximum of those latencies. In the case of TriMedia, the reduction is from 10 to 4 cycles. After this reduction however, the execute part usually has a longer latency, especially due to the evaluation stack accesses in a Java interpreter, which are always memory accesses.

This latency is easily reduced by caching the top s elements of the stack in local variables, which are mapped onto registers by the compiler. The best value for s is a trade-off between limiting the number of memory accesses to the evaluation stack on the one hand, and minimizing the register pressure and book-keeping operations relating to pipelining and stack-caching on the other, because driving these techniques too far results in too much code to implement it, which fills up the available issue slots. In practice, a value of $s = 2$ performs best on a TriMedia.

The following C code illustrates stack caching for the `iadd` bytecode, which takes two integers from the stack, adds them, and puts the result back on the stack:

```
tos = tos + nos;    /* Add top two elements on stack */
nos = sp[2];        /* Fetch new data into stack cache */
sp += 1;            /* Update stack pointer */
...                 /* IFD part */
```

The two local variables holding the top two stack elements are called `tos` (top of stack) and `nos` (next on stack). Unlike in previously published stack caching techniques [14], the primary goal of stack caching for us is to reduce the dependence height in the execute part of the bytecode and not to reduce the number of operations. Unlike [14], we do not maintain how many cache elements are valid by means of interpreter state. In our case, tos contains valid data when there is at least one element on the stack, and nos contains valid data when there are at least two elements on the stack.

After execution of a bytecode that consumes a variable number of stack elements, such as the invoke bytecodes, the cache is refilled by executing:

```
tos = sp[0];        /* load top-of-stack into cache */
nos = sp[1];        /* load next-on-stack into cache */
```

After using pipelining and stack caching, sufficient parallelism has been exposed that can be exploited by the global instruction scheduler of the TriMedia compiler [15].

3.4 Control Flow Bytecodes

In the case of control flow bytecodes, the IFD part is dependent on the execute part. In the case of a non-taken jump the pipeline is updated normally, but in the case of a taken jump the pipeline has to be flushed and has to be restarted at the jump target. The result is that taken jumps require more execution time than non-taken jumps. Pipelined processors without delay slots or branch prediction exhibit the same behavior in this respect.

3.5 Example TriMedia Assembly Code

Figure 3 shows the TriMedia assembly code for the iadd bytecode. It was produced by our compiler and slightly modified to improve clarity. Figure 3 shows four instructions, each containing five operations, in which empty issue slots are filled with nop operations. Immediate operands appear between parentheses. Register moves are implemented by an iadd operation with r0, containing a hard-wired zero value, as first operand.

Note that the jump operation is scheduled in the first instruction of the block and that the other operations are scheduled in parallel with the jump or in the three delay slots of the jump operation. To understand the code in figure 3, the reader should be aware that all operations in an instruction are issued in parallel and that the results of three-cycle latency load operations are written to registers three instructions after being issued. For example, the values that are moved from r14 and r21 in instruction 3 are not the values that are loaded in instruction 2, but the values that will be overwritten by the two loads, in the cycle after instruction 4.

4 Evaluation

In this section we describe several measurements to evaluate the presented techniques. As our evaluation platform we used Sun's Personal Java [11] running on

```
(* instruction 1 *)
iadd r22 r23 -> r22,        /* tos = tos + nos */
ijmpt r1 r13,               /* goto t1 */
iadd r0 r16 -> r9,          /* b1 = b2 */
ld32d(4) r12 -> r23,        /* nos = sp[1] */
nop;

(* instruction 2 *)
iadd r0 r17 -> r16,         /* b2 = b3 */
iadd r0 r10 -> r17,         /* b3 = b4 */
iadd r0 r20 -> r10,         /* b4 = b5 */
ld32x r18 r20 -> r14,       /* t3 = table[b4] */
uld8d(6) r11 -> r21;        /* b6 = pb[6] */

(* instruction 3 *)
iadd r0 r15 -> r13,         /* t1 = t2 */
iadd r0 r14 -> r15,         /* t2 = t3 */
isubi(4) r12 -> r12,        /* decrement stack pointer */
iadd r0 r21 -> r20,         /* b5 = b6 */
nop;

(* instruction 4 *)
iaddi(1) r11 -> r11,        /* increment bytecode counter */
nop, nop, nop, nop;
```

Fig. 3: TriMedia assembly code for the `iadd` bytecode

top of the pSOS real-time operating system. Furthermore, we used a cycle-true simulator of TriMedia that is configured for 128 MByte of main memory. We use SPEC JVM98 for benchmarking. The seven benchmarks of SPEC JVM98 are listed in table 1.

4.1 Execution Speed

First we are interested in the execution times of individual bytecodes. We determined this by inspecting the TriMedia assembly code. Table 2 shows the number of VLIW instructions required to execute a bytecode. In the absence of cache misses, the number of VLIW instructions corresponds to the number of machine cycles required to execute the bytecode. Since pipelining is intended to reduce the interpretation overhead of simple bytecodes, we only list the simple bytecodes in table 2. Long integer and double precision floating point are not supported by the TriMedia architecture and are implemented by library calls. They are therefore regarded as complex bytecodes and have consequently not been included in table 2.

Table 2 clearly shows that most simple bytecodes are executed by four VLIW instructions or close to it. Taken jumps require more cycles because the inter-

Benchmark	Description	Input description	Bytecodes
_201_compress	LZH data compression	SPEC JVM98 -s1 option	27,993,191
_202_jess	Expert shell system	SPEC JVM98 -s1 option	8,151,873
_209_db	Data management	SPEC JVM98 -s1 option	1,773,230
_213_javac	The JDK Java compiler	SPEC JVM98 -s1 option	6,151,375
_222_mpegaudio	MPEG-3 audio decode	SPEC JVM98 -s1 option	115,891,206
_227_mtrt	Raytracer	SPEC JVM98 -s1 option	33,842,764
_228_jack	Parser generator	SPEC JVM98 -s1 option	176,706,788

Table 1: Benchmarks used for evaluation

Bytecode type	Instruc-tions	Example bytecodes
Simple arithmetic	4	iadd, fadd, isub, fsub, imul, fmul, ineg, fneg, ishl
Taken/non-taken jump	15/7	ifeq, ifne, iflt, ifge, if_icmpeq, if_icmpne
Load constant	4	aconst_null, iconst_m1, iconst_0, iconst_1, fconst_0
	5	dconst_0, dconst_1, ldc_quick
	6	ldc_w_quick
	8	ldc2_w_quick
Push constant	4	bipush
	6	sipush
Load	5	iload, lload, fload, dload, aload
	4	iload_0, iload_1, iload_2, fload_0, fload_1, fload_2
Store	5	istore, lstore, fstore, dstore, astore
	4	istore_0, istore_1, istore_2, dstore_0, dstore_1
Array load	9	iaload, laload, faload, daload, aaload, baload
Array store	16	iastore, lastore, fastore, dastore, bastore
Stack manipulation	4	pop, pop2, dup, dup_x1, dup_x2, dup2, swap
Local increment	6	iinc
Control flow	12	goto, jsr, goto_w, jsr_w
Field access	7	getfield_quick, putfield_quick
	8	getfield2_quick, putfield2_quick
	21	getstatic_quick, putstatic_quick, getstatic2_quick

Table 2: Overview of execution times of simple bytecodes

preter pipeline has to be flushed and reloaded with bytecodes at the jump target, as described in section 3.4.

Various heap access bytecodes are relatively slow because of the internal data structures used by Sun Personal Java. All accesses to heap objects (class objects as well as array objects) are performed via handles. Although this facilitates heap compaction, an extra indirection, i.e. a load operation, is required to access data.

Static field accesses are relatively slow because each reference requires an expensive test to determine whether static initializers have to be called. Several sequential loads are required to perform this test in Personal Java.

Array stores are also relatively slow. This is caused by the run-time checks that have to be performed (null pointer check and bound check) and by the fact that the array reference operand is the third stack operand which is not cached in the stack cache. This operand is the most time-critical of the three operands of array store bytecodes (array reference, index, and data to be stored). A stack cache of three elements will improve the speed of array stores, but several other bytecodes are likely to take more time.

4.2   Individual Contributions of Different Techniques

In order to measure the individual contributions of the techniques described in section 3, we compiled the JVM in three different ways: (1) no threading and pipelining, (2) threading but no pipelining, and (3) threading and pipelining. In all three cases stack caching was enabled. Table 3 shows the instruction count reduction: on average, threading reduces the instruction count by 16.6%, pipelining gives a further reduction of 19.4% over the threaded version. The combined reduction is 32.5%. Furthermore, table 4 shows the cycle count reduction: on average, threading reduces the cycle count by 14.4%, pipelining gives a further reduction of 14.6% over the threaded version. The combined reduction is 26.4%.

The reduction in cycle count is obviously less than the reduction in instruction count because threading and pipelining does only reduce the number of compute cycles and not the number of stall cycles where the processor is waiting on the memory. In fact, threading and pipelining may increase the number of memory cycles because they increase the code size of the interpreter, which leads to more instruction cache misses, and pipelining results in speculative decoding, which causes more data cache references and misses.

The results listed in tables 3 and 4 show a clear correlation between the effectiveness of threading and pipelining. These techniques are most effective for applications in which the majority of the execution time is spent by interpretation of the simple bytecodes. Profile analysis shows that this is indeed the case: _202_jess, _209_db, _213_javac, and _227_mtrt spend a lot of their time in complex bytecodes, the run-time system, garbage collector, and long integer arithmetic emulation code.

5   Related Work

Ertl suggests in his thesis to move part of the dispatch code of the interpreter to earlier bytecodes for machine with sufficient instruction level parallelism [16]. This is a first step into the direction of pipelined interpreters which results in a pipeline of two stages.

Proebsting proposes superoperators to reduce the interpretation overhead [17]. Several of operators are combined together into one superoperator. The interpretation overhead is shared between several operations.

The same idea is used by Piumarta and Riccardi with the difference that their interpreter is dynamically extended with superoperators [18]. They implemented

Benchmark	Threading off/ Pipelining off	Threading on/ Pipelining off	Threading on/ Pipelining on
_201_compress	548,294,965	419,622,175 (23.4%)	291,935,454 (30.3%)
_202_jess	315,140,012	278,841,909 (11.5%)	242,821,721 (12.9%)
_209_db	64,614,881	56,152,260 (13.0%)	48,126,498 (14.2%)
_213_javac	235,200,152	206,235,014 (12.3%)	178,900,872 (13.2%)
_222_mpegaudio	2,785,393,145	2,157,813,532 (22.5%)	1,623,357,369 (24.7%)
_227_mtrt	1,319,173,260	1,163,465,508 (11.8%)	1,023,474,854 (12.0%)
_228_jack	3,676,668,870	2,882,897,278 (21.5%)	2,056,280,297 (28.6%)
Average		(16.6%)	(19.4%)

Table 3: The effects of threading and pipelining on instruction count. The instruction count reduction with respect to the previous column is shown between parentheses. The combined reduction of threading and pipelining is 32.5%.

Benchmark	Threading off/ Pipelining off	Threading on/ Pipelining off	Threading on/ Pipelining on
_201_compress	582,876,139	455,567,117 (21.8%)	334,036,387 (26.7%)
_202_jess	424,461,155	390,515,530 (8.0%)	364,608,239 (6.6%)
_209_db	92,906,063	84,712,746 (8.1%)	78,876,026 (6.9%)
_213_javac	303,094,306	270,041,792 (10.9%)	248,756,893 (7.9%)
_222_mpegaudio	2,860,981,158	2,247,040,013 (21.4%)	1,718,591,626 (23.5%)
_227_mtrt	1,471,970,773	1,319,425,388 (10.4%)	1,195,740,789 (9.3%)
_228_jack	4,135,817,332	3,333,366,670 (19.4%)	2,624,348,279 (21.2%)
Average		(14.4%)	(14.6%)

Table 4: The effects of threading and pipelining on cycle count. The cycle count reduction with respect to the previous column is shown between parentheses. The combined reduction of threading and pipelining is 26.4%.

this by a 'cut-and-past' style of code generation where the code to implement a superoperator is generated by concatenating the code of the elementary operators.

We have also used pipelined interpreter technology for other purposes than JVM. We implemented a code compaction system which compiles code to a very dense bytecode-based application-specific virtual machine [19]. Like the JVM interpreter, we used a three-stage pipeline for this.

In another project, we studied a pipelined interpreter for the MIPS instruction set; using only four pipeline stages it was capable of executing many of the MIPS instructions in six clock cycles on TriMedia without any pre-decoding. The first pipeline stage fetches the MIPS instruction, the second stage maps all opcode fields of a MIPS instruction onto one bytecode, the third stage performs the decode by means of a table lookup, and the fourth stage is the jump/execute stage.

We expect that pipelining of threaded interpreters will be useful for super-scalars and explicitly parallel instruction computers (EPIC), such as the IA64 architecture [20], as well. In case of IA-64, the rotating register file can be used for shifting bytecodes and the prepare-to-branch instructions can be used to improve the predictability of the jump to the next block.

6   Conclusions

The paper has describes how the execution speed of a JVM interpreter on a VLIW processor can be improved substantially by pipelining. While one byte-code is in its execute stage, the next bytecode is in its decode stage, and the next bytecode of that is in its fetch stage. Pipelining is implemented by both source code rewriting and compiler modifications. Rewriting of the interpreter source code requires compiler expertise. This is not a severe problem because compiler and interpreter technology are very related to each other.

On the TriMedia VLIW processor, with load and jump latencies of three and four cycles, respectively, pipelining makes it possible to execute many of the simple bytecodes, such as additions and multiplications, in four clock cycles.

References

1. Tim Lindholm and Frank Yellin. *The Java Virtual Machine Specification*. Addison-Wesley, Reading, Massachusetts, 1996. 35
2. Harlan McGhan and Mike O'Conner. PicoJava: A Direct Execution Engine for Java Bytecode. *IEEE Computer*, 31(10):22–30, October 1998. 35
3. Ali-Reza Adl-Tabatabai, Michal Cierniak, Guei-Yuan Lueh, Vishesh M. Parikh, and James M. Stichnoth. Fast, Effective Code Generation in a Just-In-Time Java Compiler. In *Proceedings of the 1998 ACM SIGPLAN Conference on Programming Language Design and Implementation*, pages 280–290, Montreal, Canada, 1998. 35
4. Andreas Krall. Efficient JavaVM Just-in-Time Compilation. In *Proceedings of the 1998 International Conference on Parallel Architectures and Compilation Techniques*, pages 205–212, Paris, France, October 1998. 35
5. Andreas Krall, Anton Ertl, and Michael Gschwind. JavaVM Implementation: Compilers versus Hardware. In John Morris, editor, *Computer Architecture 98 (ACAC '98)*, Australian Computer Science Communications, pages 101–110, Perth, 1998. Springer. 36
6. Gert A. Slavenburg. *TM1000 Databook*. TriMedia Division, Philips Semiconductors, TriMedia Product Group, 811 E. Arques Avenue, Sunnyvale, CA 94088, www.trimedia.philips.com, 1997. 36, 37
7. Gerrit A. Slavenburg, Selliah Rathnam, and Henk Dijkstra. The TriMedia TM-1 PCI VLIW Mediaprocessor. In *Hot Chips 8*, Stanford, California, August 1996. 36, 37
8. Vicky H. Allan, Reese B. Jones, Randall M. Lee, and Stephan J. Allan. Software Pipelining. *ACM Computing Surveys*, 27(3), September 1995. 36
9. Alfred V. Aho, Ravi Sethi, and Jeffrey D. Ullman. *Compilers: Principles, Techniques and Tools*. Addison-Wesley Series in Computer Science. Addison-Wesley Publishing Company, Reading, Massachusetts, 1985. 36, 38

10. The Kaffe Homepage: www.kaffe.org. 37
11. The Personal Java Homepage: java.sun.com/products/personaljava. 37, 43
12. James R. Bell. Threaded Code. *Communications of the ACM*, 16(6):370–372, 1973. 38
13. Paul Klint. Interpretation Techniques. *Software — Practice & Experience*, 11(9):963–973, September 1981. 38
14. M. Anton Ertl. Stack Caching for Interpreters. In *Proceedings of the SIGPLAN '95 Conference on Programming Language Design and Implementation*, pages 315–327, La Jolla, California, June 1995. 43
15. Jan Hoogerbrugge and Lex Augusteijn. Instruction Scheduling for TriMedia. *Journal of Instruction-Level Parallelism*, 1(1), February 1999. 43
16. M. Anton Ertl. *Implementation of Stack-Based Languages on Register Machines*. PhD thesis, Technische Universität Wien, Austria, 1996. 46
17. Todd A. Proebsting. Optimizing an ANSI C Interpreter with Superoperators. In *Proceedings of the Fifteenth Annual ACM Symposium on Principles of Programming Languages*, pages 322–332, 1995. 46
18. Ian Piumarta and Fabio Riccardi. Optimizing direct threaded code by selective inlining. In *Proceedings of the 1998 ACM SIGPLAN Conference on Programming Language Design and Implementation*, Montreal, Canada, June 1998. 46
19. Jan Hoogerbrugge, Lex Augusteijn, Jeroen Trum, and Rik van de Wiel. A Code Compression System Based on Pipelined Interpreters. *Software — Practice & Experience*, 29(11):1005–1023, September 1999. 47
20. Intel, Santa Clara, CA. *IA-64 Application Developer's Architecture Guide*, 1999. 48

Automatic Removal of
Array Memory Leaks in Java

Ran Shaham[1,2]*, Elliot K. Kolodner[2], and Mooly Sagiv[1]

[1] Tel-Aviv University
{rans,sagiv}@math.tau.ac.il
[2] IBM Haifa Research Laboratory
kolodner@il.ibm.com

Abstract. Current garbage collection (GC) techniques do not (and in general cannot) collect all the garbage that a program produces. This may lead to a performance slowdown and to programs running out of memory space.

In this paper, we present a practical algorithm for statically detecting memory leaks occurring in arrays of objects in a garbage collected environment. No previous algorithm exists. The algorithm is conservative, i.e., it never detects a leak on a piece of memory that is subsequently used by the program, although it may fail to identify some leaks. The presence of the detected leaks is exposed to the garbage collector, thus allowing GC to collect more storage.

We have instrumented the Java virtual machine to measure the effect of memory leaks in arrays. Our initial experiments indicate that this problem occurs in many Java applications. Our measurements of heap size show improvement on some example programs.

1   Introduction

Java's run-time GC does not (and in general cannot) collect all the garbage that a program produces. GC typically collects objects that are no longer reachable from a set of *root* references. However, there are some objects that the program never accesses again, even though they are reachable. This may lead to a performance slowdown and to programs running out of memory space. This may also have a negative effect on Java usability.

1.1   A Running Example

A standard Java implementation of a stack data structure is shown in Figure 1(a). After a successful `pop`, the current value of `stack[top]` is not subsequently used. Current garbage collection techniques fail to identify memory leaks of this sort; thus, storage allocated for elements popped from the stack may not be freed in a timely manner. This example class serves as the running example throughout this paper.

---

* Supported in part by the U.S.-Israel BSF under grant 96-00337

A. Watt (Ed.): CC/ETAPS 2000, LNCS 1781, pp. 50–66, 2000.

1.2   Existing Solutions

A typical solution to avoid these memory leaks is to explicitly assign null to array elements that are no longer needed. For example, a stack implementation, which avoids these leaks is shown in Figure 1(b), where null is explicitly assigned to stack[top].

```
public Class Stack {
  private Object stack[];
  private int top;
  public Stack(int len) {
    stack = new Object[len];
    top = 0;
  }
  public synchronized Object pop() {
    if (0 < top) {
      top--;
s:       return stack[top];
    }
    throw new ESExc();
  }
  public synchronized
              void push(Object o) {
    if (top < stack.length) {
s':     stack[top]=o;
        top++;
        return;
    }
    throw new FSExc();
  }
  public synchronized void print() {
    for (int i=0; i<top; i++) {
s'':  System.out.println(stack[i]);
    }
  }
}
```

```
public Class Stack {
  private Object stack[];
  private int top;
  public Stack(int len) {
    stack = new Object[len];
    top = 0;
  }
  public synchronized Object pop() {
    if (0 < top) {
      Object tmp;
      top--;
      tmp = stack[top];
      stack[top]=null;
      return tmp;
    }
    throw new ESExc();
  }
  public synchronized
              void push(Object o) {
    if (top < stack.length) {
      stack[top]=o;
      top++;
      return;
    }
    throw new FSExc();
  }
  public synchronized void print() {
    for (int i=0; i<top; i++) {
      System.out.println(stack[i]);
    }
  }
}
```

(a)   (b)

Fig. 1. (a) The runing example, Stack class. (b) With explicitly assigning null. (ESExc and FSExc are subclasses of RuntimeException)

Such solutions are currently being employed in the JDK library, e.g., in the jdk.util.Vector class and by some "GC-aware" programmers. These solutions have the following drawbacks:

- Explicit memory management complicates program logic and may lead to bugs; by trying to avoid memory leaks, a programmer may inadvertently free an object prematurely.
- GC considerations are not part of the program logic; thus, they are certainly not a good programming practice. In fact, the whole idea of GC aware programs defeats some of the purposes of automatic GC.
- The solution of explicitly assigning `null` may slow the program, since such `null` assignments are performed as part of the program flow. For example, consider the method `removeAllElements` of class `java.util.Vector` shown in Figure 2(b). The only reason for the loop is to allow GC to free the array elements. In contrast, our compile-time solution eliminates the need for such a loop. The method can be rewritten as shown in Figure 2(a); thus, at least `elementCount` instructions are saved. In Section 5 we give a potential interface to GC, which will allow unit-time operation in this case.

```
                                void removeAllElements() {
void removeAllElements() {         for (int i=0; i < elementCount; i++)
    elementCount=0; }                  elementData[i]= null;
                                   elementCount=0;  }
            (a)                              (b)
```

Fig. 2. (a) A "clean" implementation. (b) "GC-aware" implementation

Consider the `Vector` class in the `java.util` package, which implements a dynamic array of objects. Though it has already been instrumented (in Sun's implementation) with assignment to `null` in appropriate places in order to avoid leaks, it suffers from some of the limitations outlined above. Furthermore, our experimental results show that instead of using a "standard" implementation of such abstract data types (ADTs), programmers use a "tailored" implementation in many cases, due to considerations such as speed, or strong typing. Examples include rewriting a non-synchronized version of `Vector` or a well-typed version of `Vector`, maintaining only objects of a specific class. There are some Java language extensions for parameterized types, e.g., [3], being considered, and work showing how to reduce the cost of synchronization, e.g., [2], which may eliminate the need for some of these tailored implementations. Nevertheless, the above limitations lead us to conclude that programmers should be freed from dealing with these memory management considerations and that the leaks should be detected by automatic means, e.g., by compiler analyses.

1.3   Main Results and Related Work

Section 2 presents our motivating experiments for showing that array memory leaks pose a real problem, and that the problem is worth solving, performance-wise. We performed a simple string search on Java source files and found some occurrences of the array memory leak problem. For several programs we also measured the potential benefit of solving the problem and found that there are cases where there is a significant saving of memory.

This research was inspired by work on liveness analysis for Java for local variables holding references [1]. This liveness analysis leads to a reduced *root set*, enabling more memory to be reclaimed. However, such techniques are not applicable in general to arrays of objects. Treating an array as a single reference variable yields an overly conservative result; an array represents a set of references, where every array element is a potential reference, while a reference variable represents only one potential reference. For example, the field `stack` in the Stack class is *live* after s, but the location denoted by `stack[top]` is *dead* after s.

Identifying liveness requires flow sensitive analysis that may take non-linear time and could fail to scale for large programs. Moreover, due to the capability of Java to load classes in run-time, not all the code is necessarily available even when a program starts running. Therefore, our algorithm can operate on Java bytecode and analyze one class at a time by conservatively approximating potential method invocations. Despite these conservative assumptions, our algorithm is capable of finding memory leaks in many interesting cases, including the implementation of various array-based ADTs, e.g., dynamic arrays, stacks and cyclic queues. Indeed, we believe that this will allow our algorithm to scale for large programs, while locating most of the leaks in well written programs that make use of private or protected fields for encapsulation. In Section 3 we briefly discuss the *approximated supergraph* to allow a simple class level analysis of Java.

In Section 4, we give an algorithm for identifying live regions of arrays. Technically, identifying live array regions is more complex than the problem of identifying live scalars, since in many cases it is necessary to identify relationships between index variables. In the `print` method of the running example, knowing that i is less than `top` before s'' is important in order to determine that elements of stack beyond `top` cannot possibly be used in the `println` invocation. Relationships between variables have also been used to analyze array accesses for parallelizing compilers and in the context of other array reference analyses (e.g., [11,17]). These techniques can also be extended to detect the minimal and maximal values used as array indices; this allows the removal of checks for array bound violations [8,9]. One of the most precise methods was proposed by Cousot and Halbwachs [6]; it automatically identifies linear relationships between variables by scanning the control flow graph in a forward direction. In [13] it is shown that this general technique can be also used to analyze live array regions. Our chief observation is that live array regions can be also represented using linear relationships between variables.

We show how the result of a forward direction dataflow analysis, which identifies relationships between variables, is integrated into a backward analysis of the control flow, which determines the live regions of the array.

Both phases use the *constraint graph* suggested in [4, Chapter 25.5, pp.539–543] as a simple representation of program variable relationships. The constraint graph allows us to efficiently represent a special case linear relationship of the form $x \leq y + c$, where x and y are program variables and c is an integer constant. In [13] we explain how to handle more general sets of constraints and more interesting classes of programs.

In Section 5, we explain how a GC algorithm can exploit the results of our analysis algorithm. Our algorithm can also be applied to a Java program with potential leaks in order to determine the necessary null assignments. null assignment statements are added at program points where the array elements become dead. In the running example, our algorithm detects that before program point s, array element stack[top] is live, while after s, array element stack[top] is dead. Thus stack[top] can be assigned to null, as shown in Figure 1(b).

A prototype of the algorithm was implemented in Java, and used to find dead array regions for the running example in 0.21 CPU seconds. The prototype has no front-end, so the input to the prototype is the approximated supergraph of a class. The extended version of the algorithm as described in [13] was also implemented, and used to find live array regions for java.util.Vector class. Interestingly, the analysis located a bug in the method lastIndexOf(Object elem, int index) (to be fixed by Sun Microsystems). We noticed the bug due to the overly imprecise live array regions.

Some programming languages, such as CLU [10], provide built-in dynamic arrays that can be used to implement stacks and vectors. However, our algorithm can handle cases beyond dynamic arrays such as cyclic queues where the regions of live array elements are not necessarily continuous. Furthermore, our algorithm does not require extensions to the Java language.

2   Motivating Experiments

Frequency of the Problem The experiment to determine the frequency of occurrence was conducted before implementing the algorithm. Instead, we used lexical scanning of Java source files. We searched for classes having a field, which is an array of objects, and integer field(s), preferably containing the string "count" in their names. Also, we looked for methods containing the string "remove". The motivation for such searches, was to find re-implementations of the java.util.Vector class, keeping in mind that the methods like removeAllElements and removeElementAt use explicit assignments to null to prevent memory leaks.

About 5600 Java source files were scanned, including the *Java Development Kit* version 1.1.6 source files. In 1600 files, an array of objects is defined. In 20 files the problem was detected in 25 statements, i.e., several files contained more than one instance. Out of the 25 statements, 13 did not have the desired null assignment, i.e., they contained a potential memory leak.

Potential Benefits We conducted an experiment similar to that conducted in [1] using a modified JVM, in order to evaluate the potential benefits of removing leaks. We used Sun's JDK 1.2, Classic VM, as the basis. After every 100KB of allocation, we invoke the GC, perform all possible finalizations, and perform GC again. We calculate the heap size as a function of bytes allocated, sampled every 100KB. To simulate a potential memory leak, two versions of `java.util.Vector` class are used, the original one, and a version with leaks, i.e., without the explicit assignments to `null` in the `removeElementAt` and `removeAllElements` methods. Then we compared the allocation integral, calculated as the area under the heap size curve.

We measured the allocation integral in two programs from Spec JVM98 [15], *javac*, the Java compiler, and *db*, a benchmark simulating a database, on the original and modified Spec inputs. These are the only programs in the Spec suite using vectors. The measurements were done on a 400 MHz Intel Pentium-II CPU with 128MB of memory, running Windows NT 4.0.

In *javac* we obtain 1.35% average allocation integral improvement. The original input to *db* yields no improvement. However, using the modified input to *db*, which contains many delete commands, the improvement is 26.65%, concluding (as in [1]) that the expected main benefit is preventing bad surprises .

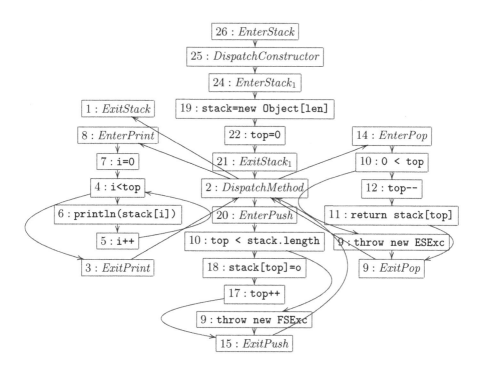

Fig. 3. The approximated supergraph of the running example.

3   Class Level Analysis of Java Programs

In this section we briefly discuss the *approximated supergraph* of a class. The main idea is to approximate the execution paths on all the class instances, while allowing the derivation of interesting information on objects encapsulated at the class level. Thus, paths that do not modify or use encapsulated data are not included in the approximated supergraph.

The *program supergraph*(see [14,12]) integrates the program call graph and the individual control flow graphs of each of the procedures in the program. To allow interprocedural class level analysis, we use the *approximated supergraph*. The approximated supergraph of the class C is an approximation of supergraphs occurring at any instance of C. Since the idea of approximated supergraph is not a core part of this work and due to space limitations, we choose not to elaborate on the subject. Details regarding the approximated supergraph including extensions to include the full spectrum of Java constructs are found in [13]. The approximated supergraph of the running example is shown in Figure 3.

Encapsulation at the class level is ensured by using *private* fields, local variables and method parameters, and by not allowing objects referenced by these variables to "escape" outside the class level scope. In the running example, top is a private field, i is local variable, len is a method parameter, stack is a private field, and in addition is not passed as a parameter or returned as a result, thus its referenced array can not escape outside the class level scope. Therefore, they are all encapsulated in Stack, and the analysis of Stack class using the approximated supergraph is conservative.

4   The Algorithm

In this section, we give an efficient algorithm for computing *liveness* information for arrays. In Section 4.1, we define the problem by extending the classical definition of liveness of scalar variables. In Section 4.2 we define constraint graphs that provide an efficient representation for special form of inequalities between index variables. In addition, we show that constraint graphs can represent liveness information. In Section 4.3 an iterative algorithm for identifying live regions for arrays at every supergraph node is given. This algorithm uses the constraint graph and the previously computed forward information, to obtain quite precise liveness information. This section is concluded in Section 4.4, in which we briefly describe the iterative forward algorithm, which computes inequalities between index variables at every supergraph node.

For expository purposes, we assume that the program supergraph contains one designated encapsulated array A of type T[] .

4.1   The Liveness Problem for Arrays

Recall that a scalar variable var is *live* before a program point p, if there exists an execution sequence in the program including p and a use of var such that

(i) p occurs before the use of var and (ii) var is not assigned between p and the use.

We now generalize this definition for arbitrary program expressions that evaluate to a location or reference (or equally have a defined L-value).

Definition 1. *An expression* e *is* **live before a program point** p, *if there exists an execution sequence,* $\pi_1.\pi_2$ *such that (i) the path* π_1 *ends at program point* p, *(ii)* e *denotes a location (or reference)* l *at the end of* π_1, *and (iii)* l *is used at the end of* π_2 *without prior assignment along* π_2.

In the running example (see Figure 1), the location denoted by stack[top] in s is live before s, but not before any other point in the class. For example, it is not live before the end of the method pop since on any sequence from that point to a usage of a location denoted by stack[top] in s, this location must be assigned a new value at s'. Indeed, the main idea in this definition is to allow the expression e to denote more than one location for different execution paths. In the running example, stack[i] is live before s'' for all $0 \leq i < top$. This is the kind of information important for GC (see Section 5).

Notice that Definition 1 coincides with the classic liveness definition for a scalar variable and in this case l is the (activation record) location of the scalar.

4.2 The Constraint Graph

We now define the constraint graph, which efficiently represents inequalities between program variables. Operations on the inequalities are implemented by path calculations on the constraint graph.

Definition 2. *The* **constraint graph** *is a finite labeled directed graph with a set of vertices* V *of the encapsulated integer variable or field, including a special vertex* 0, *and in addition another special vertex, denoted* $, *for representing liveness constraints to be discussed later. The constraint graph is captured by a weight function* $w: V \times V \to \mathbb{Z} \cup \{-\infty, \infty\}$. *Pictorially, we draw an edge from* v_1 *to* v_2 *if* $w(v_1, v2) < \infty$.

Such a directed graph w *represents the inequalities:*

$$\bigwedge_{x,y \in V} x \leq y + w(x,y) \tag{1}$$

This interpretation of w is used in the forward phase of the algorithm. The constraint graph, which represents the inequalities after supergraph node 5 (i = i + 1) of the running example, is shown in Figure 4. The -1 edge from 0 to i represents the inequality $0 \leq i + (-1)$, or $0 < i$. Usually, isolated vertices are omitted from the figures. An edge, which its weight is implied by the sum of the weights along a directed path in the graph connecting the source and the target vertices of that edge, is also not included in the figures.

The reader is referred to [4, Chapter 25.5, pp.539–543] for explanations on the properties of constraint graphs.

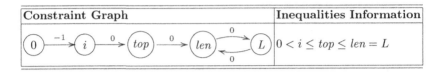

Fig. 4. The constraint graph after supergraph node 5. L stands for stack.length

Our chief insight is that live regions can also be represented using constraint graphs, with one additional designated vertex, denoted by $. This node represents constraints on the live array indices of the array. For example, the constraint graph in the first row of Figure 5 corresponds to the liveness information $0 \leq \$ < top$. This constraint graph represents the fact that array elements stack[0], stack[1], ..., stack[top − 1] are live. Another example is the constraint graph corresponding to a conditional live region which is presented in the second row of Figure 5. It signifies that array elements stack[0], stack[1], ..., stack[top − 1] are live, and in addition the live region is conditional because of the −1 edge connecting vertex i to vertex top. In other words, if $i \geq top$ then none of the array elements is alive. This can happen when the stack is empty and top = 0.

Constraint Graph	Liveness Information
$0 \xrightarrow{0} \$ \xrightarrow{-1} top$	$\{stack[\$] \mid 0 \leq \$ < top\}$
$0 \xrightarrow{0} i \quad \$ \xrightarrow{-1} top$	$\{stack[\$] \mid 0 \leq \$ < top, 0 \leq i < top\}$

Fig. 5. Constraint graphs representing liveness information

In general a constraint graph w represents the following liveness information:

$$\{A[\$] \mid \bigwedge_{x,y \in V} x \leq y + w(x,y)\} \tag{2}$$

where live regions come into play when either x or y are $. This interpretation of w is used in the backward phase of the algorithm. The constraint graph in Figure 5 represents the liveness information:

$$\{stack[\$] \mid 0 \leq \$ + 0 \wedge \$ \leq top + (-1) \wedge 0 \leq i + 0 \wedge i \leq top + (-1)\} \tag{3}$$

The operations on constraint graphs are defined in Figure 6. The most basic operation is $TC(w)$, which yields a constraint graph whose edges are labeled with the shortest path (the least weight) between any two vertices. $TC(w)(x, y)$ corresponds to *strongest implied constraint* between x and y. We implemented $TC(G)$ using Floyd's all-pairs-shortest-path algorithm.

The constraint graph *represents a contradiction* if there exists a negative directed cycle in the graph. A contradiction represents either an infeasible execution path, or the fact that there are no future uses of the array. We denote these two cases by $\bot$, $dead(A)$ respectively. The case of $w = dead(A)$ can only occur when w signifies liveness constraints. *eliminateNegativeCycles* detects contradicted constraint graphs, and $TC_{\bot}(w)$ extends $TC(w)$ by taking care of these special cases.

We define an order on constraint graphs to respect information order, i.e., $w_1 \sqsubseteq w2$ if $w_1 = \bot$, or $w_1 = dead(A)$ and $w_2 \neq \bot$ or for every $x, y \in V$, $w_1(x, y) \leq w_2(x, y)$.

For convibiency, our algorithm only operates on *closed* constraint graphs w, i.e., $TC_{\bot}(w) = w$. In this case, the order on closed constraint graphs is a *partial order* with *join*, $\sqcup$, (for merging information along different control flow paths), *meet*, $\sqcap$ (for partially interpreting program conditions) and *widening*, ∇ (for accelerating the termination of the iterative algorithm) operators shown in Figure 6. The operations in Figure 6 are exemplified in Section 4.3.

4.3   Backward Computation of Live Regions

In this section, we give an iterative algorithm for computing live regions in arrays. The algorithm operates on the approximated supergraph. The algorithm is *conservative*, i.e., the identified live regions must include "actual" live regions. When the iterative algorithm terminates, for every supergraph node n, and for every program point p that corresponds to n, if $A[i]$ is live before p then i satisfies all the constraints in the constraint graph that the algorithm yields at n.

The algorithm starts by assuming that the array is dead at $Exit\langle Class \rangle$ supergraph node (*ExitStack* in the running example). Then it backward propagates liveness information along supergraph paths. The fact that the algorithm scans the supergraphs nodes in a backward direction may not come as a surprise, since the algorithm is an extension of the scalar variables liveness algorithm. Indeed, liveness information captures information about future usages.

Formally, the backward phase is an iterative procedure that computes the constraint graph $w_b[n]$ at every supergraph node n, as the least solution to the following system of equations:

$$w_b[n] = \begin{cases} dead(A) & n = Exit\langle Class \rangle \\ w_b[n] \nabla (w_f[n] \sqcap \bigsqcup_{m \in succ(n)} w_b[n, m]) & \text{otherwise} \end{cases}$$

$$w_b[n, m] = [\![st(\langle n, m \rangle)]\!]_{b_{\bot}}^{\sharp} (w_b[m], w_f[n, m])$$

(4)

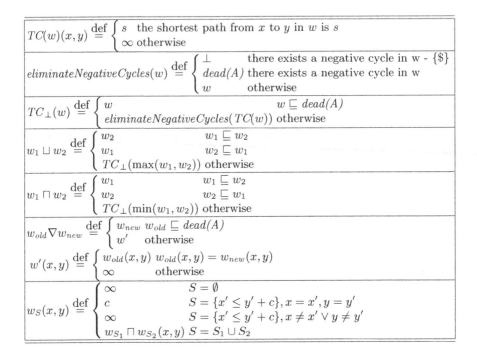

Fig. 6. The utility functions used in the forward and backward analysis algorithms. w_S constructs a constraint graph corresponding to the strongest implied constraints in S

where $st(\langle n, m \rangle)$ is either the statement at supergraph node n or the condition holding along the arc $\langle n, m \rangle$, $[\![st(\langle n, m \rangle)]\!]^\sharp_{b_\perp}$ is defined in Figure 7, and $w_f[n], w_f[n, m]$ are given in Equation (5).

In the following subsections, we briefly explain the operators and the transfer functions used in the analysis:

Join Join is used when the supergraph flow splits (see Equation (4)). $\sqcup$ shown in Figure 6 yields the intersection of the (strongest implied) constraints occurring on all splitting supergraph paths, i.e., the maximal weight.

In Figure 8, the constraint graph after supergraph node 4, `i < top` is obtained by joining the constraint graphs before node 6, `println(stack[i])` and node 3, *ExitPrint*. The edge connecting vertex i to vertex $ shown is not included, since it appears only in the constraint graph from `println(stack[i])` and not in the constraint graph from *ExitPrint*.

Integrating Forward Information The motivation to integrate forward information into the backward information comes from the observation that the

statement	$[\![\text{statment}]\!]^{\sharp}_{f}(w)$	$[\![\text{statment}]\!]^{\sharp}_{b}(w, w_f)$
$\texttt{i} = \texttt{j} + \texttt{c}$	$w \sqcap$ $w_{\{i \leq j+c, j \leq i+(-c)\}}$	$\begin{cases} dead(A) & w = dead(A) \\ TC_{\perp}(w') & \text{otherwise} \end{cases}$ $w'(x,y) = \begin{cases} min(w(j,y), w(i,y) - c) & x = j \\ min(w(x,j), w(x,i) + c) & y = j \\ \infty & x = i \vee y = i \\ w(e) & \text{otherwise} \end{cases}$
$\texttt{A} =$ $\texttt{new T}[\texttt{i} + \texttt{c}]$	$[\![A.length =$ $i + c]\!]^{\sharp}_{f}(w)$	$dead(A)$
$\texttt{use A}[\texttt{i} + \texttt{c}]$	w	$w \sqcup (w_f \sqcap w_{\{\$ \leq i+c, i \leq \$+(-c)\}})$
$\texttt{use A}[\texttt{exp}]$	w	$w_{\emptyset}$
$\texttt{def A}[\texttt{i} + \texttt{c}]$	w	$\begin{cases} dead(A) & w = dead(A) \\ TC_{\perp}(w') & \text{otherwise} \end{cases}$ $w'(x,y) = \begin{cases} c-1 & x = \$, y = i, w(x,y) = c \\ -c-1 & x = i, y = \$, w(x,y) = -c \\ w(x,y) & \text{otherwise} \end{cases}$
$\texttt{i} \leq \texttt{j} + \texttt{c}$	(true arc) $w \sqcap w_{\{i \leq j+c\}}$ (false arc) $w \sqcap w_{\{j \leq i+(-1-c)\}}$	
Transfer Function Extension		
$[\![st(\langle n,m\rangle)]\!]^{\sharp}_{f_{\perp}}(w) \overset{\text{def}}{=} \begin{cases} \perp & w = \perp \\ [\![st(\langle n,m\rangle)]\!]^{\sharp}_{f}(w) & \text{otherwise} \end{cases}$		
$[\![st(\langle n,m\rangle)]\!]^{\sharp}_{b_{\perp}}(w, w_f) \overset{\text{def}}{=} \begin{cases} \perp & w = \perp \vee w_f = \perp \\ [\![st(\langle n,m\rangle)]\!]^{\sharp}_{b}(w, w_f) & \text{otherwise} \end{cases}$		

Fig. 7. The forward and backward transfer functions for simple statements. w_f is the forward information constraint graph occurring in the same supergraph node of w. $w_{\{\text{set of constraints}\}}$ is defined in Figure 6. $\texttt{exp}$ is an arbitrary expression other than $\texttt{i+c}$. A condition node is interpreted along its true and false arcs. Transfer functions are extended to handle the case when w is $\perp$. Statement, which involves only constant expressions, can be handled simply by using a designated zero variable. Other statements are handled conservatively

liveness of an expression, $\texttt{A}[i]$, before supergraph node n, depends on two sources of information (see Definition 1): (i) The value of i on supergraph paths from node $Enter\langle Class\rangle$ leading to node n, which determines the location l denoted by $\texttt{A}[i]$, and (ii) The usage of location l on supergraph paths emanating from node n.

Therefore, integrating the (previously computed) forward information regarding the value of i and the backward information regarding the liveness of $\texttt{A}[i]$ can have a dramatic impact on the precision of the analysis.

Figure 9 shows the integration of the forward and backward information before node 6. Using the forward phase information, $0 \leq i < top \leq len = L$, leads to a precise liveness information, $\{stack[\$] | 0 \leq \$ < top, 0 \leq i < top\}$.

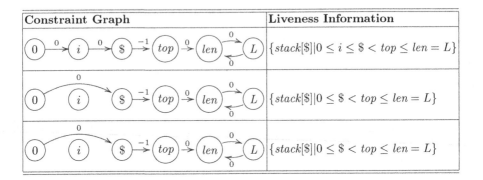

Fig. 8. The constraint graph before `println(stack[i])`, *ExitPrint*, and their join

The integration of forward and backward information is captured in Equation (4) by the ⊓ operation.

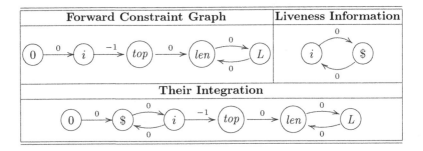

Fig. 9. The integrated constraint graph

Use of an Array Element For a statement using `A[i+c]`, the algorithm enlarges the live region to include the current (forward) value of $i + c$. This means that the constraints on $ are relaxed such that $ $ = i + c$ is satisfiable. First, we integrate the forward information and the fact that `A[i + c]` is live. Then, the resulting constraint graph is joined with the constraint graph after the statement to obtain the constraint graph before the statement.

Figure 9 corresponds to integration of the forward and backward information before node 6, occurring in the first visit of that node. Then we join it with the current liveness information after node 6, which is *dead(A)*.

Assignment to an Array Element For a statement assigning to `A[i+c]`, the algorithm can shrink the live region to exclude the current (forward) value of $i + c$. This means that the constraints on $ can be made stronger to exclude the liveness of `A[i + c]`.

In the constraint graph this corresponds to decrementing the c edge from vertex $\$$ to vertex i by 1 and decrementing the $-c$ edge from vertex i to vertex $\$$ by 1. In Figure 10 the constraint graph before supergraph node 18, `stack[top]=o`, by shrinking the live region $\$ \leq top$ to $\$ \leq top + (-1)$.

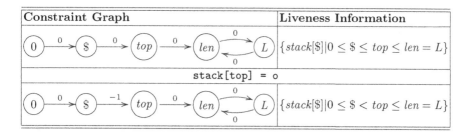

Fig. 10. The constraint graph before an assignment statement to an array element

Assignment Statements For the statement `i = j + c`, the liveness information is obtained by substituting occurrences of i with $j + c$. If i occurs in the left side of a constraint, then the constraint is normalized. For example, for the constraint $i \leq j' + c'$, after substituting $j + c$ for i, the normal form becomes $j \leq j' + (c' - c)$.

In Figure 11 the constraint graph before supergraph node 12, `top = top + (-1)`, is obtained by incrementing 0 edge from vertex $\$$ to vertex top by -1, and decrementing -1 edge from vertex top to vertex len by -1.

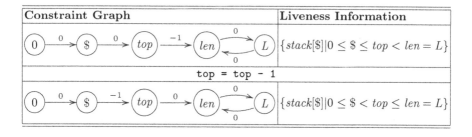

Fig. 11. The constraint graph before an assignment statement

Widening ∇ (see [5]) shown in Figure 6 accelerates the termination of the algorithm by taking the strongest implied constraints from the former visit of a supergraph node that remain true in the current visit of supergraph node.

Conditions The liveness information allows us to partially interpret program conditions in many interesting cases. This is a bit tricky, since supergraph nodes are visited in a backward direction.

The conditions of the form $i \leq j + c$ are handled by creating a constraint graph having one c edge from vertex i to vertex j, and then integrating it with the liveness information along the true edge (see Figure 7).

4.4   Forward Computation of Inequalities between Variables

The forward phase is an iterative algorithm for computing inequalities between integer variables and fields. The algorithm is *conservative*, i.e., every detected inequality at a supergraph node must hold on every execution through a program point represented by that node.

Formally, the forward phase is an iterative procedure that computes the constraint graph $w_f[n]$ at every supergraph node n, as the least solution to the following system of equations:

$$w_f[n] = \begin{cases} w_0 & n = Enter\langle Class \rangle \\ w_f[n] \nabla \bigsqcup_{m \in pred(n)} w_f[m, n] & \text{otherwise} \end{cases} \tag{5}$$
$$w_f[m, n] = [\![st(\langle m, n \rangle)]\!]_f^{\sharp}(w_f[m])$$

where $[\![st(\langle m, n \rangle)]\!]_f^{\sharp}$ is shown in Figure 7.

Since the forward phase is not new (e.g., a more precise version is given in [6]), in this paper, we only explain the backward phase.

5   GC Interface to Exploit Algorithmic Results

The output of the algorithm is a set of constraints associated with each program point that describe what sections of an array are alive at that point. A constraint may depend on the instance and local variables of the class and may include simple functions on those variables, e.g., top - 1 for the Stack class. We choose to exploit instance variables constraints that hold at all program points at which a thread can be stopped for garbage collection. The points at which a thread can be stopped are precisely the gc-points of a type-accurate collector [1,7]. We judiciously choose where to put gc-points so that the "best" constraint holds. For example, the constraint for the Stack class is that the elements of the stack array from 0 through top - 1 are alive, provided that there is no gc-point between the beginning of pop and statement s.

The chosen constraints are information that is logically associated with a specific class. Thus, it makes sense to store the constraints in the class data structure (or class object) together with the other information specific to the class, e.g., method table and description of fields. Notice that if a class has more than one array as an instance variable, then a set of constraints can be associated with each array field. A class-wide flag is also set in the class structure to indicate that it has at least one such array field.

When a tracing GC [16] (either mark-sweep or copying) encounters an object during its trace, it checks the class-wide flag in the object's class structure. If the flag is set, the collector traces the arrays reachable from the object, limiting its trace of the arrays according to their associated constraints.

6 Conclusion

We have presented a practical algorithm for determining the live regions of an array. The information produced by the algorithm can be used by GC in order to limit its trace of arrays, thereby leading to the collection of more garbage. Our experiments show a potential improvement of memory consumption.

The algorithm can determine a precise liveness information for some array based implementation of ADTs, namely stack and double stack (a stack growing in both directions). In addition, the extended version of the algorithm (maintaining at most two sets of constraint graphs per supergraph node) , described in [13] handles precisely dynamic vector. Further work is needed to analyze more Java programs and to detect more kinds of leaks occurring in arrays.

References

1. Ole Agesen, David Detlefs, and Elliot Moss. Garbage Collection and Local Variable Type-Precision and Liveness in Java Virtual Machines. In *SIGPLAN Conf. on Prog. Lang. Design and Impl.*, June 1998. 53, 55, 64
2. David F. Bacon, Ravi Konuru, Chet Murthy, and Mauricio Serrano. Thin Locks: Featherweight Synchronization for Java. In *SIGPLAN Conf. on Prog. Lang. Design and Impl.*, June 1998. 52
3. Gilad Bracha, Martin Odersky, David Stoutamire, and Philip Wadler. Making the future safe for the past: Adding genericity to the java programming language. In *Conf. on Object-Oriented Prog. Syst., Lang. and Appl.*, Vancouver, B.C., 1998. 52
4. Cormen, Leiserson, and Rivest. *Algorithms*. MIT Press and McGraw-Hill, 1994. 54, 57
5. P. Cousot and R. Cousot. Systematic design of program analysis frameworks. In *Symp. on Princ. of Prog. Lang.*, pages 269–282, New York, NY, 1979. ACM Press. 63
6. P. Cousot and N. Halbwachs. Automatic discovery of linear restraints among variables of a program. In *Symp. on Princ. of Prog. Lang.*, January 1978. 53, 64
7. Amer Diwan, Eliot Moss, and Richard Hudson. Compiler support for garbage collection in a statically typed language. In *SIGPLAN Conf. on Prog. Lang. Design and Impl.*, pages 273–282, San Francisco, CA, June 1992. 64
8. Rajiv Gupta. Optimizing array bound checks using flow analysis. *Let. on Prog. Lang. and Syst.*, 2(1–4):135–150, March–December 1993. 53
9. Priyadarshan Kolte and Michael Wolfe. Elimination of redundant array subscript range checks. In *SIGPLAN Conf. on Prog. Lang. Design and Impl.*, 1995. 53
10. Barbara Liskov et al. CLU reference manual. In *Lec. Notes in Comp. Sci.*, volume 114. Springer-Verlag, Berlin, 1981. 54
11. William Pugh. The Omega Test: a Fast and Practical Integer Programming Algorithm for Dependence Analysis. In *Communications of the ACM*, August 1992. 53

12. T. Reps, S. Horwitz, and M. Sagiv. Precise interprocedural dataflow analysis via graph reachability. In *Symp. on Princ. of Prog. Lang.*, New York, NY, 1995. 56
13. Ran Shaham. Automatic removal of array memory leaks in Java. Master's thesis, Tel-Aviv University, Tel-Aviv, Israel, September 1999. Available at "http://www.math.tau.ac.il/~ rans/thesis.zip". 53, 54, 56, 65
14. M. Sharir and A. Pnueli. Two approaches to interprocedural data flow analysis. In S.S. Muchnick and N.D. Jones, editors, *Program Flow Analysis: Theory and Applications*, chapter 7, pages 189–234. Prentice-Hall, Englewood Cliffs, NJ, 1981. 56
15. SPEC JVM98. Standard Performance Evaluation Corporation (SPEC), Fairfax, VA, 1998. Available at http://www.spec.org/osg/jvm98/. 55
16. Paul R. Wilson. Uniprocessor garbage collection techniques. In *Memory Management, International Workshop IWMM*, September 1992. 65
17. Michael Wolfe. *High Performance Compilers for Parallel Computing*. Addison-Wesley, 1995. 53

A Static Study of Java Exceptions Using JESP⋆

Barbara G. Ryder, Donald Smith, Ulrich Kremer,
Michael Gordon, and Nirav Shah

Department of Computer Science, Rutgers University
110 Frelinghuysen Road, Piscataway, NJ 08854-8019, USA
fax: 732-445-0537
{ryder,dsmith,uli,fabfour,nshah}@cs.rutgers.edu

Abstract. **JESP** is a tool for statically examining the usage of user
thrown exceptions in Java source code. Reported here are the first findings over a dataset of 31 publicly available Java codes, including the
JavaSpecs. Of greatest interest to compiler writers are the findings that
most Java exceptions are thrown across method boundaries, trys and
catches occur in equal numbers, finallys are rare, and programs fall
into one of two categories, those dominated by throw statements and
those dominated by catch statements.

1 Introduction

Java already has been embraced as a Web programming language and is beginning to gain acceptance as a language for general applications. In response
to the acceptance and use of this and other OO languages, compile-time analysis and code transformations that produce optimized code for features found in
such languages(e.g., polymorphism, exceptions, etc.) are being studied. This paper summarizes how exceptions are used in current Java codes. The information
gathered shows that exceptions are ubiquitous and that their use often falls into
specific patterns.

Exception handling is common in Java programs for the Web, but it is also
true that exceptions will play a significant role in general purpose applications.
The use of exceptions in general applications is due to several emerging trends.
Key among these are: the development of automated systems with complex
control paths, and the shift toward exception-based programming paradigms
seen in most introductory language and data-structures texts.

Automated systems are being built around legacy codes that were designed
to be controlled by humans and are now being controlled by programs. Not
surprisingly, *human-friendly* codes are proving to be *program-*un*friendly*, neces-
sitating the adaptation of these codes for use under program, as opposed to
human, control. These legacy codes have been built over several years by several
people, have been validated against extensive test suites, and are now trusted
tools. Revalidation of such codes is very expensive in time and money thus con-
straining adaptations of these codes to minimize the need for revalidation. One

⋆ The research reported here was supported, in part, by NSF grant CCR-9808607.

A. Watt (Ed.): CC/ETAPS 2000, LNCS 1781, pp. 67–81, 2000.

of the most promising strategies to facilitate the adaptation of legacy codes under the constraint of limited revalidation is the introduction of wrappers[12,11,8] that handle unexpected situations. Wrappers provide a mechanism that detects when a code has failed and passes control to a module designed to manage the failure. Java exceptions, in conjunction with their catch and throw operators, provide an ideal mechanism for implementing wrappers.

In addition to the development wrapper-based automated systems, a general shift toward exception-based programming paradigms is being observed. There are several reasons for this shift including program correctness, program clarity, and elimination of side effects. These reasons have been noted by many in the community. Texts and references now contain persuasive arguments, such as the following.

> Exceptions provide a clean way to check for errors without cluttering code. Exceptions also provide a mechanism to signal errors directly rather than use flags or side effects such as fields that must be checked. Exceptions make the error conditions that a method can signal an explicit part of the method's contract. *p.151*[1]

These two trends, along with the growth in popularity of object-oriented languages such as Java, make it clear that exceptions will play an increasing role in program design, and thus present a new challenge to optimizing compilers.

The Java exception model is very strict as to what program state must be made available to the user when an exception occurs.

> Exceptions in Java are *precise*: when the transfer of control takes place, all effects of the statements executed and expressions evaluated before the point from which the exception is thrown must appear to have taken place. No expressions, statements, or parts thereof that occur after the point from which the exception is thrown may appear to have been evaluated. If optimized code has speculatively executed some of the expressions or statements which follow the point at which the exception occurs, such code must be prepared to hide this speculative execution from the user-visible state of the Java program. *p.205*[9]

In order to produce efficient optimized code that meet these specifications, safety conditions must be guaranteed for any optimizing transform used by the compiler. Since exceptions produce new and distinctive control-flow patterns, new static analysis techniques must be developed that accurately estimate control flow[5,4,6,10,14]. Speculation of instructions must be consistent with what is required by this exception model[2,13,7]. Practical compile-time analyses and code transformations should take advantage of common patterns of exception usage, especially in calculating possible profitability of transformations or the appropriateness of approximation in analysis.

We partition exceptions into two classes: those that are not usually thrown by a user and those that are usually thrown by a user. The former are usually thrown by the runtime system and are objects in the *RuntimeException* class;

for example, *NullPointerException* and *ArrayBoundsException* are among these. The latter usually appear in a **throw** statement of a user's Java program and are often, but not always, a user-defined subclass of *Exception*. Both kinds of exceptions complicate program control flow. The empirical study reported here is an examination of Java program source codes using the Prolangs JESP tool to determine their patterns of user thrown exceptions. These initial results (and further planned static and dynamic studies) will serve as a basis for focusing compiler writers' attention on those uses of exceptions which actually occur in real codes. Additionally, it will allow compiler writers to de-emphasize those that may be difficult to transform, but do not occur very often (e.g., nested **finallys**).

Outline. Section 2 presents the dataset used in this study. The **JESP** tool and empirical measurements obtained in the study are explained and interpreted in Section 3. Ramifications of the findings for optimizing compilers are listed in Section 4. Related work is mentioned in Section 5. Section 6 states the conclusions and briefly describes future work.

2   Description of Data

As an initial study, a representative set of popular Java applications and applets were gathered. Included are a large number of programs from JARS, the Java Review Service,[1] rated in their top twenty percent by utility. These programs include:

- **IceMail** - a Java email client
- **JFlex** - a lexical analyzer generator
- **RabbIT** - a web proxy
- **WebHunter** - a file downloader
- **LPR**- a class library that allows printing to a standard LPD (Unix) printer over the network.
- **Creature** - an artificial life simulator
- **Statistician** - lists method statistics for a class
- **Vigenere** - encrypts text based on the vigenere algorithm
- **JavaBinHex** - a BinHex decompresser
- **JHLZip** - compresses an uncompressed zip file
- **JHLUnzip** - decompresses a compressed zip file
- **Othello** - a Reversi applet

A large number of Java programs that are currently being developed also were included. Among these programs are McGill University's **Soot beta 4**[15], a Java bytecode analysis and transformation framework and its accompanying tools. Additional programs, such as the **Hot Path Browser**[2] and **JavaCC**[3] came

---

[1]   http://www.jars.com

[2]   http://www.bell-labs.com/project/HPB/

[3]   http://www.suntest.com/JavaCC/

from Lucent Technologies/Bell Laboratories and Sun Microsystems, respectively. The **Hot Path Browser** allows the user to view the most frequently executed paths of a program given the correct path information. **JavaCC** is a parser generator. The final two programs are from SBKTech; **Jas** a Java bytecode assembler and **Jell** a parser generator.

3   Findings

3.1   Experimental Framework

To gather the static measurements of the sample set of applications, a set of tools collectively known as **JESP** (Java Exception Static Profiler) were built using the **JTrek** library from Compaq/Digital[4] The **JTrek** library is a Java API that allows developers to instrument, profile, and decompile Java classes. It allows for rapid development of both static and dynamic profiling tools. Specifically, the Trek class library models Java code as a hierarchy of objects. The Trek API allows a developer to scan through a program's bytecode instructions, with classes representing the program's class files, and the fields, methods, local variables, statements, and instructions within them.

3.2   Data Gathered

The 31 Java programs evaluated in this study are shown in Figure 1. They were obtained from JavaSpecs[5] as well as from public sources on the Internet and ranged in size from 48 to 96,000 lines of code. **JESP** analyzed each program and produced summaries of exception usage and structure based on JDK 1.1.5. The usage and structure of exceptions and exception constructs are reported in the sections that follow.

General Descriptive Data Figure 1 describes the programs that were evaluated. The codes are ordered from smallest to largest based on number of lines of code. Additional fields giving size in bytes, number of classes[6], number of classes with an `implements` clause, total number of methods, and percentage of methods with exception constructs (i.e., `throw`, `try`, `catch`, `finally`) are also shown.

Examination of Figure 1 shows that multiple inheritance, as indicated by an implements clause, is used infrequently in smaller programs of the dataset (i.e., under 5,000 lines of code). Figure 2(a) shows that lines of code per class has little or no correlation with program size and Figure 2(b) corroborates the prevailing view that Java methods are short. For the programs examined the number of lines of code per method had little or no correlation with program size and averaged 33 (median 26) over all programs. Note: **Statistician** (id 7, with 6996 lines of code) is an outlier because it has only one class.

---

[4] http://www.digital.com/java/download/jtrek/index.html

[5] http://www.specbench.org

[6] Figure 1 list number of files. In Java, files and non-internal classes are 1-1 mappable.

	Program	Lines of Code	Bytes	Files Analyzed	Implements	Total Methods	% of Meth. w/ Exceptions
1	227 mtrt	48	859	1	1	4	0%
2	JHLUnzip	187	3,262	1	0	3	67%
3	spec	283	5,420	2	0	11	18%
4	JavaBinHex	300	4,851	1	0	4	50%
5	Vigenere	305	9,333	3	2	22	18%
6	999 checkit	332	5,899	3	1	8	25%
7	Statistician	387	6,996	1	0	2	50%
8	JHLZip	425	5,473	2	0	11	27%
9	Javacc-JJTree-JJDoc	602	21,573	6	0	22	14%
10	LPR	777	14,731	3	0	52	25%
11	201 compress	927	17,821	12	1	44	2%
12	209 db	1028	10,156	3	1	34	21%
13	WebHunter	1610	36,114	6	9	81	11%
14	200 check	1818	40,381	17	7	107	19%
15	io	2631	58,057	8	0	98	13%
16	reporter	2743	71,703	18	3	114	21%
17	Othello	2804	41,427	18	0	164	9%
18	205 raytrace	3751	57,000	25	1	176	4%
19	harness	4882	83,899	23	2	185	12%
20	Jas	4920	210,807	121	89	422	14%
21	RabbIT	5276	128,552	43	15	267	17%
22	Joie	6773	147,757	63	3	630	8%
23	Soot-SableUtil	7155	86,006	67	23	484	12%
24	202 jess	10579	396,536	151	106	690	11%
25	Jell	10747	140,252	51	20	337	1%
26	Creature	11142	98,932	46	15	152	4%
27	HotPath Browser	11512	259,697	108	43	891	5%
28	Jflex	11796	192,839	53	16	420	7%
29	Soot-Jasmin	17152	253,292	99	22	664	8%
30	ICEMail	25974	457,246	135	72	966	13%
31	Soot beta 4	96144	1,033,630	651	276	3096	4%

Fig. 1. Programs in dataset

Try, catch, throw, and finally statements This section reports on constructs that play a role in exception processing. **JESP** totals the number of try, catch, throw and finally statements along with the number of throws declarations used in a program. Methods declared to throw multiple exceptions are handled the same as methods declared to throw only one exception - each are counted only once.

Across the entire dataset, Figure 3 shows that on average 16% (median 13%) of the methods contain some kind of exception construct and that this percentage is insensitive to program size. This confirms the belief that exceptions will be ubiquitous in Java programs and highlights the fact that optimization transformations which are effective vis-a-vis exceptions will be necessary for efficient code generation.

Figures 4(a) and 4(b) display how many catch, throw and try statements occur in the dataset. Results for finally statements are not presented in the figure since they are rarely used; 26 of the 31 programs do not contain any finally clause. Similarly, throws were rare in the smaller programs; none of the programs smaller than 1615 lines of code contained a throw. Note that the number of catch and try statements in each program seem equal.

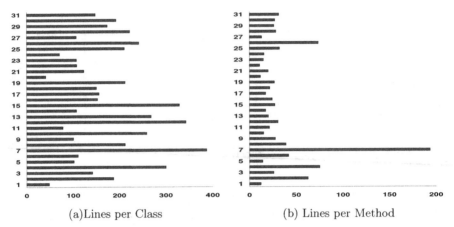

(a)Lines per Class   (b) Lines per Method

Fig. 2. Average number of lines of code

Figure 5 displays the ratio of **try** to **catch** statements. 50% of the programs have exactly 1 **catch** per **try** and only 1 program exceeds 1.5 **catches** per **try**. This implies that **try** clauses almost always contain 1 **catch** statement and very rarely contain 2 or more **catch** statements. The fact that **trys** usually contain only 1 **catch** provides strong evidence that specialization and inlining transformations may be effectively employed to improve performance.

A surprising feature of our dataset is that almost every program is dominated by either **catches** or **throws** and seldom have similar numbers of each. Figure 6 shows the breakdown by percent of **catch** and **throw** statements. Only one procedure, **io** (id 16, with 2632 lines of code), has the number of throws and catches nearly equal. In all other cases the ratio of catches to throws is greater than 3-to-1 or less than 1-to-3. This is indicative of a difference in the kinds of applications being measured. Applications with more **throws** than **catches** are hypothesized to be libraries, which must be robust over all possible uses of their methods. Similarly, applications with more **catches** than **throws** are probably clients of libraries that are handling the exceptions returned by library routines rather than passing them up the Java runtime stack. This, along with lack of **finally** statements, indicates that exceptions are fully processed where, and when, they are first caught.

We were very interested in seeing how exceptions are used in **finally** clauses and to see if potential complications to control flow were observed in practice. Unfortunately **finally** statements were so rare in our dataset that reporting on exceptions in **finally** statements is impossible.

Distance between a throw and its corresponding catch JESP was used to measured specific patterns of exception constructs within **try** statements and to report the number of **throws** not enclosed in a **try** statement. We considered four distinct usage patterns for **try** statements. Trys that contain:

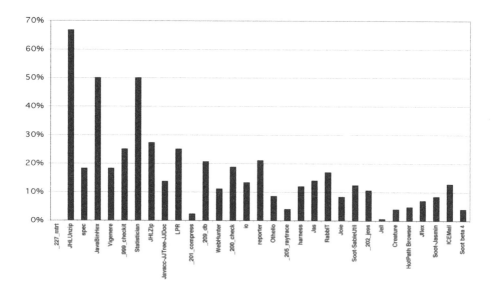

Fig. 3. Percentage of methods with try, catch, and throw constructs

- one or more throws and a corresponding catch,
- no throws and a catch,
- one or more throws and no catches, and
- no throws and no catches

Each try construct could optionally contain a finally; however for the dataset evaluated this had little impact. We found, as expected, that throws do not occur in try statements but rather occur outside of try statements. Figures 7(a) and 7(b) summarize our data. These observations support our belief that exception handling seems to be done by passing the exception up the current call stack. A try without a throw probably contains a method call that may throw an exception.[7] A throw not in a try is probably in a method called directly or indirectly from a try block. Thus, the next question to be investigated both statically and dynamically is "How far up the call stack is an exception object passed, on average?" This knowledge will aid in tailoring optimizations of this exception usage, especially for non-aborting control-flow exceptions.

Characterizing Exceptions JESP was also used to categorize the class of the object that is being thrown as either a Java-defined exception, User-defined exception, or Unknown. A Java-defined exception is an instance of an exception class that is defined in the JDK 1.1.5. User-defined exceptions are classified as

---

[7] It is possible for a try block to be used to catch exceptions such as *ArrayBoundsException* or other subclasses of *RuntimeException* which can be generated without a method call; however, we believe this use of try blocks is very rare.

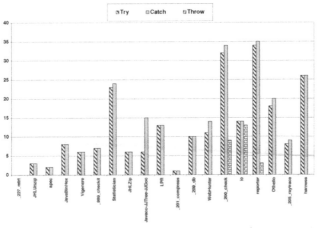

(a)Small Programs(under 5000 lines)

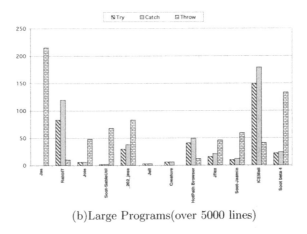

(b)Large Programs(over 5000 lines)

Fig. 4. Try, catch, throw counts per program

exception objects that are instances of classes not defined in the JDK. These can include exception classes defined in any library code that the program uses. Figure 8 reports these results and clearly shows that user defined exceptions are much more prevalent than Java-defined exceptions. In two cases, library code was not available and we found programs that did not define an exception class yet did throw one or more user-defined exceptions. These are not included in Figure 8.

The prevalence of user-defined exceptions is strong supporting evidence that exceptions are not only ubiquitous but also gaining acceptance as a mainstream control flow mechanisms in Java. The implications are clear for optimizing compilers. They will have to produce efficient code from source that contains user-defined exceptions and catch/throw patterns that manage control flow.

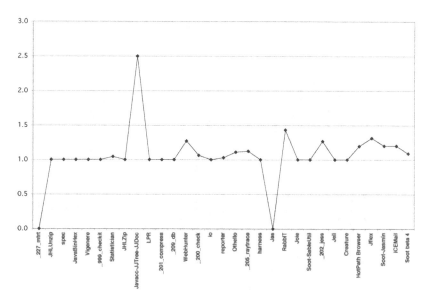

Fig. 5. Average number of catches per try

The final category of data that **JESP** gathered is information regarding the number of exception classes that the program contains as well as the shape of the exception tree hierarchy that the program defines. An exception class was considered to be any class that extends *Throwable* or any of its subclasses, excluding classes that extend *Error*. To analyze the shape of the exception tree, **JESP** gathers the maximum breadth and depth of the tree. Results of this analysis indicate that user-defined exceptions change the exception tree very little. Without any user-defined exceptions, the JDK's base exception tree has a maximum breadth of eleven and a maximum depth of four. With user-defined exceptions the breadth and depth changed very little if at all. More work is needed to separate the user- and Java-defined trees so representative figures can be reported. Preliminary indications are that user-defined exception hierarchies are very shallow (i.e., in our dataset no program had a user-defined hierarchy deeper than 2).

4   Ramifications

The gathered statistics about the use of exceptions in Java are preliminary. More experiments, in particular dynamic program instrumentation, are needed to give a more detailed picture of exceptions and their use in Java. However, some interesting conclusions and conjectures can already be made.

- **finally** clauses are only used rarely in our benchmark suite. This suggests that the development of techniques to optimize **finally** clauses and handle

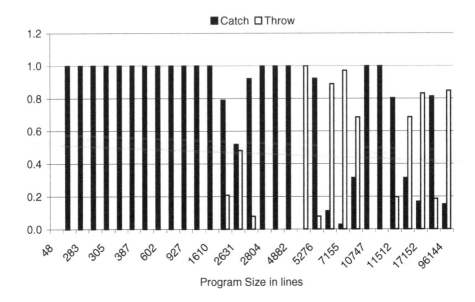

Fig. 6. Catch vs. Throw

the potential complexity they introduce into exception handling may not be profitable.

- The typical **try** blocks contains only one **catch** clause. This suggests that users have a particular exception event in mind when writing a typical **try** block and indicates a *local* treatment of exceptions may be possible. In such cases a compiler, supported by the appropriate analysis, may be able to determine which **catch** clause will process an exception thrown from a specific program point.
- The combination of **throw** statements being rare in **try** blocks, **try** blocks containing only one **catch** each, and the user-defined exception hierarchy being shallow indicates that the *static* and *dynamic* distance between **throw** and **catch** events in the call graph or on the run time stack may be short.
- There are a significant number of explicit **throw** statements outside of **try** blocks. This suggests that exception handling cannot be dealt with inside a single method. However, more work is needed to determine if exceptions are handled within methods of the same class or passed across classes. If exceptions are thrown and caught in the same class more aggressive analyses and optimizations are possible.

In Section 1 exceptions were classified as either *usually thrown by a user* or *usually not thrown by a user*; this study gathers information about the former. There is another useful classification of exceptions as either *abortive* or *control* exceptions. Abortive exceptions do not allow program recovery, but lead to the termination of the program, possibly after some clean-up or diagnostic analysis

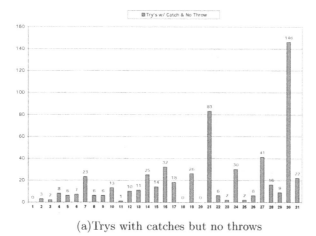

(a)Trys with catches but no throws

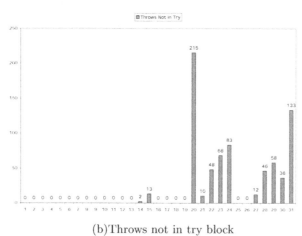

(b)Throws not in try block

Fig. 7. Exception constructs

has been performed in the corresponding `catch` clause. In contrast, a control exception signals some abnormal, but anticipated program condition from which the program is expected to recover. In this case, the corresponding `catch` clause contains recovery code and initiates the continuation of program execution in an updated program state.

Since abortive exceptions lead to program termination, the benefit of optimized code for these exceptions is minimal. Since they are abortive, their expected frequency should be rather low in debugged and tested codes and any optimization will only speedup the final cleanup stages before termination. Therefore, efforts to optimize the execution of an abortive exception itself are not beneficial. This is not true for control exceptions since they represent a likely control flow path in the program. An aggressive optimizing compiler should op-

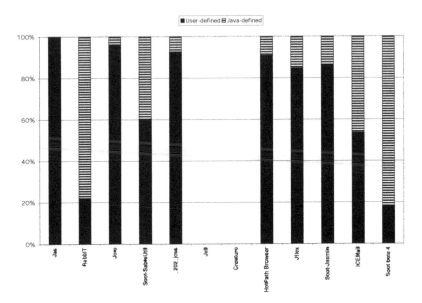

Fig. 8. User-defined versus Java-defined exceptions

timize the execution of control exceptions and should try to limit the effects of all exceptions on the safety and benefits of other transformations.

Possible Optimizations

Knowing statically the binding between a thrown exception and the `catch` clause that will process the exception has two advantages that can be exploited by an optimizing compiler:

- No runtime check is necessary to determine if the next current method will handle the exception.
- The code contained in the corresponding `catch` clause can be moved to the site where the exception is thrown, allowing better code locality. In addition, the runtime stack can be updated with a single multi-frame pop operation. This optimization assumes that no statement such as a `finally` occurs in any intermediate method invocation between the `throw` and `catch` methods. This safety property can be easily verified by a compile-time analysis.

5   Related Work

There has been much recent interest in the problems presented to compilation and analysis of programs by Java exceptions. Of course, any Java compiler must handle exceptions; for space reasons all Java compilers under development cannot be presented here. Therefore, this discussion focuses on research which reports exception usage.

Sinha and Harrold[10] present new control-flow representations to model exception flow for data-flow and control-dependence analyses. They performed a quick static study of a seven Java programs and found that that on average 23% of their methods contained a `try` or a `throw`. Their dataset included: **jacorb, javacup, jdk, jlex, swing, tdb,** and **toba**. They use this data to substantiate the hypothesis that analysis algorithms will have to take account of exceptions in Java because of their prevalence.

Chatterjee, Ryder and Landi[5] presented a new flow-sensitive analysis, called *relevant context inference (RCI)* for a subset of Java that can model exception control flow. This analysis stresses optimized memory usage by only requiring the code for a method to be in memory three times during the analysis. Exception control flow is modeled as another context preserved by the algorithm (with alias and type contexts). Chatterjee's thesis[4] shows how to use RCI to calculate def-use associations in the presence of exceptions.

Krall and Probst[13] performed a small static study of five Java programs (i.e., **JavaLex, javac, espresso, Toba, java_cup**) used as data for their *CA-CAO* compiler. They measured number of try blocks versus number of method calls in these programs and found that the latter was two orders of magnitude larger than the former. They also reported on the number of null pointer checks in these programs which was more comparable to the number of method invocations.

Choi *et.al.*[6] present a new intermediate representation, a factored control flow graph, used in the IBM *Jalapeno* dynamic Java compiler that accommodates exits caused by possible implicit exceptions such as *NullPointerException*. They report static counts of the number of basic blocks with exception handler edges for implicit exceptions, both for the traditional basic block and their new design.

The *Marmot* optimizing Java compiler from Microsoft[7] also optimizes implicit exceptions. Their transformations make it possible to catch *NullPointerExceptions* using hardware.

Robaillard and Murphy[14] report on **Jex**, a static tool for identifying user-defined exception control flow in Java programs. Given a Java source file and the user-called packages (denoted by the user), **Jex** derives a representation of exception flow through the program. Exceptions generated by the Java API were also counted. For each Java method, **Jex** produces a summary of those exceptions possibly thrown by its execution. The empirical study reported focused on the use of subsumption in `catch` clauses. About 44% of the exceptions within `try` blocks were not caught with the most precise exception type available. The goal was to give this information to a programmer to increase their understanding of possible exception flow in their program.

Brookshier[3] measured and reported on the cost of exception processing for control exceptions when the handler is not close to the method throwing the exception on the runtime stack. He describes the cost of a `throw` as due to creation of an exception object, an invocation of the handler, a search of the stack for the current method, a search for a `try` block range, and then the search for a matching `catch`. He notes that cost of a `throw` is related to the depth of nested frames, so that speed can be improved if the catch clause is in the same method or relatively close on the runtime stack. Measured on a 300MHz Pentium II with Symantec's 1.1 JIT, there was a slowdown of 80 milliseconds per exception in a program written so that the handler is several stack frames from the throw.

6   Conclusions and Future Work

The studies reported here with the Prolangs **JESP** tool are an attempt to discern the generality with which explicit exception constructs (i.e., try, catch, finally, throw) occur in Java codes. The most important results were that a substantial percentage of methods (on average 16%) in a Java program contain exception constructs, so exception usage is ubiquitous, but exception constructs are fairly sparse (the number of trys match number of catches). Finallys are rare and thrown exceptions are usually not caught within the same method. User-defined exception hierarchies are shallow. Another interesting finding was the observed dramatic categorization of programs which display many more throws than catches and *vice versa*.

As with all initial studies, this one raises more questions than it answers. Future work includes measurement of the:

- dynamic behavior of user-thrown exception,
- use of control and abortive exceptions,
- number of user- and Java-defined exceptions caught, and
- number of times a catch clause catches an exception thrown from within the try block.

Acknowledgments. We sincerely thank Seth Cohen from Compaq Corporation whose help with **JTrek** was invaluable.

References

1. K. Arnold and J. Gosling. *The Java Programming Language, Second Edition.* Addison-Wesley, 1997. 68
2. M. Arnold, M. Hsiao, U. Kremer, and B.G. Ryder. Instruction scheduling in the presence of java's runtime exceptions. In *Proceedings of Workshop on Languages and Compilers for Parallel Computation (LCPC'99)*, August 1999. 68
3. D. Brookshier. Exception handling: Simpler, faster, safer. *Java Report*, 3(2), February 1998. 79
4. R. Chatterjee. *Modular Data-flow Analysis of Statically Typed Object-oriented Programming Languages.* PhD thesis, Department of Computer Science, Rutgers University, October 1999. 68, 79
5. Ramkrishna Chatterjee, Barbara G. Ryder, and William. A Landi. Relevant context inference. In *Conference Record of the Twenty-sixth Annual ACM SIGACT/SIGPLAN Symposium on Principles of Programming Languages*, January 1999. 68, 79

6. J.-D. Choi, D. Grove, M. Hind, and V. Sarkar. Efficient and precise modeling of exceptions for the analysis of java programs. In *Proceedings of the ACM SIG-PLAN/SIGSOFT Workshop on Program Analysis for Software Tools and Engineering*, pages 1–11, September 1999. 68, 79

7. R. Fitzgerald, T.B. Knoblock, E. Rif, B. Steensgaard, and D. Tarditi. Marmot: An optimizing compilr for java. Technical Report Technical Report MSR-TR-99-33, Microsoft Research, June 1999. 68, 79

8. Andrew Gelsey, Don Smith, Mark Schwabacher, Khaled Rasheed, and Keith Miyake. A search space toolkit. *Decision Support Systems - special issue on Unification of Artificial Intelligence with Optimization*, 18:341–356, 1996. 68

9. J. Gosling, B. Joy, and G. Steele. *The Java Language Specification*. Addison-Wesley, 1996. 68

10. M.J. Harrold and S. Sinha. Analysis of programs with exception-handling constructs. In *Proceedings of the International Conference on Software Maintenance*, November 1998. 68, 79

11. J. Keane. *Knowledge-based Management of Legacy Codes for Automated Design*. PhD thesis, Rutgers University, October 1996. 68

12. J. Keane and T. Ellman. Knowledge-based re-engineering of legacy programs for robustness in automated designs. In *Proceedings of the Eleventh Knowledge-Based Software Engineering Conference*, 1996. 68

13. A. Krall and M. Probst. Monitors and exceptions: How to implement java efficiently. In *Proceedings of 1998 ACM Java Workshop*, 1998. 68, 79

14. M. Robillard and G. Murphy. Analyzing exception flow in java programs. In *Proceedings of the 7th Annual ACM SIGSOFT Symposium on the Foundations of Software Engineering*, September 1999. 68, 79

15. Raja Vallee-Rai, Laurie Hendren, Vijay Sundaresan, Patrick Lamand Etienne Gagnon, and Phong Co. Soot - a java optimization framework. In *CASCON99*, Toronto, Ontario, September 1999. 69

Fast Escape Analysis and Stack Allocation
for Object-Based Programs

David Gay[1]* and Bjarne Steensgaard[2]

[1] EECS Department, University of California, Berkeley
dgay@cs.berkeley.edu
[2] Microsoft Research
rusa@microsoft.com

Abstract. A fast and scalable interprocedural escape analysis algorithm is presented. The analysis computes a description of a subset of created objects whose lifetime is bounded by the lifetime of a runtime stack frame. The analysis results can be used for many purposes, including stack allocation of objects, thread synchronization elimination, dead-store removal, code motion, and iterator reduction. A method to use the analysis results for transforming a program to allocate some objects on the runtime stack is also presented. For non-trivial programs, typically 10%-20% of all allocated objects are placed on the runtime stack after the transformation.

1 Introduction

Several program optimizations require that objects be accessible from only one thread and/or have a bounded lifetime. For example, in order for an object to be allocated in a stack frame of a thread's runtime stack, the lifetime of the object has to be bounded by the lifetime of the stack frame. Escape analyses compute bounds of where references to newly created objects may occur.

This paper presents a fast interprocedural escape analysis algorithm for whole-program analysis of object-oriented programs written in Java™-like programming languages. The complexity of the algorithm is linear in the size of the program plus the size of the static call graph. The algorithm is simple and the analysis results are good enough to be useful in practice. The algorithm also demonstrates that a limited form of polymorphic analysis is possible in linear time.

There are many potential uses for the analysis results. For example, if a Java object is known to be accessible only to the thread creating the object, then most synchronization operations on the object can be eliminated and dead stores to fields of the object are easier to identify. Java's memory consistency model dictates that all memory reads and writes are fully performed at synchronization points, but if an object is known only to a single thread then it is not detectable

---

* The work was performed while the author was working at Microsoft Research.

A. Watt (Ed.): CC/ETAPS 2000, LNCS 1781, pp. 82–93, 2000.
© Springer-Verlag Berlin Heidelberg 2000

if reads and writes to the fields of the object are moved around synchronization points.

The usefulness of the analysis results are demonstrated in this paper by a stack allocation transformation. A subset of the objects whose lifetime is bounded by the lifetime of a runtime stack frame are allocated in the stack frame instead of on the heap. If a method creates and returns an object then the object may instead be pre-allocated in the caller's stack frame (a common scenario for iterator objects in Java). Some objects allocated in a stack frame can be replaced by local variables for the object fields (another common scenario for iterator objects). Called methods of the reduced object can either be inlined to use the field variables, or the field variables passed as arguments to specialized methods.

In Section 2 the escape analysis algorithm is presented. The value of the analysis results is demonstrated by using the analysis results for a stack allocation transformation described in Section 3 and for an object reduction transformation described in Section 4. The efficacy of the escape analysis results is discussed in Section 5, Section 6 discusses related work, and Section 7 concludes.

2   Escape Analysis

The objective of the analysis is to keep track of objects created during the execution of a method. The objects may be created directly in the method or in methods called by the method. An object is considered to have *escaped* from the scope of a method if a reference to the object is returned from the method, or if a reference to the object is assigned to a field of an object.

The above stated rules can be almost directly encoded as constraints on elements of a simple type system. Solving the constraint system can be done in time and space linear in the number of constraints.

The constraints can be derived directly from the subject program. The program is assumed to be in Static Single Assignment (SSA) form [CFR$^+$91]. In SSA form, each local variable is assigned exactly once. When two or more different definitions of a variable can reach a control-flow merge point, all the definitions are renamed and the value of the variable at the merge point is "calculated" by a special *φ-function* which takes all the new variables as arguments. The constraint derivation will be presented for the representative set of statements listed in Fig. 1. The use of SSA makes the dataflow explicit without needing to consider the control-flow statements, so only the **return** and **throw** control statements are interesting. The **return** statement is annotated with the method in which it occurs. The **new** statement creates an object of the specified class but does not initialize the object apart from filling the memory block with zeros as required by the JVM [LY99].

A *fresh method* returns an object created during the execution of the method. A *fresh variable* is a variable whose defining statement either creates an object directly (via **new**) or indirectly (via a call of a fresh method). For each fresh variable, the analysis must determine if the value assigned may escape in any

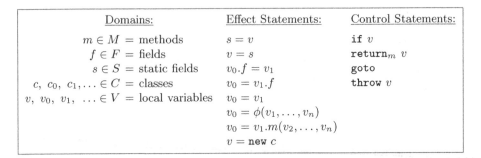

Fig. 1. representative intermediate language statements

way. For each variable the analysis determines whether the values assigned to the variable may be returned; this serves the dual purpose of keeping track of values that escape a method by being returned from it, and allows polymorphic tracking of values through methods that may return an object passed as an argument to the method.

The analysis computes two boolean properties for each local variable, v, of reference type. The property *escaped*(v) is true if the variable holds references that may escape due to assignment statements or a **throw** statement. The property *returned*(v) is true if the variable holds references that escape by being returned from the method in which v is defined.

Properties are introduced to identify variables that contain freshly allocated objects and methods returning freshly allocated objects. The set of Java reference types (classes) is augmented with a $\perp$ and a $\top$ element to form a flat lattice, τ, with partial order $\leq$. The proper elements of τ are *discrete*; the least upper bound of two distinct proper elements is $\top$. The τ property *vfresh*(v) is a Java reference type if v is a fresh variable (as defined above) assigned a freshly allocated object of exactly that type, and is either $\top$ or $\perp$ otherwise. Intuitively, the $\perp$ value means "unknown" and the *top* value means "definitely not fresh". *vfresh* is $\top$ for all formal parameter variables. The τ property *mfresh*(m) is a Java reference type if the method m is a fresh method (as defined above) returning a freshly allocated object of exactly that type, and is either $\top$ or $\perp$ otherwise.

Each statement of a program may impose constraints on these properties. The constraints imposed by the interesting representative statements are shown in Fig. 2. No attempts are made to track references through assignments to fields, so any reference assigned to a field is assumed to possibly escape from the method in which the assignment occurs. In the rule for method invocation, if a reference passed as an argument to a method may be returned from the method then the *escaped* and *returned* properties are propagated as if there was an assignment from the actual parameter to the left-hand-side variable. The function *methods-invoked* returns a set of methods that may be invoked at the call site as indicated by the given call graph. The function *formal-var* returns the formal parameter variable indicated by the given method and parameter index.

return$_m$ v:
  $true \Rightarrow returned(v)$
  $vfresh(v) \le mfresh(m)$
  $escaped(v) \Rightarrow (\top \le mfresh(m))$

throw v:
  $true \Rightarrow escaped(v)$

$v = $ **new** c:
  $c \le vfresh(v)$

$s = v$:
  $true \Rightarrow escaped(v)$

$v = s$:
  $\top \le vfresh(v)$

$v_0.f = v_1$:
  $true \Rightarrow escaped(v_1)$

$v_0 = v_1.f$:
  $\top \le vfresh(v_0)$

$v_0 = v_1$:
  $escaped(v_0) \Rightarrow escaped(v_1)$
  $returned(v_0) \Rightarrow returned(v_1)$
  $\top \le vfresh(v_0)$

$v_0 = \phi(v_1 \ldots v_n)$:
  $\top \le vfresh(v_0)$
  $\forall i \in [1 \ldots n]$:
    $escaped(v_0) \Rightarrow escaped(v_i)$
    $returned(v_0) \Rightarrow returned(v_i)$

$v_0 = v_1.m(v_2 \ldots v_n)$
  $\forall i \in [2 \ldots n]$:
  $\forall g \in methods\text{-}invoked(v_1.m)$:
    let $f = formal\text{-}var(g, i)$,
        $c = returned(f)$ in
    $c \Rightarrow (escaped(v_0) \Rightarrow escaped(v_i))$
    $c \Rightarrow (returned(v_0) \Rightarrow returned(v_i))$
    $escaped(f) \Rightarrow escaped(v_i)$
    $mfresh(g) \le vfresh(v_0)$

Fig. 2. constraints for *escaped,returned, vfresh,* and *mfresh* implied by the syntactic forms of statements.

The number of constraints generated from the program is linear in the size of the program plus the size of the call graph measured as the total number of corresponding actual/formal parameter pairs at all call sites.

Most of the constraints are boolean implications. The minimal solution to these constraints may be found by initializing all properties to be false and updating the properties as constraints are added. The properties values change monotonically. A true property will always stay true. A property that is false at one point may become true as more constraints are added. When adding a constraint where the trigger is a property whose value is false, a pending list for that property value may be used to ensure the constraint is processed again, should the property value become true. Similarly, pending lists can be used to re-process $\le$ constraints when the left-hand element changes value; the constraints are based on a lattice of height 3, so each constraint is processed at most 3 times. It follows that a minimal solution to the set of constraints can be found in time and space linear in the number of constraints.

For method calls, the implication constraints conditioned on *returned(f)* calls makes the analysis *non-sticky*, meaning that one invocation of a method does not affect the analysis results for another invocation of the same method (except for recursive method invocations). This kind of "polymorphism" is rarely seen for algorithms with linear time complexity.

The number of constraints can be limited to the size of program if the call graph is computed by an analysis like Rapid Type Analysis [BS96], or in general if the co-domain of *methods-invoked* is a power-set that can be partially ordered by the subset operator. This can be achieved by summarizing the properties for all methods in each set in the co-domain of *methods-invoked*. The summary for each set is computed by adding constraints from the summary of the largest other set it contains that is in the co-domain of *methods-invoked* and from the individual methods not in the contained set. The rule for adding constraints for method invocations should of course be modified to use the summary properties for the set of methods possibly invoked.

Constraints for parts of a program can be computed independently and subsequently linked together to obtain a solution valid for the entire program. It follows that a partial solution for library code can be precomputed and thus doesn't need to be recomputed for every program. If partial solutions for *all* parts of a program are linked together, the analysis results will be the same as if the analysis was performed on the entire program as a whole.

A conservative result can also be obtained in the absence of parts of a program. If unknown methods may be called, a conservative approximation to their effects is to assume that all formal parameters escape and that each formal parameter may be returned as a result of the method.

3   Stack Allocation

The efficacy of the escape analysis results is demonstrated by using the analysis results for stack allocation of objects.

To keep it simple, the stack allocation transformation allocates objects in the stack frame of a method. No separate stack of objects is used. To avoid the use of a frame pointer, the stack frame size must be computed at compile time. No attempt is made to stack allocate arrays since the length of the arrays may not always be known at compile time[1]. Objects created in a loop can only be stack allocated if objects from different loop iterations have non-overlapping lifetimes, so the used memory area can be reused in subsequent iterations.

Some methods create objects and return a reference to the newly created object. The object cannot be stack allocated in the stack frame of the method creating the object. Instead, memory for the object may be reserved in the stack frame of a calling method, and a pointer to the reserved memory area may be passed to a specialized version of the object-creating method. Initialization of the object is done in the specialized method.

A new effect statement is added to create an object on the stack:

$$v = \texttt{newStack}\ c.$$

It is left to the compiler backend to reserve memory in the stack frame and to translate the `newStack` operator into a computation of the address of the reserved memory.

---

[1] It is possible to stack allocate arrays whose length is known at compile time, but the details will not be presented in this paper.

An extra property, $loop(v)$, is introduced to identify when stack allocation is impossible due to overlapping lifetimes. $loop(v)$ is a boolean property that is true if the local variable v is modified in a loop and objects referenced in different iterations of the loop have overlapping lifetimes. The property is only interesting for variables containing references that do not otherwise escape.

Given a method in SSA form, objects created by a given **new** statement in a given method execution can only have mutually overlapping lifetimes if an object may escape or if a reference to an object is stored in a local variable used as an argument to a ϕ expression at a loop header.

Figure 3 shows the constraints on the *loop* property imposed by the interesting representative statements. For the purposes of exposition, it is conservatively assumed that all ϕ expressions occur at loop headers.

$v_0 = v_1:$
  $loop(v_0) \Rightarrow loop(v_1)$

$v_0 = \phi(v_1 \ldots v_n):$
  $\forall i \in [1 \ldots n]:$
    $true \Rightarrow loop(v_i)$

$v_0 = v_1.m(v_2 \ldots v_n)$
  $\forall i \in [2 \ldots n]:$
  $\forall g \in methods\text{-}invoked(v_1.m):$
    let $f = formal\text{-}var(g, i),$
      $c = returned(f)$ in
    $c \Rightarrow (loop(v_0) \Rightarrow loop(v_i))$

Fig. 3. constraints for *loop* implied by the syntactic form of statements.

For each statement of the form

$$v = \textbf{new } c$$

any object created is only used within the method and the object has non-overlapping lifetimes with other objects created by the statement if $escaped(v)$, $returned(v)$, and $loop(v)$ all are false. In that case, the **new** operator may be replaced by the **newStack** operator to allocate the object on the runtime stack.

Methods that return a freshly created object may be specialized to instead take a freshly created object as an extra argument. The freshly created object may be created on the stack at those call sites where the object originally returned does not escape. At the remaining call sites, the unspecialized method may be called or the specialized method may be called with a freshly created object on the heap.

Initialization of objects must be carefully considered. The JVM semantics dictate that any freshly allocated block of memory be filled with zeros. A block of memory allocated in a runtime stack frame can be filled with zeros at allocation time. If a pointer to such a memory block is passed as an extra argument to a specialized method, then the memory block is only known to be filled with zeros for one use. To ensure that the memory block is only used once, a depth-first traversal of each method m is performed, ensuring that for each return variable v the following holds:

- The definition of v does not occur in a loop in m, and
- All paths in m from the definition of v terminate with a statement: **return** v.

If either condition is not satisfied, the following constraint is added to indicate that a specialized method should not be created:

$$\top \leq \mathit{mfresh}(m).$$

For each method m, for which $\mathit{mfresh}(m)$ is a proper element, a specialized version, m', of the method is created with an extra formal parameter, site. For each variable v, in m, for which $\mathit{vfresh}(v)$ and $\mathit{returned}(v)$ both are true ($\mathit{loop}(v)$ and $\mathit{escaped}(v)$ are both false), the body of m is specialized as follows:

- If the definition of v is a statement of the form $v = $ **new** c, eliminate the statement.
- If the definition of v is a statement of the form $v = h(v_1, \ldots, v_n)$, specialize the statement to be $h'(v_1, \ldots, v_n, \mathit{site})$, where h' is the specialized version of h.
- Substitute all uses of v with uses of site.

The language fragment shown in Fig. 1 does not include methods without return values, but the specialized methods do not need to return a value and may be specialized accordingly.

Each statement in the program of the form

$$v_0 = v_1.m(v_2, \ldots, v_n),$$

for which $\mathit{vfresh}(v_0)$ is a proper element c and the properties $\mathit{returned}(v_0)$, $\mathit{escaped}(v_0)$, or $\mathit{loop}(v_0)$ all are false, is modified to invoke a specialized method

$$v_1.m'(v_2, \ldots, v_n, v_0).$$

The objects returned from the called method in the original program may be allocated in the stack frame of the calling method, so a statement

$$v_0 = \texttt{newStack } c$$

is inserted before the method invocation.

4   Object Reduction

Some objects may be replaced by local variables representing the fields of the objects. A requirement for doing so is that the conditions for stack allocation as described in the previous section are met. In addition, all the uses of the objects must be inlined to use the local variables rather than the fields.[2] This object

---

[2] In some cases the field values may be passed as arguments to methods instead of the object reference, but that experiment was not attempted for this paper.

reduction is often possible for objects of type `java.util.Enumeration`, and has the advantage of removing a large fraction of the overhead due to using iterator objects.

Inlining may of course cause code growth. Object reduction is a trade-off between code growth and object elimination. Object reduction is usually advantageous for iterator objects.

5   Empirical Results

The stack allocation and object reduction transformations have been implemented in the Marmot compiler [FKR+99]. The efficacy of the transformations is evaluated on the set of benchmarks described in Table 1. For these benchmarks, the stack allocation transformation typically places 10–20% (and 73% in one case) of all allocated objects on the stack as shown in Table 2.

Performance improvements due to the transformations will depend greatly on quality of the underlying compiler and the details of the machine (especially the memory subsystem) the program is being executed on. Performance improvements in general come from less work for the memory allocator and garbage collector, increased data locality, and the optimizations enabled by doing object elimination. Improvements in running time were typically 5–10% for non-trivial programs compiled with Marmot [FKR+99], an optimizing Java to native code (x86) compiler.[3] The analyses and transformations for stack allocation and object reduction increase compile time by approximately 1%.

The generated code and the garbage collection systems are high quality. The Marmot backend does not currently try to reuse memory in the stack frame for stack allocated objects with non-overlapping lifetimes. Doing so would likely yield further performance improvements.

Table 1. Benchmarks

Name	LOC	Description
marmot	88K	Marmot compiling itself
jessmab	11K	Java Expert Shell System solving "Bananas and Monkeys" problem
jessword	11K	Java Expert Shell System solving the "Word game" problem
jlex	14K	JLex generating a lexer for sample.lex
javacup	8.8K	JavaCup generating a Java parser
parser	5.6K	The JavaCup generated parser parsing Grm.java
slice	1K	Viewer for 2D slices of 3D radiology data

---

[3] Performance numbers for a larger and partially overlapping set of benchmarks are presented in [FKR+99].

Table 2. Objects allocated on the stack

Name	% Code increase	Stack increase	Allocated objs	bytes	% Stack allocated objects	bytes	% Reduced objects	bytes
marmot	8.5	24.4KB	98M	2289MB	20.6	13.9	11.1	7.1
jessmab	1.2	936 B	510K	19MB	19.1	10.5	0.3	0.2
jessword	1.2	1080 B	305K	11MB	9.7	5.3	0.1	0.1
jlex	2.5	328 B	41K	1.6MB	15.7	7.2	1.8	0.5
javacup	6.9	328 B	785K	21MB	12.6	8.8	1.8	1.3
parser	0.3	116 B	1201K	32MB	1.7	1.2	0.0	0.0
slice	3.3	220 B	463K	16MB	72.9	62.4	72.2	62.1

The data demonstrates that a significant fraction of all objects can be identified as allocatable on the runtime stack using a very simple analysis algorithm. The increase in stack size is relatively small.

6 Related Work

Escape analysis and stack allocation or compile-time garbage collection based on same have been performed on functional languages like SML or Lisp [Bla98, Deu97, Hug92, ISY88, Moh95, PG92], and recently for Java [CGS+99, Bla99, BH99, WR99]. The precision of the escape analyses considered for functional languages is much greater than the precision of the algorithm presented in this paper. For instance, some of them can find that a function's result does not contain elements from the spine of its second argument (a list). This extra precision appears to be necessary for effective stack allocation in these list-oriented languages. The only algorithm with a near-linear complexity is that of Alain Deutsch [Deu97] (the complexity is $n \log^2 n$ where n is the program's size). A study of the performance of this algorithm on some SML benchmarks was performed by Bruno Blanchet [Bla98]. On the only large program considered, this algorithm placed 25% of allocated bytes on the stack and gave a performance improvement of 3-4%. An extension of this work to Java [Bla99] gives an average speedup of 21%, but is also eliminating some synchronization operations.

Phase 1 of the algorithm of Bogda and Hölzle [BH99] is similar to the escape analysis of this paper, except that it is flow-insensitive. Also Bogda and Hölzle apply their analysis to synchronization elimination rather than stack allocation. Choi et al [CGS+99] and Whaley and Rinard [WR99] present escape analyses for Java based on building points-to style graphs. These analyses achieve greater precision, and allocate more objects on the stack, at the expense of a much more complex analysis. Direct use of alias and points-to analysis [CWZ90, Deu90, Hic93, JM81, SF96, VHU92] and other miscellaneous techniques [Bar77, BS93, JM90, JL89, Sch75] have also been considered for compile-time garbage collection. These analyses are generally expensive and their effectiveness is unclear.

Dolby and Chien's object inlining techniques [DC98] can also be applied to stack allocation, but the details are only alluded to.

The presented escape analysis assumes that any reference assigned to a field escapes. It seems likely that incorporating a points-to analysis algorithm (like [Ste96]) could help the escape analysis to allow stack allocation of objects referenced in fields of other stack allocated objects.

A general discussion of the kinds of constraint problems that can be solved in linear time appears in [RM98].

7   Conclusion

The simple escape analysis algorithm presented has demonstrated its usefulness by using the results as the basis for a simple stack allocation system that allocates Java objects on the call stack instead of on the heap. This system is effective, allocating 10–20% of all objects on the stack. When used in Marmot, the transformations described yield speedups of 5–10% on a collection of non-trivial benchmark programs.

References

[Bar77]   Jeffrey M. Barth. Shifting garbage collection overhead to compile time. *Communications of the ACM*, 20(7):513–518, July 1977. 90

[BH99]   Jeff Bogda and Urs Hölzle. Removing Unnecessary Synchronization in Java. In *Proceedings of the 1999 ACM SIGPLAN Conference on Object-Oriented Programming, Systems, Languages & Applications (OOPSLA'99)*, pages 35–46. ACM Press, October 1999. 90

[Bla99]   Bruno Blanchet. Escape Analysis for Object-Oriented Languages: Application to Java. In *Proceedings of the 1999 ACM SIGPLAN Conference on Object-Oriented Programming, Systems, Languages & Applications (OOPSLA'99)*, pages 20–34. ACM Press, October 1999. 90

[Bla98]   Bruno Blanchet. Escape analysis: Correctness proof, implementation and experimental results. In *Conference Record of POPL '98: The 25th ACM SIGPLAN-SIGACT Symposium on Principles of Programming Languages*, pages 25–37, San Diego, California, January 98. 90

[BS93]   E. Barendsen and S. Smetsers. Conventional and uniqueness typing in graph rewrite systems. In Rudrapatna K. Shyamasundar, editor, *Proceedings of Foundations of Software Technology and Theoretical Computer Science*, volume 761 of *LNCS*, pages 41–51, Bombay, India, December 1993. Springer-Verlag. 90

[BS96]   David F. Bacon and Peter F. Sweeney. Fast static analysis of C++ virtual function calls. In *Proceedings of the Conference on Object-Oriented Programming Systems, Languages, and Applications*, volume 31, 10 of *ACM SIGPLAN Notices*, pages 324–341, New York, October6–10 1996. ACM Press. 85

[CFR+91]   Ron Cytron, Jeanne Ferrante, Barry K. Rosen, Mark N. Wegman, and F. Kenneth Zadeck. Efficiently computing static single assignment form and the control dependence graph. *ACM Transactions on Programming Languages and Systems*, 13(4):451–490, October 1991. 83

[CGS⁺99] Jong-Deok Choi, M. Gupta, Mauricio Serrano, Vugranam C Shreedhar, and Sam Midkiff. Escape Analysis for Java. In *Proceedings of the 1999 ACM SIGPLAN Conference on Object-Oriented Programming, Systems, Languages & Applications (OOPSLA'99)*, pages 1–19. ACM Press, October 1999. 90

[CWZ90] David R. Chase, Mark Wegman, and F. Kenneth Zadeck. Analysis of pointers and structures. *ACM SIGPLAN Notices*, 25(6):296–310, June 1990. 90

[DC98] Julian Dolby and Andrew A. Chien. An Evaluation of Automatic Object Inline Allocation Techniques. In *Proceedings of the 1998 ACM SIGPLAN Conference on Object-Oriented Programming, Systems, Languages & Applications (OOPSLA'98)*, pages 1–20. ACM Press, October 1998. 91

[Deu90] Alan Deutsch. On determining lifetime and aliasing of dynamically allocated data in higher-order functional specifications. In ACM-SIGPLAN ACM-SIGACT, editor, *Conference Record of the 17th Annual ACM Symposium on Principles of Programming Languages (POPL '90)*, pages 157–168, San Francisco, CA, USA, January 1990. ACM Press. 90

[Deu97] Alain Deutsch. On the complexity of escape analysis. In *Conference Record of POPL '97: The 24th ACM SIGPLAN-SIGACT Symposium on Principles of Programming Languages*, pages 358–371, Paris, France, January 97. 90

[FKR⁺99] Robert Fitzgerald, Todd B. Knoblock, Erik Ruf, Bjarne Steensgaard, and David Tarditi. Marmot: An optimizing compiler for Java. Technical Report MSR-TR-99-33, Microsoft Research, June 1999. Accepted for publication in Software — Practice & Experience. 89

[Hic93] James Hicks. Experiences with compiler-directed storage reclamation. In R. John M. Hughes, editor, *Record of the 1993 Conference on Functional Programming and Computer Architecture*, volume 523 of *Lecture Notes in Computer Science*, Copenhagen, June 1993. Springer-Verlag. 90

[Hug92] Simon Hughes. Compile-time garbage collection for higher-order functional languages. *Journal of Logic and Computation*, 2(4):483–509, August 1992. 90

[ISY88] Katsuro Inoue, Hiroyuki Seki, and Hikaru Yagi. Analysis of functional programs to detect run-time garbage cells. *ACM Transactions on Programming Languages and Systems*, 10(4):555–578, October 1988. 90

[JL89] S. B. Jones and D. Le Métayer. Compile-time garbage collection by sharing analysis. In *Proceedings of the Conference on Functional Programming Languages and Computer Architecture '89, Imperial College, London*, pages 54–74, New York, NY, 1989. ACM. 90

[JM81] Neil D. Jones and Steven S. Muchnick. Flow analysis and optimization of Lisp-like structures. In Steven S. Muchnick and Neil D. Jones, editors, *Program Flow Analysis: Theory and Applications*, pages 102–131. Englewood Cliffs, N.J.: Prentice-Hall, 1981. 90

[JM90] Thomas P. Jensen and Torben Mogensen. A backwards analysis for compile-time garbage collection. In Neil D. Jones, editor, *ESOP'90 3rd European Symposium on Programming, Copenhagen, Denmark, May 1990. (Lecture Notes in Computer Science, vol. 432)*, pages 227–239. Springer-Verlag, 1990. 90

[LY99] Tim Lindholm and Frank Yellin. *The Java Virtual Machine Specification*. Addison-Wesley, second edition edition, 1999. 83

[Moh95]   Markus Mohnen. Efficient compile-time garbage collection for arbitrary data structures. Technical Report 95-08, RWTH Aachen, Department of Computer Science, 1995. 90

[PG92]   Young Gil Park and Benjamin Goldberg. Escape analysis on lists. In *Proceedings of the ACM SIGPLAN'92 Conference on Programming Language Design and Implementation (PLDI)*, pages 116–127, 1992. 90

[RM98]   Jakob Rehof and Torben Æ. Mogensen. Tractable constraints in finite semilattices. *Science of Computer Programming*, 35(2-3):191–221, 1998. 91

[Sch75]   J. T. Schwartz. Optimization of very high level languages – I. Value transmission and its corollaries. *Computer Languages*, 1(2):161–194, 1975. 90

[SF96]   Manuel Serrano and Marc Feeley. Storage use analysis and its applications. In *Proceedings of the 1st International Conference on Functional Programming*, June 1996. 90

[Ste96]   Bjarne Steensgaard. Points-to analysis in almost linear time. In *Proceedings of the 23rd ACM SIGPLAN-SIGACT Symposium on Principles of Programming Languages*, pages 32–41, St. Petersburg, Florida, January 1996. 91

[VHU92]   Jan Vitek, R. Nigel Horspool, and James Uhl. Compile-time analysis of object-oriented programs. In *Proceedings of the 4th Int. Conf. on Compiler Construction, CC'92*, Paderborn, Germany, 1992. Springer-Verlag. 90

[WR99]   John Whaley and Martin Rinard. Compositional Pointer and Escape Analysis for Java Programs. In *Proceedings of the 1999 ACM SIGPLAN Conference on Object-Oriented Programming, Systems, Languages & Applications (OOPSLA'99)*, pages 187–206. ACM Press, October 1999. 90

Constant Propagation on the Value Graph: Simple Constants and Beyond

Jens Knoop and Oliver Rüthing

Universität Dortmund,
Baroper Str. 301, D-44221 Dortmund, Germany
{knoop,ruething}@ls5.cs.uni-dortmund.de
http://sunshine.cs.uni-dortmund.de/

Abstract. We present a new algorithm for *constant propagation* (*CP*), which works on the *value graph* of a program. This algorithm combines the (1) *efficiency* of the sparse CP-algorithms of Reif and Lewis [24,25], Ferrante and Ottenstein [9], and Wegman and Zadeck [30,31] with the (2) *conceptual simplicity* of their classic conventional counterparts of Kildall [19], and Kam and Ullman [16], while (3) outperforming them in power. It detects a proper superset of the *simple constants* detected by the classical CP-algorithms, while avoiding the exponential worst-case behaviour of the CP-algorithm for *finite constants* of Steffen and Knoop [28] allowing its optimality for acyclic control flow. The class detected is a well-balanced compromise between power and performance. In fact, we show that CP is co-NP-hard for acyclic control flow making the existence of efficient optimal algorithms for acyclic control flow most unlikely. Nonetheless, the new algorithm is open for extensions, e.g. towards conditional constants in the fashion of [30,31] in order to capture to a certain extent the determinism of conditional branching.

1 Motivation

Constant propagation (*CP*) is one of the most widely used optimisations in practice (cf. [1,18,23,32]). Intuitively, it aims at replacing terms which always yield a unique constant value at run-time by this value as illustrated in Figure 1.

Pioneering for CP has been the algorithm of Kildall [19], which detects the class of so-called *simple constants*. Intuitively, a term is a simple constant, if it is a constant, or if all its operands are simple constants. Though simple constants fail optimality even for acyclic programs, i.e., there are terms being constant without being a simple constant, the class of simple constants is still dominating in practice and computed by state-of-the-art optimising compilers. This may have two reasons. First, the general problem of detecting constancy of terms is undecidable (cf. [24,25]); second, decidable supersets of simple constants, which have been proposed in the literature are usually based on simple heuristics of quite limited power as the one of Kam and Ullman [16], or are accompanied by computationally expensive algorithms like the one of Steffen and Knoop [28] deciding the class of *finite constants*. In the worst case, this algorithm is exponential in the program size, but unique in being optimal for acyclic programs.

A. Watt (Ed.): CC/ETAPS 2000, LNCS 1781, pp. 94–110, 2000.

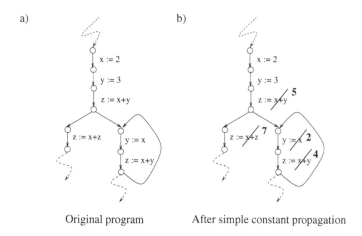

Fig. 1. Illustrating (simple) constant propagation.

The research on CP can actually roughly be split into two major groups. First, approaches aiming at making CP available for more general program settings like the interprocedural (cf. [3,8,12,22,27]) or (explicitly) parallel one (cf. [20,21]), which (usually) focus on proper subsets of simple constants like *copy constants* or *linear constants*. Second, approaches (cf. [9,24,25,30,31])[1] aiming at improving the efficiency of the classical algorithms for simple constants of Kildall [19], and Kam and Ullman [16].

Fundamental for the success of the algorithms of the second group, which are known as *sparse* CP-algorithms, is the use of specific representations of control and data-flow information like the *global value graph* [24,25],[2] the *program dependence graph* [9], or the *SSA* form of a program [30,31].

The approach we propose here starts from the line of these algorithms. It performs CP on the *value graph* of a program [2].[2] The value graph represents uniformly and concisely the control and the data flow of a program, and has originally been designed and used so far as a means for efficiently detecting equivalent program terms [2,26].

In this article, we demonstrate that it is well-suited for CP, too. In fact, the new algorithm combines the (1) *efficiency* of the sparse algorithms of Reif and Lewis [24,25], Ferrante and Ottenstein [9], and Wegman and Zadeck [30,31] with the (2) *conceptual simplicity* of their classic conventional counterparts of Kildall [19], and Kam and Ullman [16], while (3) outperforming them in power. It detects a proper superset of the simple constants detected by its classical

---

[1] Wegman and Zadeck start from a basic algorithm capturing simple constants, while actually aiming at an algorithm capturing a more general class called *conditional constants*, which capture some aspects of conditional program branching.

[2] The *global value graph* introduced by Reif and Lewis should not be confused with the *value graph* introduced by Alpern, Wegman, and Zadeck [2] underlying our approach. These are different data structures (see also Section 5.4).

counterparts as illustrated in Figure 2, while avoiding the exponential worst-case behaviour of the CP-algorithm for finite constants of Steffen and Knoop [28] allowing the optimality of their algorithm for acyclic flow.

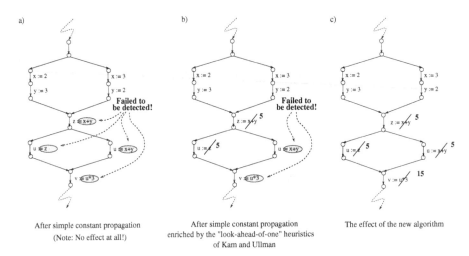

Fig. 2. Motivating example.

Moreover, the new algorithm, which works for arbitrary control flow, is scalable. While its basic version detects the class of simple constants, the class detected by the full algorithm goes well-beyond. It is a well-balanced compromise between power and performance. In fact, we show that CP is co-NP-hard for acyclic control flow. This makes the existence of efficient optimal algorithms for acyclic control flow most unlikely. Nonetheless, the new algorithm is open for extensions, e.g. towards conditional constants in the fashion of [30,31] in order to capture to some extent the determinism of conditional branching.

2   Preliminaries

As usual we represent programs by *directed flow graphs* $G = (N, E, s, e)$ with node set N, edge set E, a unique start node s, and a unique end node e, which are assumed to have no predecessors and successors, respectively. Edges represent the branching structure and the statements of a program, while nodes represent program points. Unlabelled edges are assumed to represent "skip."

By $pred(n) =_{df} \{ m \mid (m, n) \in E \}$ and $succ(n) =_{df} \{ m \mid (n, m) \in E \}$ we denote the set of immediate predecessors and successors of a node n. Additionally, by $source(e)$ and $dst(e)$, $e \in E$, we denote the *source node* and the *destination node* of edge e. A *finite path* in G is a sequence $(e_1, \ldots, e_q)$ of edges such that $dst(e_j) = source(e_{j+1})$ for $j \in \{1, \ldots, q-1\}$. It is called a path from m to n, if $source(e_1) = m$ and $dst(e_q) = n$. By $\mathbf{P}[m, n]$ we denote the set of all finite paths from $\mathbf{m}$ to $\mathbf{n}$. Without loss of generality we assume that every node of a flow graph G lies on a path from $\mathbf{s}$ to $\mathbf{e}$.

3   Simple Constants: The Conventional Approach

In this section we recall the essence of the classical algorithms of Kildall [19], and of Kam and Ullman [16] for *simple constants*. Simultaneously, this establishes the basics for our new value-graph based CP-algorithm.

Semantics of Terms. Let terms $t \in \mathbf{T}$ be inductively built from variables $v \in \mathbf{V}$, constants $c \in \mathbf{C}$, and operators $op \in \mathbf{Op}$ of arity $r \geq 1$.[3] The *semantics* of terms is then induced by an *interpretation* $I = (\mathbf{D}' \cup \{\bot, \top\}, I_0)$, where $\mathbf{D}'$ denotes a non-empty data domain, $\bot$ and $\top$ two new data not in $\mathbf{D}'$, and I_0 a function mapping every constant $c \in \mathbf{C}$ to a datum $I_0(c) \in \mathbf{D}'$, and every r-ary operator $op \in \mathbf{Op}$ to a total function $I_0(op) : \mathbf{D}^r \to \mathbf{D}$, $\mathbf{D} =_{df} \mathbf{D}' \cup \{\bot, \top\}$ being strict in $\bot$ and $\top$ with $\bot$ prioritised over $\top$ (i.e., $I_0(op)(d_1, \ldots, d_r) = \bot$, whenever there is a j, $1 \leq j \leq r$, with $d_j = \bot$, and $I_0(op)(d_1, \ldots, d_r) = \top$, whenever there is no j, $1 \leq j \leq r$, with $d_j = \bot$, but a j, $1 \leq j \leq r$, with $d_j = \top$). $\Sigma =_{df} \{\sigma \mid \sigma : \mathbf{V} \to \mathbf{D}\}$ denotes the set of *states*, and $\sigma_\bot$ the distinct *start state* assigning $\bot$ to all variables $v \in \mathbf{V}$. This choice reflects that we do not assume anything about the context of a program being optimised. The *semantics* of a term $t \in \mathbf{T}$ is then given by the inductively defined evaluation function $\mathcal{E} : \mathbf{T} \to (\Sigma \to \mathbf{D})$:

$$\forall t \in \mathbf{T} \; \forall \sigma \in \Sigma. \; \mathcal{E}(t)(\sigma) =_{df} \begin{cases} \sigma(x) & \text{if } t = x \in \mathbf{V} \\ I_0(c) & \text{if } t = c \in \mathbf{C} \\ I_0(op)(\mathcal{E}(t_1)(\sigma), \ldots, \mathcal{E}(t_r)(\sigma)) & \text{if } t = op(t_1, \ldots, t_r) \end{cases}$$

For convenience we assume $\mathbf{D}' \subseteq \mathbf{T}$, i.e., we identify the set of data $\mathbf{D}'$ with the set of constants $\mathbf{C}$. By means of the *state transformation function* $\theta_\iota : \Sigma \to \Sigma$, $\iota \equiv x := t$, which is defined by

$$\forall \sigma \in \Sigma \; \forall y \in \mathbf{V}. \; \theta_\iota(\sigma)(y) =_{df} \begin{cases} \mathcal{E}(t)(\sigma) & \text{if } y = x \\ \sigma(y) & \text{otherwise} \end{cases}$$

we obtain the set of states $\Sigma_{\mathbf{n}} =_{df} \{\theta_p(\sigma_\bot) \mid p \in \mathbf{P}[\mathbf{s}, \mathbf{n}]\}$, which are possible at a program point $\mathbf{n} \in N$.[4] By means of $\Sigma_{\mathbf{n}}$, we can now define the set $\mathcal{C}_{\mathbf{n}}$ of all terms yielding at run-time a unique constant value at a program point $\mathbf{n} \in N$:

$$\mathcal{C}_{\mathbf{n}} =_{df} \{(t, d) \in \mathbf{T} \times \mathbf{D}' \mid \forall \sigma \in \Sigma_{\mathbf{n}}. \; \mathcal{E}(t)(\sigma) = d\}$$

Unfortunately, the sets $\mathcal{C}_{\mathbf{n}}$, $\mathbf{n} \in N$, are generally not decidable (cf. [24]). Simple constants recalled next are an efficiently decidable subset of $\mathcal{C}_{\mathbf{n}}$, which are computed by state-of-the-art optimisers.

---

[3] Note, during the development of our algorithm we will consider terms with at most one operator, and assume that all operators are binary.

[4] In the definition of $\Sigma_{\mathbf{n}}$, θ_p denotes the straightforward extension of the state transformation functions to paths.

Simple Constants. Intuitively, a term is a *simple constant (SC)* (cf. [19]), if it is a constant or if all its operands are simple constants. For example, all right-hand side terms in the example of Figure 1(a) are simple constants, while those (except for the right-hand side terms 2 and 3) in the example of Figure 2(a) are not. The classical algorithms of Kildall, and Kam and Ullman rely on data-flow analysis for computing SCs. Its essence is recalled in the following section.

Data-Flow Analysis. In essence, *data-flow analysis (DFA)* aims at computing information about the program states, which may occur at specific program points at run-time. Theoretically well-founded are DFAs based on *abstract interpretation* (cf. [6]). An abstract semantics is usually specified by a *local semantic functional* $[\![\ ]\!] : E \rightarrow (\mathcal{C} \rightarrow \mathcal{C})$ giving abstract meaning to every program statement, i.e., to every edge $e \in E$ of a flow graph G, in terms of a transformation function on a complete lattice $(\mathcal{C}, \sqcap, \sqsubseteq, \bot, \top)$. Its elements express the DFA-information of interest.

Local semantic functionals can easily be extended to capture finite paths, which provides the key to the *meet over all paths (MOP)* approach in the sense of Kam and Ullman [16]. It yields the intuitively desired solution of a DFA-problem by directly mimicking possible program executions: it "meets" all informations belonging to a program path leading from $\mathbf{s}$ to a program point $\mathbf{n} \in N$.

The *MOP*-Solution: $\forall c_0 \in \mathcal{C}.\ MOP(\mathbf{n})(c_0) = \sqcap \{\,[\![p]\!](c_0) \mid p \in \mathbf{P}[\mathbf{s}, \mathbf{n}]\,\}$

Unfortunately, this is in general not effective. The *MOP*-approach is thus complemented by the *maximal fixed point (MFP)* approach in the sense of Kam and Ullman [16]. Intuitively, it approximates the *greatest* solution of a system of equations imposing consistency constraints on an annotation of the program with DFA-information with respect to some start information $c_0 \in \mathcal{C}$:

$$\mathbf{mfp(n)} = \begin{cases} c_0 & \text{if } \mathbf{n} = \mathbf{s} \\ \sqcap\{\,[\![(\mathbf{m}, \mathbf{n})]\!](\mathbf{mfp(m)}) \mid (\mathbf{m}, \mathbf{n}) \in E\,\} & \text{otherwise} \end{cases}$$

The greatest solution of this equation system, which we denote by $\mathtt{mfp}_{c_0}$, can effectively be computed, if the semantic functions $[\![e]\!]$, $e \in E$, are monotonic, and the lattice $\mathcal{C}$ satisfies the descending chain condition. It defines the solution of the *MFP*-approach, which is usually considered the minimal acceptable criterion of the quality of a data-flow analysis (cf. [11,16]):

The *MFP*-Solution: $\forall c_0 \in \mathcal{C}\ \forall \mathbf{n} \in N.\ MFP(\mathbf{n})(c_0) =_{df} \mathtt{mfp}_{c_0}(\mathbf{n})$

The following theorem, which relates both solutions, is central. It gives sufficient conditions for the safety (correctness) and precision (optimality) of the *MFP*-solution with respect to the *MOP*-solution (cf. [16,19]):

Theorem 1 (Safety and Coincidence Theorem).

1. Safety: $MFP(\mathbf{n}) \sqsubseteq MOP(\mathbf{n})$, *if all* $[\![e]\!]$, $e \in E$, *are monotonic.*
2. Coincidence: $MFP(\mathbf{n}) = MOP(\mathbf{n})$, *if all* $[\![e]\!]$, $e \in E$, *are distributive.*

Computing Simple Constants. Considering $\mathbf{D}$ a flat lattice, the set of states Σ together with the pointwise ordering is a complete lattice, too. Having this in mind, the computation of SCs relies on the local semantic functional $[\![\ ]\!]_{sc} : E \to (\Sigma \to \Sigma)$ defined by $[\![\ e\ ]\!]_{sc} =_{df} \theta_e$ for each $e \in E$, and the start state $\sigma_\perp$. Since the number of variables in a program is finite, we have (cf. [16]):

Lemma 1. Σ *is of finite height, and all functions* $[\![\ e\ ]\!]_{sc}$, $e \in E$, *are monotonic.*

In general, the functions $[\![\ e\ ]\!]_{sc}$, $e \in E$, are not distributive (cf. [16]). However, as pointed out before, monotonicity together with the finite height of the data-flow lattice is sufficient for the effective computability of the *MFP*-solution of the SC-problem, which we denote by $MFP^{sc}_{\sigma_\perp}$.[5] It induces the formal definition of *simple constants*: $\mathcal{C}^{sc}_{\mathbf{n}} =_{df} \mathcal{C}^{sc,mfp}_{\mathbf{n}} =_{df} \{(t,d) \in \mathbf{T} \times \mathbf{D}' \mid \mathcal{E}(t)(MFP^{sc}_{\sigma_\perp}(\mathbf{n})) = d\}$.

Defining dually the set of constants $\mathcal{C}^{sc,mop}_{\mathbf{n}} =_{df} \{(t,d) \in \mathbf{T} \times \mathbf{D}' \mid \mathcal{E}(t)(MOP^{sc}_{\sigma_\perp}(\mathbf{n})) = d\}$ induced by the $MOP^{sc}_{\sigma_\perp}$-solution, we obtain by means of Theorem 1(1) (cf. [16]):

Theorem 2 (SC-Correctness). $\forall\, \mathbf{n} \in N.\ \mathcal{C}_{\mathbf{n}} \supseteq \mathcal{C}^{sc,mop}_{\mathbf{n}} \supseteq \mathcal{C}^{sc,mfp}_{\mathbf{n}} = \mathcal{C}^{sc}_{\mathbf{n}}$.

The algorithms of Kildall, and Kam and Ullman are both instances of the *MFP*-approach recalled above. While Kam and Ullman present their algorithm using *environments* in the sense of states introduced above, Kildall uses *structured partitions* for this purpose which results in a higher complexity of his algorithm.

4   Constant Propagation on the Value Graph

In this section we present the basic version of the new algorithm for CP working on the value graph. We thus recall first its definition.

4.1   The Value Graph of Alpern, Wegman and Zadeck

The value graph of Alpern, Wegman and Zadeck is a data structure, which uniformly and concisely combines the control and the data flow of a program [2]. It is constructed on top of the *static single assignment* (*SSA*) form of a program (cf. [7]), which we illustrate here on an informal and intuitive level considering the program of Figure 3(a) as example.

In essence, in the SSA form of a program the variables of the original program are replaced by new versions such that every variable has a unique initialization point. At join points of the control flow pseudo-assignments $x_k := \phi_{\mathbf{n}}(x_{i1}, \dots, x_{ik})$ are introduced meaning that x_k gets the value of x_{ij} if the join node is entered via the jth ingoing edge.[6] The SSA form of our running example is shown in Figure 3(b).

Based upon the SSA form of a program the *value graph* is constructed. It represents the value transfer of SSA variables along the control flow of the program. Following the description in [23] the value graph is defined as a labelled directed graph where

---

[5] Note that a lattice of finite height trivially satisfies the descending chain condition.
[6] ϕ-operators are indexed by their corresponding join node.

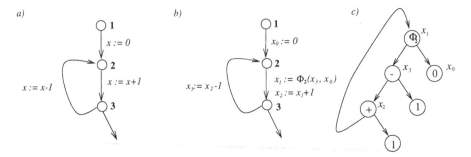

Fig. 3. The construction of the value graph: (a) the original program with x being a simple constant of value 1 on the exit of the loop, (b) the program transformed into SSA form and (c) the corresponding value graph.

- the nodes correspond to occurrences of nontrivial assignments, i.e., assignments whose right-hand sides contain at least one operator, and to occurrences of constants in the program.[7] Every node is labelled with the corresponding constant or operator symbol, and additionally with the set of variables whose value is generated by the corresponding constant or assignment. An operator node is always annotated with the left-hand side variable of its corresponding assignment. Note, the generating assignment of x of a trivial assignment $x := y$ is defined as the generating assignment of y. For a trivial assignment $x := c$ variable x is attached to the annotation of the corresponding node associated with c. For convenience, the constant or operator label is written inside the circle visualizing the node, and the variable annotation outside.
- Directed edges point to the operands of the right-hand side expression associated with the node. Moreover, edges are labelled with natural numbers according to the position of operands.[8]

Figure 3(c) shows the value graph corresponding to Figure 3(b). It is worth noting that it is cyclic which is due to self-dependencies of variables in the loop.

In the following we assume without loss of generality that all operators, i.e., ordinary ones as well as ϕ-operators, are binary.[9] In fact, this assumption is not crucial for our reasoning, but simplifies the formal development. It can easily be extended to capture k-ary operators as well. Moreover, for a node n in the value graph we denote its operator or constant label by $\text{lab}[n]$.[10] If it is an inner node, its left and right child nodes are denoted by $l(n)$ and $r(n)$, respectively.

---

[7] For the sake of simplicity it is assumed that variables are initialized.
[8] We omit this labelling in our examples making the implicit assumption that edges are ordered from left to right.
[9] For ϕ-operators this assumption can always be achieved by "linearizing" join nodes having more than two incoming edges.
[10] For clarity, we denote flow graph nodes by boldface letters and value graph nodes by italic ones.

4.2 Computing Simple Constants on the Value Graph

Simple constants can be computed very efficiently on the value graph, as propagation of information is directly reflected in this structure. Essentially, this resembles to Wegman and Zadeck's sparse CP-algorithm on SSA-form [31]. However, the value graph allows a much simpler conceptual presentation as the problem reduces to a data-flow evaluation on the value graph. In details, the analysis on the value graph computes the greatest fixed point of a data-flow annotation dfi[·] by the following iterative procedure:

Start Annotation: For each node n in the value graph initialize:

$$\text{dfi}[n] = \begin{cases} I_0(c) & \text{if } n \text{ is a leaf node with } c =_{df} \text{lab}[n] \\ \top & \text{otherwise} \end{cases}$$

Iteration Step:

1. For a node n labelled with an ordinary operator ω:

$$\text{dfi}[n] = I_0(\omega)(\text{dfi}[l(n)], \text{dfi}[r(n)]) \quad \textbf{(Evaluating terms)}$$

2. For a node n labelled with a ϕ-operator $\phi_{\mathbf{n}}$:

$$\text{dfi}[n] = \text{dfi}[l(n)] \sqcap \text{dfi}[r(n)] \quad \textbf{(Merging DFA-info's at join nodes)}$$

Figure 4 illustrates the iteration for the value graph of Figure 3(c). Note, in contrast to the classical algorithm of Kam and Ullman [16], which works on flow graphs storing a complete environment as data-flow information at every flow graph node, our algorithm works on the value graph storing a single data at every value graph node.

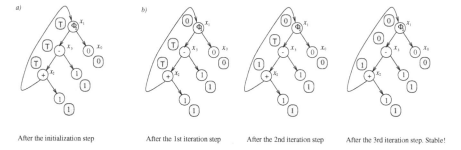

After the initialization step   After the 1st iteration step   After the 2nd iteration step   After the 3rd iteration step. Stable!

Fig. 4. The data-flow analysis on the value graph of Figure 3(c): (a) the start annotation and (b) the greatest fixed point annotation.

The time complexity of the algorithm is linear in the size of the value graph which, in the worst case, is of order $\mathcal{O}(|N||\mathbf{V}|)$. In practice, however, it usually behaves much better, and is expected to be linear [23]. Moreover, we have:

Theorem 3 (Basic Algorithm).
The basic version of the new VG-based algorithm for CP detects the class of simple constants.

In the following section we show how to enhance this algorithm in order to detect proper supersets of the class of simple constants almost without losing efficiency.

5   Beyond Simple Constants

The value graph provides an elegant handle to design more powerful, yet still efficient algorithms that are capable of detecting much broader classes of constants than the class of simple ones. This concern has already been addressed in the past. However, state-of-the-art approaches are either limited to a few ad-hoc effects, like the "look-ahead-of-one" heuristics of Kam and Ullman [16],[11] or are expensive in terms of computational complexity as e.g. the ambitious approach of Steffen and Knoop [28] computing the set of *finite constants*. As the most significant and distinguishing characteristics their algorithm is unique to detect in acyclic programs all constants. This, however, comes at the price of an exponential worst-case time complexity. In the light of the following contribution of this article, however, this is not too surprising. We demonstrate that the problem is intractable in general. Thereafter, we propose an algorithm which captures a reasonable and large subclass of finite constants which can efficiently be detected, and generalises on previous approaches going beyond simple constants, in particular the one of Kam and Ullman.

5.1   Constant Propagation for Acyclic Control Flow is Co-NP-Hard

We give a polynomial time reduction from 3-SAT, the satisfiability problem for clauses with three disjuncts (cf. [10]). To this end let $V = \{v_1, \ldots, v_k\}$ be a set of Boolean variables. A *clause* of size s over V is a disjunction of s variables or negated variables in V. A *truth assignment* is a function $t : V \to \mathbb{B}$, where $\mathbb{B}$ denotes the set of Boolean truth values. Then the 3-SAT problem is as follows:

3-SAT
Instance: A set of clauses $C = \{c_1, \ldots, c_n\}$ over V all being of size 3.
Question: Is there a truth assignment t such that all clauses in C are satisfied?

3-SAT is known as an NP-complete problem (cf. [10]). In the following we give a polynomial time reduction of its co-problem, i.e., the question whether at least one clause is not satisfied by any truth assignment, to the constant propagation problem on acyclic flow graphs. We illustrate the reduction by means of a 3-SAT instance over the variables $\{v_1, \ldots, v_k\}$ given by :

$$\underbrace{(v_3 \vee \overline{v_5} \vee v_6)}_{c_1} \wedge \ldots \wedge \underbrace{(v_2 \vee \overline{v_3} \vee v_5)}_{c_n}$$

---

[11] In essence, this heuristics delays computing the meet of DFA-informations at join nodes of the control flow across them which results in a look-ahead of one statement (or basic block). The limitations of this heuristics are illustrated in Figure 2(b).

This Boolean expression is coded into the flow graph depicted in Figure 5, where integer program variables x_i and $\overline{x_i}$ are introduced for every Boolean variable v_i. Now, it is easy to see that $r2$ is a constant of value 1 at the exit of the program fragment if and only if 3-SAT is not satisfiable.[12] In fact, this follows from the following facts: $r1$ is different from 0 on any program path if and only if the underlying instance of 3-SAT is not satisfiable.[13] Since in this case $r1$ is in the range $\{1, \dots, k\}$, the resulting variable $r2$ is assigned to 1.

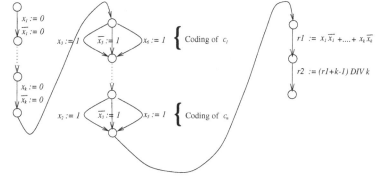

(I) Initializiation   (II) Coding of Clauses   (III) "Non-Satisfiability Reduction"

Fig. 5. The co-NP-hardness reduction: $r2$ evaluates to 1 if and only if the underlying 3-SAT instance is not satisfiable.

Hence, the existence of efficient algorithms, which are complete for acyclic control flow, is most unlikely. In the following section we thus present an algorithm efficiently determining a major fragment of the set of finite constants.

5.2   An Efficiently Decidable Subset of Finite Constants

Basically, our extension to the algorithm for simple constants refines the domain the local semantic functions are operating on. Instead of using data elements of $\mathbf{D}'$ for the analysis we introduce ϕ-*constants* over $\mathbf{D}'$. These are expressions composed of constants and ϕ-operators. Formally, $\mathbf{D}^\phi$ is defined inductively as the smallest set satisfying:

1. $\mathbf{D}' \subseteq \mathbf{D}^\phi$
2. If $\phi_\mathbf{n}$ is a ϕ-operator occurring in the SSA program and $d_1, d_2 \in \mathbf{D}^\phi$ such that neither d_1 nor d_2 contains $\phi_\mathbf{n}$, then $\phi_\mathbf{n}(d_1, d_2) \in \mathbf{D}^\phi$.

---

[12] Note that $+$ and . denote addition and multiplication in the program.
[13] Note that a truth assignment that satisfies all clauses would yield a path where for every $i \in \{1, \dots, k\}$ not both x_i and $\overline{x_i}$ are set to 1.

Adding a bottom and a top element to $\mathbf{D}^\phi$ makes $\mathbf{D}^\phi \cup \{\bot, \top\}$ a complete partial order[14] that relates ϕ-constants with other elements in the following way:

$$\phi_\mathbf{n}(r_1, r_2) \sqsubseteq r \Longleftrightarrow_{df} (r_1 \sqsubseteq r \ \vee \ r_2 \sqsubseteq r) \vee (r = \phi_\mathbf{n}(r_3, r_4) \wedge r_1 \sqsubseteq r_3 \ \wedge \ r_2 \sqsubseteq r_4)$$

If r_1 and r_2 are ϕ-constants and $\omega \in \mathbf{Op}$ then $\omega(r_1, r_2)$ will be called an *evaluation candidate*. This is because such expressions are constructed during the analysis where they are immediately evaluated to data in $\mathbf{D}^\phi \cup \{\bot, \top\}$.

The Analysis. The analysis on the value graph works essentially by annotating nodes of the value graph by elements of the new domain $\mathbf{D}^\phi \cup \{\bot, \top\}$. The essential difference to the setting for the detection of simple constants is that ϕ-nodes are now possibly evaluated by constructing ϕ-constants whenever both operands are different ϕ-constants. ϕ-constants are then used to gain precision by evaluating ordinary operators in a way which is sensitive to ϕ-operands. The evaluation function $\mathcal{E}^+$ maps evaluation candidates to data in $\mathbf{D}^\phi \cup \{\bot, \top\}$.

1. $\mathcal{E}^+(d) = d$ if $d \in \mathbf{D}$

2. $\mathcal{E}^+(\phi_\mathbf{n}(r_1, r_2)) = \begin{cases} \bot & \text{if } \mathcal{E}^+(r_1) \text{ or } \mathcal{E}^+(r_2) \text{ contains } \phi_\mathbf{n} \\ \mathcal{E}^+(r_1) & \text{if } \mathcal{E}^+(r_1) \sqsubseteq \mathcal{E}^+(r_2) \\ \mathcal{E}^+(r_2) & \text{if } \mathcal{E}^+(r_2) \sqsubseteq \mathcal{E}^+(r_1) \\ \phi_\mathbf{n}(\mathcal{E}^+(r_1), \mathcal{E}^+(r_2)) & \text{otherwise} \end{cases}$

3. $\mathcal{E}^+(\omega(r_1, r_2)) =$
$\begin{cases} I_0(\omega)(r_1, r_2) & \text{if } r_1, r_2 \in \mathbf{D} \\ \mathcal{E}^+(\phi_\mathbf{n}(\omega(r_1, r_{21}), \omega(r_1, r_{22}))) & \text{if } r_1 \in \mathbf{D}, r_2 = \phi_\mathbf{n}(r_{21}, r_{22}) \\ \mathcal{E}^+(\phi_\mathbf{n}(\omega(r_{11}, r_2), \omega(r_{12}, r_2))) & \text{if } r_1 = \phi_\mathbf{n}(r_{11}, r_{12}), r_2 \in \mathbf{D} \\ \mathcal{E}^+(\phi_\mathbf{n}(\omega(r_{11}, r_{21}), \omega(r_{12}, r_{22}))) & \text{if } r_1 = \phi_\mathbf{n}(r_{11}, r_{12}), r_2 = \phi_\mathbf{n}(r_{21}, r_{22}) \\ \bot & \text{otherwise} \end{cases}$

Important is the "otherwise" case in the second item. Here ϕ-constants are constructed, which, as operands of ordinary operators, are evaluated in a distributive fashion (cp. lines two to four of the third item). Note, finally, that in item three the evaluation of $\mathcal{E}^+$ yields $\bot$, if r_1 and r_2 are ϕ-constants with different top level ϕ-operators. This is in order to avoid the combinatoric explosion reflecting the co-NP-hardness of CP.

The analysis on the value graph is particularly easy to describe. It computes the greatest fixed point of an annotation satisfying:[15]

---

[14] Note that $\mathbf{D}^\phi \cup \{\bot, \top\}$ is not a lattice as unique greatest lower bounds do not exist due to the distinction of ϕ-operators. For instance, $\phi_\mathbf{n}(2, 3)$ and $\phi_\mathbf{m}(2, 3)$ are both incomparable lower bounds of 2 and 3. However, in our application the meet-operation is always uniquely determined by the evaluation context.

[15] The ϕ-constants of the annotation can efficiently be represented using a shared representation.

Start Annotation: For each node n in the value graph initialize:

$$\text{dfi}[n] = \begin{cases} \mathcal{E}^+(\text{lab}[n]) & \text{if } n \text{ is a leaf node} \\ \top & \text{otherwise} \end{cases}$$

Iteration Step: For a node n labelled with an ordinary or ϕ-operator ω:

$$\text{dfi}[n] = \mathcal{E}^+(\omega(\text{dfi}[l(n)], \text{dfi}[r(n)]))$$

Note that the evaluation of terms (Case (1) and (3)) as well as the merge of data-flow information at join nodes (Case (2)) is both encoded in the function $\mathcal{E}^+$. Figure 6 provides an example that is suitable to elucidate the mechanism of the analysis.

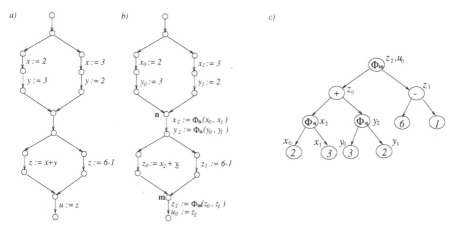

Fig. 6. (a) An example illustrating the function of our extended algorithm, (b) the program in SSA form, and (c) the corresponding value graph.

It should be noted that although u is a constant of value 5, it is neither a simple constant nor is detected by Kam and Ullman's "look-ahead-of-one" heuristics. However, our extended algorithm is capable of detecting this constant. Figure 7 shows the iteration sequence which becomes already stable after two iterations.

The most important point is the evaluation of the $+$-labelled node in the second iteration step which in details is due to the following sequence of transformations:

$$\begin{aligned}
\mathcal{E}^+(+(\phi_\mathbf{n}(2,3), \phi_\mathbf{n}(3,2))) &= \\
\mathcal{E}^+(\phi_\mathbf{n}(+(2,3), +(3,2))) &= \qquad [\text{Since } \mathcal{E}^+(+(2,3)) = \mathcal{E}^+(+(3,2))] \\
\mathcal{E}^+(+(2,3)) &= 5
\end{aligned}$$

Main Results. In the following we briefly collect the most important results on the extended algorithm. First of all, it is easy to show that the extended analysis

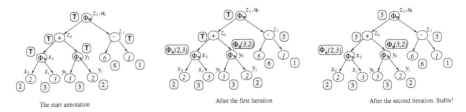

The start annotation   After the first iteration   After the second iteration. Stable!

Fig. 7. Illustrating the extended analysis for Figure 6(c).

always stays above a corresponding analysis in the simple constant setting. That means that the elements of the current annotation are always greater or equal than the elements of the annotation that would be computed by a corresponding iteration strategy in the simple constant analysis.[16] Hence, we particularly have:

Theorem 4 (Extended Algorithm on Arbitrary Control Flow).
On programs with arbitrary control flow the extended algorithm detects at least any simple constant.

As demonstrated in Section 5.1 detecting all constants is intractable even on acyclic programs. However, the extended algorithm is able to detect a major fragment of these constants which is characterised through the operators involved in building candidates for constant propagation. The key observation for this is that a variable which is not of a constant value at a program point n cannot contribute to the construction of a constant term if the operators of the term are injective in each argument and some operand variable is defined at a program point behind n. Injectivity holds for a wide range of operators like $+, -$ or division for real numbers but certainly not for operators like integer division used in the example of Figure 5. Multiplication is an injective operator for any argument if the respective other one can be proven different from 0. We have:

Theorem 5 (Extended Algorithm on Acyclic Control Flow).
On programs with acyclic control flow the extended algorithm detects every constant which is composed of operators only which are injective in their relevant arguments.

In the worst case the run-time complexity of the extended algorithm is of third order in the size of the value graph. This is due to the fact that an annotation can grow up to the size of the value graph. Hence, this sets an upper bound for the number of iterations at each node where each evaluation of an annotation has costs that are linear in the size of the resulting structure. In practice, we rather expect that the annotations are reasonably small, as most of them will quickly evaluate to $\bot$.

---

[16] Note that $\mathbf{D}$ is contained in $\mathbf{D}^\phi \cup \{\bot, \top\}$ as a sub-cpo.

5.3   Further Extensions: Towards Conditional Constants

The approach we presented so far is open for extensions. Particularly interesting are extensions towards taking conditional branching into account. Wegman and Zadeck [30,31] and Click and Cooper [4] presented two completely different approaches for this. While Click and Cooper's approach proceeds by mutually feeding the results of simple constant propagation with those of a dead path analysis, Wegman and Zadeck's approach, which can be considered a specialisation of Wegbreit's general algorithm for performing global flow analysis taking conditional branches into account (cf. [29]), enhances Kildall's approach by means of "executable flags" on (flow graph) edges. In both approaches the effect is that information is not propagated along paths which are known to be infeasible. Additionally, it allows them to make use of branch conditions in specific branches, e.g., a condition like $x = 1$ allows them to propagate this information along the then-branch of an if-then-else statement.

Both variants can be put on top of the CP-approach we proposed here. For example, the "executable flags" of Wegman and Zadeck can essentially be mimicked by "executable flags" on ingoing edges of ϕ-nodes. Along the lines of Wegman and Zadeck's approach this allows the CP-algorithm on the value graph to neglect paths which are known to be not executable.

5.4   Related Work

Though it has certainly been considered before (cf. [5,17]), CP has particularly been pioneered by the investigations of Kildall [19], and Kam and Ullman [15,16]. The class of simple constants they introduced became the state-of-the-art of CP-algorithms, though it is suboptimal even on acyclic programs. Besides a few approaches aiming at detecting more general classes of constants like those of Kam and Ullman [16], Wegman and Zadeck [30,31], and Steffen and Knoop [28], and adaptations of CP to advanced program settings like the interprocedural (cf. [3,8,12,22,27,31]) or (explicitly) parallel one (cf. [20,21]), there is a large group of approaches aiming at computing simple constants more efficiently.

This latter group includes the algorithms of Reif and Lewis [24,25], Ferrante and Ottenstein [9], and Wegman and Zadeck [30,31]. They are known as sparse CP-algorithms. This also applies to the algorithm of Kennedy proposed in [18]. It is even more efficient, however, less powerful as it is in contrast to the sparse "optimistic" algorithms a "pessimistic" one. In contrast to the optimistic algorithms, which essentially work by disproving constancy of a term, pessimistic ones have to explicitly prove constancy, which in the presence of loops acts like a worst-case assumption.

Common to the optimistic sparse algorithms is that they work on specific representations of the control and data flow of a program. Most similar to the value graph of Alpern, Wegman, and Zadeck [2] our algorithm operates on, are the *global value graph* used by Reif and Lewis [24,25], and the SSA form (cf. [7]) used by Wegman and Zadeck [30,31]. In fact, the value graph of [2] can be considered a representation, which uniformly combines the spirit underlying SSA and the global value graphs of Reif and Lewis.

6   Conclusions

The value graph has been designed and used so far as a means for efficiently detecting value equivalences of program terms [2,26]. In this article, we demonstrated that it is not restricted to this application, but well-suited for other optimisations, too. We developed a new algorithm making constant propagation available on the value graph. Even more important, this algorithm enjoys particularly nice properties. It combines the (1) *efficiency* of the sparse CP-algorithms (cf. [24,25,9,30,31]) with the (2) *conceptual simplicity* of their classic conventional counterparts (cf. [19,16]), while simultaneously (3) outperforming them in power. In fact, the class of constants it detects is a proper superset of the simple constants detected by the classical algorithms, which still constitute the state-of-the-art in nowadays compilers. Moreover, the new algorithm is open for extensions. In Section 5.3 we sketched already an extension towards conditional constants along the lines of [30,31] and [4]. Other extensions we are currently investigating include extensions to variable range analysis (cf. [13,14]) and to interprocedural constant propagation in the fashion of [3,31].

References

1. A. V. Aho, R. Sethi, and J. D. Ullman. *Compilers: Principles, Techniques and Tools.* Addison-Wesley, 1985. 94
2. B. Alpern, M. N. Wegman, and F. K. Zadeck. Detecting equality of variables in programs. In *Conf. Rec. 15th Symp. Principles of Prog. Lang. (POPL'88)*, pages 1 – 11. ACM, NY, 1988. 95, 99, 107, 108
3. D. Callahan, K. D. Cooper, K. W. Kennedy, and L. M. Torczon. Interprocedural constant propagation. In *Proc. ACM SIGPLAN Symp. on Compiler Construction (SCC'86)*, volume *21*, 7 of *ACM SIGPLAN Not.*, pages 152 – 161, 1986. 95, 107, 108
4. C. Click and K. D. Cooper. Combining analyses, combining optimizations. *ACM Trans. Prog. Lang. Syst.*, 17(2):181 – 196, 1995. 107, 108
5. J. Cocke and J. T. Schwartz. Programming languages and their compilers. Courant Inst. Math. Sciences, NY, 1970. 107
6. P. Cousot and R. Cousot. Abstract interpretation: A unified lattice model for static analysis of programs by construction or approximation of fixpoints. In *Conf. Rec. 4th Symp. Principles of Prog. Lang. (POPL'77)*, pages 238 – 252. ACM, NY, 1977. 98
7. R. Cytron, J. Ferrante, B. K. Rosen, M. N. Wegman, and F. K. Zadeck. Efficiently computing static single assignment form and the control dependence graph. *ACM Trans. Prog. Lang. Syst.*, 13(4):451 – 490, 1991. 99, 107
8. E. Duesterwald, R. Gupta, and M. L. Soffa. A practical framework for demand-driven interprocedural data flow analysis. *ACM Trans. Prog. Lang. Syst.*, 19(6):992 – 1030, 1997. 95, 107
9. J. Ferrante and K. J. Ottenstein. A program form based on data dependency in predicate regions. In *Conf. Rec. 10th Symp. on Principles of Prog. Lang. (POPL'83)*. ACM, NY, 1983. 94, 95, 107, 108
10. M. R. Garey and D. S. Johnson. *Computers and Intractability — A Guide to the Theory of NP-Completeness.* W. H. Freeman & Co, San Francisco, CA, 1979. 102
11. S. L. Graham and M. N. Wegman. A fast and usually linear algorithm for global flow analysis. *J. ACM*, 23(1):172 – 202, 1976. 98
12. D. Grove and L. Torczon. Interprocedural constant propagation: A study of jump function implementation. In *Proc. ACM SIGPLAN Conf. on Prog. Lang. Design and Impl. (PLDI'93)*, volume *28*,6 of *ACM SIGPLAN Not.*, pages 90 – 99, 1993. 95, 107

13. W. H. Harrison. Compiler analysis of the value range of variables. *IEEE Trans. Softw. Eng.*, 3(SE-3):243 – 250, 1977. 108
14. H. Johnson. Dataflow analysis for intractable systems software. In *Proc ACM SIGPLAN Symp. on Compiler Construction (SCC'86)*, volume 21, 7 of *ACM SIGPLAN Not.*, pages 109 – 117, 1986. 108
15. J. B. Kam and J. D. Ullman. Global data flow analysis and iterative algorithms. *J. ACM*, 23(1):158 – 171, 1976. 107
16. J. B. Kam and J. D. Ullman. Monotone data flow analysis frameworks. *Acta Informatica*, 7:305 – 317, 1977. 94, 95, 97, 98, 99, 101, 102, 107, 108
17. K. Kennedy. Variable subsumption with constant folding, August 1973. Courant Institute of Mathematical Sciences, New York University, SETL Newsletter 112. 107
18. K. Kennedy. A survey of data flow analysis techniques. In S. S. Muchnick and N. D. Jones, editors, *Program Flow Analysis: Theory and Applications*, chapter 1, pages 5 – 54. Prentice Hall, Englewood Cliffs, NJ, 1981. 94, 107
19. G. A. Kildall. A unified approach to global program optimization. In *Conf. Rec. 1st Symp. Principles of Prog. Lang. (POPL'73)*, pages 194 – 206. ACM, NY, 1973. 94, 95, 97, 98, 107, 108
20. J. Knoop. Parallel constant propagation. In *Proc. 4th Europ. Conf. on Parallel Processing (Euro-Par'98)*, LNCS 1470, pages 445 – 455. Springer-V., 1998. 95, 107
21. Jaejin Lee, S. P. Midkiff, and D. A. Padua. A constant propagation algorithm for explicitly parallel programs. *Int. J. Parallel Programming*, 26(5):563 – 589, 1998. 95, 107
22. R. Metzger and S. Stroud. Interprocedural constant propagation: An empirical study. *ACM LOPLAS*, 2(1-4):213 – 232, 1993. 95, 107
23. S. S. Muchnick. *Advanced Compiler Design and Implementation*. Morgan Kaufmann, San Francisco, CA, 1997. 94, 99, 101
24. J. H. Reif and R. Lewis. Symbolic evaluation and the global value graph. In *Conf. Rec. 4th Symp. Principles of Prog. Lang. (POPL'77)*, pages 104 – 118. ACM, NY, 1977. 94, 95, 97, 107, 108
25. J. H. Reif and R. Lewis. Efficient symbolic analysis of programs. Technical Report 37-82, Aiken Computation Laboratory, Harvard University, 1982. 94, 95, 107, 108
26. O. Rüthing, J. Knoop, and B. Steffen. Detecting equalities of variables: Combining efficiency with precision. In *Proc. 6th Static Analysis Symposium (SAS'99)*, LNCS 1694, pages 232 – 247. Springer-V., 1999. 95, 108
27. M. Sagiv, T. Reps, and S. Horwitz. Precise interprocedural dataflow analysis with applications to constant propagation. *TCS*, 167(1-2):131 – 170, 1996. (Special issue devoted to *TOPLAS'95*). 95, 107
28. B. Steffen and J. Knoop. Finite constants: Characterizations of a new decidable set of constants. *TCS*, 80(2):303 – 318, 1991. (Special issue devoted to *MFCS'89*). 94, 96, 102, 107
29. B. Wegbreit. Property extraction in well-founded property sets. *IEEE Trans. Softw. Eng.*, 1(SE-3):270 – 285, 1975. 107
30. M. N. Wegman and F. K. Zadeck. Constant propagation with conditional branches. In *Conf. Rec. 12th Annual Symp. on Principles of Prog. Lang. (POPL'85)*, pages 291 – 299. ACM, New York, 1985. 94, 95, 96, 107, 108
31. M. N. Wegman and F. K. Zadeck. Constant propagation with conditional branches. *ACM Trans. Prog. Lang. Syst.*, 13(2):181 – 210, 1991. 94, 95, 96, 101, 107, 108
32. R. Wilhelm. Global flow analysis and optimization in the MUG2 compiler generating system. In S. S. Muchnick and N. D. Jones, editors, *Program Flow Analysis: Theory and Applications*, chapter 5, pages 132 – 159. Prentice Hall, Englewood Cliffs, NJ, 1981. 94

Simple Generation of Static Single-Assignment Form

John Aycock and Nigel Horspool

Department of Computer Science,
University of Victoria,
Victoria, B. C., Canada V8W 3P6
{aycock,nigelh}@csc.uvic.ca

Abstract. The static single-assignment (SSA) form of a program provides data flow information in a form which makes some compiler optimizations easy to perform. In this paper we present a new, simple method for converting to SSA form, which produces correct solutions for nonreducible control-flow graphs, and produces minimal solutions for reducible ones. Our timing results show that, despite its simplicity, our algorithm is competitive with more established techniques.

1 Introduction

The static single-assignment (SSA) form is a program representation in which variables are split into "instances." Every new assignment to a variable — or more generally, every new definition of a variable — results in a new instance. The variable instances are numbered so that each use of a variable may be easily linked back to a single definition point.

Figure 1 gives a example of SSA form for some straight-line code. As its name suggests, SSA only reflects static properties; in the example, V_1's value is a dynamic property, but the static property that all instances labelled V_1 refer to the same value will still hold.

$$
\begin{array}{ccc}
\texttt{read V} & \Longrightarrow & \texttt{read } V_1 \\
\texttt{V} \leftarrow \texttt{V + 1} & & V_2 \leftarrow V_1 + 1
\end{array}
$$

Fig. 1. SSA form of some straight-line code.

A problem arises at join points, where two or more control-flow paths merge. Multiple definitions of a variable may reach the join point; this would result in a violation of the single-assignment property. The problem is illustrated in Fig. 2a; what definition should the final instance of V be associated with?

To work around this problem, imaginary assignments are introduced at join points from trivial ϕ-functions. A ϕ-function has one argument for each incoming

A. Watt (Ed.): CC/ETAPS 2000, LNCS 1781, pp. 110–125, 2000.

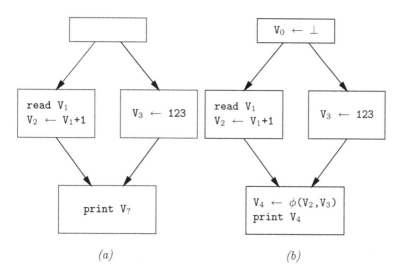

Fig. 2. Why ϕ?

control-flow path; the kth argument to a ϕ-function is the incoming value along the kth path.

Figure 2b shows the inserted ϕ-function. An initial assignment to V has been added so that instances of V always have a corresponding definition.

ϕ-functions are always inserted at the beginning of a basic block, and are considered to be executed simultaneously before execution of any other code in the block. A program must be converted out of SSA form before it is executed on a real machine.

Why use SSA form? Proponents of SSA have cited many advantages:

1. Every use of a variable is dominated by a definition of that variable [2,4]. Some optimization algorithms may be made more efficient by taking advantage of this property [4,21].
2. SSA chains are simpler to store and update than use-def chains [10].
3. Use-def chains may cause some optimizations to be missed that would be caught with a SSA-based algorithm [27].
4. Distinct uses of a variable in the source program — reusing a loop variable for another purpose, for example — become distinct variables in SSA form. This may allow more optimizations to be performed [3].

2   Converting to SSA Form

SSA form, and the conversion to SSA form, is closely coupled to dominance. If a definition of a variable V dominates a use of V, then that use may be linked back to a single definition. At join points, several definitions of V may reach a use of V, and so a ϕ-function is needed. Where ϕ-functions are needed, then, is where a definition *stops* dominating: this is the dominance frontier.

This is the basis of the algorithm by Cytron et al. [10], which is by far the most often-cited method for converting into SSA form. The idea is to precompute the dominance frontiers, then use that information to place a minimal number of ϕ-functions. The ϕ-functions are themselves definitions with a dominance frontier, so the process must be repeated — ϕ-functions must be placed in all basic blocks in the *iterated* dominance frontier.

The argument has been made that only the minimal number of ϕ-functions required should be inserted; otherwise, some optimizations could be missed [10,27]. While other forms of "minimal" SSA exist, such as those those taking liveness of variables into account, we do not consider them here.

3   Converting to SSA Form, Revisited

Appel [3] gives a gentle introduction to SSA form. He begins by suggesting a wasteful but obviously correct method for converting to SSA:

> 'A *really crude approach* is to split every variable at every basic-block boundary, and put ϕ-functions for every variable in every block.'
> [3, page 17]

He then recounts the dominance frontier algorithm of Cytron et al. [10] which inserts a minimal number of ϕ-functions. Appel's presentation raises the question: could a minimal number of ϕ-functions be discovered by starting with the "really crude approach" and iteratively deleting extraneous ϕ-functions?

3.1   Our Algorithm

Our algorithm finds a set of ϕ-functions for a given variable in a reducible control-flow graph. Intuitively, a reducible control-flow graph is one which does not have multiple entries into a loop. This is an important class of control-flow graphs because many modern languages, such as Oberon and Java, only admit reducible control-flow graphs; there is also empirical evidence suggesting that people tend to write programs with reducible control-flow graphs even if they can do otherwise [17].

We assume that there are no unreachable nodes in the control-flow graph, although the algorithm will still derive a correct solution in this case.

Our algorithm proceeds in two phases:

RC phase. Apply Appel's "really crude" approach as quoted above.
Minimization phase. Delete ϕ-functions of the form

$$V_i \leftarrow \phi(V_i, V_i, \ldots, V_i)$$

and delete ϕ-functions of the form

$$V_i \leftarrow \phi(V_{x_1}, V_{x_2}, \ldots, V_{x_k}), \text{where } x_1, \ldots, x_k \in \{i, j\}$$

replacing all other occurrences of V_i with V_j. Repeat this until no further minimizations are possible.

Once the above phases have determined the set of ϕ-functions to insert, then another pass over the control-flow graph renames instances of variables to their SSA forms. This is not unique to our algorithm, and will not be mentioned further.

An example is shown in Figs. 3–6. The original program is listed in Fig. 3a; the result after the RC phase is Fig. 3b. Figures 4 and 5 show the sets of ϕ-functions converging for i and j, respectively, and Fig. 6 gives the final result. Normally, the program variables would not be renamed until after the minimization phase, but they have been renamed earlier for illustrative purposes.

```
                                    i₀ ← ⊥
                                    j₀ ← ⊥
                                    i₁ ← 123
                                    j₁ ← i₁ * j₀
                                    repeat
                                        i₂ ← φ(i₁, i₆)
        i ← 123                         j₂ ← φ(j₁, j₅)
        j ← i * j                       write j₂
        repeat                          if (j₂ > 5) then
            write j                         i₃ ← φ(i₂)
            if (j > 5) then                 j₃ ← φ(j₂)
                i ← i + 1                    i₄ ← i₃ + 1
            else                        else
                break                       i₅ ← φ(i₂)
            end                             j₄ ← φ(j₂)
        until (i > 234)                     break
                                        end
                                        i₆ ← φ(i₄)
                                        j₅ ← φ(j₃)
                                    until (i₆ > 234)
                                    i₇ ← φ(i₆, i₅)
                                    j₆ ← φ(j₅, j₄)

              (a)                              (b)
```

Fig. 3. Before and after the RC phase.

3.2   Correctness

In this section we prove the correctness of the algorithm. By "correct," we mean that our algorithm always produces a set of ϕ-insertions that is a (possibly improper) superset of the minimal solution. Note that nothing in this proof

$$i_2 \leftarrow \phi(i_1, i_6)$$
$$i_3 \leftarrow \phi(i_2)$$
$$i_5 \leftarrow \phi(i_2)$$
$$i_6 \leftarrow \phi(i_4)$$
$$i_7 \leftarrow \phi(i_6, i_5)$$

$$\Longrightarrow$$

$$\begin{bmatrix} i_3 \equiv i_2 \\ i_5 \equiv i_2 \\ i_6 \equiv i_4 \end{bmatrix}$$

$$i_2 \leftarrow \phi(i_1, i_4)$$
$$i_7 \leftarrow \phi(i_4, i_2)$$

Fig. 4. Minimization phase convergence for i.

$$j_2 \leftarrow \phi(j_1, j_5)$$
$$j_3 \leftarrow \phi(j_2)$$
$$j_4 \leftarrow \phi(j_2)$$
$$j_5 \leftarrow \phi(j_3)$$
$$j_6 \leftarrow \phi(j_5, j_4)$$

$$\Longrightarrow$$

$$\begin{bmatrix} j_3 \equiv j_2 \\ j_4 \equiv j_2 \\ j_5 \equiv j_4 \equiv j_2 \\ j_6 \equiv j_2 \end{bmatrix}$$

$$j_2 \leftarrow \phi(j_1, j_2)$$

$$\Longrightarrow$$

$$\begin{bmatrix} j_2 \equiv j_1 \end{bmatrix}$$

(none)

Fig. 5. Minimization phase convergence for j.

```
i0 ← ⊥
j0 ← ⊥
i1 ← 123
j1 ← i1 * j0
repeat
      i2 ← φ(i1, i4)
      write j1
      if (j1 > 5) then
            i4 ← i2 + 1
      else
            break
      end
until (i4 > 234)
i7 ← φ(i4, i2)
```

Fig. 6. After the minimization phase (and renaming).

requires the control-flow graph to be reducible, so our algorithm produces a correct, but not necessarily minimal, solution for nonreducible graphs as well.

Lemma 1. *The RC phase produces a correct solution.*

Proof. Since the RC phase places ϕ-functions in all basic blocks, the minimal placement of ϕ-functions must be contained within the initial placement upon completion of the RC phase. □

Lemma 2. *The minimization phase produces a correct solution.*

Proof. There are two transformations performed in this phase:

1. Deleting $V_i \leftarrow \phi(V_i, V_i, \ldots, V_i)$. This can be safely deleted because it corresponds to the assignment $V_i \leftarrow V_i$ on all predecessor edges,[1] which has no effect on the program state. A minimal solution could not contain this because it is clearly superfluous.
2. Deleting $V_i \leftarrow \phi(V_{x_1}, V_{x_2}, \ldots, V_{x_k}), x_1, \ldots, x_k \in \{i, j\}$, and replacing all other occurrences of V_i with V_j. The ϕ-function assignment corresponds to the set of assignments $\{V_i \leftarrow V_i, V_i \leftarrow V_j\}$. As before, $V_i \leftarrow V_i$ has no effect and can be ignored. In the case of $V_i \leftarrow V_j$, it means that V_i must have the value V_j at all points in the program due to the single-assignment property. It is therefore safe to replace all V_i with V_j. Since V_i's only rôle is as an alternate name for V_j, it could not be part of a minimal solution.

□

Theorem 1. *Our algorithm produces a correct solution.*

Proof. By Lemmas 1 and 2, our algorithm cannot remove needed ϕ-functions, and must arrive at a (possibly improper) superset of the minimal solution. □

3.3   Proof of Minimality

In this section we prove that, for reducible control-flow graphs, our algorithm produces a minimal placement of ϕ-functions.

This proof draws from T_1-T_2 reduction of control-flow graphs [14]. To briefly summarize T_1-T_2 reduction, transformation T_1 is removal of a self-edge; transformation T_2 allows a node n_1 to eliminate a node n_2 if n_1 is the unique predecessor of n_2, and n_2 is not the initial node.

We construct the instance relationship graph, or IR-graph, as a directed graph derived from the control-flow graph that shows the relationships between instances of a variable in SSA form.[2] Every variable gives rise to a different IR-graph. Each instance V_i of a variable becomes a node in the IR-graph; for each

---

[1] These are placed on edges for the purposes of this proof, to avoid the critical edge problem cited by [6,20].

[2] The IR-graph is only used for the purposes of this proof; it is not used by our algorithm.

ϕ-function $V_i \leftarrow \phi(V_{x_1}, V_{x_2}, \ldots, V_{x_k})$, we add k edges to the IR-graph:

$$V_{x_1} \rightarrow V_i$$
$$V_{x_2} \rightarrow V_i$$
$$\vdots$$
$$V_{x_k} \rightarrow V_i$$

Not all instances are defined in terms of ϕ-functions. We call definitions that do not correspond to left-hand sides of ϕ-function assignments "real definitions." An instance V_i which corresponds to a real definition requires some special attention:

Case 1. V_i is not live[3] across a basic block boundary. This case corresponds to a temporary instance of V created and killed within a single basic block B. V_i will not appear in any ϕ-function. (The *final* definition of V in B will be cited by ϕ-functions in B's successor blocks.) V_i will appear as a disconnected node in the IR-graph and may be deleted; it is not taken into account by our algorithm since it doesn't appear in any ϕ-function. V_i is irrelevant to a ϕ-placement algorithm based on dominance frontiers too, because the definition giving rise to V_i in B only dominates a set of successor instructions in B, so B doesn't appear in any dominance frontier as a result of the definition.

Case 2. V_i is live across a basic block boundary. V_i must then appear as an argument to at least one ϕ-function. In the IR-graph, the V_i node will appear to be a "root" of the graph, since it will have an in-degree of zero. Let R be the set of roots of the IR-graph. So that we may take advantage of graph reduction techniques, we always augment the IR-graph with a "supersource" node V_S [13], which becomes the root of the IR-graph, and has an edge from it to every element of R. The supersource will be shown later to be inert with respect to the proof.

Case 3. V_i's definition reaches the exit point of the control-flow graph, but does not cross any basic block boundaries. As in Case 1, V_i will not appear in any ϕ-function, will appear as a disconnected node in the IR-graph, and may be deleted.

After the RC phase, when all basic blocks contain a ϕ-function, the IR-graph's structure will ape the structure of the control-flow graph. For example, Fig. 7a shows the control-flow graph for the code in Fig. 3a; the corresponding IR-graph for i is given in Fig. 7b.

In the IR-graph, the nature of the minimization phase is now apparent:

1. Deleting $V_i \leftarrow \phi(V_i, V_i, \ldots, V_i)$ is equivalent to applying T_1 to the IR-graph.
2. Deleting $V_i \leftarrow \phi(V_{x_1}, V_{x_2}, \ldots, V_{x_k}), x_1, \ldots, x_k \in \{i, j\}$, and replacing all other occurrences of V_i with V_j is equivalent to applying T_2 (possibly in combination with T_1) to the IR-graph.

---

[3] We consider liveness to include uses of V_i as arguments to ϕ-functions.

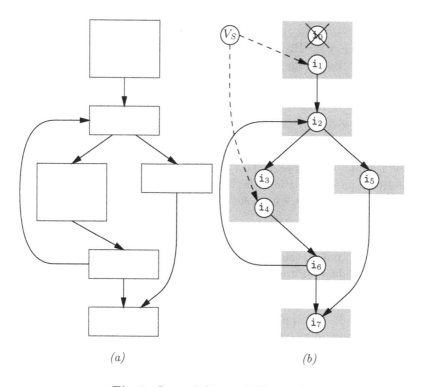

(a)   *(b)*

Fig. 7. Control-flow and IR graphs.

Fig. 8. The (*)-graph.

The structure of the IR-graph is important too:

Lemma 3. *The IR-graph is nonreducible only if the control-flow graph is nonreducible.*

Proof. Assume that the control-flow graph is reducible and the IR-graph is nonreducible. Then the IR-graph must contain the (*)-graph [14], which is illustrated in Fig. 8. Each edge in the IR-graph arises in one of two ways:

1. The edge results from paths in the control-flow graph. If every edge in the (*)-graph came from the control-flow graph, then the control-flow graph was itself nonreducible [14], yielding a contradiction.
2. The edge is added from the supersource V_S. V_S has no in-edges, so if any edge from V_S were to form part of the (*)-graph, it would have to connect to a V_i node which is part of a cycle in the graph. However, by definition of the IR-graph construction, the V_i nodes that V_S would connect to have no other in-edges, thus they cannot be part of a cycle. □

Since we are only considering reducible control-flow graphs, the IR-graph cannot initially contain the (*)-graph by Lemma 3. Furthermore, the (*)-graph cannot be introduced through T_1-T_2 reduction [14]. This means that the IR-graph must be reducible by T_1-T_2 transformations into the single node V_S.

T_1 and T_2 comprise a finite Church-Rosser transformation [14]. This means that if T_1 and T_2 are applied to a graph until no more transformations are possible, then a unique graph will result [1] — in this case, the single node V_S. Furthermore, this unique result does not depend on the order in which T_1 and T_2 are applied [13].

Given this freedom, we choose an ordering of T_1-T_2 reductions which corresponds to the manner in which our algorithm operates. A parse of a reducible flow graph is an ordered sequence of reductions together with the nodes to which the reductions are applied [13,14]. We select a full parse of the IR-graph which may be partitioned in two:

1. The first part performs as many T_1 and T_2 reductions as possible without eliminating any root nodes in R.
2. The final part applies T_1 and T_2 transforms to the remainder of the IR-graph, reducing it into the single node V_S. $\Pi(R)$ refers to the set of nodes yet to be reduced in the latter partition; by definition, $R \subseteq \Pi(R)$. $V_S \notin \Pi(R)$ because V_S can never be eliminated.

Lemma 4. *The minimization phase computes $\Pi(R) - R$.*

Proof. The transformations performed in the minimization phase can only remove V_i instances resulting from ϕ-functions; they cannot remove V_i instances corresponding to real definitions. This is the same as applying T_2 to the IR-graph, subject to the proviso that no elements of R be deleted. Because the minimization phase repeats until no further transformations are possible, it is computing $\Pi(R) - R$. □

Lemma 5. $\Pi(R) - R$ *is the iterated dominance frontier of R, $DF^+(R)$.*

Proof. The RC phase inserts a ϕ-function per basic block, so every V_i resulting from a ϕ-function has a one-to-one correspondence to a node in the control-flow graph. By definition, $\Pi(R) - R$ cannot contain any V_i from real definitions, so we may discuss the IR-graph nodes in $\Pi(R) - R$ and the control-flow graph nodes in $DF^+(R)$ interchangeably.

$\Pi(R) - R \subseteq DF^+(R)$. A reducible flow graph can be thought of as being decomposed by "regions." [26] A region is a subflowgraph, and the header node of a region dominates all nodes in the region save itself [14]. When the regions which have the elements of R as their headers are eliminated via T_1 and T_2, then what remains is the set of nodes which are not strictly dominated by elements of R. In other words, we are left with the dominance frontier of R, $DF(R)$.

The nodes in $DF(R)$ will themselves be headers of regions which have been reduced via T_1 and T_2. Inductively repeating this process, we get the iterated dominance frontier of R.

$DF^+(R) \subseteq \Pi(R) - R$. Suppose that there were a basic block $B \in DF^+(R)$ such that its corresponding IR-graph node $V_B \notin \Pi(R) - R$. This means that V_B must have already been eliminated by T_1 and T_2 earlier in the reduction parse. For this to happen, V_B must have been strictly dominated by some node in the IR-graph. It could not then be in $DF^+(R)$, a contradiction.   □

Theorem 2. *Our algorithm computes the minimal ϕ-function placement for reducible control-flow graphs.*

Proof. By Lemmas 4 and 5, our algorithm computes the iterated dominance frontier of R, where R is the set of real definitions of V. This iterated dominance frontier has been shown to be the minimal ϕ-function placement [10].   □

3.4   Improvements to the Basic Algorithm

Our algorithm can be improved upon; three improvements are immediately apparent:

Improvement 1. *One-pass RC phase.*

When inserting ϕ-functions during the RC phase, the instances of a variable coming from predecessor blocks must be known; complete processing of a block requires that all of its predecessor blocks be processed first. Even the best case — a depth-first ordering of the blocks — may require backpatching of information along back edges.

A slight change in numbering fixes this. If the instance of a variable V coming out of a block B_i is always V_i, then a block may be completely processed simply by knowing the block numbers of its predecessors — information likely to be available anyway. This means that the RC phase can run linearly regardless of how the blocks are ordered.

Improvement 2. *Mapping table.*

A naïve implementation of the minimization phase, which literally renamed all instances of V_i to V_j when deleting a ϕ-function, would clearly be wasteful. Instead, a mapping table can be used, which would map V_i to V_j; all references to variable instances in ϕ-functions would be filtered through this table.

This technique is well-known, under several different names: the equivalence problem [12,18], set merging [15], disjoint set union [25].

Improvement 3. *Basic blocks with single predecessors.*

Some ϕ-functions will always be deleted immediately. If a block has only a single predecessor, then it can't be a join point, so a ϕ-function need not be placed there during the RC phase.

At first sight, this improvement is incompatible with Improvement 1, which assumes ϕ-functions in every block. When combined with Improvement 2, however, this difficulty can be overcome. Upon finding a block with a single predecessor, the mapping table can simply be primed accordingly, instead of creating the ϕ-function.

4   Timing Results

We implemented our algorithm with the above improvements as a drop-in replacement for the Cytron et al. algorithm [10] used in the Gardens Point Modula-2 compiler. Timings were conducted on a 200 MHz Pentium with 64 M of RAM and a clock granularity of 10 ms, running Debian GNU/Linux version 2.1. To minimize transient timing errors, we ran each test five times; the times reported are the arithmetic mean of those five runs.

Figure 9 shows the time both algorithms take on a sample of thirty source files, comprising approximately 26,000 lines of code. (This code is the Modula-2 compiler's front end.) For all but a few of the files, our algorithm is competitive, sometimes faster than Cytron's.

What is often overlooked is the fact that SSA-generation algorithms do not operate in a vacuum. It is revealing to look at our algorithm in context. Figure 10 shows that, compared to the entire compilation, our algorithm takes an insignificant amount of time — this "total time" does not even include the time taken by the compiler's front end! Given that SSA generation time is not even a remotely dominant factor in compilation time, a simple algorithm such as ours may reasonably be used.

5   Related Work

In this section we survey other methods for converting to SSA form. These methods have been categorized based on the largest class of control-flow graph (CFG) they operate on: reducible or nonreducible.

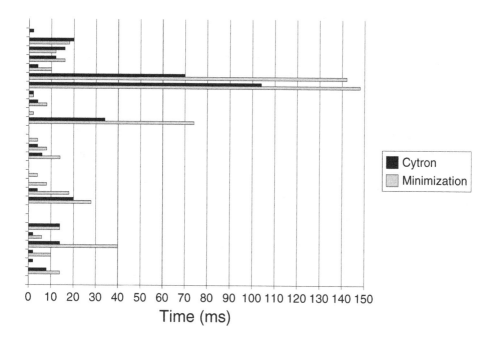

Fig. 9. Timing results.

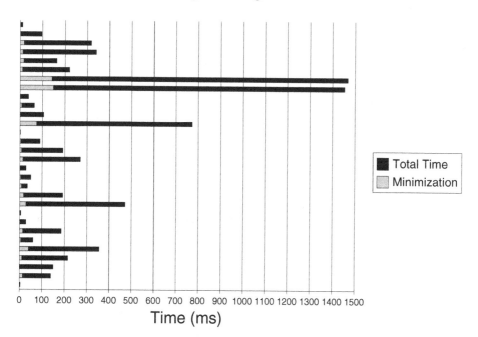

Fig. 10. Results in context.

5.1   Reducible CFGs

Brandis and Mössenböck [5] generate SSA form in one pass for structured control-flow graphs, a subset of reducible control-flow graphs, by delicate placement of ϕ-functions. They describe how to extend their method to reducible control-flow graphs, but require the dominator tree to do so.

Cytron, Lowry, and Zadeck [11] predate the use of ϕ-functions, and employ a heuristic placement policy based on the interval structure of the control-flow graph, similar to that of Rosen, Wegman, and Zadeck [22]. The latter work is interesting because they look for the same patterns as our algorithm does during our minimization phase. However, they do so after generating SSA form, and then only to correct 'second order effects' created during redundancy elimination.

5.2   Nonreducible CFGs

The work of Cytron et al. [10] is the method for generating SSA form we described in Sect. 2. Cytron and Ferrante [9] later refined their method so that it runs in almost-linear time.

Johnson, Pearson, and Pingali [16] demonstrate conversion to SSA form as an application of their "program structure tree," a decomposition of the control-flow graph into single-entry, single-exit regions. They claim that using this graph representation allows them to avoid areas in the control-flow graph that do not contribute to a solution.

The genesis of SSA form was in the 1960s with the work of Shapiro and Saint [23,19]. Their conversion algorithm was based upon finding equivalence classes of variables by walking the control-flow graph.

Finally, Sreedhar and Gao [24] devised a linear-time algorithm for ϕ-function placement using DJ-graphs, a data structure which combines the dominator tree with information about where data flow in the program merges.

All of the algorithms for nonreducible control-flow graphs described in this subsection have been proven to yield a minimal placement of ϕ-functions.

6   Future Work

There are a number of avenues for further work. First, we would like to determine the time complexity of our algorithm, although this is unlikely to matter in practice — there is evidence suggesting that some of these algorithms only rarely achieve worst-case performance [9,10].

Second, our algorithm may be extendible to other forms of minimal SSA, such as "pruned" SSA form, which only places a ϕ-function if the variable is live at that point [7].

Third, we are currently throwing away useful information. The algorithm of Cytron et al. that we compare our algorithm to in Sect. 4 only determines where ϕ-functions should be placed. Our algorithm determines this too, of course, but also knows upon completion what the arguments to the ϕ-functions are, something Cytron's algorithm does not know until variable renaming. It is possible that we can concoct a faster and/or simpler variable renaming algorithm as a result.

7   Applications

Our algorithm is particularly suitable in applications where a simple algorithm would be preferred, without the baggage of extra data structures. One might argue that the "extra" information computed by other algorithms will be used later: in fact, Cytron et al. suggest this [10]. However, in the two compilers we found employing SSA, neither made further use of the iterated dominance frontier information.

Some optimizations necessitate the re-generation of minimal SSA form. For example, re-minimization is required in the SSA-based partial redundancy elimination algorithm of [8], for which they suggest re-running the ϕ-insertion algorithm. Other optimizations may force SSA re-generation by changing the structure of the control-flow graph. Our algorithm may be useful in these situations.

8   Conclusions

We have presented a new, simple method of generating SSA form which finds a minimal ϕ-function placement for an important class of control-flow graph — reducible ones — and which finds a correct placement for all control-flow graphs, even nonreducible ones. Our timings indicate that it is competitive with the prevalent method of generating SSA form, especially when viewed in context.

9   Acknowledgments

Many thanks to John Gough for use of the Gardens Point Modula-2 compiler. The IFIP Working Group 2.4 made a number of helpful comments; in particular, Bob Morgan suggested applying our algorithm for re-minimization. The anonymous referees made many helpful comments. This work was supported in part by a grant from the National Science and Engineering Research Council of Canada.

References

1. A. V. Aho, R. Sethi, and J. D. Ullman. Code Optimization and Finite Church-Rosser Systems. In *Design and Optimization of Compilers*, R. Rustin, ed. Prentice Hall, 1971, pp. 89–105. 118
2. B. Alpern, M. N. Wegman, and F. K. Zadeck. Detecting Equality of Variables in Programs. *Proceedings of the Fifteenth Annual ACM Symposium on Principles of Programming Languages*, 1988, pp. 1–11. 111
3. A. W. Appel. SSA is Functional Programming. *ACM SIGPLAN 33*, 4 (April 1998), pp. 17–20. 111, 112

4. A. W. Appel. *Modern Compiler Implementation in Java*. Cambridge, 1998. 111

5. M. M. Brandis and H. Mössenböck. Single-Pass Generation of Static Single-Assignment Form for Structured Languages. *ACM TOPLAS 16*, 6 (November 1994), pp. 1684–1698. 122

6. P. Briggs, T. Harvey, and T. Simpson. Static Single Assignment Construction, Version 1.0. Unpublished document, 1995. 115

7. J.-D. Choi, R. Cytron, and J. Ferrante. Automatic Construction of Sparse Data Flow Evaluation Graphs. *ACM POPL '91*, pp. 55–66. 122

8. F. Chow, S. Chan, R. Kennedy, S.-M. Liu, R. Lo, and P. Tu. A New Algorithm for Partial Redundancy Elimination based on SSA Form. *ACM PLDI '97*, pp. 273–286. 123

9. R. K. Cytron and J. Ferrante. Efficiently Computing ϕ-Nodes On-The-Fly. *ACM TOPLAS 17*, 3 (May 1995), pp. 487–506. 122

10. R. Cytron, J. Ferrante, B. K. Rosen, M. N. Wegman, and F. K. Zadeck. Efficiently Computing Static Single-Assignment Form and the Control Dependence Graph. *ACM TOPLAS 13*, 4 (October 1991), pp. 451–490. 111, 112, 119, 120, 122, 123

11. R. Cytron, A. Lowry, K. Zadeck. Code Motion of Control Structures in High-Level Languages. *Proceedings of the Thirteenth Annual ACM Symposium on Principles of Programming Languages*, 1986, pp. 70–85. 122

12. M. J. Fischer. Efficiency of Equivalence Algorithms. In *Complexity of Computer Computations*, R. E. Miller and J. W. Thatcher, eds. Plenum Press, 1972. 120

13. M. S. Hecht. *Flow Analysis of Computer Programs*, North-Holland, 1977. 116, 118

14. M. S. Hecht and J. D. Ullman. Flow Graph Reducibility. *SIAM Journal of Computing 1*, 2 (June 1972), pp. 188–202. 115, 118, 119

15. J. E. Hopcroft and J. D. Ullman. Set Merging Algorithms. *SIAM Journal of Computing 2*, 4 (December 1973), pp. 294–303. 120

16. R. Johnson, D. Pearson, and K. Pingali. The Program Structure Tree: Computing Control Regions in Linear Time. *ACM PLDI '94*, pp. 171–185. 122

17. D. E. Knuth. An Empirical Study of FORTRAN Programs. *Software — Practice and Experience 1*, 1971, pp. 105–133. 112

18. D. E. Knuth. *The Art of Computer Programming, Volume 1: Fundamental Algorithms*, Addison Wesley, 1997. 120

19. D. B. Loveman and R. A. Faneuf. Program Optimization — Theory and Practice. *Conference on Programming Languages and Compilers for Parallel and Vector Machines*, 1975, pp. 97–102. 122

20. R. Morgan. *Building an Optimizing Compiler*, Digital Press, 1998. 115

21. S. S. Muchnick. *Advanced Compiler Design and Implementation*. Morgan Kaufmann, 1997. 111

22. B. K. Rosen, M. N. Wegman, and F. K. Zadeck. Global Value Numbers and Redundant Computations. *Proceedings of the Fifteenth Annual ACM Symposium on Principles of Programming Languages*, 1988, pp. 12–27. 122

23. R. M. Shapiro and H. Saint. The Representation of Algorithms. Rome Air Development Center TR-69-313, Volume II, September 1969. 122

24. V. C. Sreedhar and G. R. Gao. A Linear Time Algorithm for Placing ϕ-Nodes. *Proceedings of the Twenty-Second Annual ACM Symposium on Principles of Programming Languages*, 1995, pp. 62–73. 122

25. R. E. Tarjan. Efficiency of a Good But Not Linear Set Union Algorithm. *JACM 22*, 2 (April 1975), pp. 215–225. 120

26. J. D. Ullman. Fast Algorithms for the Elimination of Common Subexpressions. *Acta Informatica 2*, 1973, pp. 191–213. 119

27. M. N. Wegman and F. K. Zadeck. Constant Propagation with Conditional Branches. *ACM TOPLAS 13*, 2 (April 1991), pp. 181–210. 111, 112

Demand-Driven Construction of Call Graphs[*]

Gagan Agrawal

Department of Computer and Information Sciences, University of Delaware
Newark DE 19716
(302)-831-2783
agrawal@cis.udel.edu

Abstract. Call graph construction has been an important area of research within the compilers and programming languages community. However, all existing techniques focus on exhaustive analysis of all the call-sites in the program. With increasing importance of just-in-time or dynamic compilation and use of program analysis as part of the software development environments, we believe that there is a need for techniques for demand-driven construction of the call graph. We present a demand-driven call graph construction framework in this paper, focusing on the dynamic calls due to polymorphism in object-oriented languages. We use a variant of Callahan's Program Summary Graph (PSG) and perform analysis over a set of influencing nodes. We show that our demand-driven technique has the same accuracy as the corresponding exhaustive technique. The reduction in the graph construction time depends upon the ratio of the cardinality of the set of influencing nodes to the set of all nodes.

1 Introduction

With increasing focus on interprocedural optimizations in compilers for imperative and object-oriented languages and with increasing use of results of interprocedural program analysis in software development environments, the problem of call graph construction has received a significant attention [1,4,5,7,11,12,13,14]. A call graph is a static representation of dynamic invocation relationships between procedures (or functions or methods) in a program. A node in this directed graph represents a procedure and an edge $(p \rightarrow q)$ exists if the procedure p can invoke procedure q. In object-oriented languages, a call graph is typically constructed as a side-effect of interprocedural class analysis or type analysis [4]. Interprocedural class analysis computes a set of classes or types for each program variable such that each run-time value bound to a variable is a direct instance of one of the classes bound to the variable. The set of classes associated with the arguments of a dynamically dispatched message send at a callee site determine the set of callee methods or procedures.

A number of techniques have been developed for call graph construction in the last two decades. These techniques not only vary in their cost and precision, but also in the programming languages features they target. Some of the

---

[*] This research was supported by NSF CAREER award ACI-9733520

A. Watt (Ed.): CC/ETAPS 2000, LNCS 1781, pp. 125–140, 2000.

techniques are specifically for object-oriented languages [1,4,5,11,12], some other primarily target procedure-valued pointers in imperative languages [7,13], and others primarily target functional languages [14]. However, a common characteristic of all these techniques is that they perform *exhaustive analysis*, i.e. given a code, they compute the set of procedures that can be called at each of the call-sites in the code.

We believe that with increasing popularity of just-in-time or dynamic compilation and with increasing use of program analysis in software development environments, there is a strong need for *demand-driven call graph analysis* techniques. In a dynamic or just-in-time compilation environments, aggressive compiler analysis and optimizations are applied to selected portions of the code, and not to other less frequently executed or never executed portions of the code. Therefore, the set of procedures called needs to be computed for a small set of call-sites, and not for all the call-sites in the entire program.

Similarly, when program analysis is applied in a software development environment, demand-driven call graph analysis may be preferable to exhaustive analysis. For example, while constructing static program slices [9], the information on the set of procedures called is required only for the call-sites included in the slice and depends upon the slicing criterion used. Similarly, during program analysis for regression testing, only a part of the code needs to be analyzed, and therefore, demand-driven call graph analysis can be significantly quicker than an exhaustive approach.

In this paper, we present a framework for performing demand-driven call graph analysis. We use a variant of the Callahan's Program Summary Graph (PSG) for performing flow-sensitive analysis for reaching definitions. There are three major steps in our techniques. We initially assume a sound call graph using Class Hierarchy Analysis (CHA). Then, we construct a set of *influencing nodes* that influence the set of procedures invoked at the call-sites we are interested in. Finally, we perform propagation analysis on the set of influencing nodes.

The rest of the paper is organized as follows. In Section 2, we formulate the problem. The program representation used for our analysis is presented in Section 3. Our demand-driven analysis technique is presented in Section 4. We conclude in Section 5.

2   Problem Definition

In this section, we revisit the exhaustive call graph analysis problem, and then give our definition of the problem of demand driven call graph construction. We describe the language features our solution targets. We then state the main challenges in performing demand driven analysis for call graph construction and relate it to the existing solutions for exhaustive call graph construction.

2.1   Problem Definition

Consider a program for which the call graph is to be constructed. Let $P = \{p_1, p_2, \ldots, p_n\}$ be the set of procedures in the given program. Let $\mathcal{P}$ be the power

```
Class A {                    A::P(A *x, A *y) {
    void P(A *x, A *y);          x.Q(y) ;              cs1
    void Q(A* y);                y.Q(y) ;              cs2
    void R() ;               }
}                            main() {
Class B: public A {          A* a;
    void P(A *x, A *y) ;      A* b;
    void Q(A *y) ;
    void R() ;                       ...                s3
}                                a.R() ;               cs3
A::Q(A *y) {                      a = new B ;          s4
    y = new A ;      s1          b = new A ;           s5
}                                a.P(b,a) ;            cs4
B::Q(A *y) {                     a = new A ;           s6
    y = new B ;      s2          a.P(a,b) ;            cs5
}                            }
```

Fig. 1. Object-oriented program used as a running example in this paper. Definitions of functions A::R, B::R and B::P are not provided here.

set of P. Let $C = \{c_1, c_2, \ldots, c_m\}$ be the set of dynamic call-sites, that is, the call sites for which the set of procedures possibly invoked is not statically known (without non-trivial analysis). The problem of exhaustive call graph analysis is the same as constructing the mapping

$$M : C \rightarrow \mathcal{P}$$

In other words, we compute, for each call-site in the program , the set of procedures that can be possibly be invoked.

In contrast, the demand-driven call graph analysis involves constructing the set of procedures called at a specific call-site, or a (small) set of call-sites. Given a particular call-site c_i, we compute the mapping from c_i to a subset of P. Formally, this can be expressed as

$$m_i : c_i \rightarrow \mathcal{P}$$

2.2 Language Model

We now state the language features we focus on. We are interested in treating common object-oriented languages like C++ and Java. At the same time, we are interested in focusing on a set of simple language features, so that we can present the details of our technique with simplicity.

A class has members fields and member methods or procedures. A member procedure pname of a class pclass is denoted as pclass::pname. A base class can be extended by another class. In such a case, the base class is called a *superclass* and the class extending the base class is called a *subclass*. A class can only extend one superclass, treating languages with multiple inheritance is beyond the scope of this paper. The *set of subclasses* of a given class c is constructed transitively by including the class c, and any class that extends c or any class already included in the set. Similarly, the *set of superclasses* of a given class c is constructed transitively by including the class c, the class that the class c extended or any class that is extended by a class already included in the set.

We assume a statically-typed language in which a new object reference is created by a statement of the type r = new Classname; . Such a statement gives the type Classname to the variable r. The type of this instance of the variable r can only change as a result of another new statement.

The procedure calls are made as *static procedure calls*, in which an explicitly declared procedure is directly called by its name, or as *dynamic procedure calls*. A dynamic procedure call is of the format r.pname(paramlist). We assume that the actual procedure invoked at this call-site depends only upon the type of r. If r is of type Classname, then the procedure invoked at this call-site is the procedure pname defined in the class Classname (if it exists) or the procedure with the name pname declared in the nearest superclass of Classname. However, the type of r is usually not known through static declarations. If the static declaration of r is of class Declname, r can be dynamically assigned to an object of any subclass of Declname.

An example code that will be used as a running example is shown in Figure 1. We assume that all parameters are passed by reference and all procedures are declared to be virtual (i.e. can be over-written by a derived class). All member methods and fields are assumed to be public for simplicity. The class A is the base class, from which the class B is derived. Procedures P, Q and R are each defined in both these classes.

2.3   Overview of the Solution

We now give an overview of the problems involved in computing the mapping $m_i : c_i \rightarrow \mathcal{P}$. Let the call-site c_i have the format r.pname().

We first need to compute the types that r can possibly have at the program point c_i. Since a new type can only be assigned to r by a statement of the type r = new Classname;, we need to examine such *instantiations* of r that reach c_i. Let p be the statement where c_i is placed. There are three possibilities for each reaching instantiation of r:

1. It is defined in the procedure p.
2. The procedure p has another call-site c_j, such that the instantiation of r reaching c_i is passed as a reference parameter at the call-site c_j.
3. The instantiation of r reaching c_i is a formal parameter for the procedure p.

Case 1: This case is trivial because the reaching types of r can be determined by intraprocedural analysis within the procedure p. For example, in Figure refex:code, the dynamic calls at call-sites cs4 and cs5 can be resolved by intraprocedural propagation. The following non-trivial analysis is required for cases 2 and 3.

Case 2: We need to analyze the procedures that can possibly be invoked at the call-site c_j to be able to determine the type of r. This is relatively easy if the call-site c_j is a static call-site. However, if the call-site c_j is a dynamic call-site, we need to perform additional analysis to be able to determine the set of procedures invoked at the call-site c_j, and then need to perform reaching definitions analysis in the procedures invoked at c_j. For example, in Figure 1, for resolving the call-site cs2, we need to look at the possible values of the reference parameter y at the end of the procedure calls possible at the call-site cs1.

Case 3: To determine the types associated with r when entering the procedure p, we need to analyze all the call-sites at the which the procedure p is invoked. In the absence of the call graph, however, we do not know the set of call-sites that can invoke the procedure p. Therefore, we need to start with a conservative estimate of the set of call-sites at which the procedure p may be invoked. Analyzing these call-sites, we need to determine:

– Can the procedure p be invoked at this call-site ?
– If so, what are the types associated with the actual parameter at this call-site corresponding to the formal parameter r ?

For example, in Figure 1, for resolving the call-site cs1, we need to look the possible values of the reference parameter x at the entry of the proceedure A::P.

The previous work in demand-driven flow-sensitive data-flow analysis [6,8] (which does not apply to call graph analysis) formulates the problem as that of *query propagation*. The initial data-flow problem to be solved on a demand-basis is itself a query, whose solution is described in terms of queries at successor or predecessor nodes.

We can also describe the analysis for cases 2 and 3 as query propagation problems. Consider initially the case 2. If the call-site c_j is a dynamic call site, we need to answer the query

$$m_j : c_j \rightarrow \mathcal{P}$$

to answer our initial query. Irrespective of whether the call-site c_i is a dynamic call-site or a static call-site, we will need to know the types associated with r at the end of the call to each of the procedures that can possibly be invoked at this call-site.

The query propagation for case 3 can be stated as follows. We need to determine the set of call-sites C', such that for each

$$\forall c_k \in C' \quad (m_k : c_k \rightarrow \mathcal{P}_k) \quad \rightarrow \quad p \in \mathcal{P}_k$$

2.4   Overview of Call Graph Analysis Techniques

For ease in explaining our demand-driven call graph construction technique, we describe an existing classification of call graph analysis techniques [4]. All possible call graphs constructued by various algorithms, including the initial call graphs assumed and the results after each stage of the algorithm, can be described by a lattice. The *top-most* element of the lattice (denoted by $G_\top$) has no edges between any of the procedures. The *bottom-most* element of the lattice is denoted by $G_\perp$ and includes edges to all procedures in the entire program at each call-site. An *ideal graph* is the one in which each edge corresponds to an actual procedure invocation during one of the possible executions of the program. Obviously, the ideal graph is uncomputable.

Actual call graphs at each stage in various algorithms can be classified as *optimistic* or *sound*. An optimistic graph has fewer edges than the ideal graph, i.e., additional edges need to be inserted to model invocations during actual executions. A sound graph has more edges than ideal graph, so some edges can be deleted to improve the accuracy of the analysis. The process of adding more edges to an optimistic graph (to move it down the lattice) is referred to as the *monotonic refinement*. The process of deleting some edges from a sound graph (to move it up the lattice) is referred to as *non-monotonic improvement*.

3   Program Summary Graph

We use the interprocedural representation Program Summary Graph (PSG), initially proposed by Callahan [2], for presenting our demand-driven call graph analysis technique. We initially give the original definition of PSG and then describe several extensions of PSG that we use for our purpose.

A program summary graph is a representation of the complete program that is much concise as compared to the Myers' Supergraph or Interprocedural Control Flow Graph (ICFG) [10], but is more detailed than a call graph, and allows *flow-sensitive* interprocedural analysis.

Data-flow within procedures and between procedures is represented through edges between nodes of the following four types:

- *Entry nodes*; there is one entry node for each formal parameter of each procedure.
- *Exit nodes*; there is one exit node for each formal parameter of each procedure.
- *Call nodes*; there is one call node for each actual parameter at each call-site.
- *Return nodes*; there is one return node for each actual parameter at each call-site.

Edges between these nodes can be classified as *intraprocedural* and *interprocedural*. Intraprocedural edges summarize data-flow within the procedures. These edges are inserted after solving the standard data-flow problem of reaching definitions within each procedure. Specifically, the intraprocedural edges are inserted:

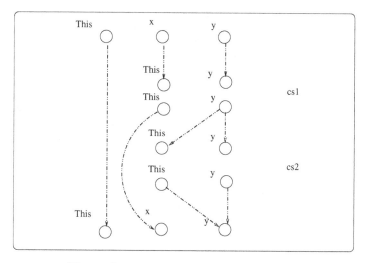

Fig. 2. Procedure A::P's portion of PSG

- From an entry node to a call node if the value of the corresponding formal parameter at the procedure entry reaches the corresponding actual parameter at the call-site.
- From an entry node to an exit node if the value of the corresponding formal parameter at the procedure entry reaches a procedure return statement.
- From a return node to a call node if the value of the corresponding actual parameter at the call return reaches the corresponding actual parameter at the call node.
- From a return node to an exit node if the value of the corresponding actual parameter at call return reaches a procedure return statement.

Interprocedural edges in the graph represent bindings of actual parameters to the formal parameters and vice-versa. Specifically, interprocedural edges are inserted:

- From a call node to an entry node to represent the binding of an actual parameter at the call-site to the formal parameter at procedure entry.
- From an exit node to a return node to represent the binding of a formal parameter at the procedure exit to the actual parameter at the call return.

To perform demand-driven call graph analysis, we make the following three extensions to the original definition construction method of PSG.

This pointer as a parameter: Consider a call site of the form
`r->pname(paramlist)`. For our analysis, besides having call and return nodes corresponding to each actual parameter in the list `paramlist`, we also need to have a call and return node for the object reference `r`. We refer to such nodes as nodes for THIS pointer, consistent with the C++ terminology. We also insert one THIS pointer node each at procedure entry and return for each procedure.

Internal Intraprocedural Nodes: We insert new *internal* intraprocedural nodes in the graph besides entry, exit, call and return nodes. These intraprocedural nodes represent statement that provide a new type to a variable. In the language model we assumed, these are statements of the type `r = new Classname`. New intraprocedural edges are inserted from internal nodes as follows. If a definition given in an internal nodes reaches an actual parameter at a call-site, a new edges is inserted from the internal node to the corresponding call node. If a definition given in an internal node reaches a procedure return statement, a new edge is inserted from the internal node to the corresponding exit node.

Demand Driven Construction: The Program Summary Graph is not fully constructed at the beginning of the analysis, since it will require knowing the call graph. Instead, the program summary graph is constructed on a demand basis. If v is the call node for which we are determining the types, we perform a reachability analysis on the portion of the graph constructed and check if v is reachable from one of the nodes of a procedure p. If so, the CFG of the procedure p is constructed, and intraprocedural edges of the procedure p's portion of PSG are inserted. The portion of PSG constructed in performing the propagation analysis is referred to as the Partial Program Summary Graph (PPSG) and set of nodes in the PPSG is referred to as the *set of influencing nodes*.

Procedure `A::P`'s portion of PSG is shown in Figure 2.

4   Demand-Driven Call Graph Construction

In this section, we describe the various phases of our algorithm for constructing call graph on a demand-driven basis and analyze the complexity of our technique.

4.1   Overview of the Algorithm

We are considering the problem of computing the set of procedures that can be invoked at a call-site c_i, of the form `r->pname()`. The most important goal for our algorithm is to analyze as few procedures as possible while determining the set of procedures that can be invoked at the call-site c_i. Our algorithm initially assumes a sound or conservative call graph, i.e., one with much larger number of edges than what can be taken during actual executions. This initial sound call graph is constructed using the results of Class Hierarchy Analysis (CHA) [3]. Such an initial sound call graph is also not constructed explicitly for the entire program, but is constructed on a demand basis. Each procedure's components are added only after it is known that this procedure may influence the types associated with the object reference `r` at the call-site c_i.

There are two main phases in our algorithm. Initially, we perform reachability analysis using the sound call graph to determine the set of influencing nodes and to construct the Partial Program Summary Graph (PPSG). The second phase involves performing data-flow propagation on the PPSG to improve the precision of the call graph using reaching types information.

4.2   Initial Sound Call Graph

As we described earlier in Section 2, call graph analysis techniques either start from an optimistic graph and add more edges, or can start from a sound or conservative graph and delete edges. We prefer to start from a sound graph and delete edges since it allows us to compute the set of influencing nodes. One possible initial sound graph is $G_{\perp}$, in which each call-site can invoke all procedures. Obviously, starting from such an initial call graph will defeat the purpose of demand-driven analysis as all the nodes in the entire program will get added to the set of influencing nodes. We can construct a relatively accurate initial call graph by performing relatively inexpensive Class Hierarchy Analysis (CHA) [3].

CHA involves having knowledge of all the classes declared in the entire program, including which class extends another class, and the set of procedures declared in each of the classes. Consider a call-site of the form r->rname(), such that the declared type of r is rclass. Let $\mathcal{R}$ be the set of subclasses of rclass. For each class in the set $\mathcal{R}$, we determine the nearest superclass (including itself) in which a procedure with the name rname is declared. Let us denote such a set of classes by $\mathcal{R}'$. Then, as a result of class hierarchy analysis, we know that the possible procedures that can be called at this call-site are of the form pclass::rname, where pclass belongs to the set $\mathcal{R}'$.

Alternatively, consider a procedure p of the form pclass::pname. By knowing all class declarations in the program, we can determine the set of subclasses of pclass. By further examining the procedures declared in each of these classes, we can narrow this set down to classes for which pclass is the earliest superclass for which the procedure pname is defined. Let us denote such a set by $\mathcal{S}$. The procedure p can be called at any dynamic call-site of the form r->pname where the declared type of the reference r belongs to the set $\mathcal{S}$.

4.3   Preliminary Definitions

In presenting our technique, we use the following definitions.

$pred(v)$: The set of predecessors of the node v in the PPSG. This set is initially defined during the construction of PPSG and is not modified as the type information becomes more precise.

$proc(v)$: This relation is only defined if the node v is an entry node or an exit node. It denotes the name of the procedure to which this node belongs.

TYPES(v): The set of types associated with a node v in the PSG during any stage in the analysis. This set is initially constructed using Class Hierarchy Analysis, and is later refined through data-flow propagation.

THIS_NODE(v): This is the node corresponding to the THIS pointer at the procedure entry (if v is an entry node), procedure exit (if v is an exit node), procedure call (if v is a call node) or call return (if v is a return node).

THIS_TYPE(v): If the vertex v is a call node or a return node, THIS_TYPE(v) returns the types currently associated with the call node for the THIS pointer at this call-site. This relation is not defined if v is an entry or exit node.

PROCS(S): Let S be the set of types associated with a call node for a THIS pointer. Then, PROCS(S) is the set of procedures that can actually be invoked at this call-site. This function is computed using Class Hierarchy Analysis (CHA).

Let v be the this pointer node at the call site
Let p be the procedure to which v belongs
Initialize $Workset$ to $\{v\}$
Initialize $Procset$ to $\{p\}$
Initialize all nodes to be not $marked$
$Construct\_PSG\_Portion(p)$

$While$ $Workset$ is not empty
   Select and remove vertex u from $Workset$
   case (type of u):
      call or exit:
         $foreach$ predecessor w of u
            If w is not $marked$
               $Workset = Workset \cup \{w\}$
      return:
         If THIS_NODE(u) is not $marked$
            $Workset = Workset \cup$ THIS_NODE(u)
         $foreach$ possibly called function q
            If $q \notin Procset$
               $Procset = Procset \cup \{q\}$
               $Construct\_PSG\_Portion(q)$
         $foreach$ predecessor w of u
            If w is not $marked$
               $Workset = Workset \cup \{w\}$
      entry:
         $Workset = Workset \cup$ THIS_NODE(u)
         $foreach$ possible callee function q
            If $q \notin Procset$
               $Procset = Procset \cup \{q\}$
               $Construct\_PSG\_Portion(q)$
         $foreach$ predecessor w of u
            If w is not $marked$
               $Workset = Workset \cup \{w\}$

Fig. 3. Constructing the Partial Program Summary Graph (PPSG)

4.4 Constructing the Set of Influencing Nodes

We now describe how we compute the set of nodes in the PSG for the entire program that influence the set of procedures invoked at the given call-site c_i.

The PSG for the entire program is never constructed. However, for ease in presenting the definition of the set of influencing nodes, we assume that the PSG components of all procedures in the entire program are connected based upon the initial sound call graph.

Let v be the call node for the THIS pointer at the call-site c_i. Given the hypothetical complete PSG, the set of influencing nodes (which we denote by S) is the minimal set of nodes such that:

- $v \in S$
- $(x \in S) \wedge (y \in pred(x)) \rightarrow y \in S$
- $x \in S \rightarrow$ THIS_NODE$(x) \in S$

Starting from the node v, we include the predecessors of any node already in the set, till we reach internal nodes that do not have any predecessors. For any node included in the set, we also include the corresponding node for the THIS pointer (denoted by THIS_NODE) in the set.

Such a set of influencing node and the partial PSG can be constructed by an iterative algorithm, which is shown in Figure 3. Two main data-structures maintained in the algorithm are *Workset* and *Procset*. *Workset* is the set of nodes whose predecessors have not been analyzed yet. *Procset* is the set of procedures that have been analyzed and whose portions of the PSG has been constructed.

The algorithm progresses by removing a node from the *Workset*. If this node is a call or exit node, all the predecessors of this node are within the same procedure. These predecessors are added to the *Workset*. If the node u (removed from the *Workset*) is a return node, the predecessors of this node are the exit nodes of the procedures that can be invoked at this call-site. Such a set of procedures is known (not necessarily accurately) from our construction of the initial sound call graph. Let q be any such procedure. If q is not in the set *Procset* (i.e. it has not been analyzed yet), then the function $Construct\_PSG\_Portion(q)$ is invoked. This function analyzes the CFG of the procedure q to construct its portion of the PSG. For each callee of q that has been analyzed, edges from its call nodes to entry nodes of q and edges from exit nodes of q to its return nodes are inserted. Similarly, for each function called by q that has been analyzed, we insert edges from call nodes at q to its entry nodes from its exit nodes to the return nodes at q. After all such procedures called at this call-site have been analyzed and edges have been inserted, we add the predecessors of the node u to the *Workset*.

The edges inserted at these call-sites are obviously based upon an initial sound call graph, that needs to be refined by our analysis. For this purpose, we need to know the types associated with the THIS_NODE at the call-site corresponding to the return node. For this reason, we also add THIS_NODE(u) to the *Workset*.

The actions taken for an entry node are very similar to the actions taken for a return node. The only difference is that instead of analyzing the procedures that can be called at that call-site, we analyze the procedures that have a call-site that can invoke this procedure.

4.5 Call Graph Refinement

The next step in the algorithm is to perform iterative analysis over the set of nodes in the Partial Program Summary Graph (PPSG) to compute the set of types associated with a given initial node. This problem can be modeled as computing the data-flow set TYPES with each node in the PPSG and refining it iteratively. The initial values of TYPES(v) are computed through class hierarchy analysis that we described earlier in this section. If a formal or actual parameter is declared to be a reference to class cname, then the actual runtime type of that parameter can be any of the subclasses (including itself) of cname.

The refinement stage can be described by a single equation, which is shown in Figure 4. Consider a node v in PPSG. Depending upon the type of v, three cases are possible in performing the update:

1. v is a call or exit node,
2. v is an entry node, and
3. v is a return node.

In Case 1., the predecessors of the node v are the internal nodes, the entry nodes for the same procedure, or the return nodes at one of the call-sites within this procedure. The important observation is that such a set of predecessors does not change as the type information is made more precise. So, the set TYPES(v) is updated by taking union over the sets of TYPES(v) over the predecessors of the node v.

We next consider case 2, i.e., when the node v is an entry node. $proc(v)$ is the procedure to which the node v belongs. The predecessors of such a node are call nodes at all call-sites at which the function $proc(v)$ can possibly be called, as per the initial call graph assumed by performing class hierarchy analysis. Such a set of possible call-sites for $proc(v)$ gets restricted as interprocedural type propagation is performed. Let p be a call node that is a predecessor of v. We want to use the set TYPES(p) in updating TYPES(v) only if the call-site corresponding to p invokes $proc(v)$. We determine this by checking the condition $proc(v) \in$ PROCS(THIS_TYPE(p)). The function THIS_TYPE(p) determines the types currently associated with the THIS pointer at the call-site corresponding to p and the function PROCS determines the set of procedures that can be called at this call-site based upon this type information.

Case 3 is very similar to the case 2. If the node v is a return node, the predecessor node p to v is an exit node. We want to use the set TYPES(p) in updating TYPES(v) only if the call-site corresponding to v can invoke the function $proc(p)$. We determine this by checking the condition $proc(p) \in$ PROCS(THIS_TYPE(v)). The function THIS_TYPE(v) determines the types currently associated with the THIS pointer at the call-site corresponding to v and the function PROCS determines the set of procedures that can be called at this call-site based upon this type information.

$$\text{TYPES}(v) = \begin{cases} \text{TYPES}(v) \cap (\bigcup_{p \in pred(v)} \text{TYPES}(p)) \\ \qquad \text{if v is call or exit node} \\ \text{TYPES}(v) \cap (\bigcup_{(p \in pred(v)) \wedge (proc(v) \in \text{PROCS}(\text{THIS\_TYPE}_{(p)}))} \text{TYPES}(p)) \\ \qquad \text{if v is an entry node} \\ \text{TYPES}(v) \cap (\bigcup_{(p \in pred(v)) \wedge (proc(p) \in \text{PROCS}(\text{THIS\_TYPE}_{(v)}))} \text{TYPES}(p)) \\ \qquad \text{if v is a return node} \end{cases}$$

Fig. 4. Data-Flow Equation for Propagating Type Information

4.6   Complexity Analysis

We now calculate the worst-case complexity of the technique proposed earlier. We initially analyze the complexity of the phase for creating the PPSG and then analyze the complexity of the call graph refinement phase. We define the following terms for our presentation:

N :   The number of nodes in PPSG
E :   The number of edges in the PPSG
D :   The maximum depth of a class hieararchy

Creating PPSG: The algorithm for constructing the set of influencing nodes was presented in Figure 3. We are focussing on analysis of large codes comprising a very large number of procedures. Therefore, we assume that the cost of constructing and analyzing a single procedure is small and the function *Construct_PSG_Portion* can be executed in a constant time. Then the overall cost of the execution of the algorithm presented in Figure 3 is $O(N + E)$. This is because each node is removed once from the *Workset* (and the total number of elements ever added in the *Workset* is N) and each edge is followed once to consider the source of the edge.

Iterative Analysis: The iterative analysis is performed over a graph with N nodes and E edges. The maximum number of times that the types associated with a node can change is bounded by D, the maximum depth of the class hierarchy. Since the total number of nodes in the graph is N, the maximum possible length of any acyclic path in the graph is also N. Therefore, the iterative analysis needs to be repeated over a maximum of a $N \times D$ steps. Each step in the iterative analysis requires updating the types of N nodes, which will take $O(N)$ time, assuming that the number of predecessors of a node is bounded by a small constant. Therefore, the complexity of iterative analysis is $O(N^2 D)$.

  The efficiency of our technique depends upon the size of the PPSG constructed. If the PPSG is almost as large as the complete PSG for the entire program, our algorithm basically reduces to the classical 0-CFA construction technique proposed by Shivers [14]. If PPSG is significantly smaller than the

PSG for the entire program, our technique is very efficient as compared to the exhaustive techniques.

4.7 Theoretical Results

As we mentioned in the previous subsection, our analysis is similar to Shiver's 0-CFA, except that we perform demand-driven analysis using propagation only on PPSG, whereas Shiver's 0-CFA is an exhaustive technique requiring propagation over the PSG for the entire program. One important issue is the accuracy of our demand driven technique as compared to the similar exhaustive technique. We show below that the accuracy of our demand-driven technique is the same as the accuracy of Shiver's 0-CFA technique.

Theorem 1 *The sets* $\text{TYPES}(v)$ *computed by our technique for any node* v *in the set* S *is identical to the set constructed by 0-CFA exhaustive technique.*

Proof: The basic idea behind the proof is as follows. Any node that can influence the value of $\text{TYPES}(v)$ is included in the set S. Therefore, a propagation just over the set S results in as accurate results as propagating over the entire PSG.

There are two interesting consequences of this theorem. Suppose, we initially computed the types for a node v by performing demand-driven analysis and the set of influencing nodes S that is computed includes a node w. If we later require the type information for the node w, we can just use the information computed while performing demand-driven analysis for node v. Further, suppose we need to compute types information for a node z. While computing the set of influencing nodes, we include a node y, which was previously included in a set of influencing nodes. We can just use the previously computed types information for y, and do not need to continue to include predecessors of y in the new set of influencing nodes.

5 Conclusions

For performing interprocedural program analysis and transformations on programs with polymorphism, we need to know which methods can be called at each of the call-sites. In a number of scenarios, it can be important to compute this information on a demand-basis for certain call-sites only, rather than the entire program. Examples of such scenarios are 1) performing optimizations during just-in-time or dynamic compilation, 2) performing program analysis (like slicing) for software development, and 3) performing scalable analysis for very large programs.

In this paper we have presented, to the best of our knowledge, first solution to the problem of demand-driven resolution of call-sites in object-oriented programs. Our technique is based upon computing a set of influencing nodes, and then applying data-flow propagation over such a set.

We have two major theoretical results. We have shown that the worst-case complexity of our analysis is the same as the well known 0-CFA exhaustive analysis technique, expect that our input is cardinality of the set of influencing nodes, rather than the total number of nodes in the graph. Thus, the advantage of our demand-driven technique depends upon the relative size of set of influencing nodes and the total number of nodes. Second, we have shown that they type information computed by our technique for all the nodes in the set of influencing nodes is as accurate as the 0-CFA exhaustive analysis technique.

References

1. David Bacon and Peter F. Sweeney. Fast static analysis of c++ virtual function calls. In *Eleventh Annual Conference on Object-Oriented Programming Systems, Languages, and Applications (OOPSLA '96)*, pages 324–341, October 1996. 125, 126

2. D. Callahan. The program summary graph and flow-sensitive interprocedural data flow analysis. In *Proceedings of the SIGPLAN '88 Conference on Programming Language Design and Implementation*, Atlanta, GA, June 1988. 130

3. Jeffrey Dean, Craig Chambers, and David Grove. Selective specialization for object-oriented languages. In *Proceedings of the ACM SIGPLAN'95 Conference on Programming Language Design and Implementation (PLDI)*, pages 93–102, La Jolla, California, 18–21 June 1995. *SIGPLAN Notices* 30(6), June 1995. 132, 133

4. Greg DeFouw, David Grove, and Craig Chambers. Fast interprocedural class analysis. In *Proceedings of the POPL'98 Conference*, 1998. 125, 126, 130

5. Amer Diwan, J. Elliot Moss, and K. Mckinley. Simple and effective analysis of statically typed object-oriented programs. In *Eleventh Annual Conference on Object-Oriented Programming Systems, Languages, and Applications (OOPSLA '96)*, pages 292–305, October 1996. 125, 126

6. Evelyn Duesterwald, Rajiv Gupta, and Mary Lou Soffa. Demand-driven computation of interprocedual data flow. In *Conference Record of POPL '95: 22nd ACM SIGPLAN-SIGACT Symposium on Principles of Programming Languages*, pages 37–48, San Francisco, California, January 1995. 129

7. Mary W. Hall and Ken Kennedy. Efficient call graph analysis. *ACM Letters on Programming Languages and Systems*, 1(3):227–242, September 1992. 125, 126

8. S. Horwitz, T. Reps, and M. Sagiv. Demand interprocedural dataflow analysis. In *In SIGSOFT '95: Proceedings of the Third ACM SIGSOFT Symposium on the Foundations of Software Engineering*, pages 104–115, 1995. 129

9. Susan Horwitz, Thomas Reps, and David Binkley. Interprocedural slicing using dependence graphs. *ACM Transactions on Programming Languages and Systems*, 12(1):26–60, January 1990. 126

10. E. Myers. A precise interprocedural data flow algorithm. In *Conference Record of the Eighth ACM Symposium on the Principles of Programming Languages*, pages 219–230, January 1981. 130

11. Jens Palsberg and Patrick O'Keefe. A type system equivalent to flow analysis. In *Conference Record of POPL '95: 22nd ACM SIGPLAN-SIGACT Symposium on Principles of Programming Languages*, pages 367–378, San Francisco, California, January 1995. 125, 126

12. Hemant Pande and Barbara Ryder. Data-flow-based virtual function resolution. In *Proceedings of the Third International Static Analysis Symposium*, 1996. 125, 126

13. B. Ryder. Constructing the call graph of a program. *IEEE Transactions on Software Engineering*, SE-5(3):216–226, May 1979. 125, 126

14. O. Shivers. The semantics of Scheme control-flow analysis. In *Proceedings of the Symposium on Partial Evaluation and Semantics-Based Program Manipulation*, volume 26, pages 190–198, New Haven, CN, June 1991. 125, 126, 137

A Framework for Loop Distribution on Limited On-Chip Memory Processors*

Lei Wang, Waibhav Tembe, and Santosh Pande**

Compiler Research Laboratory, Department of ECECS, ML 0030,
University of Cincinnati, PO Box 210030, Cincinnati, OH 45221-0030
leiwang,wtembe,santosh@ececs.uc.edu

Abstract. This work proposes a framework for analyzing the flow of values and their re-use in loop nests to minimize data traffic under the constraints of limited on-chip memory capacity and dependences. Our analysis first undertakes fusion of possible loop nests intra-procedurally and then performs loop distribution. The analysis discovers the *closeness factor* of two statements which is a quantitative measure of data traffic saved per unit memory occupied if the statements were under the same loop nest over the case where they are under different loop nests. We then develop a greedy algorithm which traverses the program dependence graph (PDG) to group statements together under the same loop nest legally. The main idea of this greedy algorithm is to transitively generate a *group* of statements that can legally execute under a given loop nest that can lead to a minimum data traffic. We implemented our framework in Petit [2], a tool for dependence analysis and loop transformations. We show that the benefit due to our approach results in eliminating as much as 30 % traffic in some cases improving overall completion time by a 23.33 % for processors such as TI's TMS320C5x.

1 Introduction

1.1 On-Chip Memory and Data Traffic

Due to significant advances in VLSI technology, 'mega-processors' made with a large number of transistors has become a reality. These processors typically provide multiple functional units which allow exploitation of parallelism. In order to cater to the data demands associated with parallelism, the processors provide a limited amount of on-chip memory. The amount of memory provided is quite limited due to higher area and power requirements associated with it. Even though limited, such on-chip memory is a very valuable resource in memory hierarchy. Due to tight integration and careful layouts, the latency delays amongst the on-chip resources are significantly smaller; thus, on-chip memory can serve as an ultra-fast cache as shown by Panda, Nicolau and Dutt [15]. One of the significant uses of on-chip memory is to store spill values as shown by

---

* Supported in part by NSF through grant no. #EIA 9871345
** Contact author for future communications about this paper

A. Watt (Ed.): CC/ETAPS 2000, LNCS 1781, pp. 141–156, 2000.

Cooper et. al. [17]. Another important use of on-chip memory is to hold the instructions from short loops along with the associated data for very fast computation. Such schemes are very attractive on embedded processors where, due to the presence of dedicated hard-ware on-chip (such as very fast multipliers-shifters etc.) and extremely fast accesses to on-chip data, the computation time of such loops is extremely small meeting almost all real-time demands. Biggest bottleneck to performance in these cases are off-chip accesses and thus, compilers must carefully analyze references to identify good candidates for *promotion* to on-chip memory. In our earlier work [6,5], we formulated this problem in terms of 0/1 knapsack and proposed a heuristic solution that gives us good promotion candidates. Our analysis was limited to single loop nest. When we attempted extending this framework to multiple loop nests (intra-procedurally), we realized that not only it is important to identify good candidates for promotion but a careful restructuring of loops must be undertaken *before performing promotion* since data traffic of loading and storing values to on-chip memory poses a significant bottleneck.

Reorganization of loop nests is quite useful for signal processing applications which typically consist of a sequence of loop nests that tend to operate on the same data elements performing operations such as DCT transform, averaging, convolution, edge detection etc. in succession. Valuable data traffic can be saved in such cases by compiler analysis of flow of values to maximize re-use. This is the focus of this work.

2   Motivating Example: On-Chip Memory and Parallelism

Consider the following loop nests to be executed on a processor that can support 300 parallel adders. Assume that the processor has on-chip memory which can hold 300 data elements (this is a typical size for most on-chip memories which ranges from 128 words to about 512 words).

```
Example:
For i=1 to 100              //L1
    m[i] = a[i] + e[i];        //S1
    n[i] = b[i] + c[i];        //S2
For i=1 to 100              //L2
    p[i] = f[i] + d[i];        //S3
    q[i] = e[i-1] + m[i] + a[i+1];//S4
```

Consider executing the above loop nests (without any restructuring), on this processor. The first loop nest L1 needs 200 parallel adders and the second one L2 also needs 200 parallel adders. Since the processor can support 300 parallel adders, both of these needs are satisfied as far as the parallelism is concerned. However, due to limited on-chip memory, both loops must be blocked. The loop L1 is blocked with size 50 since each iteration demands storage for 6 data elements. The loop L2 is blocked with size 42 since each iteration demands storage for 7 elements. Thus, one can see that although the processor can support 300 adders, loop L1 can utilize only 100 parallel adders and loop L2 can utilize only 84 parallel adders due to the limitations on data storage. The total data traffic for the above blocked loop nests is 1300 (900 input values loaded to on-chip memory and 400 output values stored from on-chip memory into main cache). This traffic is essentially sequential and poses the largest overhead on loop execution. We now show that if we restructure the loops we can significantly reduce the costly traffic and also utilize parallelism more effectively. We see that arrays a[] and e[] are used in both S1 and S4, and m[i] (output of S1) is used in S4. Thus, statements S1 and S4 exhibit a higher degree of 'closeness' to each other since their execution under one loop nest can significantly increase data re-use and reduce effective traffic. We can thus group them together. Statements S2 and S3 however share no such data re-use and thus, we can put them under separate loop nests. Using the memory capacity constraint, the blocked loops are as follows:

```
Output Loop:
For i = 1 to 100 by 75               //L1
  For j = i to min(i+74, 100)
    m[j] = a[j] + e[j];              //S1
    q[j] = e[j-1] + m[j] + a[j+1];   //S4
For i=1 to 100                       //L2
  n[i] = b[i] + c[i];                //S2
For i=1 to 100                       //L3
  p[i] = f[i] + d[i];                //S3
```

The block size for the first loop is found 75 since each iteration of the inner loop needs storage for 4 elements per iteration and since we have a memory capacity of 300 elements, we can 'block' 75 iterations together. Thus, during the execution we get fetch the entire data needed for complete execution of the blocked loop, so that no intermediate traffic is needed. Once the loop is executed, we output all the necessary data elements generated/modified in the program. No blocking is needed for other two loop nests. In the above restructured loops, the first loop nest utilizes a parallelism of 150 parallel adders whereas the second and third loop nests utilize parallelism of 100 parallel adders. One can see that these loop nests not only exhibit better parallelism but also have much lower data traffic needs. The first loop nest has total traffic of 400 (200 loads and 200 stores). The other two loop nests have traffic of 300 each (200 loads and 100 stores). Thus the total data traffic for the restructured loop nests is 1000. The total data traffic is thus reduced from 1300 to 1000 or a saving of about 23% is achieved. As mentioned earlier, the data traffic is sequential and has a higher latency and thus forms a dominant part of overall loop completion time. The reduction in data traffic has a more significant effect on reduction of overall completion time of the loop. This motivates our approach of restructuring the loop nests for minimizing data traffic. Our approach is based on determining a group of statements that should execute under a given loop nest to minimize data traffic. In the next section, we present an outline of our approach introducing terms and definitions.

3   Terms and Definitions

3.1   Outline of Our Approach

Our analysis begins by undertaking loop fusion assuming unlimited memory. We first calculate the amount of data re-use between the statements after carrying out loop fusion. We then calculate the *closeness factor* of every pair of statements. Closeness factor between two statements quantifies the amount of data reuse per unit memory required. We decorate the program dependence graph (PDG) with this information by inserting undirected edges between the nodes of the PDG that represent statements. The undirected edges have a weight equal to the closeness factor of the two statements. We then group the statements greedily under a given loop nest i.e. statements which have higher closeness factor are grouped together over those which have lesser. At every step, when we group statements, we examine if we must include some other statement(s) so as to preserve the dependences. (this step is explained in the next subsection). Sometimes we may not be able to include statements due to dependence and memory capacity constraints. In such cases, we adjust the dependence groups to eliminate *useless* re-use edges. Finally, we iterate to expand the group of statements and when we exceed the capacity of the on-chip memory we halt. We carry out the above steps of grouping and adjusting the dependence groups until there are no more re-use edges. We finally block the groups so as to fit the available memory size.

In our approach, we analyze following three types of data reuse: flow dependence reuse, input dependence reuse, and iteration reuse. We calculate the total amount of data re-use between two statements based on the total re-use associated with each of the references within those statements adding them up. Closeness Factor (CF) of two statements is defined as the ratio of the total re-use present between these statements and the total number of data elements that occupy the memory to facilitate the re-use. Thus, the CF is a measure of how good is the re-use relative to a unit of memory occupied by references corresponding to the two statements. We say that two statements are closest to each other if they have the highest closeness factor. Thus, we rank the statements in the order of closeness factor. Our approach is to legally group statements in the order of CF under the constraints of available memory size and dependencies. The motivation behind grouping two 'closest' statements together under the same loop nest is that largest amount of data traffic is eliminated by doing so. This is due to the fact that by grouping statements, we have utilized maximum possible reuse per unit memory. We propose a greedy strategy to accomplish this goal. When we start grouping the statements together, certain re-use edges from the decorated PDG become useless. In other words, it becomes impossible to group statements together under one loop nest due to the groups already formed and due to dependence constraints. The next section explains the details along with an algorithm.

4   PDG Analysis

4.1   Legality of Grouping

Our framework starts grouping statements together greedily. When we find out a statement S is the closest statement to a group A, we want to check the following to make sure we can group S and A together: (1) We first want to check if we can group S and A legally according to PDG (2) whether there is sufficient memory available (3) when the above two situations are satisfied, if grouping one more statement will really increase CF. In this section, we discuss (1), the most important condition. There are some interesting issues faced in determining legality. In Figure 1, we have found a statement group Gi having three statements S2, S3 and S6 in it. We assume that at this point, no more statement can be grouped with Gi because of on-chip memory capacity. Amongst the remaining statements S1, S4, S5 and S7, statements S5 and S7 are the closest statements and we group them into Group A. At this stage, we find out that S4 is the next closest statement to A, but we can not group it with A. The reason is S4 must execute before Gi which must execute before A and thus, S4 can not be a part of A.

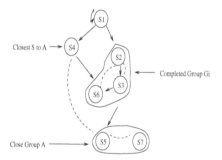

Fig. 1. Legality of grouping S4 with A

4.2   PDG Adjustment

After we find out that the grouping is legal, we need to adjust PDG for further PDG analysis use. In general, after we group S with X, one of the following scenarios may arise:

Case 1 If S and X are each other's direct and only successor/predecessor after they are grouped, S and X's other direct successors will be direct successors of this group; and their other direct predecessors will be direct predecessors of the group. In figure 2, after S2 and S3 are grouped, S1 is their predecessor and S5, S6 are their successors.

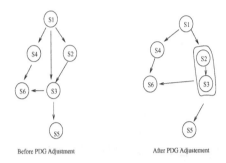

Fig. 2. Direct Predecessor/Successor Relationship

Case 2 If S and X belong to the same dependency group and they are not each other's successor and predecessor, but they have same (direct/indirect) and only successor(s)/predecessor(s), the two statements will be grouped together and their direct successors and predecessors will be the direct successors and predecessors of the group. In figure 3, after S3 and S4 are grouped together, S1 and S2 are their predecessors and S5, S6 are their successors.

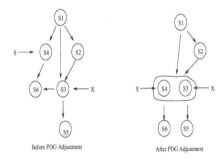

Fig. 3. Common Successor/Predecessor Relationship

Case 3 In some cases we cannot directly include a statement in a group without including some other statements. If two closest statements are in the same group and are each other's non-direct successor and predecessor (suppose S is X's predecessor). In this case, we have to resort to the following:

1. Find out all the statements between them in the PDG, that is, find out all of intermediate statements between S and X. We call this set as the intermediate statement set of S and X : ISGroup(S,X).
2. Count total data storage requirements of statements S, X and ISGroup(S,X), and compare it with available memory. If it can fit, group S, X and IS-Group(S,X). If the capacity is not big enough, S and X can not be grouped

together and the re-use edge must be discarded. From figure 4, one can see that if capacity is big enough, statements S1, S2, S3, S4 and S6 will be grouped into group G. Otherwise, input dependence reuse between S1 and S6 will be removed and no group is formed.

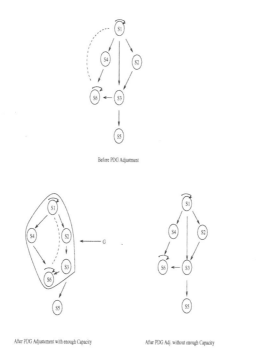

Fig. 4. Indirect Predecessor/Successor Relationship

In the above three cases, the two closest statements are in the same dependency group.

Case 4 If two closest statements belong to different dependency groups, there is no clear execution order for the two statements, that is, the two statements can be executed in any order. In figure 5, S1 must be executed before S3 and S6; however, S5 can be executed in any order with respect to S1, S3 or S6. However, when S3 and S2 are grouped together under one loop nest, it automatically fixes the order of execution of S5 with respect to S1 and can't be potentially combined with it.It can still be combined with any one of S4, S6 or S8 though. Thus, as long as the two statements S and X or one statement and a group belong to different dependency groups, they can be group together. The two dependency groups should be combined into one, predecessors and successors of S and/or X will be the predecessors and successors of the group. We have devised an

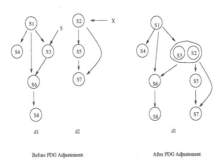

Fig. 5. S and X are in different Dependence Groups

algorithm based on these ideas to check possible groupings of the statements and the CF of the group is an indicator of the profitability. It is shown below.

```
Input : PDG for the given loop
Output: Rearranged statements.
1.For every pair of ungrouped statements
  calculate the closeness factor(CF).
2.while(some ungrouped statements can be grouped)
 2.A.select the pair of ungrouped statements with
      highest CF
 2.B.Check the possibility of grouping based on
      available memory size
 2.C.if grouping possible
   2.C.a. Form the new group
   2.C.b. Adjust the parents and children of
          all statements in the new group
   2.C.c. Find all possible ungrouped statememts
          that share data with this group and
          if such statement found
             merge that statements into the group
             (if memory size allows)
             goto 2.C.b
          else goto 2.A
     else
     set the CF of this pair to zero.
     goto 2.
```

5   Complexity

The algorithm attempts to first form a group using two statements. It then examines statements which can be included in this group to facilitate more data re-use based upon a re-use edge. This step could potentially involve examining

$O(|V|)$ nodes where $|V|$ is the number of nodes in the graph. In worst case the number of re-use edges present in the graph could be $|V^2|$. Thus, the overall complexity of the algorithm in worst case can be $O(|V^3|)$.

6   Results

Table 1. Benchmark I Data Traffic Comparison. Ideal Traffic is 280,006

OnChip MemSize	Original Traffic	Our Traffic	Traffic Improved
24	440,000	380,000	15.79%
36	410,000	341,500	16.71%
48	400,000	362,667	9.33%
60	397,142	332,500	16.28%
74	388,300	318,182	18.06%
112	388,000	304,706	21.47%
140	385,128	291,235	24.38%
172	384,953	286,482	25.19%
224	382,477	281,134	26.49%

Typically in DSP applications, a sequence of steps (such as convolution, filtering, edge detection etc.) operate successively on data. The procedure calls corresponding to these steps take place one after another. We first turned on inlining and formed a sequence of intra procedural loop nests using the DSP kernels. We then performed fusion and performed our analysis. Please refer to Appendix A for the codes of the benchmarks (the codes shown in each benchmark are sequences of loop kernels inlined intra procedurally). We used TMS320C5x for analysis. The framework has been implemented in Petit [2], a tool for data dependency analysis developed by University of Maryland. Petit provides a good support for finding the dependence distances as well as types of dependences between them.

6.1   Benchmark I

Table 1 shows the comparison of original traffic and traffic after applying our work when on chip memory size varies. The ideal (minimum possible) data traffic for the above example is about 280,006.

6.2   Benchmark II

Table 2 shows the comparison of original traffic and traffic after applying our work when on chip memory size varies for Benchmark II. It also shows the improvement. We assume the loop size N = 10000. The ideal amount of data traffic for Benchmark II is 320,005. The ideal amount of data traffic for Benchmark III

Table 2. Benchmark II data traffic comparison.

On-Chip MemSize	Original Traffic	Our Traffic	Traffic Improved
24	380,625	371,647	2.36%
36	363,750	352,466	3.10%
48	355,312	343,677	3.27%
60	350,250	338,634	3.32%
74	346,530	335,031	3.32%
112	340,945	329,664	3.31%
140	338,709	327,728	3.24%
172	337,105	326,273	3.21%
224	335,435	324,775	3.18%
268	334,614	323,986	3.17%

is 430,004. Table 3 shows the comparison when on chip memory size varies on Benchmark III. It also shows the improvement. Benchmark III is composed of

Table 3. Benchmark III data traffic comparison. Ideal Traffic was 430,004.

On-Chip MemSize	Original Traffic	Our Traffic	Traffic Improved
24	690,971	620,000	10.27%
36	597,756	572,857	4.16%
48	544,000	533,414	1.94%
60	498,987	478,888	4.03%
74	464,256	461,111	0.68%
112	455,735	450,000	1.26%
140	452,419	445,730	1.48%
172	450,073	442,363	1.71%
224	447,661	439.379	1.85%

two large groups of statements and its own data reuse is very strong. That can explain why our improvement on data traffic is around 1-2 percent most of the time. Thus, the additional gain in re-use due to our work is small.

The code for Benchmark V as shows a loop used frequently in DSP applications. The first one is a matrix multiplication code. The second one is a convolution. The results have been summarized in Table 4.

7   Related Work

We now contrast our work with existing work related to solving data locality and data re-use problems on memory hierarchy. Two important directions of work are: Tiling or iteration space blocking [12] and data-centric approaches

Table 4. Traffic comparison for benchmark IV, V and VI

Code	Original Traffic	Optimized Traffic	Saved Traffic	% Traffic Reduction
Benchmark IV	30000	21000	9000	30
Benchmark V	$18*10^6$	$11.25*10^6$	$6.75*10^6$	37.5
Benchmark VI	27692	22532	5160	18.63

such as data shackling [14]. In tiling or data blocking (which is a control centric transformation), a loop nest is tiled to maximize temporal locality [13,7,8,16]. Previous research on optimizing compilers [18] [19] [11] has proposed algorithms to detect and perform loop interchange to increase temporal locality. In data centric transformations, all the iterations that touch a data shackle are executed together giving better control to the compiler to directly focus on data than resorting to side effect of control centric transformation [14].

Our work differs from these in that we focus on data traffic as against issues of locality. This is important since in our problem, we are faced with a small amount of memory that results in excessive load/stores of short arrays between on-chip and off-chip memories. Thus, in order to minimize data traffic, we must not only concentrate on re-use of fetched values (as is typically the goal in the most memory hierarchy oriented optimizations described above) but also carefully analyze the flow and use of generated values and transitive closure of their uses and values which they generate in turn. This is because on-chip memory can be viewed somewhat intermediate between caches and register files. It is much smaller than traditional caches leading to the above differences. However, it is larger than register files. This also leads to different issues than traditional load/stores. In fact the on-chip memory is *large enough* to act as an ideal temporary store for intermediate array subsections with short live ranges. To maximally utilize the property of this temporary store, we must analyze the tradeoffs between values that get re-used across iterations (iteration re-use) input values that get re-used across two statements (due to input dependencies) and most importantly values that are produced and consumed (due to flow dependencies) in short span of iterations under the constraint of limited memory capacity and legality. Gupta et. al. [23] [22] have addressed the problem of register allocation for subscripted array variables by analyzing their liveness based on the number of iterations that elapse between definition and use. They propose a register allocation algorithm based on this liveness information. Our work addresses orthogonal problem to theirs - in our approach we are interested in determining the best grouping of statements inside a loop nest such that best re-use per memory occupied results to minimize. Our work also differs from McKinley and Kennedy [20] and Gao and Sarkar [21] in that we define a new measure of data traffic based on closeness factor than simply attempting to maximize data re-use as in their loop fusion framework. It can be shown that simply attempting to maximize data re-use can incur higher data traffic than found by using closeness factor.

8 Conclusion

We have proposed a framework on how to get a better performance by analyzing the flow of values and their re-use to effectively reduce data traffic for limited on-chip memory processors. A new concept of Closeness Factor has been developed which is the measure of data reuse between statements per unit memory requirement. The loop restructuring algorithm proposed by us helps to effectively utilize the on-chip memory while preserving the data dependences between the statements in the loop. Good performance enhancements for DSP codes are obtained using our framework. These loop restructuring transformations should be very useful for limited on-chip memory processors.

References

1. J. Eyre and J.Bier,"DSP Processors Hit the Mainstream", 'COMPUTER', 31(8):51-59, August 1998.
2. Petit, Uniform Library, Omega Library, Omega Calculater. 'http://www.cs.umd.edu/projects/omega/index.html' 141, 149
3. Texas Instruments. 'TMS 320C5x User's Guide.
4. Embedded Java. http://java.sun.com/products/embeddedjava/.
5. A. Sundaram and S. Pande, "Compiler Optimizations for Real Time Execution of Loops on Limited Memory Embedded Systems", *Proceedings of IEEE International Real Time Systems Symposium*, Madrid, Spain, pp.154–164. 142
6. A. Sundaram and S. Pande, "An Efficient Data Partitioning Method for Limited Memory Embedded Systems", *1998 ACM SIGPLAN Workshop on Languages, Compilers and Tools for Embedded Systems (in conjunction with PLDI '98)*, Montreal, Canada, Springer–Verlag, pp. 205–218. 142
7. F.Irigoin and R.Triolet, "Supernode Partitioning". in *15th Symposium on Principles of Programming Languages (POPL XV)*, pages 319–329, 1988. 151
8. J.Ramanujam and P.Sadayappan, "Tiling Multidimensional Iteration Spaces for Multicomputers." *Journal of Parallel and Distributed Computing*, 16:108–120, 1992. 151
9. U. Banerjee, "Loop transformations for restructuring compilers", Boston: Kluwer Academic, 1994.
10. W. Li, "Compiling for NUMA parallel machines", Ph.D. Thesis, Cornell University, Ithaca, NY, 1993.
11. M. Wolfe, *High Performance Compilers for Parallel Computing, Addison Wesley, 1996.* 151
12. M. Wolfe, "Iteration space tiling for memory hierarchies" in *Third SIAM Conference on Parallel Processing for Scientific Computing, December 1987.* 150
13. R. Schreiber and J. Dongarra, "Automatic Blocking of Nested Loops". *Technical report, RIACS, NASA Ames Research Center, and Oak Ridge National Laboratory, May 1990.* 151
14. I. Kodukula, N. Ahmed and K. Pingali, "Data Centric Multi-level Blocking" in *ACM Programming Language Design and Implementation 1997 (PLDI '97)*, pp. 346–357. 151

15. P. Panda, A. Nicolau and N. Dutt, "Memory Organization for Improved Data Cache Performance in Embedded Processors", *Proceedings of 1996 International Symposium on System Synthesis.* 141
16. N. Mitchell, K. Hogstedt, L. Carter and J. Ferrante, "Quantifying the Multi-level Nature of Tiling Interactions", International Journal of Parallel Programming, Vol 26, No 6, 1998, pp. 641–670. 151
17. K. Cooper and T. Harvey,"Compiler Controlled Memory", *Proceedings of the 8th International Conference on Architectural Support for Programming Languages and Operating Systems (ASPLOS)*, Oct. 3-7, 1998, San Jose, CA. 142
18. K. McKinley, S. Carr, and C.-W.Tseng, Improving data locality with loop transformation. ACM Transactions on Programming Languages and Systems (PLDI) 18(4):424-453, July 1996. 151
19. M. Wolf and M. Lam, "A data locality optimizing algorithm", in proceedings of *ACM Special Interest Group on Programming Languages (SIGPLAN) 91 Conf. Programming Language Design and Implementation(PLDI'91)*, pp. 30-44, Toronto, Canada, June 1991. 151
20. K. Kennedy and K. McKinley, "Maximizing Loop Parallelism and Improving Data Locality via Loop Fusion and Distribution" in *Languages and Compilers for Parallel Computing (LCPC) 1993.* 151
21. G. Gao, R. Olsen, V. Sarkar and R. Thekkath "Collective Loop Fusion for Array Contraction" in *Languages and Compilers for Parallel Computing (LCPC) 1992.* 151
22. E. Dusterwald, R. Gupta and M.Soffa, "A Practical Data-flow Framework for Array Reference Analysis and its Application in Optimization" in *ACM Programming Language Design and Implementation (PLDI)* 1993 pp. 68-77. 151
23. R.Gupta and R. Bodik, "Array Data-Flow Analysis for Load-Store Optimizations in Superscalar Architectures," in *Eighth Annual Workshop on Languages and Compilers for Parallel Computing (LCPC) 1995.* Also published in International Journal of Parallel Computing, Vol. 24, No. 6, pages 481-512,1996. 151

9 Appendix

Benchmark I

```
for(i=0; i<N; i++)
  tmpPtr[i] = (a1[i] * b[i]);
for(i=0; i<N; i++)
  c[i] = ((sum[i] * a1[i]) >> 15) + b[i];
for(i=0; i<N; i++)
  r[i] = rd[i];
  g[i] = gd[i];
  b[i] = bd[i];
  p[i] = (r[i]&mask[i])+((g[i]&mask[i])>>5)
            + ((b[i] & mask[i]) >> 10);
for(i=0; i<N; i++)
  k[i] = c[i];
  h[i] = b[i] + (k[i] * m[i]);
  f[i] = b[i] * k[i] + m[i];
for(i=0; i<N; i++)
  sum[i] = a[i] + a[i];
for(i=0; i<N; i++)
  tmpPtr2[i] = tmpPtr[i];
for(i=0; i<N; i++)
  R1[i] = tmpPtr[i] * tmpPtr2[i];
  G1[i] = tmpPtr[i] * tmpPtr[i];
for(i=0; i<N; i++)
  sum1[i] = mask[4+i-1]-a[4+i-1];
  sum2[i] = mask[4+i-2]-a[4+i-2];
  sum3[i] = mask[4+i-3]-a[4+i-3];
  sum4[i] = mask[4+i-4]-a[4+i-4];
  oPtr[4+i] = sum[i];
  sum5[i] = oPtr[4+i];
```

Benchmark II

```
for (i = 0; i < n; i++)
  b[i] = ia[i];
  f[i] = b[i] * k[i];
  a[i] = f[i] * k[i] + b[i];
  g[i] = a[i];
for(i=0; i < n; i++)
  c[i] = w[2*j];
  s[i] = w[2*j+1];
  m[i] = ia[i] + n2[i];
  rtemp[i] = x[i] - y[2*i+1];
  x1[i] = x[i] + y[2*i+2];
  itemp = m[i] - 2*m[i];
```

```
 x2[i] = x1[i] + 2*m[i];
 x3[i] = c[i]*rtemp[i] - s[i]*itemp[i];
 x4[i] = c[i]*itemp[i] + s[i]*rtemp[i];
for (i=0; i < n; i++)    {
 sum0[i] = x[i+0]*p[i] + x2[i+1]*p[i]
         + x3[i+2]*p[i];
 sum1[i] = x[i]*p[i] + x2[i+2]*p[i]
         + x3[i+3]*p[i];
 dist0[i] = sum0[i] - point[i];
 dist1[i] = sum1[i] - point[i];
 dist3[i] = fabsf[i];
 dist4[i] = fabsf[i];
 retval[i] = (int)&z[i+3];
```

Benchmark III

```
for(j=0; j<n2; j++)
 ia2[j] = ia1[j] + ia1[j];
 ia3[j] = ia1[j] + ia2[j];
 co1[j] = w[j*2];
 si1[j] = w[j*2+1];
 co2[j] = w[j*2];
 si2[j] = w[j*2+1];
 co3[j] = w[j*2];
 si3[j] = w[j*2+1];
for(j=0; j<n2; j++)
 i2[j] = i1[j] + n2[j];
 i3[j] = i2[j] + n2[j];
 r1[j] = x[j*2] + x[j*2];
 r3[j] = x[j*2] - x[j*2];
 s1[j] = x[j*2+1] + x[j*2+1+2];
 s3[j] = x[j*2+1] - x[j*2+1+2];
 r2[j] = x[j*2] + x[j*2+3];
 r4[j] = x[j*2] - x[j*2+3];
 s2[j] = x[j*2+1] + x[j*2+1+4];
 s4[j] = x[j*2+1] - x[j*2+1+4];
 x[j*2] = r1[j] + r2[j];
 r12[j] = r1[j] - r2[j];
 r11[j] = r3[j] - s4[j];
 r13[j] = r3[j] + s4[j];
 z[j*2+1] = s1[j] + s2[j];
 s12[j] = s1[j] - s2[j];
 s11[j] = s3[j] + r4[j];
 s13[j] = s3[j] - r4[j];
 x1[j] = co1[j]*r3[j] + si1[j]*s3[j];
 x2[j] = co1[j]*s3[j] - si1[j]*r3[j];
 x3[j] = co2[j]*r2[j] + si2[j]*s2[j];
```

```
x4[j] = co2[j]*s2[j] - si2[j]*r2[j];
x5[j] = co3[j]*r1[j] + si3[j]*s1[j];
x6[j] = co3[j]*s1[j] - si3[j]*r1[j];
i1[j] = i0[j] + n2[j];
```

Benchmark IV

```
for (i = 0; i < N; i++)
  m[i] = sd[i] + sd[i + 1];
  m5[i] = sd[i] - sd[i + 1];
  m11[i] = -sd[i] + sd[i + 1];
  m14[i] = -sd[i] - sd[i + 1];
for (i=0; i < N; i++)
  new_s = m[i] + m11[i];
  old[i] = m5[i] + m14[i];
for (i=0; i<N; i++)
  a[i] = old[i] + new_s[i];
  b[i] = - mi[i] * 2
  term[i] = a[i] + sd[i];
  trans[i] = b[i] + mi[i];
  mj[i] = trans[i];
```

Benchmark V

```
do I = 1 .. N
 do J = 1 .. N
  do K = 1 .. N
   C[I,J] = C[I,J] + A[I,K]*B[K,J] // S1
do I = 1 .. N
 do J = 1 .. N
  do K = 1 .. N
   D[K,J] = D[I,J]*C[I,K] - B[K,J] // S2
```

Benchmark VI

```
for i=1 to N
  c[i]=a[i]-b[i];                    //S1
  r[i]=d[i-9]/e[i];                  //S2
  k[i]=a[i+1]*b[i-1]+p[i]-q[i];      //S3
for i=1 to N
  n[i]=d[i]*c[i]+e[i];               //S4
  f[i]=o[i]+d[i]/e[i];               //S5
  g[i]=r[i]/m[i+1];                  //S6
  h[i]=n[i]*m[i+1]+e[5+i]-c[i+10];   //S7
```

Techniques for Effectively Exploiting a Zero Overhead Loop Buffer

Gang-Ryung Uh[1], Yuhong Wang[2], David Whalley[2], Sanjay Jinturkar[1], Chris Burns[1], and Vincent Cao[1]

[1] Lucent Technologies, Allentown, PA 18103, U.S.A.
{uh,sjinturkar,cpburns,vpcao}@lucent.com
[2] Computer Science Dept., Florida State Univ.
Tallahassee, FL 32306-4530, U.S.A.
{yuhong,whalley}@cs.fsu.edu

Abstract. A Zero Overhead Loop Buffer (ZOLB) is an architectural feature that is commonly found in DSP processors. This buffer can be viewed as a compiler managed cache that contains a sequence of instructions that will be executed a specified number of times. Unlike loop unrolling, a loop buffer can be used to minimize loop overhead without the penalty of increasing code size. In addition, a ZOLB requires relatively little space and power, which are both important considerations for most DSP applications. This paper describes strategies for generating code to effectively use a ZOLB. The authors have found that many common improving transformations used by optimizing compilers to improve code on conventional architectures can be exploited (1) to allow more loops to be placed in a ZOLB, (2) to further reduce loop overhead of the loops placed in a ZOLB, and (3) to avoid redundant loading of ZOLB loops. The results given in this paper demonstrate that this architectural feature can often be exploited with substantial improvements in execution time and slight reductions in code size.

1   Introduction

The number of DSP processors is growing every year at a much faster rate than general-purpose computer processors. For many applications, a large percentage of the execution time is spent in the innermost loops of a program [1]. The execution of these loops incur significant overhead, which is due to the increment and branch instructions to initiate a new iteration of a loop. Many code improving transformations and architectural features used to improve execution time for applications in general-purpose computers do so at the expense of substantial code growth and more power consumption. For instance, loop unrolling is a popular technique to decrease loop overhead [2]. Yet, this approach often requires a significant increase in code size. Likewise, VLIW instructions can be used to reduce loop overhead at the expense of more power. Space increasing transformations and power inefficient architectures are often unacceptable options for many DSP applications due to these limitations.

A. Watt (Ed.): CC/ETAPS 2000, LNCS 1781, pp. 157–172, 2000.

A zero overhead loop buffer (ZOLB) is an architectural feature commonly found in DSP processors. This buffer can be used to increase the speed of applications with no increase in code size and often with reduced power consumption. A ZOLB is a buffer that can contain a fixed number of instructions to be executed a specified number of times under program control. Depending on the implementation of the DSP architecture, some instructions may be fetched faster from a ZOLB than from the conventional instruction memory. In addition, the same memory bus used to fetch instructions can sometimes be used to access data when certain registers are dereferenced. Thus, memory bus contention can be reduced when instructions are fetched from a ZOLB. Due to addressing complications, transfers of control instructions are not typically allowed in such buffers. Therefore, a compiler or assembly writer attempts to execute many of the innermost loops of programs from this buffer. A ZOLB can be viewed as a compiler controlled cache since special instructions are used to load instructions into it.

This paper describes strategies for exploiting the ZOLB that is available on the DSP16000 architecture [3], which could also be applied to other DSP architectures that have ZOLBs. These strategies have the potential for being readily adopted by compiler writers for DSP processors since they rely on the use of traditional compiler improving transformations and data flow analysis techniques. Figure 1 presents an overview of the compilation process used by the authors to generate and improve code for this architecture. Code is generated using a C compiler retargeted to the DSP16000 [4]. Conventional improving transformations in this C compiler are applied and assembly files are generated. Finally, the generated code is then processed by another optimizer, which performs a number of improving transformations including those that exploit the ZOLB on this architecture. There are advantages of attempting to exploit a ZOLB using this approach. First, the exact number of instructions in a loop will be known after code generation, which will ensure that the maximum number of instructions that can be contained in the ZOLB is not exceeded. While performing these transformations after code generation sometimes resulted in more complicated algorithms, the optimizer was able to apply transformations more frequently since it did not have to rely on conservative heuristics concerning the ratio of intermediate operations to machine instructions. Second, interprocedural analysis and transformations also proved to be valuable in exploiting a ZOLB, as will be shown later in this paper.

2   Related Work

A number of hardware and software techniques have been used to reduce loop overhead. Common hardware techniques include branch prediction hardware to reduce branch mispredictions and superscalar or VLIW execution to allow other operations to execute in parallel with the loop overhead instructions [1]. However, the use of complex hardware mechanisms to minimize branch overhead results in the consumption of more power. Some current general-purpose processors have a loop branch instruction that eliminates the incrementing of a loop counter and

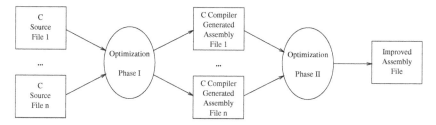

Fig. 1. Overview of the Compilation Process for the DSP16000

a comparison, but still require the branch instruction. Common software techniques include loop strength reduction with basic induction variable elimination and loop unrolling. Note that loop unrolling can significantly increase code size.

Currently available versions of ZOLBs in TI, ADI, and Lucent processors have been described [5]. Assembly language programmers for DSPs commonly use ZOLBs in the code that they write. However, optimizing compilers have been used only recently for DSP applications and programmers still tend to write critical sections by hand [6]. A preliminary version of this paper appeared in a workshop [12]. To the best of our knowledge, no other work describes how a ZOLB can be exploited by a compiler, the interaction of exploiting a ZOLB with other improving transformations, and the performance benefits that can be achieved from using a ZOLB.

3   Using the DSP16000 ZOLB

The target architecture for which the authors generated code was the DSP16000 developed at Lucent Technologies. This architecture contains a ZOLB that can hold up to 31 instructions. Two special instructions, the do and the redo, are used to control the ZOLB on the DSP16000 [7]. Figure 2(a) shows the assembly syntax for using the do instruction, which specifies that the n instructions enclosed between the curly braces are to be executed k times. The actual encoding of the do instruction includes a value of n, which can range from 1 to 31, indicating the number of instructions following the do instruction that are to be placed in the ZOLB. The value k is also included in the encoding of the do instruction and represents the number of iterations associated with an innermost loop placed in the ZOLB. When k is a compile-time constant less than 128, it may be specified as an immediate value since it will be small enough to be encoded into the instruction. Otherwise a value of zero is encoded and the number of times the instructions in the ZOLB will be executed is obtained from the cloop register. The first iteration results in the instructions enclosed between the curly braces being fetched from the memory system, executed, and loaded into the ZOLB. The remaining k-1 iterations are executed from the ZOLB. The redo instruction shown in Figure 2(b) is similar to the do instruction, except that the current contents of the ZOLB are executed k times. Figure 3 depicts some of the hardware used for a ZOLB, which includes a 31 instruction buffer, a `cloop` register initially assigned the number of iterations and implicitly decremented on each iteration, and a `cstate` register containing the number of instructions in the loop and the pointer to the current instruction to load or execute. Performance benefits are achieved whenever the number of iterations executed is greater than one.

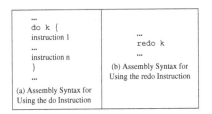

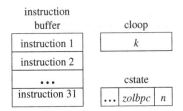

Fig. 2. DSP16000 Assembly Syntax for Using the ZOLB

Fig. 3. Example of Using the ZOLB on the DSP16000

Figure 4 shows a simple example of exploiting the ZOLB on the DSP16000. Figure 4(a) contains the source code for a simple loop. Figure 4(b) depicts the corresponding code for the DSP16000 without placing instructions in the ZOLB. The effects of these instructions are also shown in this figure. The array in Figure 4(a) and the arrays in the other examples in the paper are of type `short` Thus, the postincrement causes `r0` to be incremented by 2. Many DSP architectures use an instruction set that is highly specialized for known DSP applications. The DSP16000 is no exception and its instruction set has many complex features, which include separation of address (`r0-r7`) and accumulator (`a0-a7`) registers, postincrements of address registers, and implicit sets of condition codes from accumulator operations. Figure 4(b) also shows that the loop variable is set to a negative value before the loop and is incremented on each loop iteration. This strategy allows an implicit comparison to zero with the increment to avoid performing a separate comparison instruction. Figure 4(c) shows the equivalent code after placing the loop in the ZOLB. The branch in the loop is deleted since the loop will be executed the desired number of iterations. After applying basic induction variable elimination and dead store elimination, the increment and initialization of `a1` are removed. Thus, the loop overhead has been eliminated.

4   Placing More Loops in a ZOLB

The limiting factors that can prevent exploiting a ZOLB for an innermost loop are (1) transfers of control other than the loop branch, (2) the number of instructions in the loop exceeding the ZOLB limit, and (3) the number of iterations being unknown at run-time. In this section we describe techniques that can often address each of these factors.

| for (i = 0; i < 10000; i++) |
| a[i] = 0; |

(a) Source Code of Loop

r0 = _a	# r[0]=ADDR(_a);	cloop = 10000
a2 = 0	# a[2]=0;	r0 = _a
a1 = -9999	# a[1]= -9999;	a2 = 0
L5: *r0++ = a2	# M[r[0]]=a[2]; r[0]=r[0]+2;	do cloop {
a1 = a1 + 1	# a[1]=a[1]+1; IC=a[1]+1?0;	*r0++ = a2
if le goto L5	# PC=IC<=0?L5:PC;	}
(b) DSP16000 Assembly and Corresponding RTLs without Using the ZOLB		(c) After Using the ZOLB

Fig. 4. ZOLB Hardware

One limiting factor that prevents the exploitation of a ZOLB for many loops is that transfers of control cannot be executed from a ZOLB. This limitation can be partially overcome by the use of conditional instructions. Consider the example source code in Figure 5(a), which shows a loop with an assignment that is dependent on a condition. The assembly code in Figure 5(b) cannot be placed into a ZOLB since there is a conditional branch that is not associated with the exit condition of the loop.[1] Our compiler used predicated execution when possible to avoid this problem [1]. Figure 5(c) depicts the same loop with a conditional instruction and this loop can be transformed to be executed from a ZOLB. Unfortunately, many potential loops could not be placed in a ZOLB since predicates are assigned to a single condition code register on the DSP16000 and only a subset of the DSP16000 instructions can be conditionally executed.

	r0 = _a	r0 = _a
	a1 = -9999	a1 = -9999
for (i = 0; i < 10000;	L5: a0 = *r0	L5: a0 = *r0
i++)	a0 = a0	a0 = a0
if (a[i] > 0)	if gt goto L4	if le a2 = a2 + a0
sum += a[i];	a2 = a2 + a0	r0 = r0 + 2
(a) Original Source Code	L4: r0 = r0 + 2	a1 = a1 + 1
	a1 = a1 + 1	if le goto L5
	if le goto L5	
	(b) DSP16000 Assembly	(c) DSP16000 Assembly
	without Conditional Instructions	with Conditional Instructions

Fig. 5. Example of Using Conditional Instructions to Place More Loops in a ZOLB

A call instruction is another transfer of control that cannot be placed in the DSP16000 ZOLB. Consider the source code and corresponding DSP16000 assembly in Figures 6(a) and 6(b). The loop cannot be placed in a ZOLB since it contains a call to _abs. However, the function can be inlined as shown in

---

[1] The a0 = a0 instruction is used to set the condition codes, which are not set by the previous load instruction.

Figure 6(c) and the ZOLB can be used for the resulting loop. The DSP16000 optimizer does not inline indiscriminately due to potential growth in code size. However, the optimizer inlines functions that are called from a loop when the loop after inlining can be placed in the ZOLB (i.e. limited code growth for measurable performance benefits). Likewise, inlining of a function is performed when the function is only called from one site (i.e. no code growth) [8].

`int abs(int v)`
`{`
`    if (v < 0)`
`        v = -v;`
`    return v;`
`}`
`...`
`sum = 0;`
`for (i = 0; i < 10000; i++)`
`    sum += abs(a[i]);`
`...`
	`_abs: a0 = a0`
	`      if lt a0 = -a0`
	`      return`
	`      ...`
	`      r4 = _a`
	`      a5 = 0`
	`      a4 = -9999`
	`L5:   a0 = *r4++`
	`      call _abs`
	`      a5 = a5 + a0`
	`      a4 = a4 + 1`
	`      if le goto L5`
		`r4 = _a`
		`a5 = 0`
		`a4 = -9999`
		`L5:a0 = *r4++`
		`a0 = a0`
		`if lt a0 = -a0`
		`a5 = a5 + a0`
		`a4 = a4 + 1`
		`if le goto L5`

(a) Source Code	(b) Before Inlining	(c) After Inlining

Fig. 6. Example of Inlining a Function to Allow a Loop to Be Placed in a ZOLB

Another factor that sometimes prevented loops from being placed in the DSP16000 ZOLB was the limit of 31 instructions in the buffer. The authors implemented loop distribution to address this problem. The optimizer splits loops exceeding the ZOLB limit if the sets of dependent instructions can be reorganized into separate loops that can all be placed in a ZOLB. The optimizer first finds all of the sets of dependent instructions. The conditional branch and the instructions that contribute to setting the condition codes for that branch are treated separately since they will be placed with each set. Note that these instructions will typically be deleted once loops are placed in the ZOLB and the basic induction variable elimination and dead store elimination transformations are applied. The optimizer then checks if each set of instructions will fit in the ZOLB and combines multiple sets together when they would not exceed the maximum instructions that the ZOLB can hold.

A final factor preventing the use of the ZOLB is that often the number of iterations associated with a loop is unknown at run-time. However, sometimes such loops can still be placed in the ZOLB on the DSP16000. Consider the source code shown in Figure 7(a) and the corresponding DSP16000 assembly shown in Figure 7(b). The number of iterations is unknown since it is not known which will be the first element of array a that will be equal to n. For each iteration of a ZOLB loop on the DSP16000 the cloop register is implicitly decremented by one and then tested. The ZOLB is exited when this register is equal to zero. Thus, assigning a value of one to the cloop register will cause the loop to exit after the current iteration completes. The loop in Figure 7(b) can be transformed to be placed in the ZOLB since the cloop register can be conditionally assigned a value in a register. Figure 7(c) depicts the transformed code. The cloop register is initially set to the maximum value to which it can be assigned and a register, a3, is allocated to hold the value 1. The a[i] != n test is accomplished by the last three instructions in Figure 7(b). To force an exit from the ZOLB on the DSP16000, the cloop register must be assigned a value of 1 at least three instructions before the end of the loop due to the latency requirements of the machine. Moving three instructions after the branch, comparison, and instructions that affect the comparison often required the optimizer to perform register renaming and adjust the displacements of memory references, as shown in Figure 7(c). Since the loop can eventually exit due to the cloop register being decremented to zero without being set in the conditional assignment, another loop is placed after the ZOLB loop that will repeatedly redo the ZOLB loop until the exit condition has been satisfied. Note that unlike ZOLB loops with a known number of iterations, the number of instructions in this ZOLB loop is not less than the number of instructions before the loop was placed in the ZOLB. However, conditional branches on the DSP16000 require more cycles than conditional assignments. Other potential benefits include reducing contention to the memory system in the loop. Thus, there is a performance benefit on the DSP16000 from placing loops with an unknown number of iterations in the ZOLB.

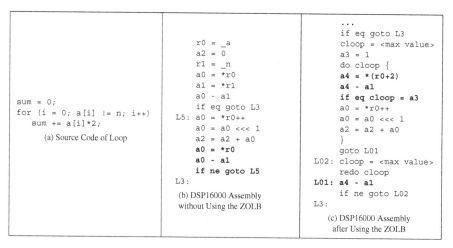

Fig. 7. Example of Placing a Loop with an Unknown Number of Iterations in a ZOLB

5   Further Reducing Loop Overhead

As shown previously in Figure 4(c), basic induction variable and dead store elimination are invoked after placing a loop in a ZOLB since often assignments to the loop variable become unnecessary due to the branch no longer being in the loop. When the value of the basic induction variable is used after the loop and is used for no other purpose in the loop, the optimizer extracts these increments of the variable from the loop. First, the increments in the loop are deleted. Next, a new increment of the variable is placed after the loop that is the product of the original increment and the number of loop iterations.

Another approach that is often used to reduce the overhead associated with outer level loops is to collapse nested loops. Figure 8(a) shows perfectly nested loops that initialize every element of a matrix. Figure 8(b) shows how the array is conceptually accessed after these loops are collapsed by our optimizer into a single loop. After the optimizer places the collapsed loop into the ZOLB, the loop overhead for both original loops are entirely eliminated. The optimizer collapses nested loops whenever possible. Even when the inner loop cannot be placed in a ZOLB, the loop overhead is reduced since the outer loop is eliminated.

`int a[50][100];`
 	
`for (i = 0; i < 50; i++)`
`    for (j = 0; j < 100; j++)`
`        a[i][j] = 0;`
 	
(a) Original Nested Loops
	`int a[5000];`
	
	`for (i = 0; i < 5000; i++)`
	`    a[i] = 0;`
	
	(b) After Loop Collapsing

Fig. 8. Example of Loop Collapsing to Eliminate Additional Loop Overhead

Figures 9(a) and 9(c) show the source and corresponding assembly code for an example of a loop nest that cannot be collapsed by our optimizer since not all of the elements of each row of the matrix are accessed. However, these two loops can be interchanged, as shown in Figures 9(b) and 9(d). After interchanging the two loops, the inner loop now has a greater number of loop iterations, which can be executed from the ZOLB as shown in Figure 9(e). More loop overhead is now eliminated by placing the interchanged inner loop in the ZOLB as opposed to the original inner loop. The optimizer attempts to interchange nested loops when the loops cannot be collapsed, the loops are perfectly nested, the number of iterations for the original inner loop is less than the number of iterations for the original outer loop, the number of instructions in the inner loop does not increase, and the resulting inner loop can be placed in the ZOLB. Figure 9(d) shows that register k was allocated to hold the value of the increment 200 so an additional instruction to increment r0 would be unnecessary. This example illustrates the advantage of performing loop interchange after code generation since otherwise it would not be known if a register was available to be used to hold the increment and the transformation may result in more instructions in the inner loop. Interchanging loops will not degrade the performance of the memory hierarchy for the DSP16000 since it has no data cache or virtual memory system.

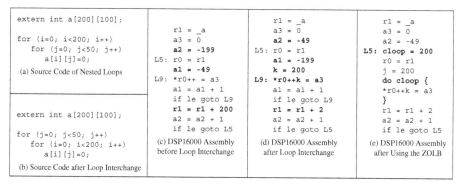

Fig. 9. Example of Loop Interchange to Increase the Iterations Executed in the ZOLB

6 Avoiding Redundant Loads of the ZOLB

The do instruction indicates that a specified number of instructions following the do will be loaded into the ZOLB. Depending upon the implementation of the DSP architecture, instructions may be fetched faster from a ZOLB than the conventional memory system. In addition, contention for the memory system may be reduced when a ZOLB is used. The redo instruction has similar semantics as the do instruction, except that the redo does not cause any instructions to be loaded into the ZOLB. Instead, the current contents of the ZOLB are simply executed the specified number of iterations.

The redo instruction can be used to avoid redundant loads of loops into the ZOLB. Consider the source code shown in Figure 10(a). It would appear that the two loops are quite different since they iterate a different number of times, access different variables, and access different types of data. However, the body of the two loops are identical as shown in Figure 10(b). The reason is that much of the characteristics of the loops have been abstracted out of the loop bodies. The number of iterations for ZOLB loops is encoded in the do instruction or assigned to the cloop register preceding the loop. The addresses of the arrays are assigned to registers associated with basic induction variables preceding the loop after loop strength reduction is performed. In addition, data moves of the same size between registers and memory are accomplished in the same manner on the DSP16000, regardless of the data types. Figure 10(c) shows the assembly code after the redundant loop is eliminated using the redo instruction.

The optimizer determines which ZOLB loops can reach each point in the control flow without the contents of the ZOLB being changed. The authors used flow analysis to determine if the loading of each ZOLB loop was necessary. A bit was associated with each ZOLB loop and one bit was also reserved to indicate that no ZOLB loops could reach a given point. Equations (1) and (2) are used to to determine which ZOLB loops could possibly reach each point in the

| extern int a[100], b[100];<br>extern float c[200], d[200];<br>...<br>for (i = 0; i < 100; i++)<br>  a[i] = b[i];<br>...<br>for (i = 0; i < 200; i++)<br>  c[i] = d[i];<br>...<br><br>(a) Source Code of Two Different Loops | ```
r1 = _a
r0 = _b
do 100 {
a0 = *r0++
*r1++ = a0
}
...
cloop = 200
r1 = _c
r0 = _d
do cloop {
a0 = *r0++
*r1++ = a0
}
```<br>(b) DSP16000 Assembly<br>after Using the ZOLB | ```
r1 = _a
r0 = _b
do 100 {
a0 = *r0++
*r1++ = a0
}
...
cloop = 200
r1 = _c
r0 = _d
redo cloop
```<br>(c) DSP16000 Assembly<br>after Avoiding the<br>Redundant ZOLB Load |

Fig. 10. Example of Avoiding a Redundant Load of the ZOLB

control flow within a function.[2] In the actual implementation, interprocedural flow analysis was used to avoid redundant loading of ZOLB loops across function calls and returns. An adjustment was required when ZOLB loop information was propagated from a return block of a function. This adjustment prevented ZOLB loops that are propagated into the entry block of a function at one call site from being propagated to the block following a call to the same function at a different call site. Likewise, it was assumed that no ZOLB loops could reach the point after a library call since it was not known if the ZOLB would be used for a different ZOLB loop in the called library function.

$$in[B] = \begin{cases} Null & \text{if B is a function entry block} \\ \bigcup_{P \in pred[B]} out[P] & \text{otherwise} \end{cases} \quad (1)$$

$$out[B] = \begin{cases} Null & \text{if B contains a call} \\ B & \text{if B contains a ZOLB loop} \\ in[B] & \text{otherwise} \end{cases} \quad (2)$$

After all of the ZOLB loop reaching information is calculated, the optimizer determines which ZOLB loops do not need to be loaded into the ZOLB. If the in[] of a current block containing a ZOLB loop indicates that only a single other ZOLB loop is guaranteed to reach that point and if all of the instructions in the other ZOLB loop are identical with the instructions in the current ZOLB loop, then the entire current ZOLB loop is replaced with a redo instruction.

Even after using flow analysis to avoid redundant loads of ZOLB loops, many loops are repeatedly loaded into the ZOLB because they are in nested loops. The optimizer was modified to have the ability to avoid these redundant loads as well. The optimizer avoids the repeated loading of the inner loop in the ZOLB by peeling an iteration of the outer loop. Only in the peeled iteration is the ZOLB loaded. All remaining iterations execute from the ZOLB using the redo

---

[2] Note that B represents a basic block in the program

instruction. The optimizer only performs the loop peeling transformation when the increase in code size is small and there are expected performance benefits (i.e. reducing memory bus contention conflicts on the DSP16000) from avoiding the repeated load of the inner loop into the ZOLB.

7   Analysis and Transformations

The order in which these transformations are applied can affect how effectively a ZOLB can be exploited. Figure 11 shows the order of the pertinent analysis and transformations that are applied on the assembly code in the second optimization phase shown in Figure 1. The complete list of types of analysis and improving transformations performed in this phase of optimization and a more thorough description and rationale for this order may be found elsewhere [9]. Likewise, a more general description of these analyses and transformations can also be obtained [13].

Basic blocks are merged (#2) when possible. This transformation does not usually improve the code directly but may provide additional opportunities for other improving transformations. For instance, placing loops in a ZOLB (#13) is only applied to loops containing a single basic block. Merging basic blocks (#2) also reduces the overhead of most types of global analysis.

Analysis is performed to allow optimizations to be performed A call graph (#1) is built to perform various types of interprocedural improving transformations [8], which includes inlining (#8) to support placing loops in a ZOLB. Loops in the program are detected (#3) to support a variety of improving transformations, which of course includes placing loops in a ZOLB (#13). Live register information is calculated (#4) since many improving transformations require allocation of registers. For instance, placing a loop with an unknown number of iterations in the ZOLB (#13) requires renaming registers to newly allocated registers to accomplish the scheduling required to force an exit from the loop at the appropriate time. Loop invariant values and basic induction variables are detected (#6) so the number of iterations for a loop may be calculated (#7). Note that detecting the number of loop iterations is a much more challenging task at the assembly level as compared to examining source level loop statements.

Some instructions with immediate values cannot be executed conditionally. When these instructions are inside a loop and a register is available, the compiler replaces the immediate value with the register and assigns the immediate value to the register outside the loop. Therefore, branches are converted into conditional assignments (#5) after finding loops (#3) and calculating live register information (#4). Branches are converted into conditional assignments (#5) before analysis is performed to determine if a loop can be placed in the ZOLB (#13) since loops with branches not associated with the exit condition of the loop cannot be placed in the ZOLB.

Inlining (#8) also removes transfers of control from a loop, namely a call instruction. Inlining (#8) was performed after detecting the number of loop iterations (#7) since it could be determined at this point if the inlining would allow the loop to be placed in the ZOLB (#13) so unnecessary code growth could be avoided.

Ranges of addresses were calculated (#9) for each memory reference to allow independent instructions in a loop to be separated via loop distribution (#10). Both loop flattening (#11) and loop interchange (#12) are performed after calculating the number of loop iterations (#7) since these transformations require this information. Perfectly nested loops are flattened (#11) before loop interchange (#12) is performed since flattening loops places more iterations in a ZOLB than interchanging loops.

Basic induction variable elimination (#14) was performed after placing loops in the ZOLB (#13) since the assignments were often unnecessary at that point. The remaining assignments to basic induction variables are extracted from loops (#15) after basic induction variable elimination (#14) to prevent unnecessary extractions of instructions.

Avoiding redundant loading of the ZOLB using flow analysis was performed after loops were placed in the ZOLB so redundant loads could be detected. Finally, loop peeling was only considered for the loops whose loading could not be avoided using flow analysis since loop peeling requires a code size increase.

1. Build call graph for the program	10. Perform loop distribution to place more loops in the ZOLB
2. Merge consecutive blocks	11. Flatten perfectly nested loops
3. Find the loops in the program	12. Perform loop interchange
4. Calculate live register info	13. Place loops in the ZOLB
5. Convert branches into conditional assignments	14. Eliminate basic induction variable
6. Find loop invariant & induction variables	15. Extract loop induction variable assignment
7. Calculate the number of loop iterations	16. Avoid redundant loading of the ZOLB
8. Perform inlining to support placing more loops in the ZOLB	17. Perform loop peeling to further avoid redundant ZOLB loading
9. Calculate ranges of addresses accessed by each memory reference	

Fig. 11. Order of the Analysis and Transformations Used to Exploit a ZOLB

8   Results

Table 1 describes the benchmarks and applications used to evaluate the impact of using the ZOLB on the DSP16000. All of these test programs are either DSP benchmarks used in industry or typical DSP applications. Many DSP benchmarks represent kernels of programs where most of the cycles occur. Such kernels in DSP applications have been historically optimized in assembly code by hand to ensure high performance [6]. Thus, many established DSP industrial benchmarks are small since they were traditionally hand coded. Standard benchmarks (e.g. SPEC) were not used since the DSP16000 was not designed to support operations on floating-point values or integers larger than two bytes.

Table 1. Test Programs

Program	Description		Program	Description
add8	add two 8-bit images		conv	convolution code
copy8	copy one 8-bit image to another		fft	128 point complex fft
fir	finite impulse response filter		fir_no	fir filter with
fire	fire encoder			redundant load elimination
inverse8	invert an 8-bit image		iir	iir filtering
lms	lms adaptive filter		jpegdct	jpeg discrete cosine transform
sumabsd	sum of absolute differences of		scale8	scale an 8-bit image
	two images		trellis	trellis convolutional encoder
vec_mpy	simple vector multiply			

Table 2 contrasts the results for loop unrolling and exploiting the DSP16000 ZOLB.[3] Execution measurements were obtained by accessing a cycle count from a DSP16000 simulator [10]. Code size measurements were gathered by obtaining diagnostic information provided by the assembler [11]. The authors compared the performance of using the ZOLB against loop unrolling, which is a common approach for reducing loop overhead. The loop unrolling showed in Table 2 was performed on all innermost loops when the number of iterations was known statically or dynamically. As shown in the results, using the ZOLB typically resulted in fewer execution cycles as compared to loop unrolling. Sometimes loop unrolling did have benefits over using a ZOLB. This occurred when an innermost loop had too many instructions or had transfers of control that would prevent it from being placed in a ZOLB. In addition, sometimes loop unrolling provided other benefits, such as additional scheduling and instruction selection opportunities, that would not otherwise be possible.[4] However, the average performance benefits of using a ZOLB are impressive, particularly when code size is important. As shown in the table, loop unrolling caused significant code size

---

[3] Only relative performance results could be given due to disclosure restrictions for these test programs.

[4] The production version of the optimizer does limited unrolling of loops. For instance, loop unrolling is applied when memory references and multiplies can be coalesced. However, unrolling is not performed when it would cause the number of instructions to exceed the limit that the ZOLB can hold [9]. Note the measurements presented in this paper did not include loop unrolling while placing loops in the ZOLB since it would make the comparison of applying loop unrolling and using a ZOLB less clear. Likewise, the production version of the optimizer performs other optimizations, such as multiply and memory coalescing and software pipelining, that were not applied for the results in this paper.

increases, while using the ZOLB resulted in slight code size decreases. The code size decreases when using the ZOLB came from the combination of eliminating branches by placing the loops in the ZOLB and applying induction variable elimination and dead store elimination afterwards. Occasionally, code size decreases were obtained by avoiding redundant loads of the ZOLB loops using the flow analysis described in Section 5. Loop peeling, which increases code size, was rarely applied since memory contentions did not occur that frequently.

Table 2. Contrasting Loop Unrolling and Using a ZOLB

Program	Unroll Factor = 2		Unroll Factor = 4		Unroll Factor = 8		Exploiting ZOLB	
	Cycles	Code Size	Cycles	Code Size	Cycles	Code Size	Cycle	Code Size
add8	-11.47%	+7.84%	-23.11%	+62.75%	-27.46%	+90.20%	-36.33%	-3.92%
conv	-33.42%	+22.58%	-47.56%	+29.03%	-54.63%	+41.94%	-47.84%	-3.23%
copy8	-23.11%	+6.25%	-42.32%	+12.50%	-51.92%	+25.00%	-62.44%	-4.17%
fft	-6.22%	+32.14%	-10.56%	+92.86%	-12.73%	+214.29%	-8.69%	-3.57%
fir	-20.35%	+21.05%	-35.25%	+147.37%	-41.98%	+255.26%	-48.42%	-10.53%
fir_no	-3.97%	+34.88%	-7.07%	+109.30%	-9.14%	+258.14%	-31.35%	-4.65%
fire	-0.75%	+36.27%	-4.22%	+110.78%	-6.20%	+255.88%	-26.88%	-21.57%
iir	-11.10%	+14.58%	-15.43%	+51.04%	-15.67%	+88.54%	-19.61%	-4.17%
inverse8	-20.27%	+8.16%	-37.34%	+18.37%	-46.64%	+48.98%	-55.50%	-4.08%
jpegdct	-8.26%	+17.56%	-8.44%	+59.54%	-8.44%	+59.54%	0.00%	0.00%
lms	-1.75%	+0.48%	-10.52%	+1.78%	-10.52%	+1.78%	-8.33%	-0.04%
scale8	-4.90%	+38.46%	-9.37%	+93.85%	-11.60%	+204.62%	-14.28%	-1.54%
sumabsd	-14.69%	+8.57%	-19.57%	+25.71%	-22.03%	+60.00%	-58.83%	-8.57%
trellis	-11.52%	+0.11%	-19.10%	+0.33%	-22.79%	+0.78%	-20.16%	-0.17%
vec_mpy	-19.08%	+63.16%	-28.49%	+336.84%	-31.15%	+531.58%	-38.16%	-15.79%
Average	**-12.72%**	**+20.81%**	**-21.22%**	**+76.80%**	**-24.86%**	**+142.44%**	**-31.79%**	**-5.73%**

Table 3 depicts the benefit of applying the improving transformations described in Sections 4 and 5. Only some of the improving transformations applied without using a ZOLB (column 2) had a performance benefit on their own. These transformations include the use of conditional instructions, inlining, and loop collapsing. The characteristics of the DSP16000 prevented conditional instructions from being used frequently. Inlining only had occasional benefits for the test programs since the optimizer only inlined functions when the function was called from a loop and inlining would allow the loop to be placed in the ZOLB. Inlining was not performed when a function had transfers of control other than a return instruction, which was the common case. Loop collapsing was applied most frequently of these transformations. The results shown in column 3 include basic induction variable elimination since it was quite obvious that this transformation could almost always be applied when a loop is placed in the ZOLB. The combination of using the ZOLB with the improving transformations (column 4) sometimes resulted in greater benefits than the sum of the benefits (columns 2 and 3) when applied separately. Most of the additional benefit came from the new opportunities for placing more loops in the ZOLB (transformations described in Section 4).

The authors also obtained the percentage of the innermost loops that were placed in the ZOLB. On average 71.56% of the innermost loops could be placed

Table 3. The Impact of Improving Transformations on Using a ZOLB

Program	Impact on Execution Cycles		
	Transformations without Using the ZOLB	Using the ZOLB without Transformations	Using the ZOLB with Transformations
add8	-2.24%	-35.09%	-37.76%
conv	-8.22%	-43.48%	-52.13%
copy8	-1.84%	-60.39%	-63.13%
fft	0.00%	-8.69%	-8.69%
fir	0.00%	-48.42%	-48.42%
fir_no	-0.03%	-31.37%	-31.37%
fire	-7.44%	0.00%	-32.31%
iir	0.00%	-19.61%	-19.61%
inverse8	-1.64%	-53.80%	-56.23%
jpegdct	0.00%	0.00%	0.00%
lms	0.00%	-8.33%	-8.33%
scale8	-3.79%	-16.92%	-17.52%
sumabsd	-23.11%	0.00%	-51.70%
trellis	-8.75%	-7.36%	-20.16%
vec_mpy	0.00%	-38.16%	-38.16%
Average	**-3.83%**	**-25.34%**	**-32.97%**

in the ZOLB without applying the improving transformations described in Section 4. However, 84.89% of the innermost loops could be placed in the ZOLB with these improving transformations applied. Transfers of control was the most common factor that prevented the use of a ZOLB. The use of conditional instructions, inlining, and the transformation on loops with an unknown number of iterations all occasionally resulted in additional loops being placed in the ZOLB.

9   Conclusion

This paper described strategies for generating code and utilizing improving transformations to exploit a ZOLB. The authors found that many conventional improving transformations used in optimizing compilers had significant effects on how a ZOLB can be exploited. The use of predicated execution, loop distribution, and function inlining allowed more loops to be placed in a ZOLB. The overhead of loops placed in a ZOLB was further reduced by basic induction variable elimination and extraction, loop collapsing, and loop interchange. The authors also found that a ZOLB can improve performance in ways probably not intended by the architects who originally designed this feature. The use of conditional instructions and instruction scheduling with register renaming allowed some loops with an unknown number of iterations to be placed in a ZOLB. Interprocedural flow analysis and loop peeling were used with the `redo` instruction to avoid redundant loading of a ZOLB. The results obtained from test programs indicate that these transformations allowed a ZOLB to be often exploited with significant improvements in execution time and small reductions in code size.

References

1. Hennessy, J., Patterson, D.: Computer Architecture: A Quantitative Approach, Second Edition, Morgan Kaufmann, San Francisco, CA (1996). 157, 158, 161
2. Davidson, J.W., Jinturkar, S.: Aggressive Loop Unrolling in a Retargetable, Optimizing Compiler. Proceedings of Compiler Construction Conference. 59–73 (April 1996). 157
3. Lucent Technologies.: DSP16000 Digital Signal Processor Core Information Manual (1997). 158
4. Lucent Technologies: DSP16000 C Compiler User Guide (1997). 158
5. Lapsley, P., Bier, J., Lee, E.: DSP Processor Fundamentals - Architecture and Features, IEEE Press (1996). 159
6. Eyre, J., Bier, J.: DSP Processors Hit the Mainstream, IEEE Computer 31(8), 51–59 (August 1998). 159, 169
7. Lucent Technologies.: DSP16000 Digital Signal Processor Core Instruction Set Manual (1997). 159
8. Wang, Y.: Interprocedural Optimizations for Embedded Systems, Masters Project, Florida State University, Tallahassee, FL (1999). 162, 167
9. Whalley, D.: DSP16000 C OPtimizer Overview and Rationale, Lucent Technologies, Allentown, PA (1998). 167, 169
10. Lucent Technologies.: DSP16000 LuxWorks Debugger (1997). 169
11. Lucent Technologies.: DSP16000 Assembly Language User Guide (1997). 169
12. Uh, G.R., Wang, Y., Whalley, D. Jinturkar, S., Burns, C., and Cao, V.: Effective Exploitation of a Zero Overhead Loop Buffer, ACM SIGPLAN 1999 Workshop on Languages, Compilers, and Tools for Embedded Systems, 10–19 (1999). 159
13. Bacon, D., Graham, S., Sharp, O.: Compiler Transformations for High-Performance Computing, ACM Computing Surveys, Volume 26 Number 4, 345–420 (1994). 167

Advanced Compiler Optimization
for CalmRISC8 Low-End Embedded Processor

Dae-Hwan Kim

MCU Team, Samsung Electronics, San #24, Nongseo-Ri, Kiheung-Eup,
Yongin-City, Kyungki-Do 449-900, KOREA
dhtail@samsung.co.kr

Abstract. CalmRISC8 is an 8-bit embedded processor, in which architectural considerations for compiler are ignored to reduce power consumption. To overcome these constrains, new techniques are presented at an intermediate code level, an assembly level, and a link-time level. Techniques include register allocation, integer promotion elimination, extensive use of library functions, instruction scheduling for bank collects, and various optimizations at link-time. Experimental results show that 56.7 % reduction in code size can be achieved.

1. Introduction

In recent years, microcontrollers and DSPs are increasingly being embedded into many electrical products such as a fax modem and a cellular telephone. A common trend found in embedded systems is to integrate a microcontroller, a ROM, a RAM, and an ASIC on a single IC. In traditional compilers, especially for general purpose processors, optimization of generating fast executable code is mainly focused on. However in some embedded processors, the compactness of code is at least as important as execution speed. As the application software often exists in an on-chip ROM, so large code size increases ROM size and eventually the cost of system. On the other hand, as the complexity of embedded software is relatively small, the execution time improvement is often marginal. Further, many embedded processors have architecture constrains to generate a compact code. Such examples are relatively small number of registers and limited instruction set, and irregular data paths. Thus code reduction by traditional techniques is not satisfactory, and to get a dense code on such architectures, new optimization techniques of overcoming architecture constraints should be applied to.

CalmRISC8 [1] is an 8-bit embedded processor developed by SAMSUNG Electronics, and its main goal is to reduce power consumption. It operates on 3-volts of power and requires 30-70 microamperes per megahertz. To accomplish its low power consumption goal, architectural preferences by compiler are less considered or even ignored. The CalmRISC8 register set is organized as 4 banks with 4 registers in each bank to minimize the number of bits that the register specification consumes in instruction format. No instructions support operations on registers across different banks. This bank structure of registers greatly reduces the register allocation performance and causes a bank switching overhead to use registers in different banks.

A. Watt (Ed.): CC/ETAPS 2000, LNCS 1781, pp. 173–188, 2000.
© Springer-Verlag Berlin Heidelberg 2000

The limitation in addressing mode is another example of an architectural constraint that makes optimization difficult. In most cases, the memory operand is accessed by specifying the address in designated registers named 'index registers'. The register indirect addressing with a general purpose register (GPR) is not available.

The operations on word (a 16-bit length) on an 8-bit machine are also an obstacle. This becomes more overhead in CalmRISC8, because the registers in one bank often run short, so bank switching is required. CalmRISC8 has the 16-bit address line. The data memory of CalmRISC8 is organized as 256 pages of 256 bytes each. The high-order part of 16-bit address is page number and lower-order is page offset. In some cases, the sequential memory access is performed in a same page, thus, memory access can be optimized by deleting the latter page set instruction. Useless integer promotion from ANSI C makes many word operations also. Integer promotion means the type conversion from character to integer types when operands are character variables. When operands are character types, much of conversion can be eliminated.

Many of techniques in this paper are specific to CalmRISC8. However, basic ideas can be adapted to most DSP processors which have the multiple register bank and memory bank problem. Some of the issues occur also in non-DSP processors. For example, a VLIW may have the multiple register and memory banks.

The rest of this paper is organized as follows. Section 2 describes CalmRISC8 architecture. In section 3, overall structure of optimization is explained. In section 4, 5, 6 this paper presents intermediate, assembly, and link-time level solutions for architecture limitations in detail respectively. Experimental results are shown in section 7. This paper concludes in section 8 with some comments.

2.   CalmRISC8 Architecture

Fig. 1 shows the CalmRISC8 architecture. CalmRISC8 is an 8-bit embedded processor in which register and a data path are 8 bits long. The main characteristics of CalmRISC8 can be summarized as follows.

- CalmRISC8 follows the Harvard architecture in which program and data space is separated.
- Program memory is organized as 256 pages of 4K words for each page and data memory is 256 pages of 256 bytes each.
- For data memory addressing, index register pairs (IDH and IDL) should be used or absolute address should be specified in the instruction. CalmRISC8 has 16-bit data memory address line. The upper 8 bits of the data address that should be reside in IDH point to a specific page and the lower 8 bits specify the offset address of the page.
- It has two banks of index registers, each of which has one IDH and IDL0, IDL1.
- It has four banks of four general purpose registers in each bank.
- To change a bank of general purpose registers or index registers demands a special instruction. Current bank information is in SR0 register. The instruction for changing bank is one of 'BANK #num' or 'ORSR0 #imm' or 'ANDSR0 #imm'.

- It is a non-load/store architecture. Some operators can use memory operand as second operand. This kind of operators are AND, OR, XOR, ADD, SUB, CMP, LD.
- There are two types of branches including calls. One is a short branch (1 word) which branches into the address of the code memory in the same page, the other is a long branch (2 word) in which a target address can be in other pages.

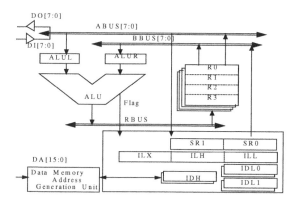

Fig. 1. CalmRISC8 Architecture

The addressing modes of CalmRISC8 can be demonstrated by 'LD' instruction. The page number of the address should be in an IDH register and offset can be in IDL0 or IDL1 or absolutely specified in the instruction. Thus, following LD instructions are possible for memory access. The displacement can be combined with index registers, and the displacement should be within 5-bit range.

```
LD    R1, @ID0  // address is 16 bits of (IDH:IDL0)
LD    R1, @ID1  // address is in (IDH:IDL1)
LD    R1, @[ID0+16]! // address is (IDH:IDL0)+16
LD    R1, @7A   // address is (IDH:7AH)
```

Due to the architecture constrains for compiler, CalmRISC8 compiler generates relatively long code without optimizations. Fig. 2 shows assembly code before optimization for the statement of 'a[i] = 0;', where 'a' is the global scope array and 'i' and 'a' are of character types. To compute the data memory address, first the value of 'i' is loaded into R3 from data memory. Then the value of 'i' is extended to integer by 'CALL __cvci_r3', which is the library function and it takes the register R3 in bank 0 and extend the sign bit into the R3 in bank 1. It is then added to the base address of 'a'. The '#<_a' represents the high part of 16 bit address of 'a' in data memory and resolved at link-time. The '#>_a' does the lower part. The 'ADD' instruction permits the immediate value as the second operand, but 'ADC' does not, so in 'ADC' in line (8) the second operand is in register. Then, the address of 'a[i]' is moved into IDH and IDL1 that are the index registers in line (13) and (15). The 'ID1' means combination of IDH and IDL1. The IDH and IDL0 are used as the stack pointer. Thus to keep the value of IDH which is written at line (13) of the 'LD IDH, R3', the IDH is saved by 'PUSH' instruction and later restored by 'POP' instruction.

```
LD      R3,@[ID0+(-1+1)]!;_i
CALL    __cvci_r3
BANK    #1
LD      R2,#<_a
BANK    #0
ADD     R3,#>_a
BANK    #1
ADC     R3,R2
BANK    #0
LD      R2,#0
PUSH    IDH
BANK    #1
LD      IDH,R3
BANK    #0
LD      IDL1,R3
LD      @[ID1]!,R2
POP     IDH
```

Fig. 2. Generated code example before optimization

3. Overall Structure of Optimization

To overcome architectural constrains for compiler, new techniques targeted for the CalmRISC8 are contrived. Optimizer runs at intermediate code, assembly code, and link-time cooperatively. The newly designed register allocation is applied for small set of registers and by using extensive assembly library functions like the line (2) in Fig. 2, the effect of expanding instruction set including addressing modes is achieved. The word operations are reduced byte operations by eliminating integer promotion. To reduce overhead of bank switching, instructions are reordered to gather same bank operations. At link-time, the cost of global variable access is minimized, word operations are reduced to byte operations again for functions whose stacks are allocated in a single page, and the 2-word branch instructions are changed into 1-word instructions when the target label is in the same page with the branch label.

General structure of optimization is shown in Fig. 3. The intermediate optimizer performs optimizations including classical optimizations [2] on DAG form of intermediate code. Implemented techniques are common subexpression elimination, copy propagation, constant propagation/folding, dead code elimination, peephole optimization, and optimal instruction ordering. In addition, it passes optimizing information to an assembly and a link optimizer. Some example of information is the condition and code block that can be deleted at link-time. All optimizations in an intermediate level are implemented in Local C Compiler (LCC) [3]

An assembly optimizer does the classical optimizations, target specific optimizations, procedural abstraction, and instruction scheduling for bank collection. Classical optimizations are performed on assembly level again, because some code redundancy is caused from machine resources and architecture limitation. An assembly optimizer analyzes information from an intermediate optimizer, changes it, and generates its own optimization information for the link-time optimizer. It takes the assembly code from intermediate optimizer and transforms code optimally and passes assembly code with pseudo code to assembler.

A link-time optimizer is a part of linker. CalmRISC8 linker plays a role of a standard linking job. Further, some code optimizations are performed. The code change at link-time is only deleting. It affects main job of linker such as external symbol reference and resolution. Deleting the code at link-time is a hard part, because this requires reallocation of code address. At some transformations like stack optimization, linker manipulates and constructs information from assembler actively in itself.

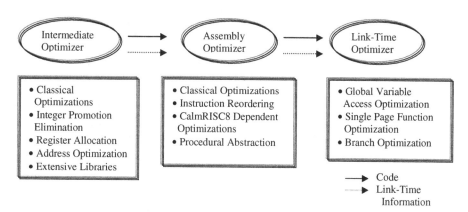

Fig. 3. Overall optimization structure

4. Intermediate Optimization

In CalmRISC8, the size of word is 16 bits and byte is 8 bits. Like other 8-bit embedded compilers, the size of character is 8 bits and short and integer types have 16-bit size. CalmRISC8 compiler allocates one register in bank 0 for character and does pair registers of the same number from bank 0 and bank 1 to the word data that demands 2 bytes. It reduces the number of library functions, compared with intra-bank register allocation, which allocates 2 registers in the same bank.

4.1 Flow Analysis OPT Register Allocation

CalmRISC8 has four general purpose registers in each bank of four, and operations on registers between different banks are not permitted. Therefore, it can not have better performance than that of four registers of no bank structure. The known dominant paradigm of register allocation is a graph coloring [4], [5], [6]. However, graph coloring does not result in good performance with small register sets such as CalmRISC8.

CalmRISC8 allocator takes the idea of the OPT page replacement algorithm in operating system. Contrary to O/S, compiler can analyze variable access sequence in most of cases, especially within a single basic block. When allocator runs out of registers, the register held by a variable that will be used at the furthest in the future will be replaced. Previously, the similar ideas are tried for local register allocation [7], [8]. However, they consume lots of spaces and time. Furthermore, they are local to a basic block.

Our method has two steps. At the first step, our OPT register allocation runs for each basic block. Before actually allocating registers, allocator constructs definition-use chains for each variable definition in an access order. Allocator tries to assign the same register to the same variable. At the second step, like the traditional data flow analysis, variable flow is analyzed for entire basic blocks. When the same variable has different registers from control flow, code is inserted to write variable content back into memory at the end of the basic block that has a variable definition. In the same way, loading operation from memory is inserted immediately before the use of that variable in descendant basic blocks.

To reduce the register pressure, temporary uses of word operations are split into two byte operations with the same register number for high-order and low-order part of operations. This reduces the number of required registers by halves, and obviates the bank-switching overhead. Word operations occur to some extent, even if user does not use much of word type variables. The address calculation and parameter passing cause some word operations.

LD R2, @i	// low part of i
BANK #1	
LD R2, @ (i+1)	// high part of i
BANK #0	
ADD R2, @j	// low part of j
BANK #1	
ADC R2, @(j +1)	// high part of j
BANK #0	
LD @k, R2	// low part of k
BANK #1	
LD @(k+1), R2	// high part of k
BANK #0	

LD R2, @i	// low part of i
ADD R2, @j	// low part of j –(2)
LD @k, R2	// low part of k
LD R2, @(i +1)	// high part of i
ADC R2, @(j+1)	// high part of j –(5)
LD @(k+1), R2	// high part of k

(a) before split   (b) after split

Fig. 4. Word operation split example. This is not perfect assembly code, but enough to illustrate the effect of idea.

Fig. 4 is the example of word operation split for the statement of 'k = i + j', where 'i', 'j', and 'k' are integer variables. In (a), values are first loaded into registers and the addition of word type is executed using 'ADD' and 'ADC' pair. After applying word operation split, code is shown in (b). The code 'LD' instruction does not affect carry information, so the instruction (5) uses the carry generated from instruction (2).

The intermediate expression tree can be split if any of word operations do not change the code correctness. Some operators on words can not be split. The shift of word by word is such an operator. The shift operator can not be transformed into two character shifts without additional code to keep the correctness. These operators are shift, type conversion, modular, and divide operator. The sequence of word operations that generate more than one carry can not be split also. The statement of 'l = i + j +k' can not be split, because that changes the carry information to be used. As an example, consider the code in Fig. 5. The line (6) should use the carry result of lower part of operation of 'i+j', that is the carry from line (2). However, if split, the (6) will use the carry of '(i+j)+k', that is the carry from line (3). It is wrong.

```
LD  R1, @i        // low part of i
ADD R1,@j         // low part of j –(2)
ADD R1,@k         // low part of k –(3)
LD  @l,R1         // low part of l
LD  R1,@(i+1)     // high part of i
ADC R1,@(j+1)     // high part of j –(6)
ADC R1,@(k+1)     // high part of k
LD  @(l+1),R1     // high part of l
```

Fig. 5. Wrong word operation split example

4.2 Instruction Set Expansion by Library Functions

The CalmRISC8 has small number of instruction set, and many of them are primitive, so intermediate code corresponds to many assembly instructions. Furthermore, compiler generates many word operations. The word operations take a form of pattern. For example, word addition is composed of 'ADD' and 'ADC' pair. A deficiency of addressing mode is another factor to cause generating long code. To overcome above circumstances, making assembly library for code generation is tried, and it results in remarkable code reduction.

Table 1. Some of library functions

LIBRARY NAME	DESCRIPTION
__addW_rx_ry	Word (16 bits) addition
__cmpW_rx_ry	Word (16 bits) compare
__loadB_rx_ry	Register indirect byte (8 bits) load support. The 'rx' is the address of data memory and 'ry' is the register into which value is loaded
__storeB_rx_ry	Register indirect byte store
__loadW_rx_ry	Register indirect word load
__LshW_rx_ry	Left shift 'rx' by 'ry'. CalmRISC8 ISA only supports 1bit shift.
__loadB_storeB_rx_ry	The value of memory addressed by 'rx' is stored into the memory of address 'ry'
__add_loadB_rx_ry_rz	C language support. In most cases, used for array element referencing. The memory content whose address is 'rx' + 'ry' is load into 'rz'

Table 1 shows some assembly libraries that compiler frequently generates. There are about 50 kinds of functions. Some functions such as 'loadB_storeB_rx_ry' are the combination of other primitive library functions. In table 1, 'rx' and 'ry' can be a register 0, 1, 2, 3. As shown in Table 1, compiler generates like this:

```
CALL addW_r2_r3
```

for 16 bits addition, rather than:

```
ADD R2,R3
BANK #1
ADC R2,R3
BANK #0
```

To make assembly level analysis and optimizations easy, the intermediate optimizer generates information of reading and writing registers of the library as pseudo code. The format is that the first digit means bank number and the second represents register number as shown below.

```
.READ_REG 03,02,13,12
.WRITE_REG 03,13
CALL addW_r2_r3
```

4.3 Integer Promotion Elimination

In an 8-bit embedded processor application, most of the variables are 8 bits or character type. According to ANSI C, the character operands are widened into integer types for operations between character variables ('integer promotion'). When semantics can be preserved, this integer promotion can be eliminated. Additionally, integer operators are changed into character ones.

```
LD      R3,@[ID0+(-1+3)]! ;_i          LD      R3,@[ID0+(-1+3)]! ; _i
CALL    $__cvci_r3                     ADD     R3,@[ID0+(-2+3)]! ; _j
LD      R2,@[ID0+(-2+3)]! ;_j          LD      @[ID0+(-3+3)]!,R3 ; _k
CALL    $__cvci_r2
CALL    $__addW_r3r2
LD      @[ID0+(-3+3)]!,R3 ;_k
```

(a) before elimination   (b) after elimination

Fig. 6. Integer promotion elimination example for the statement of "k = i + j ", when 'i', 'j', 'k' are character variables.

Fig. 6 shows the integer promotion elimination, when 'i', 'j', and 'k' are character variables. Without integer promotion elimination, compiler would generate the code for integer operations as shown in (a). First the 'i' and 'j' are converted into integers and the integer addition is executed, and then the result is written to 'k'. However, in this example, the conversions from characters to integers and integer addition are of no use, because the result is written into character variable. In other words, excluding the possibility of overflow, the addition of character is equivalent to original code in semantics. This elimination extends to argument passing. When the prototype is known, compiler compares the type of formal parameter with that of actual parameter. When the formal parameter is a character type, actual parameter of character type is not promoted into integer.

For each tree, one pass is in bottom up manner to check that the node can be converted by checking the kids' type. Take division operator of integer type as an example. Whether integer division can be converted into character division depends on the division operands. If both are in character boundary, it can be converted. However, if any of both should keep an integer value, it can not be changed. Thus for character variables 'i' and 'j', the integer division operator in 'i/2' can be converted into character division operator, because it is evident that 'i/2' has a character value. However, the divide in '(i + j)/2' can not be reduced because 'i+j' can have value of integer range.

A second pass is top-down approach to determine whether each node can be reduced. Basically, all promotions between characters including constants in character range are eliminated. However, some integer type operators keep promotions of character type from being eliminated. Some examples of these operators are assignment into integer variable, integer divide, and 16 bits address calculation. Thus, for example, in the statement of " i_i = c_i + c_j;" where 'c_i' and 'c_j' are character and 'i_i' is a integer variable, the addition of 'c_i' and 'c_j' are promoted into integers, because that result is written into a integer variable.

4.4 Address Calculation Optimization

The word type address calculation is another barrier to overcome for generating dense code. The memory accesses except the local variable whose offset in stack is determined at compile-time, which takes the form of @[ID0+offset]!, demands word operations on address calculation. Such examples are global variable access and array indexing by non-constant expression. Relatively high percentage of the word addressing is address calculation of array element, and most of the array is byte addressable from the base address of array in an 8-bit application. In this case, array indexing can be optimized by the addition of byte offset and word base address rather than that of word offset and word base address.

```
LD      R3,@[ID0+(-1+1)]!  ;_i
CALL    $__cvci_r3
BANK    #1          ;B1start
LD      R2,#<1
BANK    #0          ;B1end
LD      R2,#>1
CALL    $__lshi_r3r2
BANK    #1          ;B1start
LD      R2,#<_Gi
BANK    #0          ;B1end
LD      R2,#>_Gi
CALL    $  addW  r3r2
```

```
LD      R3,@[ID0+(-1+1)]!   ;_i
ADD     R3, @[ID0+(-1+1)]!  ;_i
BANK    #1          ;B1start
LD      R2,#<_Gi
BANK    #0          ;B1end
LD      R2,#>_Gi
CALL    $__addBW_r3r2
```

(a) before optimization   (b) after optimization

Fig. 7. Address optimization

As an example, consider the computing the address of 'Gi[i]', assuming that the size of array 'Gi' is 100 bytes and the element type of 'Gi' is integer and 'i' is the character type variable. Without the address calculation optimization, the code is shown in Fig 7 (a). First, the value of 'i' is extended to word by the 'CALL $_cvci_r3' instruction. Next, the index value is left shifted by 1-bit, because the size of integer is 2 bytes in CalmRISC8, then the offset is added to base address of 'Gi'. By moving the code of converting character to integer inside library function, code can be reduced. For this purpose, we create a new library function of 'addBW' library, that adds the second word value with the zero extended value of the first library argument. The body of 'addBW' is almost the same as 'addW'. Therefore, by sharing the same code, the total size of library functions is not increased much. In addition, to access the integer type array, the left shift of index variable by 1-bit can be reduced into an ADD operation. After the address optimization, the code is shown in (b).

5. Assembly Level Optimization

Two techniques are described here. One of well-known code compaction techniques is procedural abstraction that is more useful in low-end embedded processors and CalmRISC8 specific instruction scheduling.

5.1 Procedural Abstraction

Compiler generates the same code sequences that appear many times. In CalmRISC8, this becomes evident because it has a relatively small number of instructions and registers. Procedural abstraction makes each sequence as a separate function and changes repeated occurrence patterns into function calls [9].

Each assembly line excluding directives is mapped a symbol based on its opcode and operand types. Suffix tree [10] is built for these symbols. Thus, a whole assembly code is treated as one string. The non-terminal nodes that have at least 2 kids in tree are the candidates for a subroutine, because at least the pattern occurs 2 times. Next step is to evaluate the candidates based on the sequence occurrence count and the length of sequence. Current code size of totally repeated sequences is the multiplication of count by length. If abstraction is applied, the newly generated function code size will be addition of length and size of return instruction, and total size will be the addition of new function size and a multiplication of count by the size of call instruction. Procedural abstraction is applied for each pattern only when current total code size of patterns is greater than size that will be after abstraction.

5.2 Instruction Scheduling for Bank Operation Collects

One of main overheads of CalmRISC8 compiler is a need of bank switching. The current bank status is in SR0 (status register 0). The bit 3 and 4 have the GPR bank information and bit 2 has the index register bank information. To use other banks, bank specifying bits in SR0 should be changed by 'ANDSR0 #imm' or 'ORSR0 #imm' or 'BANK #num' instructions. If we put together the same bank operations, many pairs of bank switching instruction become redundant. Our reorder technique is relatively simple compared with other instruction scheduling. The order of instructions in the same bank is not changed.

At an assembly level, the dependency between bank blocks that are the sequential instructions of having the same bank status is analyzed. In CalmRISC8, additional dependencies happen as well as normal data dependency. One of them is a carry dependency. The typical code form of 16-bit addition is like below.

```
ADD R0,R2
BANK #1
ADC R0,R2
BANK #0
```

Above code means ADC use the carry result of ADD. Therefore, ADC depends on ADD. No carry affecting instructions can locate within them and ADC should follow ADD immediately. Fig. 8 shows code before and after scheduling. In (a), the (5) can be moved after (1), because there is no dependency between them. After a move, (4) and (6) become useless, so those can be deleted as shown in (b).

LD R3,@[ID0+(-4+1+6)]!	(1) jj(low)
BANK #1 ;B1start	(2)
LD R3,@[ID0+(-4+6)]!	(3) jj(high)
BANK #0;B1end	(4)
LD R2,@[ID0+(-6+1+6)]!	(5) kk(low)
BANK #1;B1start	(6)
LD R2,@[ID0+(-6+6)]!	(7) kk(high)
BANK #0 ;B1end	(8)
CALL __addW_r3r2	(9)

(a) code before scheduling

LD R3,@[ID0+(4+1+6)]!	(1) jj (low)
LD R2,@[ID0+(-6+1+6)]!	(5) kk(low)
BANK #1;B1start	(2)
LD R3,@[ID0+(-4+6)]!	(3) jj(high)
~~BANK #0;B1end~~	(4)
~~BANK #1;B1start~~	(6)
LD R2,@[ID0+(-6+6)]!	(7) kk(high)
BANK #0;B1end	(8)
CALL __addW_r3r2	(9)

(b) code after scheduling

Fig. 8. Instruction scheduling code example of 'jj + kk'

This idea applies to the ID (index register) banks. ID bank 1 is used as a global variable pointer, whereas ID bank 0 is used for stack pointer of a function. Before a global variable access, the bank is switched into ID bank 1. After a global variable is accessed, compiler changes ID bank 1 back to ID bank 0. Like the GPR bank collect, the operations of global variables can be collected as well.

6. Link-Time Optimization

Only a few compilers have performed optimizations at link-time [11], [12], [13], because link-time optimizations need much analysis and the effects may not be great. Some embedded compilers have burdened the link-time information such as memory allocation information of variables on the users for efficient code generation. However, it is cumbersome to the users.

6.1 Global Variable Access Optimization

Many global variables have been used in an embedded processor application. Memory is allocated to global variables at link-time, so link-time is the best for global variable access optimization. To access global variables in CalmRISC8, two parts of address, which are the page number and offset, must be specified. Normally, the IDH (index high register) of ID Bank 1 specifies the page number of a global variable. The offset is often specified absolutely as shown (2) in Fig. 9 (a). Optimization occurs when two sequential global variables are allocated into the same page. In that case, the loading of page number to IDH of the second is the same as the first one. Therefore, it becomes redundant and can be deleted.

```
ID_BANK        #1 ;  IDbank <- 1
.GLOBAL_ACCESS        _j
.GLOBAL_OPT  BEGIN
LD    IDH,#<_j              (1)
.GLOBAL_OPT  END
LD    R3,>_j               (2)
ID_BANK        #0
ID_BANK        #1 ;  IDbank <- 1
.GLOBAL_ACCESS        _k
.GLOBAL_OPT  BEGIN
LD    IDH,#<_k             (3)
.GLOBAL_OPT  END
ADD  R3,>_k
ID_BANK        #0
```

(a) intermediate information

```
ID_BANK        #1 ; IDbank <- 1
.FLOW_GLOBALS   _j,_a,_b  (1)
.GLOBAL_OPT  BEGIN
LD    IDH,#<_j
.GLOBAL_OPT  END
LD    R3,>_j
.FLOW_GLOBALS   _j,_k    (2)
.GLOBAL_OPT  BEGIN
LD    IDH,#<_k
.GLOBAL_OPT  END
ADD  R3,>_k
ID_BANK        #0
```

(b) assembly information

```
ID_BANK        #1 ; IDbank <- 1
LD    IDH,#<_j
LD    R3,>_j
ADD  R3,>_k
ID_BANK        #0
```

(c) code after link

Fig. 9. Global variable access optimization example. This figure takes the example of 'j+k', when 'j' and 'k' are allocated into the same memory page. (a) shows pseudo code generated from intermediate optimization. (b) shows assembly information. In this code, sequential ID bank switching instructions are eliminated. (c) shows code after link.

The intermediate optimizer generates the name of global variable and marks the code block that can be deleted at link-time. Assembly optimizer analyzes the global variable access sequence throughout all basic blocks in a function. It specifies the link-time condition on that following code block, so it can be deleted. This mechanism is illustrated in Fig. 9. The (1) and (3) in (a) that is between GLOBAL_OPT BEGIN and GLOBAL_OPT END mark the block that can be deleted at link-time. The assembly optimizer generates variable access flow information like (1) and (2) in (b). For example, the pseudo code in (2) gives linker information that if the variable 'j' and 'k' are allocated in the same page memory, following marked block can be deleted. The pseudo code of '.FLOW_GLOBAL' lists all the global variables that can reach at that point from control flow and immediately following global variable name. The (c) shows code after link-time optimization. Linker deletes code and recalculates linking information such as code segment size and symbol linkage caused from code layout change.

6.2 Single-Page Stack Function Optimization

To overcome the paged memory architecture, in case that the stack, or activation record, of a function is allocated within a single page at all execution paths, many high-order parts of word operations can be deleted. In other words, word operations can be converted into byte operations. Furthermore, the save and restore instructions of index register pair to keep stack pointer, which are shown at line (11) and (17) in Fig. 2, can be eliminated. It is believed the embedded application use many global variables and relatively a few local variables, so the size of stack frame is relatively small. Thus in fact, many of functions will have stack frame within a single page, not covering many pages.

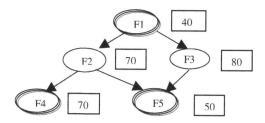

Fig. 10. Call graph and functions whose stack is allocated within a single page. In here, 'F1', 'F4', 'F5' are functions whose frames are allocated within a single page.

With these facts, like the global variable access optimization, this technique detects the functions of which stack are allocated within a single page from all paths in a call graph, and then deletes marked blocks at link-time. Intermediate optimizer generates function call information before 'CALL' instruction.

```
.fcall  _foo
CALL    _foo
```

In addition, it generates stack size information for each function.

```
.fsize    frame_size (bytes)
```

Intermediate optimizer marks code blocks that can be deleted. This marking information takes the following form.

```
.STACK_OPT BEGIN
// code that can be deleted
.STACK_OPT END
```

Assembly optimizer constructs annotated call graph that has frame size information. Linker completes the call graph for entire program and marks single page allocatable functions from all call graph paths, and deletes marked blocks.

Take the call tree in Fig. 10 for an example, and assume the size of one page is 100 bytes for simplicity, and stack frame is allocated from address 0, and grows to high address. In this example, the function 'F1', 'F4', and 'F5' have frame in a single page by all paths. For example, the stack 'F5' will be in page 2 which path it follows. If 'F5' is reached from 'F1', 'F2', and 'F5' path, the stack of 'F5' begins from the address of 110 and the end of stack is 159. Thus, the stack is in page 2. From the other path, the stack of 'F5' is in page 2 also.

6.3 Branch Address Resolution.

In CalmRISC8, branch is not a PC-relative but absolute addressing, so at compile time, it is impossible to know whether target address is in the same page. Therefore, compiler emits the long branch instruction. At link-time, while resolving the address, the branch whose target is in the same page is changes into short one. If a branch is changed into short one, it causes code layout change, and affects other code address and other branch instructions. Therefore, this address resolution is iterated until no more code layout change occurs. This stage should be the last stage of link-time optimization, because other link-time optimizations can change code layout.

7. Experiments

The results of applying optimizations are shown in Table 2. On average, 56.7 % code reductions can be achieved. The code size after optimizations ranges from 36.8 % to 56.0 % of the original code. At an average there are 47.0 % reduction at an intermediate level, 6.5 % at assembly and 3.2 % at a link-time level. Relatively minor ones are dhry and fib. They use many 16-bit variables and exceed the 5-bit displacement used in index register addressing mode. In experiments, the general applications are evaluated. If evaluations are done on embedded application, the results will be better, because our techniques are targeted for embedded application such as global variable optimization and integer promotion elimination.

Table 2. Experimental results NO_OPT means no optimizations. IO, AO, LO mean intermediate optimization, assembly optimzaiton, and link-time optimization respectively. For example, the last column shows the results of applying IO, AO, and LO. Each column shows the code size after optimization, not the reduction size. Bubble is a bubble sort program. Fib is a fibonacci permutation. Fact is a factorial calculation. Insert is a insertion sort program. Matmul is a matrix multiplication. Stan is a part of stanford benchmarks. Dhry is a part of dhrystone benchmarks.

Program	NO_OPT (Bytes)	IO (Bytes, %)	IO + AO (Bytes, %)	IO+AO+LO (Bytes, %)
Bubble	390	202 (51.8)	178 (45.6)	160 (41.0)
Fib	232	144 (62.1)	128 (55.1)	112 (48.3)
Fact	270	170 (62.9)	140 (51.8)	124 (45.9)
Insert	380	176 (46.4)	150 (39.5)	140 (36.8)
Matmul	1298	728 (56.0)	672 (51.7)	612 (47.1)
Stan	31578	16414 (51.9)	14502 (45.9)	13638 (43.1)
Dhry	1730	1204 (69.5)	1056 (61.0)	974 (56.0)
Total	35878	19038 (53.0)	16700 (46.5)	15560 (43.3)

In terms of cycle count, CalmRISC8 has a 3-stage pipeline. The first stage is instruction fetch stage, the second instruction decode and data memory access stage, and the final stage is execute and write-back stage. The number of clocks per instruction (CPI) is 1 except for long branches, which take 2 clock cycles. So reducing code size reduces cycle count also. Almost all optimizations contribute code size reduction. Procedural abstraction and library functions reduce code size, but increase execution cycle time by the generated function and call.

8. Conclusion

Embedded processors make compiler optimizations difficult. The extreme one is CalmRISC8. For embedded architectures, new optimization techniques should be applied. At intermediate level, assembly level, and link-time level the optimizations are performed, and passing information to later levels helps more optimizations being processed. Embedded architecture constrains can be overcome to great level. Several ideas can be extended to other embedded processors including DSP processors that have irregular structures like banked structure, and limited instruction set.

References

1. Samsung Corp.: CalmRISC8 Specification. Samsung Corp. (1999)
2. A. V. Aho, R. S. Sethi, and J. D. Ullman: Compilers: Principles, Techniques and Tools. Addison-Wesley (1985)
3. C. Fraser and D. Hanson: A Retargetable C Compiler: Design and Implementation. the Benjamin/Cummings, Redwood City, CA (1995)

4. G. J. Chaitin, M. A. Auslander, A. K. Chandra, J. Cocke, M. E. Hopkins, and P. Markstein: Register allocation via coloring. Journal of Computer Languages, 6 (1981) 45-57
5. P. Briggs, K. D. Cooper, K. Kennedy, and L. Torczon: Coloring Heuristics for register allocation. In Proceedings of the ACM SIGPLAN '89 Conference on Programming Language Design and Implementation, SIGPLAN Notices, 24(7) (1989) 275-284
6. F. Chow and J. Hennessy: Register allocation by priority-based coloring. SIGPLAN Notices, 19 (1984) 222-232
7. W. Hsu, C. N. Fischer, and J. R. Goodman: On the minimization of loads/stores in local register allocation. IEEE Trans. on Software Engineering, 15 (1989) 1252-1260
8. M. Farach and V. Liberatore: On Local Register Allocation. DIMACS Technical Report, July (1997) 93-33,
9. M. Z. Zastre: Compacting Object Code via Parameterized Procedural Abstraction. B.Sc. Thesis, Simon Fraser University (1993)
10. E. M. McCreight: A Space-Economical Suffix Tree Construction Algorithm. Journal of the ACM, Vol. 23. No. 2, April (1976) 262-272
11. A. Srivastava, and D. W. Wall: Link-Time Optimization of Address Calculation on a 64-bit Architecture. In SIGPLAN Conference on Programming Language Design and Implementation, (1993) 49-60
12. D W. Wall: Link-Time Code Modification. WRL Research Report 89/17, September (1989)
13. D. W. Wall: Experience with a Software-Defined Machine Architecture. ACM Transactions on Programming Languages and Systems, 14(3) (1992) 299-338

Global Software Pipelining with Iteration Preselection

David Gregg

Institut für Computersprachen, Technische Universität Wien,
Argentinierstraße 8, A-1040 Wien
Fax: (+431) 58801-18598
dave@complang.tuwien.ac.at

Abstract. Software pipelining loops containing multiple paths is a very difficult problem. Loop shifting offers the possibility of a close to optimal schedule with acceptable code growth. Deciding how often to shift each operation is difficult, and existing heuristics are rather *ad hoc*. We separate loop shifting from scheduling, and present new, non-greedy heuristics. Experimental results show that our approach yields better performance and less code growth.

1 Introduction

Instruction Level Parallelism (ILP) offers the hope of greatly faster computers by automatically overlapping the execution of many machine-level instructions to complete tasks more quickly. An important class of ILP machine is the Very Long Instruction Word computer. These simple machines provide large numbers of execution resources, but require a sophisticated compiler to schedule the instructions. A particularly important scheduling technique is software pipelining, which can produce very compact schedules for loops.

This paper focuses on global software pipelining, that is pipelining loops containing branches. Our approach is based on shifting operations across the loop entry. This technique is used in several important software pipelining algorithms [ME97,NN97,Jai91,DH99]. Most loop shifting algorithms use an iterative approach to software pipelining. These algorithms interleave acyclic scheduling of the loop body, and shifting operations from one iteration to another. Acyclic scheduling has been studied in great detail and a number of good algorithms exist. Loop shifting has been less studied, and most algorithms shift operations, one iteration at a time, and on quite an *ad hoc* basis.

The fundamental problem of loop shifting is how to know which operations should be moved across the loop back edge, and how many times. Algorithms which move operations one iteration at a time are similar to early attempts at global acyclic scheduling which percolated operations from on basic block to the next without any final intended destination. Moving an operation one iteration at a time may create a temporarily worse schedule, that can later be transformed into a better one [Rau94]. The problem is to distinguish between such good moves, and shifts that genuinely make the schedule worse.

A. Watt (Ed.): CC/ETAPS 2000, LNCS 1781, pp. 189–201, 2000.

Despite the problems of loop shifting, it has one very important advantage – it extends naturally to software pipelining loops containing branches. Loop shifting algorithms can pipeline such loops using existing acyclic scheduling techniques. Most importantly, the initiation interval (II) of the resulting pipeline is not fixed; it can vary depending on the control flow path. Other algorithms can achieve a variable II, but only at the cost of large scale code duplication or scheduling restrictions which may increase the average II. Furthermore, loop shifting naturally allows operations to be scheduled ahead of branches upon which they are control dependent. Many other approaches limit ILP by treating control dependences as data dependences.

This paper deals with software pipelining of integer code using loop shifting. Such code often contains loops with branches and low trip counts. With such loops it is important to both minimize the average II of the pipeline, and to control code growth and other resource usage. With low trip count loops the cost of loop start-up, such as cache misses from an over-large loop prolog, may be just as important as the average II for the loop. Therefore, we concentrate on shifting the loop only enough to make the minimum II attainable. Only after shifting is complete do we apply acyclic scheduling.

The paper is organised as follows. First we describe existing loop shifting techniques. Section 3 describes our novel approach to software pipelining loops containing branches. In section 4 we present experimental results from implementing the algorithm in an ILP compiler. In section 5 we look at other work in this area. And finally we outline some conclusions and open questions for our future research.

2   Shift and Schedule Algorithms

We will first describe shifting algorithms in more detail. These algorithms move operations from inside the loop across the loop back-edge and into the region of code before the start of the loop. This produces a compensation code copy of the moved operation at the end of the loop. Thus operations move from one iteration to another inside the loop. This process is often know as *shifting* the operation.

The most prominent loop shifting algorithms interleave acyclic scheduling and shifting [ME97,NN97,Jai91]. A problem with these algorithms is their rules for choosing which operations to shift. The candidates for shifting are those operations which the acyclic scheduling step has placed toward the start of the acyclic schedule. At each acyclic scheduling stage, operations are scheduled as early as possible. This strategy can work well for operations that are members of the longest dependence chains in the loop, since dependences prevent them being scheduled too early. Other operations may be scheduled far earlier than necessary.

There are a number of problems with shifting operations more often than necessary. First, functional units may be used for speculatively executing operations which could be scheduled less speculatively without delaying the schedule.

This is especially true for loops containing unpredictable branches. Secondly, the length of the register lifetimes will increase, thus increasing register pressure, and register spills. Values that are live across loop iterations may need renaming to maintain the correctness of the code. Renaming requires copy operations and/or loop unrolling, neither of which is desirable. Shifting operations increases code growth in the prolog and loop body, increasing cache misses. Finally, shifting operations can, under some circumstances, increase the length of the new loop body rather than decreasing it.

In order to avoid these problems, existing algorithms try to limit their greediness in a number of ways. Enhanced Pipeline Scheduling (EPS) uses a limited size scheduling window. At each cycle during scheduling, only the first K (usually $K = 16$) operations operations on each path are eligible to be scheduled. This limits greediness somewhat, but operations within the window can still be scheduled too early, and operations outside the window may be shifted too little. EPS also tries to schedule the loop acyclically as much as possible. Once all the operations on a given path have been scheduled once, no further shifting of the loop is allowed on that path. When all control flow paths have reached this state, scheduling is complete. Furthermore, priority is given to operations which are shifted a smaller number of times.

Resource Directed Loop Pipelining (RDLP) has weaker controls. It calculates the minimum II (MII) for each control flow path through the loop. It then alternates between acyclic scheduling and shifting all operations in the first cycle of the schedule. This process continues until the MII is reached on all path, or some limit on the number of shifts has been reached. Specifying a lower limit makes the algorithm less greedy, but reduces the opportunities for pipelining.

Both EPS and RDLP use a greedy strategy, but with some rather *ad hoc* heuristics to try to limit the greediness. The result is that many operations will be shifted too much and an occasional one shifted too little. What is really needed is a strategy that shifts operations just enough. In the next section, we present our approach to doing exactly this.

3   Iteration Preselection

Iteration Preselection is a new type of *Decomposed Software Pipelining* (DESP) algorithm [WE93]. Rather than trying to shift and schedule together, we break pipelining into two stages. First, we calculate the number of times each operation should be shifted using only an approximation of the resource constraints. We then shift each operation the appropriate number of times. In the second stage, we schedule the resulting loop body using an existing acyclic scheduling algorithm. It is only in this stage that we take full account of the resource constraints on the loop.

All DESP algorithms try to simplify software pipelining by breaking it into the two simpler problems of choosing to how many times to shift each operation in the loop body, and acyclic scheduling. Although the computational complexity of these two subproblems is not smaller than that of the software pipelining problem, good heuristics can be found for both subproblems. It can be more difficult to find such good heuristics which solve both subproblems together.

Existing DESP algorithms concentrate on loops containing a single basic block. In our opinion, however, the true strength of the DESP idea lies in global software pipelining. Global software pipelining with a variable II and reasonable code growth is an enormously difficult problem. Good heuristics can be found for the two subproblems, however. Acyclic global scheduling has been well studied and good heuristic algorithms such as Selective Scheduling [ME97] and DAG-GER [CYS98] produce excellent results. The remaining problem is heuristics for shifting operations.

3.1   Single Path Loops

Our approach to shifting single path loops involves three steps. First, we calculate the MII for the loop. Secondly, we calculate the smallest number of times that each operation needs to be shifted for this II to be reached, assuming infinite resources. Finally, we shift the operations.

We calculate the MII using Lam's [Lam88] approach to calculating the initial MII for modulo scheduling[1]. This calculation finds the precise MII based on dependences, but uses only an approximation for the effects of resources. Thus, our algorithm takes some account of resources at this step, but the detailed resource allocation is not done until acyclic scheduling.

The goal of second step is to reduce the length of the longest acyclic dependence chain in the loop to the length of the MII. Such a loop can certainly be acyclically scheduled in MII cycles on a machine with infinite resources. The *height* of an operation measures the length of the longest acyclic dependence chain from that operation to the end of the loop. To reduce the acyclic dependence length, it is necessary to shift operations whose height is greater than the II. We call the number of times that an operation *op* must be shifted the *Times to Shift* or TTS(*op*). In the absence of cyclic dependences, we can calculate the TTS with the following formula.

$$\text{TTS}(op) = (\text{height}(op) - 1) \ / \ \text{MII}$$

In the presence of cyclic dependences, the situation is more complicated. Cyclic dependences may cause the height of an operation to increase when other ops are shifted. We introduce the notion of *circular height* (*CH*) to solve this problem. Intuitively, Circular Height is a measure of the height of an operation, plus the amount that the operation's height will increase when dependent operations are shifted to below it. More formally, we calculate *CH* on the data dependence graph of the loop. The data dependence graph contains vertices representing operations, and directed edges for dependences. Each edge has a weight representing dependence distance. Edges with a zero weight are acyclic

---

[1] Our original formulation looked only at the dependence MII. The idea of using the resource MII as-well comes from the EPS++ algorithm.

dependences. Let $succ(op)$ denote the set of vertices v such that there exists an edge (op, v). We initialise the CH of each operation op to latency(op). We calculate the final CH values using the following algorithm.

```
repeat
    change = FALSE
    for each v ∈ succ(op)
        ht = latency(op) + height(v) - weight(op, v) * MII
        if ( ht > CH(op) )
            CH(op) = ht
            change = TRUE
        endif
    endfor
until change == FALSE
```

These circular heights can be used as the height in the TTS formula above to calculate the number of times to shift each operation. The final stage of loop shifting is to actually shift the operations, using existing operation movement techniques.

3.2 Multiple Paths

Calculating the number of times to shift each operation is considerably more complicated in the presence of multiple paths. First, the II for each path may be different. Secondly, several control flow paths may contain the same instruction. This single instruction may have different heights depending on which path one considers. A further complication is with *cross paths*. A cross path is the section of code dealing with control flow from one path to another. The idea of II is very difficult to apply to cross paths, since they involve moving from one path to another, perhaps every iteration.

To attempt to satisfy these conflicting requirements, we use a heuristic based on the single path case. We treat each path separately. For each path through the loop, we calculate the TTS for each operation. Branches are assigned a CH equal to the greater of their latency, or the CH of the operation op that computes the branch condition, minus the latency of op.

Based on these calculations we shift operations. If an operation falls on more than one path, we choose the maximum TTS from all the different paths. If an operation is duplicated while moving, due to the normal effects of compensation code in global scheduling, the two copies may be shifted independently.

3.3 An Example

Figure 1 shows the control flow graph for a simple loop containing two control flow paths. The MII for Path1 is one, and is two for path2. The figure also shows the circular height and TTS of each operation. All operations have a latency of one.

| | | Path1 (II = 1) | | Path2 (II = 2) | |
		Circular Height	Times to Shift	Circular Height	Times to Shift
x = f(x)		3	2	4	1
cc1 = test1(x)		2	1	2	0
if cc1		1	0	1	0
x = g(x, y)		-	-	3	1
cc2 = test2(x)		2	1	2	0
if cc2		1	0	1	0

exit, x live

Fig. 1. Example loop with variable II

First, we ensure that all loop back edges come from unconditional gotos rather than conditional branches. Where necessary, we add additional dummy basic blocks which branch back to the loop entry. This allows operations to move across the loop entry without necessarily becoming speculative. Part (a) of figure 2 shows the transformed CFG. Note that in our notation, a control flow edge that continues in a straight line represents the fall through path, while a curved control flow edge represents the taken path of a conditional branch.

Figure 1 shows that the operation $x = f(x)$ should be shifted. The loop entry is a join point in the CFG, with two incoming edges. Moving the op above this join will leave it just before the loop entry, and create a compensation copy just before the goto at the end of the loop, as in part (b). The operation $cc = test1(x)$ is moved in the same way going from part(b) to part (c). Moving from (c) to (d), the operation $x = g(x, y)$ moves speculatively above *if cc1* and out of the loop. The register x is live at this point, however, so the target register of the operation is renamed to x'. A copy operation is added at the original point in the CFG to copy x' to x, should that path be followed.

Part (e) considers the operation $cc2 = test2(x)$. This operation is on both paths but should only be shifted once on path1. On path2, it can stay in the current iteration. Moving the operation along path1, it first crosses the join point. This creates a compensation copy on path2, just above the join. A further compensation copy is created at the end of the loop, when the operation moves across the loop entry.

Finally, part (f) shows how the operation $x = f(x)$ is shifted a second time on path1. This creates a compensation copy for both joins that the operation moves across. A renaming copy operation is also needed. This operation is not shifted again on path2, since our original calculations (see figure 1) showed that it should be shifted only once on that path.

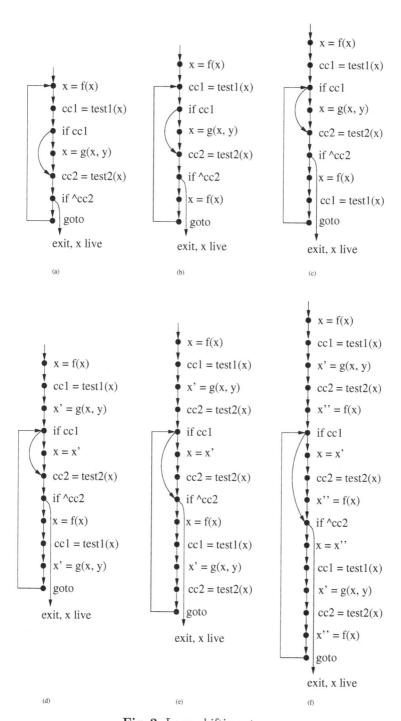

Fig. 2. Loop shifting steps

3.4 Acyclic Scheduling

Once shifting is complete, the resulting loop body is scheduled. We use a conventional DAG scheduling algorithm based on Selective Scheduling [ME97]. Any global scheduling algorithm such as trace scheduling can be used, but a general DAG approach allows operations from all paths to be scheduled together, making it more likely that the MII will be reached on all paths.

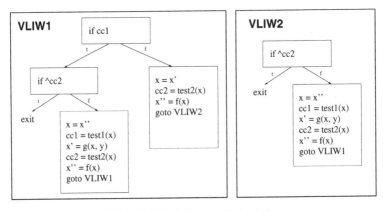

Fig. 3. Final Kernel Schedule

The final schedule for the example loop kernel appears in figure 3. The loop has been compacted into two VLIWs. The machine model is IBM's Tree VLIW, where a VLIW consists of a tree shaped control flow graph of operations. Only those operations on the path through the tree that is followed at run time are allowed to write their results back to the register file. No data dependences are allowed between operations in the same VLIW[2]. When path1 is followed, the machine repeatedly executes *VLIW1*, and achieves an II of one. When control moves to path2, the machine alternates between executing *VLIW1* and *VLIW2*, yielding an II of two.

Our approach is not limited to the Tree VLIW architecture, however. The two main features of the Tree VLIW are multi-way branching and conditional write-back. Architectures which allow only two way branching can be modeled by allowing only a single branch per VLIW. Conditional write-back can be modeled with predication, or by simply moving the operations in the VLIW above all branches in the VLIW.

---

[2] An exception to this general rule is with copy operations. An operation may read a register that is written by a copy operation in the same VLIW. These dependences on copy operations can easily be removed in a final pass over the VLIWs [ME97]

4   Experimental Results

We implemented Iteration Preselection in the Chameleon Compiler and ILP test-bed. Chameleon provides a highly optimizing ILP compiler for IBM's Tree VLIW architecture. The compiler performs many sophisticated traditional and ILP increasing optimizations. For comparison, we also implemented a version of Enhanced Pipeline Scheduling[3] with window size 16. Both algorithms used the same acyclic scheduling scheme. We compiled and scheduled benchmark programs whose inner loops contain branches and ran them on Chameleon's VLIW machine simulator.

The Chameleon compiler uses an existing C compiler (in our case *gcc*) as a front end to generate the original sequential machine code. The baseline for our speedup calculation is the number of cycles it takes to run this code on a simulated one ALU VLIW machine. This sequential code is then optimised to increase ILP, rescheduled by our software pipelining phase, and registers are re-allocated. We run this scheduled code on a machine simulator with the correct number of ALUs to calculate the number of cycles taken. The speedup is the baseline cycles, divided by the number needed for the relevant VLIW.

Benchmark	Description
wc	Unix word count utility
eight	Solve eight queens problem
bubble	Bubble sort array of random integers
bsearch	Binary search sorted array
eqn	Inner loop of eqntott

The purpose of the EPS limited scheduling window is not always understood. It exists to reduce the greediness of EPS scheduling and so *increase* the speedup while reducing code growth, register pressure and compilation time. The paper [NE93] examines the effect of varying the window size, and established 16 as a good size for balancing greediness against scheduling freedom. Our own experiments confirm this finding. In no case does increasing the window size to 32 give any but the most minor increase in speedup. Decreasing the window size below 16 usually reduces the speedup except in the case of bubble, where it sometimes produces faster code.

The speedup results for Iteration Preslection are very encouraging. Clearly, our non-greedy heuristics are shifting operations sufficiently, but no more. Our algorithm does better by preserving VLIW slots for operations which need to execute early. The only exceptions 8-ALU bubble and eqn, where our algorithm performs a lot of shifting to make a very low II achievable. The acyclic scheduler fails to pack the instructions into a schedule that length. It appears that in

---

[3] Our version does not use the original EPS register allocation scheme. Our scheduling window is also implemented slightly differently

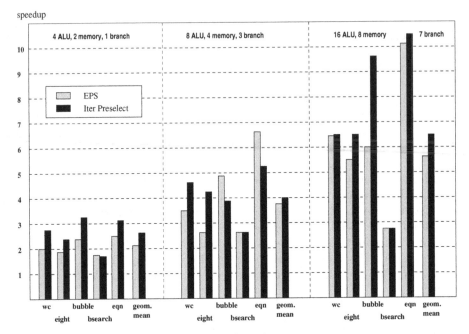

Fig. 4. Speedup

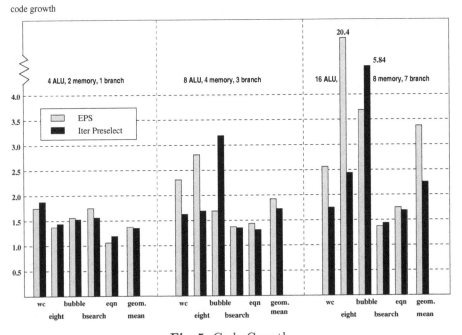

Fig. 5. Code Growth

these cases the resource MII that we compute is too optimistic in the presence of multiple paths. In general, however, iteration preselection performs better than EPS.

Iteration Preslection also controls code growth well. Again, our non-greedy strategy reduces both the size of the loop prolog and code growth from moving operations through the loop while shifting. The difference is most notable on the larger machines, where EPS's greedy scheduling combined with abundant resources place little limit on the code growth[4]. Where Iteration Preselection produces more code growth, it is normally the result of producing a pipeline with lower average II, and significant speedup. Smaller code size should also lead to faster execution time on machines with caches. We intend to demonstrate this with a cache simulator in future work.

5   Related Work

A large number of algorithms exist for global software pipelining with multiple IIs. Unrolling kernel recognition algorithms [AN90] are theoretically very powerful. In practice, however, they cause enormous code growth and their controlling heuristics restrict their power [NN97]. Several algorithms use code duplication to separate all paths in the loop and pipeline each separately. Again, the code growth from code duplication and cross paths can be huge [SM98]. A number of other strategies exist which trade code growth for restrictions on the attainable II [WPP95,SL96].

A number of DESP [WE93] algorithms exist. These algorithms use a similar strategy as ours for TTS numbers for the strongly connected components in the dependence graph. But they differ substantially in the placement of other operations. In addition to minimising the dependence length of the loop body, they also seek to remove restrictions on the acyclic scheduler. These DESP algorithms to shift operations very many times to try to convert acyclic dependences to loop carried ones. A global version of the original DESP algorithm has been proposed, but it assumes a fixed II when calculating the number of times to shift an operation, and treats control dependences as data dependences. The most recent work on GDESP separates all paths before pipelining.

EPS++ is an unpublished algorithm developed by IBM's VLIW group. This algorithm uses a non-greedy, as late as possible, acyclic scheduling algorithm for EPS. In a single path loop, this will place the operation in the same iteration as our approach. A modulo schedule is computed for the most commonly followed path, and the heights of operations are adjusted to ensure that the scheduling algorithm will place those operations in the cycle designated by the modulo

---

[4] The program *eight* is a particularly bad pathological case for EPS, combining a loop with a large initial acyclic height and a number of branches which can be scheduled almost arbitrarily early.

schedule. Software pipelining of other paths is only allowed in so far as it does not interfere with the most common path[5].

Recent work [DH99] on loop shifting by circuit re-timing has yielded fascinating theoretical results for single path loops. We do not believe this research is applicable to our work, however, since it seeks to shift operations much more than necessary. We also remain convinced that loop shifting is not the best strategy for local software pipelining. Unless a loop contains branches, modulo scheduling is likely to produce better results.

6   Conclusions and Future Work

We have presented a new decomposed algorithm for global software pipelining general purpose integer code. Our algorithm allows a variable II and speculative scheduling, while controlling code growth. We have demonstrated that the DESP framework is very suited to global software pipelining. In fact, the true potential of DESP seems to be in pipelining loops containing branches, rather than local software pipelining which already has many good solutions. The implementation of our algorithm shows that when compared with EPS it generally achieves better speedups or less code growth or both.

An open problem remains with operations which fall on several paths. Conflicting TTS numbers for different paths may cause poor scheduling decisions. Our future work will look at other strategies for choosing the TTS in this situation. We believe, however, that our experimental results show that the existing strategy is very successful for the programs tested.

Acknowledgments

We would like to thank the VLIW group at IBM's T. J. Watson Research Center for providing us with the Chameleon experimental test-bed. Special thanks to Mayan Moudgill and Michael Gschwind. Thanks also to Sylvain Lelait and Anton Ertl for their comments on this paper.

This research was supported by the Austrian Science Foundation (FWF).

References

AN90.   Alexander Aiken and Alexandru Nicolau. A realistic resource-constrained software pipelining algorithm. *Advances in Languages and Compilers for Parallel Computing*, pages 274–290, 1990. 199

CYS98.   Gang Chen, Cliff Young, and Michael Smith. Practical and profitable alternatives to greedy, single-path scheduling. Harvard University. Submitted to MICRO 31, November 1998. 192

---

[5] Initial experiments show that EPS++ produces similar or better results than ours, when execution of a loop is dominated by one path, and when EPS++ successfully identifies that path. Where this is not true, as in wc and bubble, EPS++ performs worse.

DH99.   Alain Darte and Guillaume Huard. Loop shifting for loop compaction. Technical report, Ecole Normale Sup/'erieure de Lyon, 1999. 189, 200

Jai91.   S. Jain. Circular scheduling: A new technique to perform software pipelining. In *SIGPLAN 91 Conference on Programming Language Design and Implementation*, pages 219–228, June 1991. 189, 190

Lam88.   Monica Lam. Software pipelining: An efficient scheduling technique for VLIW machines. In *Proceedings of the SIGPLAN 88 Symposium on Programming Language Design and Implementation*, pages 318–328. ACM, June 1988. 192

ME97.   S. Moon and K. Ebcioğlu. Parallelisizing nonnumerical code with selective scheduling and software pipelining. *ACM Transactions on Programming Languages and Systems*, 19(6):853–898, November 1997. 189, 190, 192, 196

NE93.   Toshio Nakatani and Kemal Ebcioğlu. Making compaction-based parallelization affordable. *IEEE Transactions on Parallel and Distributed Systems*, 4(9):1014–1029, September 1993. 197

NN97.   Steve Novack and Alexandru Nicolau. Resource directed loop pipelining: Exposing just enough parallelism. *The Computer Journal*, 10(6), 1997. 189, 190, 199

Rau94.   B. Ramakrishna Rau. Iterative modulo scheduling: An algorithm for software pipelining loops. In *27th Annual International Conference on Microarchitecture*. ACM, December 1994. 189

SL96.   M. Stoodley and C. Lee. Software pipelining of loops with conditional branches. In *29th International Symposium on Microarchitecture (MICRO-29)*, pages 262–273. IEEE/ACM, December 1996. 199

SM98.   SangMin Shim and Soo-Mook Moon. Split-path enhanced pipeline scheduling for loops with control flows. In *Micro 31*, pages 290–302. ACM/IEEE, November 1998. 199

WE93.   Jian Wang and Christine Eisenbeis. Decomposed software pipelinig. Rapports de Recherche 1838, INRIA Rocquencourt, F - 79153 Le Chesnay Cedex, January 1993. 191, 199

WPP95. Nancy J. Warter-Perez and Noubar Partamnian. Modulo scheduling with multiple initiation intervals. In *28th Annual International Conference on Microarchitecture*, pages 111–118. ACM, December 1995. 199

Analysis of Irregular Single-Indexed Array Accesses and Its Applications in Compiler Optimizations

Yuan Lin and David Padua

Department of Computer Science, University of Illinois at Urbana-Champaign
{yuanlin,padua}@uiuc.edu

Abstract. Many compiler techniques require analysis of array subscripts to determine whether a transformation is legal. Traditional methods require the array subscript expressions to be expressed as closed-form expressions of loop indices. Most methods further require the subscript expressions to be linear. However, in sparse/ irregular programs, closed-form expressions of array subscripts are not available. More powerful methods to analyze array subscripts are needed. Array accesses with no closed-form expressions available are called irregular array accesses. In real programs, many irregular array accesses are single-indexed. In this paper, we present techniques to analyze irregular single-indexed array accesses. We show that single-indexed array accesses often have properties that are useful in compiler analysis. We discuss how to use these properties to enhance compiler optimizations. We also demonstrate the application of these techniques in three real-life programs to exploit more implicit parallelism.

1 Introduction

Many compiler techniques, such as loop parallelization and optimizations, need analysis of array subscripts to determine whether a transformation is legal. Traditional methods require the array subscript expressions to be expressed as closed-form expressions of loop indices. Furthermore, most methods require the subscript expression to be linear. However, in many programs, especially sparse/irregular programs, closed-form expressions of array subscripts are not available, and many codes are left unoptimized. Clearly, more powerful methods to analyze array subscripts are needed.

For example, array privatization [9,13,17,19] is an important technique in loop parallelization. An array can be privatized if any array element that is read in one iteration of a loop is always first defined in the same iteration. For example, in the outermost do k loop in Fig.1, array $x()$ is first defined in the repeat-until loop, and then is read in the do j loop. Any element of $x()$ read in statement (2) is first defined in statement (1) in the same iteration of the do k loop. Therefore, array $x()$ can be privatized for the do k loop, and the do k loop can be parallelized. Current techniques can determine that section $[1 : p]$

A. Watt (Ed.): CC/ETAPS 2000, LNCS 1781, pp. 202–218, 2000.
© Springer-Verlag Berlin Heidelberg 2000

```
i = 1
do k=1, n
    p = 0
    i = link(i,k)
    repeat
        p = p + 1
        x(p) = y(i)            (1)
        i = link(i,k)
    until ( i == 0 )
    do j=1, p
        z(k,j) = x(j)          (2)
    end do
end do
```

Fig. 1. An example of a loop with an irregular single-indexed array

of array $x()$ is read in the do j loop, but they cannot determine that the same section also is written in the repeat-until loop because no closed-form expression for index variable p can be derived. Therefore, they fail to privatize $x()$.

In this paper, we introduce the notion of *irregular single-indexed array access*. An array access is *irregular* in a loop if no closed-form expression for the subscript of the array access in terms of loop indices is available. An array access is *single-indexed* in a loop if the array is always subscripted by the same index variable in the loop. An array access is *irregular single-indexed* in a loop if the array access is both irregular and single-indexed in the loop . For example, the access of array $x()$ in the repeat-until loop in Fig.1 is an irregular single-indexed access.

We chose to investigate irregular single-indexed array accesses for several reasons. First, in the programs we have studied, the single-indexed array accesses often follow a few patterns. These array accesses exhibit properties that are useful in compiler optimizations. Second, many irregular array accesses are single-indexed. Developing analysis methods for irregular single-indexed array accesses is a practical approach toward the analysis of general irregular array accesses, which is believed to be difficult. Third, it is easy to check whether an array access is single-indexed. Efficient algorithms can be developed to "filter" single-indexed array accesses out of general irregular array accesses.

In this paper, we present two important patterns of irregular single-indexed array accesses: *consecutively-written* and *stack-access*. We present the techniques to detect these two patterns and show how to use the properties that irregular single-indexed array accesses have to enhance compiler optimizations.

Throughout the rest of this paper, we will use "single-indexed array access" and "irregular single-indexed array access" interchangeably.

2   Consecutively Written Arrays

An array is *consecutively written* in a loop if, during the execution of the loop, all the elements in a contiguous section of the array are written in a non-increasing or a non-decreasing order. For example, in the repeat-until loop in Fig.1, array element $x(2)$ is not written until $x(1)$ is written, $x(3)$ is not written until $x(2)$ is written, and so on. Array $x()$ is written consecutively in the $1, 2, 3, \ldots$ order in the loop.

To be concise, in this paper, we consider only arrays that are consecutively written in the non-decreasing order. It is trivial to extend the techniques to handle the non-increasing cases as well.

2.1   Algorithm for Detecting Consecutively Written Arrays

In this section, we present an algorithm that tests whether a single-indexed array is consecutively written in a loop.

Since we are dealing with irregular array accesses, we must consider not only do loops, but also other kinds of loops, such as while loops and repeat until loops. In general, we consider natural loops [1]. A natural loop has a single entry node, called the *header*. The header dominates all nodes in the loop. A natural loop can have multiple exits, which are the nodes that lead the control flow to nodes not belonging to the loop.

Before we present the algorithm, we first describe a *bounded depth-first search* (bDFS) method, which is used several times in this paper.

The bDFS is shown in Fig.2. A bDFS does a depth-first search on a graph (V, E), where V is the set of vertices and E is the set of edges in the graph. bDFS uses three auxiliary functions ($f_{bound}()$, $f_{failed}()$, and $f_{proc}()$) to change its behavior during the search. The auxiliary functions are defined before the search starts. $f_{bound}()$ maps V to $(true, false)$. Suppose the current node is n_0, if $f_{bound}(n_0)$ is *true*, then bDFS does not search the nodes adjacent to n_0. The nodes whose $f_{bound}()$ values are *true* are the boundaries of the search. $f_{failed}()$ also maps V to $(true, false)$. If, for the current node n_0, $f_{failed}(n_0)$ is *true*, then the whole bDFS terminates with a return value of *failed*. The nodes whose $f_{failed}()$ values are *true* cause an early termination of the bDFS. $f_{proc}()$ does not have a return value; it does predefined computations for the current node.

Now we can show the algorithm that detects consecutively written arrays.

- **Input:** a loop L with header h and a set of exit nodes $(t_1, t_2, ..., t_n)$, a single-indexed array $x()$ in the loop, and the index variable p of $x()$.
- **Output:** answer to the question whether $x()$ is consecutively written in L.
- **Steps:**
  1. Find all the definition statements of p in the loop. If any of them are not of the form "$p = p + 1$", then return NO. Otherwise, put the definition statements in a list lst.

```
            bDFS(u)
1               visited[u] := true ;
2               f_proc(u) ;
3               if (not f_bound(u)) {
4                   for each adjacent node v of u {
5                       if (f_failed(v))
6                           return failed ;
7                       if ((not visited[v]) and (bDFS(v) == failed))
8                           return failed ;
9                   }
10              }
11              return succeeded ;
            Before the search starts, visited[] is set to false for all nodes.
```

Fig. 2. Bounded depth-first search

2. For each statement n in lst, do a bDFS on the control flow graph from n using the following auxiliary functions:

$$f_{bound}(n) = \begin{cases} true, \text{ if } n \text{ is "}x() = ..\text{"} \\ false, \text{ otherwise} \end{cases}, f_{failed}(n) = \begin{cases} true, \text{ if } n \text{ is "}p = p+1\text{"} \\ false, \text{ otherwise} \end{cases}$$

$$f_{proc}(n) = NULL$$

If any of the bDFSs returns $failed$, then return NO. Otherwise, return YES.

The algorithm starts by checking whether the index variable is ever defined in any way other than being increased by 1. If it is, we assume the array is not consecutively written. Step 2 checks whether in the control flow graph there exists a path from one "$p = p+1$" statement to another "$p = p+1$" statement[1] and the array $x()$ is not written on the path. If such a path exists, then there may be "holes" in the section where the array is defined and, therefore, the array is not consecutively written in the section. For example, the array $x()$ is consecutively written in Fig. 3.(a), but is not in Fig. 3.(b). The algorithm allows an array element to be written multiple times before the index variable is increased by 1.

2.2   Applications

Dependence Test and Parallelization Suppose a single-indexed write-only array $x()$ with index variable p is consecutively written in a loop, where the assignments of p are of the form "$p = p + 1$". If there does not exist a path from one "$x() = ..$" assignment to another "$x() = ..$" assignment such that the loop header is on the path, but there is no "$p = p+1$" statement on the path,

---

[1] These two statements can be the same statement, in which case the path is a circle.

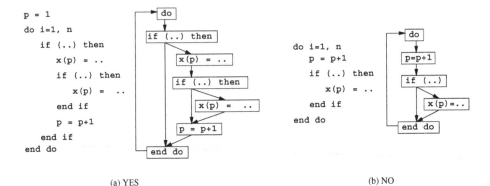

(a) YES   (b) NO

Fig. 3. Consecutively written or not?

```
do i=1, n                    do j=1, n
  x(p) = ..                    x(p) = ..     (1)
  p = p + 1                    p = p + 1
end do                         x(p) = ..     (2)
                             end do
```

Fig. 4. Data dependence for consecutively written arrays

then $x()$ does not cause any loop-carried dependence in the loop. For example, although array $x()$ is consecutively written in both loops in Fig. 4, there is no dependence between different instances of the access of $x()$ in the loop do i, but there is a loop-carried output dependence between statement (1) and (2) in loop do j.

This kind of dependence can be detected by using the following method. Here, we assume $x()$ is write-only and found consecutively written with the method described in the previous section.

1. Using the following auxiliary functions, do a bDFS on the control flow graph from the loop header, where the value of $tag1$ is initially set to $null$,

$$f_{bound}(n) = \begin{cases} true, & \text{if } n \text{ is "}x()=..\text{"} \\ & \text{or "}p = p + 1\text{"} \\ false, & \text{otherwise} \end{cases}, f_{failed}(n) = \begin{cases} true, & \text{if } tag1 \text{ is } asgn \\ false, & \text{otherwise} \end{cases}$$

$$f_{proc}(n) = \begin{cases} \text{set } tag1 \text{ to } asgn, & \text{if } n \text{ is "}x() = ..\text{"} \\ \text{set } tag1 \text{ to } incr, & \text{if } n \text{ is "}p = p + 1\text{" and } tag1 \text{ is } null \\ \text{do nothing, otherwise} \end{cases}$$

   If $tag1$ is $incr$ after the bDFS, then there is no dependence; otherwise, goto step 2.

2. Using the same auxiliary functions as in the previous step, do a bDFS on the reversed control flow graph from the loop header, with $tag1$ being replaced with $tag2$. If, after the bDFS, both $tag1$ and $tag2$ are $asgn$, then there is loop-carried output dependence for $x()$; otherwise, there is no such dependence.

Sequential version:

```
    k = k0
    do i = 1, n
        while (..) do
            a(k) = ..
            k = k+1
        end while
    end do
```

(a)

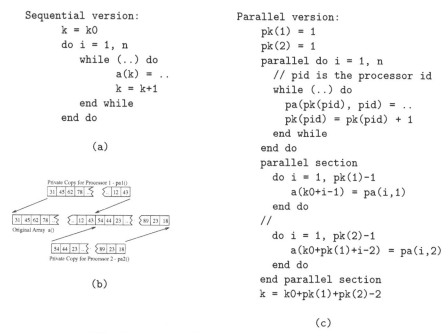

(b)

Parallel version:

```
    pk(1) = 1
    pk(2) = 1
    parallel do i = 1, n
        // pid is the processor id
        while (..) do
            pa(pk(pid), pid) = ..
            pk(pid) = pk(pid) + 1
        end while
    end do
    parallel section
        do i = 1, pk(1)-1
            a(k0+i-1) = pa(i,1)
        end do
    //
        do i = 1, pk(2)-1
            a(k0+pk(1)+i-2) = pa(i,2)
        end do
    end parallel section
    k = k0+pk(1)+pk(2)-2
```

(c)

Fig. 5. An example of *array splitting and merging*

In order to parallelize the loop with single-indexed and consecutively written arrays, we also need to eliminate the flow dependence caused by the index variable. If the index variable is not used anywhere other than in the array subscript and the increment-by-1 statements, then the *array splitting-and-merging* method [14] can be used to parallelize the enclosing loop.

Array splitting and merging consists of three phases. First, a private copy of the consecutively written array is allocated on each processor. Then, all the processors work on their private copies from position 1 in parallel. After the computation, each processor knows the number of array elements of its private copy that are written in the loop; hence, the starting position in the original array for each processor can be calculated by using the parallel prefix method. Finally, the private copies are copied back (merged) to the original array. Figure 5 shows an example when two processors are used.

Privatization Test As we have illustrated at the beginning of this paper, with consecutively written array analysis, we can extend the privatization test to process irregular single-indexed arrays and more general loops.

Suppose a single-indexed array $x()$ with index variable p is found consecutively written in a loop by using the method described in the previous section, we can use the following two steps to calculate the section of $x()$ written in the loop.

1. Using the following auxiliary functions, do a bDFS on the control flow graph from the loop header h, where the value of $tag1$ is initially set to $null$:

$$f_{bound}(n) = \begin{cases} true, & \text{if } n \text{ is ``}x() = ..\text{'' and } tag1 \text{ is } asgn \\ true, & \text{if } n \text{ is ``}p = p+1\text{'' and } tag1 \text{ is } incr \\ false, & \text{otherwise} \end{cases}$$

$$f_{failed}(n) = \begin{cases} true, & \text{if } n \text{ is ``}x() = ..\text{'' and } tag1 \text{ is } incr \\ true, & \text{if } n \text{ is ``}p = p+1\text{'' and } tag1 \text{ is } asgn \\ false, & \text{otherwise} \end{cases}$$

$$f_{proc}(n) = \begin{cases} \text{set } tag1 \text{ to } asgn, \text{ if } n \text{ is ``}x() = ..\text{'' and } tag1 \text{ is } null \\ \text{set } tag1 \text{ to } incr, \text{ if } n \text{ is ``}p = p+1\text{'' and } tag1 \text{ is } null \\ \text{do nothing, otherwise} \end{cases}$$

If the bDFS returns a $failed$, then set $tag1$ to $null$.
2. Using the same auxiliary functions as in the previous step, do a bDFS on the reversed control flow graph from each of the exit nodes (including the loop header), with $tag1$ being replaced with $tag2$. If any of the bDFSs returns a $failed$, then set $tag2$ to $null$.
3. The section where $x()$ is written in the loop is $[lower, upper]$, where

$$lower = \begin{cases} p_0, & \text{if } tag1 \text{ is } asn \\ p_0 + 1, & \text{if } tag1 \text{ is } incr \\ unknown, & \text{otherwise,} \end{cases}, upper = \begin{cases} p, & \text{if } tag2 \text{ is } asn \\ p - 1, & \text{if } tag2 \text{ is } incr \\ unknown, & \text{otherwise.} \end{cases}$$

and p_0 is the value of p before entering the loop.

For example, the section of $x()$ written in the loop in Fig. 3.(a) is $[1, p - 1]$. The section of $z()$ written in the loop in Fig. 6.(a) is $[unknown, p]$, and that of $y()$ in Fig. reffig:section.(b) is $[1, unknown]$.

Index Array Property Analysis The *indirectly accessed array* is another kind of irregular array. An array is indirectly accessed if its subscript is another array, such as $x()$ in statement "$x(ind(i)) = ..$". $x()$ is called the *host array*, and $ind()$ is

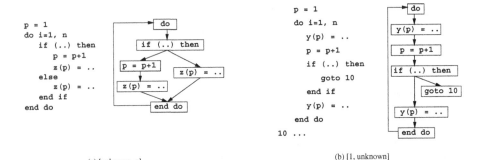

(a) [unknown, p]   (b) [1, unknown]

Fig. 6. The section of consecutively written array

```
do k = 1, n                           do i = 1,  n
   q = 0                                 p = 1
   do i = 1, p                           t(p) = ...
      if ( x(i) > 0 ) then               loop
         q = q + 1                          p = p + 1
         ind(q) = i                         t(p) = ...
      end if                              if (...) then
   end do                                   loop
   do j = 1, q                                if (p>=1) then
      jj = ind(j)                               ... = t(p)
      z(k,jj) = x(jj) * y(jj)                    p = p - 1
   end do                                     end if
end do                                      end loop
                                          end if
                                        end loop
                                     end do
```

Fig. 7. An example of a loop with an   **Fig. 8.** An example of an array stack
inner index gathering loop

called the *index array*. Traditional techniques cannot handle indirectly accessed
arrays. However, recent studies [5,14] have shown that index arrays often have
simple properties, which can be used to produce more accurate analysis of host
arrays. An *array property analysis* method has been developed to check whether
an index array has any of these key properties [15].

Consecutively written array analysis can be used to find the properties an
index array has in the array property analysis. For example, two of the key
properties are *injectivity* and *closed-form bounds*. An array section is injective
if any two different array elements in the section do not have the same value.
An array section has closed-form bounds if the lower bound and upper bound
of the values of array elements in the section can be expressed by closed-form
expressions. Detecting whether an array section has any of the two properties
is difficult, in general. However, in many cases, we only need to check whether
the array section is defined in an *index gathering loop*, such as the do i loop in
Fig.7.

In Fig.7, the indices of the positive elements of array $x()$ are gathered in
array $ind()$. After the gathering loop is executed, all the array elements in section
$ind[1 : q]$ are defined, the values of the array elements in array section $ind[1 : q]$
are injective, the lower bound of the values of the array elements in section
$ind[1 : q]$ is 1, and the upper bound is q.

With this information available at compile-time, the compiler is now able to
determine that there is no data dependence in the do j loop, and array $ind()$
can be privatized in the do k loop. Thus, the compiler can choose either to
parallelize the do k loop only, parallelize the do j loop only, parallelize both,

or parallelize the do k loop and vectorize the do j loop, depending upon the architecture for which the code is generated.

An index gathering loop for an index array has the following characteristics:

1. the loop is a do loop,
2. the index array is single-indexed in the loop,
3. the index array is consecutively written in the loop,
4. the right-hand side of any assignment to the index array is the loop index
5. one assignment to the index array cannot reach another assignment to the index array without first reaching the do loop header.

The fifth condition above ensures that the same loop index value is not assigned twice to the elements of the index array. This condition can be verified using a bDFS. After an index gathering loop, the values assigned to the index array in the loop are injective, and the range of the values assigned is bounded by the range of the do loop bound.

3   Array Stack

The stack is a very basic data structure. Many programs implement stacks using arrays because it is both simple and efficient. We call stacks implemented in arrays *array stacks*. Figure 8 illustrates an array stack. In the body of the do i loop, array $t()$ is used as a stack, and variable p is used as the stack pointer which always points to the top of the stack.

3.1   Algorithm for Detecting Array Stacks

In this section, we present an algorithm that checks whether a single-indexed array is used as a stack in a program region. A region [1] is a subset of the control flow graph that includes a header, which dominates all the other nodes in the region.

To be concise, we consider program regions in which the single index variable p is defined only in one of the following three ways:

1. $p := p + 1$,
2. $p := p - 1$, or
3. $p := C_{bottom}$, where C_{bottom} is an invariant in the program region.

We check whether a single-indexed array is used as a stack in a region by checking whether the statements involved in the array operations appear in some particular orders. These orders are shown in Table 3.1.

The left column and the top row in Table 3.1 give the statements to be checked. If there is a path in the control flow graph from a statement of the form shown in the left column of the table to a statement of the form shown in the top row, then the statement in the corresponding central entry of the table must be on the path. For example, if there is a path from a statement "$x(p) = ..$" to another statement "$x(p) = ..$", then before the control flow researches the

Table 1. Order for access of array stacks

	$p = p+1$	$p = p-1$	$x(p) = ..$	$.. = x(p)$	$p = C_{bottom}$
$p = p+1$	$x(p) = ..$	$.. = x(p)$	-	$x(p) = ..$	-
$p = p-1$	-	$.. = x(p)$	$p = p+1$	G	-
$x(p) = ..$	-	$.. = x(p)$	$p = p+1$	-	-
$.. = x(p)$	$p = p-1$	-	$p = p+1$	$p = p+1$	-

second "$x(p) = ..$" statement, it must first reach a "$p = p+1$" statement. A '-' in a table entry means there is no restriction on what kind of statement must be on the path. The 'G' represents an if statement that is "$if (p \geq C_{bottom}) then$".

Intuitively, we want to ensure that for an array stack $x()$ with index p, (1) p is first set to C_{bottom} before it is modified or used in the subscript of $x()$, (2) the value of p never goes below C_{bottom}, and (3) the access of elements of $x()$ follows the "last-written-first-read" pattern.

Table 3.1 can be simplified to Table 3.1. Any path originating from a node n of the forms in the left column of Table 3.1 must first reach any node of the forms in $S_{bound}(n)$ before it reaches any node of the forms in $S_{failed}(n)$.

Next, we present the algorithm to detect array stacks.

- **Input:** a program region R with header h, a single-indexed array $x()$ in the region, and the index variable p of $x()$.
- **Output:** answer to the question whether $x()$ is used as a stack in R. And, if the answer is YES, the minimum value C_{bottom} the index variable p can have in the region.
- **Steps:**
  1. Find all the definition statements of p in R. If any are not of a form in the set $\{p = p+1, p = p-1, p = C_{bottom}\}$ (if there are multiple "$p = C_{bottom}$" statements, the C_{bottom} must be the same), where C_{bottom} is invariant in R, then return NO. Otherwise, put the definition statements in a list lst. If there are no statements of the form "$p = C_{bottom}$", then find all if statements of the form "$if (p \geq C_{if}) then$". If all C_{if}'s are the same, set C_{bottom} to C_{if}; otherwise, return NO. If no such if statement is found, set C_{bottom} to $unknown$.

Table 2. Simplified order for array stacks

n	$S_{bound}(n)$	$S_{failed}(n)$
$p = p+1$	$\{x(p) = .., p = C_{bottom}\}$	$\{p = p+1, p = p-1,.. = x(p)\}$
$p = p-1$	$\{p = p+1, G, p = C_{bottom}\}$	$\{p = p-1, x(p) = .., .. = x(p)\}$
$x(p) = ..$	$\{p = p+1, .. = x(p), p = C_{bottom}\}$	$\{p = p-1, x(p) = ..\}$
$.. = x(p)$	$\{p = p-1, p = C_{bottom}\}$	$\{p = p+1, x(p) = .., .. = x(p)\}$

2. Find all the "$x(p) = ..$" and "$.. = x(p)$" statements in R, and add them to lst.
3. For each statement m in lst, do a bDFS on the control flow graph from this statement using the following auxiliary functions:

$$f_{bound}(n) = \begin{cases} true & n \in S_{bound}(m) \\ false & \text{otherwise} \end{cases}, f_{failed}(n) = \begin{cases} true & n \in S_{failed}(m) \\ false & \text{otherwise} \end{cases}$$

$$f_{proc}(n) = NULL$$

If any of the bDFSs returns a $failed$, then return NO. Otherwise, return YES and C_{bottom}.

3.2 Applications

Run-Time Array Bound Checking Elimination Run-time array bound checking is used to detect array bound violations. The compiler inserts bound checking codes for array references. At run-time, an error is reported if an array subscript expression equals a value that is not within the declared bounds of the array. Some languages, such as Pascal, Ada and Java, mandate array bound checking. Array bound checking also is useful in testing and debugging programs written in other languages. Since most references in computationally intense loops are to arrays, these checks cause a significant amount of overhead.

When an array is used as a stack in a program region, the amount of array bound checking for the stack array can be reduced by 50%. Only the upper bound checkings are preserved. The lower bound checking is performed only once before the header of the program region. Elimination of unnecessary array bound checking also has been studied by Markstein et al [16], Gupta [11], and Kolte and Wolfe [12]. Gupta and Spezialetti [18] proposed a method to find monotonically increasing/decreasing index variables, which also can be used to eliminate the checking by half. But, their method cannot handle array stacks, which are more irregular.

Privatization Test Array stack analysis also can improve the precision of array privatization tests. Here, we consider the loop body as a program region. When an array is used as a stack in the body of a loop, the array elements are always defined ("pushed") before being used ("popped") in the region. If C_{bottom} is a loop invariant, then different iterations of the loop will reuse the same array elements, and the value of the array elements never flow from one iteration to the other. Therefore, array stacks in a loop body can be privatized. For example, the array stack $t()$ in Fig.8 can be privatized in the outermost the do i loop.

Loop Interchanging Loop interchanging [2,20] is the single most important loop restructuring transformation. It has been used to find vectorizable loops, to change the granularity of parallelism, and to improve memory locality. Loop interchanging changes the order of nested loops. It is not always legal to perform loop interchanging since data dependence cannot be violated. Data dependence tests must be performed before loop interchanging.

Traditionally, loop interchanging is not possible when array stacks are present because current data dependence tests cannot handle irregular arrays. However, as in the privatization test, array stacks cause no loop carried dependences. If the index variables of array stacks are not used in any statements other than stack access statements, then the data dependence test can safely assume no dependence between the stack access statements. The loop interchanging test then can ignore the presence of array stacks and use traditional methods to test other arrays. By using array stack analysis, we have extended the application domain of loop interchanging.

4 Related Work

There are two closely related studies done by two groups of researchers. M. Wolfe [21] and M. Gerlek, E. Stoltz, and M. Wolfe [10] presented an algorithm to recognize and classify *sequence variables* in a loop. Different kinds of sequence variables are linear induction variables, periodic, polynomial, geometric, monotonic, and wrap-around variables. Their algorithm is based on a demand-driven representation of the Static Single Assignment form [7,6]. The sequence variables can be detected and classified in a unified way by finding strongly connected components of the associated SSA graph.

R. Gupta and M. Spezialetti [18] have extended the traditional data-flow approach to detect "monotonic" statements. A statement is monotonic in a loop if, during the execution of the loop, the statement assigns a monotonically increasing or decreasing sequence of values to a variable. They also show the application of their analysis in run-time array bound checking, dependence analysis, and run-time detection of access anomalies.

The major difference between both these studies and ours is that we focus on arrays while they focus on index variables. While both of their methods can recognize the index variable for a consecutively written array as a monotonic variable, if the array is defined in more than one statement, then none of them can detect whether the array itself is consecutively written. For example, Gerlek, Stoltz and Wolfe's method can find that the two instances of variable k in statements (1) and (2) in Fig.9 have a strictly increasing sequence of values. Gupta and Spezialetti's method can classify statements (1) and (2) as monotonic. However, neither can determine whether the access pattern of the array $x()$ is consecutively written. As for array stack analysis, as the index variable does not have a distinguishable sequence of values, both Gerlek, Stoltz and Wolfe's method and Gupta and Spezialetti's method treat the index variable as a generally irregular variable. Without taking the arrays into the account in their analysis, they can do little in detecting array stacks.

The authors believe it is often important to consider both index variables and arrays. While both of the two other methods can recognize a wide class of scalar variables beyond the variable used as the subscript of single-indexed

```
do i = 1, n
   if ( .. ) then
      x(k) = ..
      k = k + 1              (1)
   else if ( .. ) then
      x(k) = ..
      k = k + 1              (2)
   end if
end do
```

Fig. 9. Both array $x()$ and index k should be analyzed to know that $x()$ is consecutively written.

arrays in our method, they are not necessarily more powerful in analyzing the access pattern of the arrays.

5 Case Studies

In this section, we show how consecutively written array analysis and array stack analysis can be used to enhance the automatic parallelism detection in three real-world programs.

These three programs are summarized in Table 5. Column 3 in Table 5 shows the loops that can be parallelized only after the techniques presented in this paper have been used to analyze the arrays shown in Column 4. Figure 10 shows the difference in speedups when these loops are parallelized. We compare the speedups of the programs generated by our Polaris parallelizing compiler, with and without single-indexed array analysis, and the programs compiled using the automatic parallelizer provided by SGI. The experiments were performed on an SGI Origin2000 machine with 56 195MHz R10000 processors (32KB instruction case, 32KB data cache, 4MB secondary unified level cache) and 14GB memory running IRIX64 6.5. One to thirty-two processors are used for BDNA and TREE. One to eight processors are used for P3M. "APO" means using the "-apo" option when compiling the programs. This option invokes the SGI automatic parallelizer. "Polaris without SIA" means using the Polaris compiler without the single-indexed array analysis. "Polaris with SIA" means using the Polaris compiler with the single-indexed array analysis. As we have not yet implemented array stack analysis in our Polaris compiler, for TREE we show the result of manual parallelization. For all three codes, the speedups of the versions in which the single-index array analysis had been used are much better than those of the other versions.

5.1 BDNA

BDNA is a molecular dynamics simulation code from the PERFECT benchmark suite [8].

Table 3. Three real-life programs

Program Name	Lines of Codes	Major Loops	Single-indexed Arrays	% of Exe. Time
BDNA	4000	$actfor\_do\_240$	$xdt()$	31%
P3M	2500	pp_do_100	$ind0(), jpr()$	74%
		$subpp\_do\_100$	$ind0(), jpr()$	14%
TREE	1600	$accel\_do10$	$stack()$	70%

The do 240 loop in subroutine $ACTFOR$ is a loop that computes the interaction of biomolecules in water. It occupies about 31% of total computation time. The main structure of this loop is outlined in Fig.11

Consecutively written array analysis is used in the do j2 loop to find that elements in $[1, k]$ of $ind()$ are written in this loop. Furthermore, this loop is recognized as an index gathering loop; thus, the values of the elements in $ind[1, k]$ defined in this loop are bounded by $[1, i-1]$. This information is used to privatize array $ind()$ and $xdt()$ in the do i loop, which is then determined to be parallel.

5.2 P3M

P3M is an N-body code that uses the particle-mesh method. This code is from NCSA.

Most of the computation time (about 88% after using vendor provided FFT library) is spent in subroutine pp and $subpp$, whose structures are very similar. The core is a three-perfect-loop nest, which can be parallelized. Before parallelization, several single-indexed arrays in the loop must be privatized. The outline of the core loops is shown in Fig. 12. The simplified loop pattern is similar to that in Fig. 11. The difference is that both $x()$ and $ind()$ are consecutively written arrays here.

5.3 Barnes & Hut TREE Code

The **TREE** code [4] is a program that implements the hierarchical N-body method for simulating the evolution of collisionless systems [3].

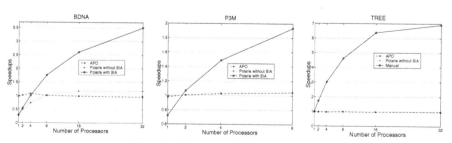

Fig. 10. Comparison of Speedups

```
                      do i1 = 1, n
                      do i2 = 1, n
                      do i3 = 1, n                sptr = 1
do i = 2, n              p = 0                    stack(sptr) = root
   do j1 = 1, i-1        repeat                   while (sptr .gt. 0) do
      xdt(j1) = ..          p = p+1                  q = stack(sptr)
   end do                   x(p) = ..               sptr = sptr - 1
   k = 0                 until (..)                 if (q is a body) then
   do j2 = 1, i-1        k = 0                          process body-body interaction
      if (..) then       do j2 = 1, p                elseif (q is far enough from p) then
         k = k+1            if (..) then                 process body-cell interaction
         ind(k) = j2           k = k+1               else
      end if                   ind(k) = j2              do k = 1, nsubc
   end do                   end if                         if (subp(q,k) .ne. null) then
   do j3 = 1, k          end do                               sptr = sptr + 1
      .. = xdt(ind(j3))  do j3 = 1, k                          stack(sptr) = subp(q,k)
   end do                   .. = x(ind(j3))                 end if
end do                   end do                          end do
                      end do                          end if
                      end do                       end while
                      end do
```

Fig. 11. BDNA   **Fig. 12.** P3M   **Fig. 13.** TREE

The core of the program is a time-centered leap-frog loop, which is inherently sequential. At each time step, it computes the force on each body and updates the velocities and positions. About 70% of the program execution time is spent in the force calculation loop. Each iteration of the force calculation loop computes the gravitational force on a single body p using a tree walk method that is illustrated in Fig.13.

In the tree walk code, single-indexed array *stack* is used as a stack to store tree nodes yet to be visited. Variable *sptr* is used as the stack pointer. As discussed in Sect.3.2, array *stack* can be privatized for the force calculation loop. As there is no other data dependence in the loop, the loop can be parallelized (i.e., the force calculation of the n bodies can be performed in parallel).

6   Conclusion

In this paper, we introduced the notion of irregular single-indexed array access. We described two common patterns of irregular single-indexed array accesses (i.e., consecutively written and stack access) and presented simple and intuitive algorithms to detect these two patterns. More importantly, we showed that array accesses following these two patterns exhibit very important properties. We demonstrated how to use these properties to enhance a variety of compiler analysis and optimization techniques, such as the dependence test, privatization test, array property analysis, loop interchanging, and array bound checking. In the case study, we showed that, for three real-life programs, the speedups of the parallelized versions generated by the Polaris compiler with single-index array access analysis are much better than those of other versions.

Acknowledgments

We wish to thank the anonymous referees for their many useful comments and suggestions. This work is supported in part by Army contract DABT63-95-C-0097; Army contract N66001-97-C-8532; NSF contract NSF ACI98-70687; and a Partnership Award from IBM. This work is not necessarily representative of the positions or policies of the Army or Government. This work also was partially supported by National Computational Science Alliance and utilized the NCSA SGI Origin2000.

References

1. Alfred V. Aho, Ravi Sethi, and Jeffrey D. Ullman. *Compilers: Principles, Techniques, and Tools.* Addison-Wesley Publishing Company, 1986. 204, 210
2. John R. Allen and Ken Kennedy. Automatic loop interchange. In *Proceedings of the SIGPLAN '84 Symposium on Compiler Construction*, pages 233–246, New York, NY 10036, USA, 1984. ACM Press, ACM Press. 212
3. J. Barnes and P. Hut. A hierarchical o(nlogn) force calculation algorithm. *Nature*, 324(4):446–449, 1986. 215
4. Joshua E. Barnes. ftp://hubble.ifa.hawaii.edu/pub/barnes/treecode/. Technical report. 215
5. W. Blume and R. Eigenmann. An overview of symbolic analysis techniques needed for the effective parallelization of the perfect benchmarks. In K. C. Tai, editor, *Proceedings of the 23rd International Conference on Parallel Processing. Volume 2: Software*, pages 233–238, Boca Raton, FL, USA, August 1994. CRC Press. 209
6. Ron Cytron, Jeanne Ferrante, Barry K. Rosen, Mark K. Wegman, and F. Kenneth Zadeck. An efficient method of computing static single assignment form. In *Proceedings of 16th Annual ACM Symposium on Principles of Programming Languages*, pages 25–35, 1989. 213
7. Ron Cytron, Jeanne Ferrante, Barry K. Rosen, Mark N. Wegman, and F. Kenneth Zadeck. Efficiently computing static single assignment form and the control dependence graph. *ACM Transaction on Programming Languages and Systems*, 13(4):451–490, October 1991. 213
8. Mike Berry et.al. The perfect club benchmarks: Effective performance evaluation of supecomputers. *International Journal of Supercomputer Applications*, 3(3):5–40, Fall 1989. 214
9. P. Feautrier. Array expansion. In *Proceedings of the Second International Conference on Supercomputing*, St. Malo, France, July 1988. 202
10. Michael P. Gerlek, Eric Stoltz, and Michael Wolfe. Beyond induction variables: Detecting and classifying sequences using a demand-driven SSA form. *ACM Transactions on Programming Languages and Systems*, 17(1):85–122, January 1995. 213
11. Rajiv Gupta. Optimizing array bound checks using flow analysis. *ACM Letters on Programming Languages and Systems*, 2(1–4):135–150, March–December 1993. 212
12. Priyadarshan Kolte and Michael Wolfe. Elimination of redundant array subscript range checks. *ACM SIGPLAN Notices PLDI 1995*, 30(6):270–278, June 1995. 212
13. Z. Li. Array privatization for parallel execution of loops. In *Proceedings of 1992 International Conference on Supercomputing, July 19–23, 1992, Washington, DC*, pages 313–322, New York, NY 10036, USA, 1992. ACM Press. 202

14. Y. Lin and D. Padua. On the automatic parallelization of sparse and irregular fortran programs. In *Proc. of 4th Workshop on Languages, Compilers, and Runtime Systems for Scalable Computers (LCR98)*, volume 1511 of *Lecture Notes in Computer Science*, pages 41–56. Springer-Verlag, Pittsburgh, PA, 1998. 207, 209

15. Y. Lin and D. Padua. Demand-driven interprocedural array property analysis. In *Proceedings of the 12th International Workshop on Languages and Compilers for Parallel Computing*, San Diego, CA, August 1999. 209

16. Victoria Markstein, John Cocke, and Peter Markstein. Optimization of range checking. In *Proceedings of the SIGPLAN '82 Symposium on Compiler Construction*, pages 114–119. ACM, ACM, 1982. 212

17. Dror E. Maydan, Saman P. Amarasinghe, and Monica S. Lam. Array-data flow analysis and its use in array privatization. In *Proceedings of the Twentieth Annual ACM Symposium on Principles of Programming Languages, Charleston, South Carolina, January 10–13, 1993*, pages 2–15, New York, NY, USA, 1993. ACM Press. 202

18. Madalene Spezialetti and Rajiv Gupta. Loop monotonic statements. *IEEE Transactions on Software Engineering*, 21(6):497–505, June 1995. 212, 213

19. Peng Tu and David Padua. Automatic array privatization. In Uptal Banerjee, David Gelernter, Alex Nicolau, and David Padua, editors, *Proceedings of the 6th International Workshop on Languages and Compilers for Parallel Computing*, Lecture Notes in Computer Science, pages 500–521, Portland, Oregon, August 12–14, 1993. Intel Corp. and the Portland Group, Inc., Springer-Verlag. 202

20. M. J. Wolfe. *Optimizing Supercompilers for Supercomputers*. PhD thesis, Dept. of Computer Science, University of Illinois at Urbana-Champaign, October 1982. 212

21. Michael Wolfe. Beyond induction variables. In *Proceedings of the Conference on Programming Language Design and Implementation (PLDI)*, volume 27, pages 162–174, New York, NY, July 1992. ACM Press. 213

Advanced Scalarization of Array Syntax

Gerald Roth

Dept of Math and Computer Science, Gonzaga University
Spokane, WA 99258
roth@cps.gonzaga.edu

Abstract. One task of all Fortran 90 compilers is to scalarize the array syntax statements of a program into equivalent sequential code. Most compilers require multiple passes over the program source to ensure correctness of this translation, since their analysis algorithms only work on the scalarized form. These same compilers then make additional subsequent passes to perform loop optimizations such as loop fusion. In this paper we discuss a strategy that is capable of making advanced scalarization and fusion decisions at the array level. We present an analysis strategy that supports our advanced scalarizer, and we describe the benefits of this methodology compared to the standard practice. Experimental results show that our strategy can significantly improve the runtime performance of compiled code, while at the same time improving the performance of the compiler itself.

1 Introduction

Fortran 90 and High-Performance Fortran (HPF)[7] are increasingly becoming the language of choice for creating high-performance applications targeted for today's high-end architectures, no matter whether those architectures are parallel, vector or superscalar. The array constructs of these languages have raised the level of abstraction from the strictly scalar constructs of Fortran 77, thus making them more expressive. Unfortunately, few compilers have taken advantage of this heightened level of abstraction. Instead they prefer to scalarize the array constructs into familiar scalar constructs which they then optimized by standard analysis and transformations.

In this paper we present a methodology for performing data dependence analysis directly on Fortran 90 array-section references. We show how direction vectors can be extended to include the dependence information. We then show how this dependence information can be used to perform advanced scalarization and loop fusion transformations. We conclude with a brief look at some preliminary performance results obtained by incorporating these methods into Sun Mircosystem's f90 compiler.

2 Standard Scalarization and Optimization

At some point during the compilation of a Fortran 90 program, array assignment statements must be translated into serial DO-loops. This process is known as

A. Watt (Ed.): CC/ETAPS 2000, LNCS 1781, pp. 219–231, 2000.

X(1:256) = X(1:256) + 1.0

```
DO I=1, 256
   X(I) = X(I) + 1.0
END DO
```

(a) array statement   (b) scalarized code

Fig. 1. Scalarization example.

X(2:255) = X(1:254) + X(2:255)

```
DO I=2, 255
   X(I) = X(I-1) + X(I)
END DO
```

(a) array statement   (b) naively scalarized code

Fig. 2. Invalid scalarization example.

scalarization [2,11,15]. The transformation replaces each array assignment statement with a loop nest containing a single assignment statement in which all array references contain only scalar subscripts.

For example, consider the array assignment statement shown in Figure 1(a). Scalarization translates the statement into the code shown in Figure 1(b), which iterates over the specified 256 elements of the array X.

Unfortunately, the naive translation of array statements into serial loops is not always safe. The Fortran 90 semantics for an array assignment statement specify that all right-hand side array elements are read before any left-hand side array elements are stored. Thus a naive translation of the code shown in Figure 2(a) into the code shown in Figure 2(b) is incorrect, since on the second and subsequent iterations of the I loop the reference X(I-1) accesses the new values of the array X assigned on the previous iteration. This violates the "load-before-store" semantics of the Fortran 90 array assignment statement.

Fortunately, data dependence information can tell us when the scalarized loop is correct. Allen and Kennedy [2] have shown that a scalarized loop is correct if and only if it does not carry a true dependence. Using this fact, most compilers perform scalarization in the following manner:

1. Perform a naive scalarization of the array statement into a scalar loop nest.
2. Compute the data dependences of the resulting code.
3. While a scalarized loop carries a true dependence, perform code transformations to either eliminate the dependence or change it into an antidependence.

The code transformations that can be applied to handle the loop carried true dependences include loop reversal, loop interchange, prefetching, and as a last resort the generation of array temporaries and copy loops. In the example above, loop reversal can be used to change the loop-carried true dependence into a loop-carried antidependence, thus creating a valid scalarization. The interested reader is referred to Allen and Kennedy [2] for a complete discussion. It is noted that the Allen and Kennedy algorithm requires two passes over the code: one pass to perform the naive scalarization followed by dependence analysis and another pass to perform code transformations to restore the semantics of the program if the initial scalarization is invalid.

After scalarization, a program will consist of many loop nests, each containing a single assignment statement. If the goal of a Fortran 90 compiler is to produce code for array expressions that is competitive with code produce for scalar programs by Fortran 77 compilers, it is critical that the Fortran 90 compiler do a good job of fusing these loops when possible. *Loop fusion* [3,16] not only reduces the total amount of loop overhead, but more importantly it can significantly increase the possibility of data reuse in a program. The importance of loop fusion in the compilation of Fortran 90 array statements cannot be over emphasized [9].

In previous work on loop fusion [5,14,16] two adjacent loops are candidates for fusion if their headers are *conformable* and no *fusion-preventing dependences* exist. Two loop headers are conformable if they specify the same number of iterations. A data dependence between two loops is fusion-preventing if after fusion the dependence becomes loop-carried and its direction is reversed [14].

By using loop fusion, in conjunction with other transformations such as statement substitution and array contraction, it is possible for a Fortran 90 compiler to generate code for a block of array assignments that is equivalent to the code produced by a Fortran 77 compiler for a corresponding hand-coded loop nest.

3   Advanced Scalarization and Loop Fusion

In this section we will describe an advanced scalarizer that performs dependence analysis at the array syntax level, directly scalarizes array statements in a single pass, and is capable of directly generating fused loops during the scalarization process.

3.1   Array Section Dependence Analysis

Before beginning a discussion on dependence analysis, it is important to clarify some terminology that is used in this section. An *array reference* is a subscripted variable reference. A *subscript* is one element from a subscript list. A triplet, as seen in Figure 1(a), is one type of subscript. It is assumed that Fortran 90 whole array references, array references without a subscript list, are represented internally within the compiler to include a subscript list containing the appropriate number of null triplets.

Data dependences are often represented using *direction vectors* and/or *distance vectors* [15]. The direction vector is an ordering vector, containing $<$, $=$, $>$, or $*$, that specifies the relation of the source and target iterations involved in the dependence. The distance vector contains the vector difference of the source and target iterations. These vectors are convenient methods for characterizing

```
          DO I = 1, N-1
    S₁:     A(I,2:N-1,1:N) = A(I,1:N-2,1:N) + A(I,2:N-1,1:N)
    S₂:     B(I,2:N-1,1:N) = A(I,3:N,1:N) + A(I+1,2:N-1,1:N)
          END DO
```

Fig. 3. Fortran 90 code fragment.

the relationship between the values of the loop indices of the two array references involved in the dependence. In this work we discuss only direction vectors, although the algorithms discussed could easily be adapted to work with distance vectors.

Direction vectors are useful in determining if a dependence is *loop-carried* or *loop-independent* [1]. For loop-carried dependences, the direction vector also tells us which loop *carries* the dependence and in which direction. The vectors contain an element for each loop which encloses both statements involved in the dependence. The positions in the vectors from left to right correspond to the surrounding loop indices from outermost to innermost.

To extend direction vectors for array-section references, we add vector elements to account for the implied loops of the triplets. The number of elements added to a vector corresponds to the number of triplets that the two array references have in common. In most cases these vector elements are only considered when the two array references are conformable, in which case they have the same number of triplets. These new direction vector elements appear to the right of those elements corresponding to surrounding loops. We order the elements from left to right as they appear in the subscript list, although any consistent ordering will do. In fact some people may want to use the opposite ordering since they want the rightmost direction vector position, corresponding to the innermost loop, to be associated with the leftmost subscript due to the column-major storage layout of Fortran arrays. We chose the left to right ordering for its ease of understanding since it matches the order in which the triplets appear in the program text.

Consider the code fragment shown in Figure 3. Any dependences among statements S_1 and S_2 due to the references to array A would have an associated direction vector containing three elements: the first corresponding to the I loop, the second corresponding to the first triplet, and the third corresponding to the second triplet. This fragment of code contains the following four dependences: $S_1\bar{\delta}_{(=,>,=)}S_1$, $S_1\bar{\delta}_{(=,=,=)}S_1$, $S_1\delta_{(=,>,=)}S_2$, and $S_2\bar{\delta}_{(<,=,=)}S_1$, where δ indicates a true (or flow) dependence, and $\bar{\delta}$ indicates an antidependence.

3.2   Scalarization Dependences

Given this extension to the concept of a direction vector, there is a subclass of dependences that deserve some special attention: those dependences which have an "=" in all non-triplet direction vector positions. We call these dependences *scalarization dependences* [11]. Since scalarization dependences arise from parallel constructs in the Fortran 90 program, they do not have the same behavior as non-parallel dependences. Note that it is valid for *any* of the three direction specifiers to appear in the triplet-related vector positions. Thus for scalarization dependences, it is no longer the case that a true dependence with a ">" as the first non-"=" direction is equivalent to an antidependence with the direction reversed, as has been previously noted by others [2,4].

By definition, scalarization dependences are loop-independent with regard to surrounding loops. This has several implications. First, any such dependence of a statement on itself is always an antidependence (ignoring input dependences). Secondly, all inter-statement scalarization dependences flow in lexicographical order, from the earlier statement to the later statement. Next, scalarization dependences have no effect on the parallelization of surrounding loops, regardless of what direction the triplet-related positions contain. Finally, it is especially important to point out that such dependences do not affect the ability to parallelize the DO-loops that get generated during the scalarization of the Fortran 90 code. This is due to the fact that the array-section subscripts are explicitly parallel constructs.

However, this does not mean that we can ignore scalarization dependences. These dependences play an important role when the compiler scalarizes the Fortran 90 program into its Fortran 77 equivalent. This aspect of the dependences is addressed in more detail in the next subsection.

Consider again the code in Figure 3. This fragment of code contains three scalarization dependences: $S_1 \bar{\delta}_{(=,>,=)} S_1$, $S_1 \bar{\delta}_{(=,=,=)} S_1$, and $S_1 \delta_{(=,>,=)} S_2$. The code also has the dependence $S_2 \bar{\delta}_{(<,=,=)} S_1$ which is carried by the I loop.

The actual dependence testing algorithms used to test array syntax references are described in previous works [10,11] and are not presented here.

3.3   One-Pass Scalarization

As described in Section 2, the typical scalarizer requires two passes over the code to produce a valid scalarization: one to perform a naive scalarization and a second to apply code transformations to restore program semantics when necessary. Using the dependence information described in the preceding subsection, we propose a new algorithm that eliminates the need for the first pass and is able to determine a valid scalarization before attempting any transformations.

Our new scalarization algorithm begins by performing dependence analysis directly on Fortran 90 array statements. When attempting to scalarize an array statement, we only need to be concerned with the scalarization dependences of that statement on itself. As discussed in the preceding subsection, such dependences are always antidependences and may contain any of the three direction specifiers in triplet positions. If we perform naive scalarization on a triplet that has a forward (<) or loop independent (=) antidependence, the resulting loop has an equivalent dependence. However, if we naively scalarize a triplet that carries a backward $(>)$ antidependence, the resulting loop carries a forward true dependence indicating an incorrect scalarization. Thus we must be careful to address the antidependences that contain an "$>$" in the position corresponding to a triplet we are scalarizing.

Our algorithm proceeds to scalarize the statement one triplet at a time, paying particular attention to those triplets that carry backward antidependences. There are several methods we can use to handle these dependences; basically the same methods that the two-pass algorithm uses to address loop carried true dependences.

First we can choose the order in which the triplets are scalarized. If we choose a triplet position that contains only "$<$" and "$=$" elements in the scalarization dependences, we can perform a naive scalarization of that triplet and know that it is correct. Afterward we can eliminate from further consideration those dependences which contained an "$<$" in that position, since those dependences are carried by the scalarized loop. This is advantageous when the eliminated dependences contained non-"$=$" elements in other positions.

Second, if all dependences contain either a "$>$" or "$=$" in a given position, the corresponding triplet can be correctly scalarized with a reversed loop. Again, those dependences that were carried at that triplet position can be eliminated. Failing these, we can continue to attempt all the transformations that the two-pass algorithm utilized, including prefetching.

If there are triplets remaining that cannot be scalarized by any of the transformations, we generate a temporary array whose size equals the remaining array section. We then create two adjacent loop nests for the remaining triplets. The first nest performs the desired computation and stores it in the temporary array, and the second copies the results from the temporary array into the destination array.

As an example, consider the statement in Figure 4(a) and its corresponding scalarization dependences in Figure 4(b). After scanning the dependences, we see that the second triplet can safely be scalarized using the naive method. This eliminates the first two dependences from further consideration since they both contain an "$<$" in the position corresponding to the second triplet. That leaves us with a single dependence of $(>, =)$ and only the first triplet to scalarize. The direction vector quickly tells us that the remaining triplet can safely be scalarized by generating a reversed loop. The resulting code is shown in Figure 5.

3.4   Scalarization Plus Loop Fusion

As discussed in Section 2, loop fusion is an important optimization associated with scalarization. After scalarization, a program will consist of many loop nests, each containing a single assignment statement. The duty of loop fusion is to combine these loop nests when possible to reduce loop overhead and to increase the possibility of data reuse. As prevously discussed, loop fusion is safe when the loop headers are conformable and no fusion-preventing dependences exist.

These criteria can be non-trivial to verify in the general case of fusing Fortran 77 loops; although the task can be easier for scalarized loops since the

```
A(2:N-1,2:N-1) = A(1:N-2,3:N)              (>,<)
             + A(3:N,3:N)                  (<,<)
             + A(1:N-2,2:N-1)              (>,=)
```

(a) array statement   (b) dependence vectors

Fig. 4. One-pass scalarization example.

```
DO J = 2, N-1
  DO I = N-1, 2, -1
    A(I,J) = A(I-1,J+1)
           + A(I+1,J+1)
           + A(I-1,J)
  END DO
END DO
```

Fig. 5. Generated scalar code.

structure of the loop headers is completely under the control of the compiler. Unfortunately, in many Fortran 90 compilers, scalarization and loop fusion are far removed from one another, the former occuring in the compiler front end while the latter occurs in the compiler back end. This seperation has several drawbacks. First, each must compute the necessary data dependence information anew, since it is not likely to remain valid given the transformations are so distant from each other. Secondly, intermediate transformations that alter the loops may impede fusing the scalarized loops.

To address this problem, we have combined scalarization and fusion into a single integrated optimization. The goal of this unified optimization is to scalarize multiple array statements into a single loop nest, while maintaining program semantics and avoiding the generation of array temporaries at all costs [1].

The fusing scalarizer depends upon scalarization dependences, just as our single-statement scalarizer did. However, we are now considering inter-statement dependences along with the intra-statement dependences. As with scalarizing a single statement, we must pay special attention to triplets that carry backward ($>$) dependences, whether they are true dependences or antidependences. If two statements that have an inter-statement, backward-carried dependence are naively scalarized and fused into a single loop nest then the dependence becomes forward-carried in the opposite direction and its meaning becomes inverted (*e.g.*, true becomes anti and vice versa).

As an example, consider again the code in Figure 3. This fragment of code contains the inter-statement scalarization dependence $S_1\delta_{(=,>,=)}S_2$. If the two

---

[1] The cost of allocating and freeing array temporaries far outweighes any possible benefits of loop fusion, and thus temp arrays should be avoided whenever possible.

statements were naively scalarized and fused, the dependence relationship of the resulting code would be $S_2\overline{\delta}_{(=,<,=)}S_1$, indicating that the transformation did not maintain program semantics. However, just as in scalarizing a single statement that had backward dependences, it is possible to use loop reversal to maintain the dependence relationship and program semantics.

Our fusing scalarizer has the following general outline. First, all array statements requiring scalarization are identified. Each array statement is then considered in lexicographical order. Dependence analysis is performed on the statement to identify all intra-statement scalarization dependences. If the dependences indicate that an array temporary is required for valid scalarization, the statement is scalarized by itself (with an array temp) and we move onto the next statement.

However, if the statement can be scalarized without an array temporary, we begin considering fusing subsequent array statements. This is accomplished by seeding a *fusion group* with the given statement. The purpose of the fusion group is to identify those array statements that can be scalarized and fused as a single group. Subsequent array statements are then considered for inclusion in the fusion group. To be included, an array statement must satisfy the following requirements:

1. The array statement must be adjacent to the last statement in the fusion group.
2. The statement must be conformable with the other statements in the group. Since all statements already in the group are known to be conformable, it is only necessary to test the candidate statement against any one representative of the group. Note that due to the typically regular nature of array syntax used in practice, this criteria is usually quite easy to verify, unlike determining conformance of general Fortran 77 loop headers.
3. The candidate statement must be scalarizable without a temporary array. This is determined by performing dependence analysis on the candidate statement and examining all intra-statement scalarization dependences as described in the preceding subsection.
4. Finally, the entire fusion group must be scalarizable into a single loop nest without a temporary array if the candidate is included. This can be determined by performing dependence analysis between the candidate statement and each statement in the fusion group, adding all inter-statement dependences to the set of dependences already present in the fusion group. The intra-statement dependences identified in the preceding step are also included. Then the entire set of dependences is examined to determine if a valid scalarization exists.

Statements are added to the fusion group in this manner, one at a time, until a statement is encountered which violates one of the above criteria. At that point, the entire fusion group is scalarized into a single loop nest, with the scalarization dependences dictating the order and format of the loops. The strategy is the same as that used in scalarizing a single statement as described in the preceding subsection. After the fusion group has been scalarized the process

S_1: `A(2:N-1,2:N-1) = A(1:N-2,3:N) + A(3:N,3:N) + A(1:N-2,2:N-1)`
S_2: `B(2:N-1,2:N-1) = A(2:N-1,2:N-1) + A(2:N-1,1:N-2) + B(1:N-2,2:N-1)`

Fig. 6. One-pass scalarization plus fusion example.

```
DO J = 2, N-1
  DO I = N-1, 2, -1
    A(I,J) = A(I-1,J+1) + A(I+1,J+1) + A(I-1,J)
    B(I,J) = A(I,J) + A(I,J-1) + B(I-1,J)
  END DO
END DO
```

Fig. 7. Generated scalar code.

begins again, starting with the last statement that was not added to the fusion group.

As an example, consider the two statements in Figure 6. Statement S_1 has the following set of intra-statement scalarization dependences: $S_1 \bar{\delta}_{(>,<)} S_1$, $S_1 \bar{\delta}_{(<,<)} S_1$, and $S_1 \bar{\delta}_{(>,=)} S_1$. Statement S_2 has this intra-statement scalarization dependences: $S_2 \bar{\delta}_{(>,=)} S_2$. And finally, the inter-statement scalarization dependences are: $S_1 \delta_{(=,=)} S_2$, and $S_1 \delta_{(=,<)} S_2$.

As was shown in the preceding subsection, our algorithm easily determines the S_1 can be scalarized without an array temporary. It would thus start a fusion group. Next S_2 is considered. Since S_2 has only one intra-statement dependence, we know we can scalarize it without the aid of a temporary array. We must next consider all the scalarization dependences between S_1 and S_2, both inter-statement and intra-statement dependences. These dependences indicate that the second triplet can directly be scalarized with a naive loop. After eliminating all dependences that are carried by that naive loop, the remaining dependences indicate that the final triplet can be safely scalarized by generating a reverse loop. Since scalarization is possible without an array temporary, statement S_2 will be added to the fusion group, and the scalarization process continues. If there were no more statements to be considered, code for the fusion group containing S_1 and S_2 would be generated as seen in Figure 7.

4   Experimental Results

The algorithms and scalarization/fusion strategy presented in this paper have been partially implemented in Sun Microsystem's f90 compiler. Previously, the compiler had a very simple scalarizer that always generated a compiler temporary array and multiple loop nests per array statement. The compiler still uses the simple scalarizer at lower optimization levels.

To measure the performance improvements attained with the new advanced scalarizer, we collected a set of Fortran 90 benchmarks that make heavy use of array syntax statements. The benchmarks collected include three from the NAS Parallel Benchmark suite (EP, SP, and BT)[2], and six benchmarks from the Quetzal Suite (Channel, Gas_Dyn, Monte_Carlo, Scattering, Fatigue, and Capacita). Each test case was compiled twice, once with the existing simple scalarizer and once with the new advanced scalarizer. All test cases were compiled at -O4, regardless of which scalarizer was used, so that the compiler's optimizing backend would attempt a full compliment of scalar optimizations, including loop fusion, after scalarization was performed.

The nine benchmarks contained 557 array statements requiring scalarization. The simple scalarizer generated an array temporary and multiple loop nests for each of these array statement. In contrast, the advanced scalarizer was able to scalarize all but two without the need for an array temporary and multiple loops. In addition, the loop fusion capability of the advanced scalarizer was able to fuse 326 of the remaining 555 array statements into 83 separate loop nests; that is a reduction of 44% in the total number of loop nests generated. The average fused loop contained 4 array statements, while the maximum number of statements fused into a single loop nest was 8.

The run-time performance results are shown in Figure 8. As can be seen, the speed-ups attained on the nine benchmarks ranged from 1.2 all the way up to a factor of 21.8 for the Capacita benchmark [3]. The average speed-up, disregarding the Capacita number, was 2.3. The following are the primary reasons for the significant improvements in runtime performance:

1. The advanced scalarizer generated an array temporary for only two of the 557 array statements scalarized. Whereas the simple scalarizer generated an array temporary and multiple loop nests for each statement.
2. The advanced scalarizer was successful in fusing multiple array statements into single loop nests while the nests were being generated. Due to the presence of the array temporaries, the optimizing back end was not able to fuse many loops produced by the simple scalarizer.
3. The advanced scalarizer generated in-line code for several array reduction intrinsics (e.g., SUM/PRODUCT, MINVAL/MAXVAL, and ANY/ALL), as well as the DOT_PRODUCT intrinsic function. The simple scalarizer depended upon library routines to handle all such intrinsics.
4. The advanced sclarizer produced code that looks exactly like the code the compiler front end would produce for equivalent Fortran 77 code. This assists the backend since it is geared toward optimizing standard Fortran 77 loop nests.

---

[2] We used the HPF version of the NAS Parallel Benchmarks, as produced by The Portland Group.

[3] The dramatic improvement for the Capacita benchmark is the result of extremely poor code generated by the simple scalarizer for a single statement that combined an array reduction intrinsic with a whole array operation.

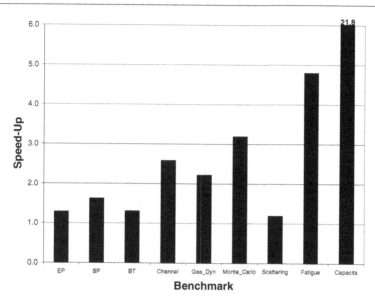

Fig. 8. Run time performance speed-ups

We now consider the affects of the advanced scalarizer on compile time. One might expect that the analysis required to perform advanced scalarization and fusion to come at a high cost. However, just the opposite is true. Performing dependence analysis at the array statement level is generally inexpensive, since the array syntax used in practice tends to be very regular in nature. And since the fusing scalarizer produces fewer loop nests, there is less work to be done by all subsequent compiler phases.

For all nine benchmarks discussed previously, the compiler actually ran faster with the advanced scalarizer than without it. Figure 9 summarizes the compile time speed ups obtained when the advanced scalarizer was used. Speed-ups ranged from 1.2 to 7.8; the average was 3.2.

5   Related Work

Many people have recognized the need to fuse loops generated by the scalarization of Fortran 90 array statements [2,6,13,16]. However, all of these only consider fusion *after* array statements have been scalarized.

The ZPL compiler [8] is an exception. In a manner similar to the work presented here, the ZPL compiler performs array-level analysis to determine a valid strategy for scalarization and fusion prior to making any code transformations. It aggressively rearranges array statements to promote loop fusion for the purpose of array contraction. It is closely related to our previous work on compiling HPF [12]. However, in both of these cases the target architecture was

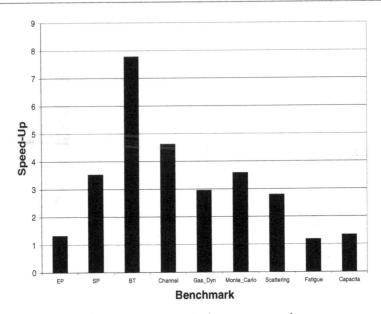

Fig. 9. Compile time performance speed-ups

a distributed-memory parallel machine. For that reason, neither of these prior works would perform any fusion if there were inter-statement loop carried dependences, since such dependences would entail the addition of interprocessor communication into the scalarized loop nest, resulting in slower performance. For example, neither compiler would have performed the fusion displayed in Figure 7.

6   Conclusion

In this paper we have presented a strategy for combining scalarization and loop fusion into a single integrated algorithm. The strategy relies upon advanced analysis and transformations performed at the level of Fortran 90 array statements. The strategy has been implemented in a commercial compiler, and preliminary performance results show a significant improvement in both compile time and run time over the naive strategy previously implemented.

Future work on this scalarization strategy would include the analysis to permit statement reordering so as to promote additional loop fusion, as well as applying this strategy to the scalarization and fusion of array statements in WHERE-blocks.

Acknowledgments

I'd like to thank Robert Corbett, Larry Meadows, and Prakash Narayan of Sun Microsystems for their support of this work.

References

1. J. R. Allen and K. Kennedy. Automatic translation of Fortran programs to vector form. *ACM Transactions on Programming Languages and Systems*, 9(4):491–542, October 1987. 222
2. J. R. Allen and K. Kennedy. Vector register allocation. *IEEE Transactions on Computers*, 41(10):1290–1317, October 1992. 220, 221, 223, 229
3. D. F. Bacon, S. L. Graham, and O. J. Sharp. Compiler transformations for high-performance computing. *ACM Computing Surveys*, 26(4):345–420, December 1994. 221
4. M. Burke and R. Cytron. Interprocedural dependence analysis and parallelization. In *Proceedings of the SIGPLAN '86 Symposium on Compiler Construction*, Palo Alto, CA, June 1986. 223
5. D. Callahan. *A Global Approach to Detection of Parallelism*. PhD thesis, Dept. of Computer Science, Rice University, March 1987. 221
6. M. Chen and J. Cowie. Prototyping Fortran-90 compilers for massively parallel machines. In *Proceedings of the SIGPLAN '92 Conference on Programming Language Design and Implementation*, San Francisco, CA, June 1992. 229
7. High Performance Fortran Forum. High Performance Fortran language specification. *Scientific Programming*, 2(1-2):1–170, 1993. 219
8. E Lewis, C. Lin, and L. Snyder. The implementation and evaluation of fusion and contraction in array languages. In *Proceedings of the SIGPLAN '98 Conference on Programming Language Design and Implementation*, Montreal, Canada, June 1998. 229
9. John D. McCalpin. A case study of some issues in the optimization of Fortran 90 array notation. *Scientific Programming*, 5:219–237, 1996. 221
10. G. Roth. *Optimizing Fortran90D/HPF for Distributed-Memory Computers*. PhD thesis, Dept. of Computer Science, Rice University, April 1997. 223
11. G. Roth and K. Kennedy. Dependence analysis of Fortran90 array syntax. In *Proceedings of the International Conference on Parallel and Distributed Processing Techniques and Applications (PDPTA '96)*, Sunnyvale, CA, August 1996. 220, 223
12. G. Roth and K. Kennedy. Loop fusion in High Performance Fortran. In *Proceedings of the 1998 ACM International Conference on Supercomputing*, Melbourne, Australia, July 1998. 229
13. G. Sabot, (with D. Gingold, and J. Marantz). CM Fortran optimization notes: Slicewise model. Technical Report TMC-184, Thinking Machines Corporation, March 1991. 229
14. J. Warren. A hierachical basis for reordering transformations. In *Conference Record of the Eleventh Annual ACM Symposium on the Principles of Programming Languages*, Salt Lake City, UT, January 1984. 221
15. M. J. Wolfe. *Optimizing Supercompilers for Supercomputers*. The MIT Press, Cambridge, MA, 1989. 220, 221
16. M. J. Wolfe. *High Performance Compilers for Parallel Computing*. Addison-Wesley, Redwood City, CA, 1996. 221, 229

Techniques for Reducing the Overhead of Run-Time Parallelization

Hao Yu and Lawrence Rauchwerger*

Dept. of Computer Science
Texas A&M University
College Station, TX 77843-3112
{h0y8494,rwerger}@cs.tamu.edu

Abstract. Current parallelizing compilers cannot identify a significant fraction of parallelizable loops because they have complex or statically insufficiently defined access patterns. As parallelizable loops arise frequently in practice, we have introduced a novel framework for their identification: speculative parallelization. While we have previously shown that this method is inherently scalable its practical success depends on the fraction of ideal speedup that can be obtained on modest to moderately large parallel machines. Maximum parallelism can be obtained only through a minimization of the run-time overhead of the method, which in turn depends on its level of integration within a classic restructuring compiler and on its adaptation to characteristics of the parallelized application. We present several compiler and run-time techniques designed specifically for optimizing the run-time parallelization of sparse applications. We show how we minimize the run-time overhead associated with the speculative parallelization of sparse applications by using static control flow information to reduce the number of memory references that have to be collected at run-time. We then present heuristics to speculate on the type and data structures used by the program and thus reduce the memory requirements needed for tracing the sparse access patterns. We present an implementation in the Polaris infrastructure and experimental results.

1 Run-Time Parallelization Requires Static Compiler Analysis

To achieve a high level of performance for a particular program on today's supercomputers, software developers are often forced to tediously hand–code optimizations tailored to a specific machine. Such hand–coding is difficult, increases the possibility of error over sequential programming, and the resulting code may not be portable to other machines. The large human effort that is involved in

---

* Research supported in part by NSF CAREER Award CCR-9734471, NSF Grant ACI-9872126, NSF Grant EIA-9975018, DOE ASCI ASAP Level 2 Grant B347886 and a Hewlett-Packard Equipment Grant

A. Watt (Ed.): CC/ETAPS 2000, LNCS 1781, pp. 232–248, 2000.

parallelizing code makes parallel programming a task for highly qualified scientists and has kept it from entering mainstream computing. The only avenue for bringing parallel processing to every desktop is to make parallel programming as easy (or as difficult) as programming current uniprocessor systems. This can be achieved through good programming languages and, mainly, through automatic compilation.

Restructuring, or parallelizing, compilers address this need by detecting and exploiting parallelism in sequential programs written in conventional languages as well as parallel languages (e.g., HPF). Although compiler techniques for the automatic detection of parallelism have been studied extensively over the last two decades (see, e.g., [10,19]), current parallelizing compilers cannot extract a significant fraction of the available parallelism in a loop if it has a complex and/or statically insufficiently defined access pattern. Typical examples are complex simulations such as SPICE [9], DYNA–3D [18], GAUSSIAN [7], CHARMM [1].

In previous work [14] we have shown that a viable method to improve the results of classic, static automatic parallelization is to employ run–time techniques that can trace 'relevant' memory references and decide whether a loop is parallel or not. Run–time techniques can succeed where static compilation fails because they have access to the input data. For example, input dependent or dynamic data distribution, memory accesses guarded by run–time dependent conditions, and subscript expressions can all be analyzed unambiguously at run–time. In contrast, at compile–time the access pattern of some programs cannot be determined, sometimes due to limitations in the current analysis algorithms but most often because the necessary information is just not available, i.e., the access pattern is a function of the input data. For example, compilers usually conservatively assume data dependences in the presence of subscripted subscripts. Although more powerful analysis techniques could remove this last limitation when the index arrays are computed using only statically–known values, nothing can be done at compile–time when the index arrays are a function of the input data [5,16,20].

In [12] we have presented the general principles of run–time parallelization implementation. Briefly, such run–time parallelization can be effective, i.e., obtain a large fraction of the available speedup, by reducing the associated run–time overhead. This can be achieved through a careful exploitation of *all or most* available *partial* static information by the compiler to generate a minimal run–time activity (for reference tracing and subsequent analysis). To achieve significant performance gains both compiler and run–time techniques need to take into account the specific characteristic of the applications. While it is difficult and may be, for now, impractical to specialize the compilation technology to each individual code, we have found two important classes of reference patterns that need to be treated quite differently: dense and sparse accesses.

In our previous work we have mostly discussed how to efficiently implement the LRPD test for the dense case. In this paper we will emphasize the compiler and run–time techniques required by sparse applications. As we will show later, the run–time disambiguation of sparse reference patterns requires a rather different new implementation and presents serious challenges in obtaining good speedups.

We will first present some generally applicable techniques to reduce the run-time overhead of run-time testing through shadow reference aggregation. More specifically we will show how we can reduce the number and instances of memory references traced during execution by using statically available control- and data-flow information. Then we will present specific shadow structures for sparse access patterns. Finally we will present experimental results obtained through implementation in the Polaris infrastructure to illustrate the benefits of our techniques.

2   Foundational Work - The LRPD Test for Dense Problems

We have developed several techniques [13,14,15] that can detect and exploit loop level parallelism in various cases encountered in irregular applications: (i) a speculative method to detect fully parallel loops (The LRPD Test), (ii) an inspector/executor technique to compute wavefronts (sequences of mutually in-dependent sets of iterations that can be executed in parallel) and (iii) a technique for parallelizing while loops (do loops with an unknown number of iterations and/or containing linked list traversals). In this paper we will mostly refer to the LRPD test and how it is used to detect fully parallel loops. To make this paper self-contained we will now briefly describe a simplified version of the speculative LRPD test.

2.1   The LRPD Test

The LRPD test speculatively executes a loop in parallel and tests subsequently if any data dependences could have occurred. If the test fails, the loop is re-executed in a safe manner, e.g., sequentially. To qualify more parallel loops, *array privatization* and *reduction parallelization* can be speculatively applied and their validity tested after loop termination.[1] For simplicity, reduction parallelization is not shown in the example below; it is tested in a similar manner as independence and privatization.

Consider a do loop for which the compiler cannot statically determine the access pattern of a shared array A (Fig. 1(a)). We allocate the shadow arrays for marking the write accesses, A_w, and the read accesses, A_r, and an array A_{np}, for flagging non-privatizable elements. The loop is augmented with code (Fig. 1(b))

---

[1] *Privatization* creates, for each processor cooperating on the execution of the loop, private copies of the program variables. A shared variable is privatizable if it is always written in an iteration before it is read, e.g., many temporary variables. A *reduction variable* is a variable used in one operation of the form $x = x \otimes exp$, where $\otimes$ is an associative and commutative operator and x does not occur in exp or anywhere else in the loop. There are known transformations for implementing reductions in parallel [6,17,8].

that will mark during speculative execution the shadow arrays every time A is referenced (based on specific rules). The result of the marking can be seen in Fig. 1(c). The first time an element of A is written during an iteration, the corresponding element in the write shadow array A_w is marked. If, during any iteration, an element in A is read, but never written, then the corresponding element in the read shadow array A_r is marked. Another shadow array A_{np} is used to flag the elements of A that *cannot* be privatized: an element in A_{np} is marked if the corresponding element in A is both read and written, and is read first, in any iteration.

A post-execution analysis, illustrated in Fig. 1(c), determines whether there were any cross-iteration dependencies between statements referencing A as follows. If $any(A_w(:) \wedge A_r(:))^2$ is true, then there is at least one flow- or anti-dependence that was not removed by privatizing A (some element is read and written in different iterations). If $any(A_{np}(:))$ is true, then A is not privatizable (some element is read before being written in an iteration). If *Atw*, the total number of writes marked during the parallel execution, is not equal to *Atm*, the total number of marks computed after the parallel execution, then there is at least one output dependence (some element is overwritten); however, if A is privatizable (i.e., if $any(A_{np}(:))$ is false), then these dependencies were removed by privatizing A.

```
do i=1,5
  z = A(K(i))
  if (B1(i) .eq. .true.) then        do i=1,5
    A(L(i)) = z + C(i)                  markread(K(i))
  endif                                 z = A(K(i))
enddo                                   if (B1(i) .eq. .true.) then
                                          markwrite(L(i))
B1(1:5) = (1 0 1 0 1)                      A(L(i)) = z + C(i)
K(1:5) = (1 2 3 4 1)                     endif
L(1:5) = (2 2 4 4 2)                   enddo

       (a)                    (b)
```

Operation	Value				
	1	2	3	4	5
Aw	0	1	0	1	0
Ar	1	1	1	1	0
Anp	1	1	1	1	0
Aw(:) ∧ Ar(:)	0	1	0	1	0
Aw(:) ∧Anp(:)	0	1	0	1	0
Atw	3				
Atm	2				

(c)

Fig. 1. Do loop (a) transformed for speculative execution, (b) the `markwrite` and `markread` operations update the appropriate shadow arrays, (c) shadow arrays after loop execution. In this example, the test fails.

2.2   Overhead of the LRPD Test for Dense Access Patterns

The overhead spent performing the LRPD test scales well with the number of processors and data set size of the parallelized loop. For dense access patterns the best choice for the shadow structures are *shadow arrays* conformable to the arrays under test because they provide fast random access to its elements and can be readily analyzed in parallel during the post-execution phase. The efficiency

---

^{2} **any** returns the "OR" of its vector operand's elements, i.e., $any(v(1:n)) = (v(1) \vee v(2) \vee \ldots \vee v(n))$.

of the algorithm will be high because (almost) all allocated shadow space will be used. We can break down the time spent testing a loop with the LRPD test into the following components:

1. The *initialization of shadow structures* - takes time proportional to the dimension of the shadow structures (arrays).
2. *Checkpointing* the state of the program before entering speculation takes time proportional to the number of distinct shared data structures that may be modified by the loop. The work involved is approximately equal to saving all modified shared arrays and thus very program dependent.
3. The overhead associated with the execution of the *speculative loop* is equal to the time spent marking (recording) the references to the arrays under test, i.e., proportional with their dynamic count.
4. The final *analysis of the marked shadow structures* will be, in the worst case, proportional to the number of distinct memory references marked on each processor and to the (logarithm of the) number of processors. For dense access patterns this phase is equivalent to the parallel merge of p shadow arrays.
5. If the speculation fails, the *safe re-execution of the loop* may cost as much as the restoration of the checkpointed variables and a sequential re-execution of the original loop.

Each of these steps is fully parallel and scales with the number of processors. Another important measure of performance of run-time parallelization is its *relative efficiency*. We define this efficiency as the ratio between the speedup obtained through our techniques and the speedup obtained through hand-parallelization. In case hand-parallelization is not possible due to the dynamic nature of the code then we measure an ideal speedup. Another measure of performance is the *potential slowdown*, i.e., the ratio between sequential, un-parallelized execution time and the time it takes to speculate, fail, and re-execute. Our goal is to simultaneously maximize these two measures (equal to 1) and thus obtain an optimized application with good performance.

While we do not consider increasing efficiency and reducing potential slowdown as being orthogonal, in this paper we will present, to a large extent, avenues to improve *relative efficiency*, i.e., how to increase speedups obtained for successful speculation.

2.3   Some Specific Problems in Sparse Code Parallelization

The run-time overhead associated with loops exhibiting a sparse access pattern has the same break-down as the one described in the previous section. However the scalability and relative efficiency of the technique is, for practical purposes, jeopardized if we use the same implementation as the one used for dense problems

The essential difficulty in sparse codes is that the dimension of the array tested may be orders of magnitude larger than the number of distinct elements referenced by the parallelized loop. Therefore the use of shadow arrays can become prohibitively expensive: In addition to allocating much more memory than necessary (causing all the associated problems) the work of the initialization, analysis and checkpointing phases would not scale with data size and/or number of processors. We would have to traverse many more elements than have been actually referenced by the loop and thus drastically reduce the relative efficiency of our general technique.

For these reasons we have concluded that sparse codes need a compacted shadow structure. However, such data structures (e.g., hash tables, linked lists, etc) do not have, in general, the desirable random, fast access time of arrays. This in turn will increase the overhead represented by the actual marking (tracing) of references under test, during the execution of the speculative loop.

Another important optimization specific to the sparse codes is the parallelization of reductions. This is a very common operation in scientific codes and has also to be specialized for the case of sparse codes. We have developed such techniques [3] but they will not constitute the focus of this paper.

Sparse codes rely almost exclusively on indirect, often multi–level addressing. Furthermore, such loops may traverse linked lists (implemented with arrays) and use equivalenced offset arrays to build C-like structures. These characteristics, as we will show later, result in a statically completely un-analyzable situation in which even the most standard transformations like loop distribution and constant propagation, cannot be performed (all statements end up in one strongly connected component). It is therefore clear that different, more aggressive techniques are needed. We will further show that a possible solution to these problems is the use of compiler heuristics to speculate on the type of data structures used by the original code, which can be verified at run-time.

A representative and complex example can be found in SPICE 2G6, a well known and much used circuit simulation code, in subroutine BJT. The unstructured loop (implemented with `goto` statements) traverses a linked list and evaluates the model of a transistor. Then it updates the global circuit matrix (a sparse reduction). All shared memory references are to arrays that are equivalenced to the same name (`value`) and use several levels of indirection. Because almost all references may be aliased, no classic compiler analysis can be directly applied.

3   Overhead Minimization

Our simple performance model of the LRPD test gives us general directions for performance improvement. To reduce slowdown we need to improve the probability of successful parallelization and reduce the time it takes to fail a speculation. The techniques handling this problem are important but will not be detailed in this paper. Instead, we will now present several methods to reduce the run-time overhead associated with run-time parallelization: First we will present a generally applicable technique that uses compile time (static) information to reduce the number of references that need to be traced (marked) during speculative execution. Then in Section 4 we will present a method for sparse codes that speculates about the data structures and reference patterns of the original loop and customizes the shape and size of the shadow structures.

3.1   Redundant Marking Elimination

Same-Address Type Based Aggregation While in previous implementations we have traced every reference to the arrays under test we have found that such an approach incorporates significant redundancy. We only need to detect attributes of the reference pattern that will insure correct parallelization of loops. For this purpose memory references can be classified, similar to [4] as: (1) Read only (RO), (2) Write-first (WF), (3) Read-first-write (RW), (4) Not referenced (NO).

NO or RO references can never introduce data dependences. WF references can always be privatized. RW accesses must occur in only one iteration (or processor) otherwise they will cause flow-dependences and invalidate the speculative parallelization. The overall goal of the algorithm is to mark only the necessary and sufficient sites to unambiguously establish the type of reference: WF,RO,RW or NO by using the dominance (on the control graph) relationship.

Based on the control flow graph of the loop we can aggregate the marking of read and/or write references (*to the same address*) into one of the categories listed above and replace them with a single marking instruction. The intuitive and elementary rule for combining Reads and Writes *to the same address* is shown in Figure 2.

The algorithm relies on a DFS traversal of the control dependence graph (CDG) and the recursive combination of the elementary constructs (elementary CDG's) shown in Figure 2. First all Read and Write references are initialized to RO and WF respectively. Then, at every step of the CDG traversal we attempt to aggregate the siblings with the parent of the subgraph, remove the original marks and add the new one at the root of the subgraph. When marks of siblings cannot be directly replaced with a mark of the parent (because they are not of the same type) then references (marks) and their predicates are OR'ed together and passed to the next level. Simplification of boolean expressions will enhance the chance of success. The final output of the algorithm is a loop with fewer marks than the number of memory references under test. Of course, the effectiveness of this method is program dependent and thus does not always lead to significant improvement (fewer marks).

It is important to remark that if predicates of references are loop invariant then the access pattern can be completely analyzed before the loop execution in an inspector phase. This inspector would be equivalent to a LRPD test (or simpler run-time check) of a generalized address descriptor. Such address descriptors have been implemented in a more restricted form (for structured control-flow graphs) in [11].

Grouping of Related References We say that **two memory addresses are related** if they can be expressed as a function of the same base pointer. For example, when subscripts are of the form *ptr +affine function*, then all addresses starting at the pointer *ptr* are related. For example, in SPICE, we find many indices to be of the form *ptr + const*, where *const* takes values from 1 to 50. In fact they are constructed through offset `equivalence` declarations for the

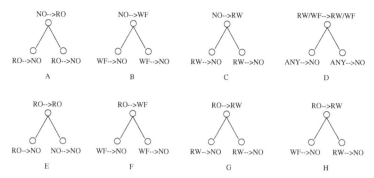

Fig. 2. Simple aggregation situations. The currently visited node is root of an elementary *cdg*. XX before aggregation is transformed into YY after aggregation. ANY denotes R or W. In (D), if the root is RW or WF, then it remains that way and the previous marks of the children, if any, are removed.

purpose of building C-like structures (`struct`). The *ptr* takes a different value at every iteration.

Intuitively, two related references of the same type can be aggregated for the purpose of marking if they are executed under the same control flow conditions, or more aggressively, if the predicates guarding one reference imply the other reference.

More formally, we will define a *marking group* as set of subscript expressions of references to an array under run-time test that satisfies the following conditions:

• The addresses are derived from the same base pointer.

• For every path from the entry of the considered block to its exit all *related* array references are of the same type (same attribute from the list WF, RO, RW, NO).

The *grouping algorithm* tries to find a minimum number of disjoint sets of references of maximum cardinality (subscript expressions) to the array under test. These groups can then be marked as a single abstract reference. The net result is:

• A reduced number of marking instructions (because we mark several individual references at once) and

• A reduced size (dimension) of the shadow structure that needs to be allocated because we map several distinct references into a single marking point.

Algorithm Outline A. CDG and colorCDG construction. We represent control dependence relationships in a control dependence graph, with the same vertices as the CFG and an edge $(X - cd \rightarrow Y)$ whenever Y is control dependent on X. Figure 4(a) shows the CDG for the loop example in Figure 5. In Figure 4(a), each edge is marked as a predicate expression. For multiple nodes that are control dependent on one node with the same predicate expression, (e.g., Node S2, S3, S4 are control dependent on node S1 with predicate expression A) we put a branch node between S1 and S2, S3, S4 with label A. We name the resulting graph a colorCDG: The white node is the original CDG node and the black node is a branch node. The corresponding colorCDG for example in Figure 5 is shown in Figure 4(b), where node S1 represents an IF   statement which leads two branch nodes. Each of these two nodes leads to multiple cdg nodes which are control dependent on the edge (S1,A) and (S1,NOT A).

B. Recursive Grouping. For each CDG node, in DFS order, the `extract_grp` function returns the group sets of the current child colorCDG. Siblings are visited in control flow order. In our example, the grouping heuristic is applied in three places: S1, S2, S3. Since references in one CDG node have the same predicate, the `compute_local_grp` function only needs to put subscripts with same base pointer and access type into one group. In `grp_union`, we do the same work as that in `compute_local_grp` except the operators are groups of subscripts. When two groups with common elements (same subscript expressions) cannot be combined, we compute their intersection (a set operation) which can generate three new groups:

$out\_group1 = group1 - group2$
$out\_group2 = group1 \cap group2$
$out\_group3 = group2 - group1$

The access type and predicate properties of out_group1 and out_group3 retain those of group1 and group2. The access type and predicate properties of out_group2 are the union of that of group1 and group2. This algorithm is sketched in Figure 3.

```
                                    Begin
                                    S1 localGrp = compute_local_grp(N, Bcond)
                                    if (N leads branch nodes) then
                                       for (each branch node B leaded from N)
extract_grp (N, Bcond)                 Grouping  branchGrp
                                       Predicate new_Bcond = Bcond AND
Input:                                                      (Predicate of branch B)
   CdgNode      N                       for (each cdg node N1 rooted in B) do
   Predicate    Bcond                      subGrp = extract_grp(N1, new_Bcond)
Output:                             S2    branchGrp = grp_union(branchGrp, subGrp)
   Grouping     localGrp                end
                                    S3 localGrp = grp_intersect(localGrp, branchGrp)
                                       end
                                    return localGrp
                                    End
```

Fig. 3. Recursive grouping algorithm

C. Marking the Groups. In this step, we simply mark the groups where the first element of a group is referenced.

Global Reference Aggregation With the same rules as before we can even group references to addresses formed with different base pointers. In other words, we need not analyze references to each array individually but can group them together as long as they follow the same access pattern. This straight forward extension will not lead to smaller shadow structures (because we have to collect all pointer values) but may reduce the calls to marking routines.

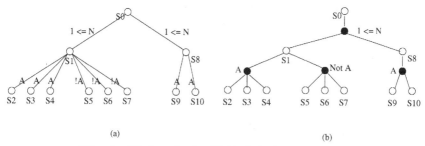

(a)   (b)

Fig. 4. CDG and colorCDG of the loop example

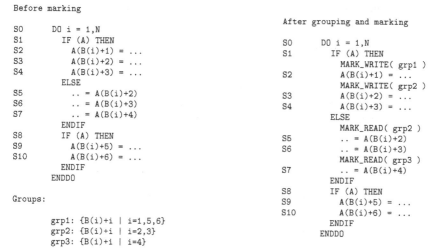

Fig. 5. Example of loop, obtained groups and resulting loop marked for speculative execution

A different possibility is that different base pointer groups follow the exact same reference pattern, e.g., two completely different arrays are traversed in the same manner. In this case only one of the arrays will be marked, the tracing of the second one being redundant.

For example, in the program SPICE this global aggregation is made somewhat more difficult because the different base pointers point into the same global array. So even if the access to different base pointers can be marked at the same time we cannot merge their shadow representation. Each pointer will have its own stride even if they can be marked together. Still, this optimization can lead to performance improvements.

The situation is more favorable in P3M where several arrays under test have the same access pattern and are referenced under the same conditions. The different arrays can be mapped to a single shadow array that, when analyzed after loop execution, can qualify the correctness of the parallelization. Furthermore, even if only some of the references to different arrays can be grouped together we can still significantly reduce the run-time overhead.[3]

4   Shadow Structures for Sparse Codes

Many sparse codes use linked structure traversals when processing their data structures. The referenced pointers can, in principle, take any value (in address space) and give the overall 'impression' of being very sparse and random. For example, in SPICE 2G6 the device evaluation loops (in subroutine `load` and its descendants, e.g., BJT) traverse linked lists and process C-like structures pointed to by each node in the list. Because the program does its own memory management out of a large statically allocated array, all pointers index into the same space (the code uses different array names but they are overlaid). This makes the task of efficiently shadowing and representing memory references seem extremely difficult.

However a static analysis reveals a single statement strongly connected component, a recurrence between address and data, that is initialized before the loop and whose values are used as indices in the loop body. It is of the form `loc = NODPLC(loc)`. Furthermore, we can find more such recurrences in the loop body, with the difference that they are initialized within loop.

After this type of static analysis we can speculate with a high degree of confidence that the code traverses a linked list and that the addresses it references are in some 'advantageous' order which is amenable to optimization.

We have therefore identified the base-pointers used by the loop (the various names of overlaid names) and classified their accesses as:

(A) monotonic accesses with constant stride, (B) monotonic accesses with variable stride and (C) random access patterns.

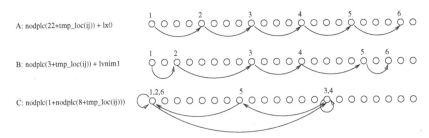

A: nodplc(22+tmp_loc(ij)) + lx0

B: nodplc(3+tmp_loc(ij)) + lvnim1

C: nodplc(1+nodplc(8+tmp_loc(ij)))

Fig. 6. (A)access region with constant stride, (B) access region with non-constant stride but monotonic, (C) access region with non-constant stride and not monotonic (random). Examples are from the BJT loop in SPICE.

Figures 6 and 7 show examples of such accesses. For each of these possible reference patterns we have adopted a specialized representation.

---

[3] This part of the algorithm has not yet been implemented.

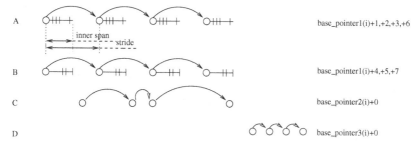

Fig. 7. (A) and (B) have the same base pointers, inner span, and stride. Actual array reference indices are different, because they are in two groups. To verify no overlap between A and B, only check whether 'stride > inner span'; (A) and (C) have different base pointers, and C doesn't have constant stride. To verify for no overlap between A and C, merge A and C and check for collisions; (C) and (D) To verify for no overlap between C and D, compare ranges. Examples have been abstracted from loop BJT in SPICE.

- monotonic constant strides can be recorded in a triplet [offset,stride,count]
- monotonic addresses with variable stride can be recorded in an array with the additional fields [min,max] of their value
- random addresses can be stored in hash tables (if we expect a large number of them) or simple lists which are to be sorted later. Range information will also be maintained and recorded.

The run-time marking routines are adaptive, i.e., they will verify the class of the access pattern and use the simplest possible form of representation. Ideally all references can be stored as a triplet, dramatically reducing the space requirements. In the worst case, the shadow structures will be proportional to the number of marked references. **The type of reference**, i.e., WF, RO, RW and NO will be recorded in a **bit vector** which could be as long as the number recorded references.

After loop execution the analysis of the recorded references will again use algorithms that range from the simplest to the most time consuming. We will test the data dependence conditions by detecting if pointers (and their associated groups, as defined in Section 3.1) collide through the following hierarchical procedure:

- Check for overlap of address ranges traversed by the base pointers (linked lists) using min/max information.
- If there is overlap then check (analytically) triplets for collisions; Check collision of monotonic stride lists by merging them into one array
- Sort random accesses stored in lists (if they exist) and merge into other the previous arrays. (Self collisions will be detected during sorting)
- Merge hash tables (if they exist) into the previous arrays. (Self collisions will be detected at insertion time)

When (if) a collision is detected, then the type of reference will be read from the bit vector for that particular address and any possible data dependence will be detected.

This scheme uses shadow data structures that are, in general, more expensive (no random access) to access and analyze than the shadow arrays used in dense problems. However, if the speculation about the code's reference pattern is correct then storage requirements are minimized and only inexpensive operations will be performed. Of course, should the speculation fail then the only advantage of this technique is its compact storage. As we will show in Section 5.1, we have devised reasonably accurate compile time heuristics for a successful speculation.

5 Experimental Results

5.1 Run-Time Overhead Reduction

We have implemented the previously presented method of reducing marking points in a program through the grouping algorithm in the POLARIS compiler infrastructure [2].

The grouping algorithm has been implemented as part of our run-time parallelization pass, the last optimization/transformation step before the code generation pass in Polaris. We ran it on several important loops from the Perfect Benchmarks (SPICE2G6, Ocean), SPEC (TFFT2) and a N-body code from NCSA (P3M). In Figure 8 we compare the number of references to the arrays under run-time test in the original code, the number of references that were marked in a previous implementation of the LRPD test (that already had some optimizations based on simple dominator relation between references) and the resulting number of static marking after applying the grouping technique. The reduction is significant in all cases and does indeed contribute to improved performance. The actual performance improvement is more impacted by the *dynamic* counts of the marking code and is also quite significant.

Program : Loop	Static				Dynamic		
	# of refe-rences	# of marks before group	# of marks after group	reduc-tion %	# of marks before group	# of ma rks after group	reduc-tion %
SPICE2G6:BJT_do	259	150	13	91.3%	68	11	83.88%
P3M:PP_do100	24	24	12	50%	5081	3020	40.57%
OCEAN:Ftrvmt_do9109	18	6	3	50%	258/128	129/64	50%
TFFT2:Cfftz_do#1	18	18	8	55%	98304	30720	68.75%

Fig. 8. Reduction of static/dynamic marking points using the grouping al gorithm

We have applied the technique to several loops from SPICE, OCEAN (PERFECT codes), P3M (an NCSA benchmark) and TFFT2, a SPEC benchmark.

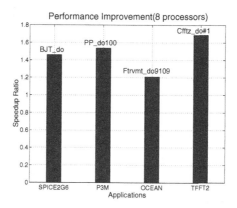

Fig. 9. Performance improvement through redundant marking elimination using grouping. $Speedup - Ratio = \frac{Execution-time-of-loop(before-grouping)}{Execution-time-of-loop(after-grouping)}$

We will now use the main loop in subroutine BJT from SPICE as our case study and give statistical results for all the other loops.

A Case Study: SPICE 2G6 We have chosen as the target of our detailed experiment the loop in subroutine BJT of the SPICE 2G6 code. This loop has an almost identical access pattern as most of the device evaluation step and represents between 31% and 57% of the total execution time of the code. The SPICE2G6 program is a very sparse code and thus offered us the opportunity to evaluate both our grouping methods (which are also applicable to dense codes) as well as the choice of shadow structures and sparse reduction validation and optimized parallelization.

The unstructured loop has first been brought to a structured do loop form (a separate pass we have developed in Polaris). Then, through a different technique we have recently developed, we have distributed the dominating recurrence outside the loop: This is in fact the loop containing the linked list traversal that controls the traversal of all data structures of the loop and has the form LOC = NODPLC(LOC). This first loop is executed sequentially and all pointers are collected in a temporary array of pointers that is used by the remainder of the BJT loop (and has random access).

Then we have used the run-time pass of the compiler to instrument the minimal number of reference groups for run-time marking. The loop invariant part of the marked addresses has been hoisted outside the loop and set up as an inspector loop. It represents the flow insensitive traversal of all base pointers (13 of them) that the loop can reference. These are the base pointers of all marking groups. The predicates guarding their actual execution are loop variant and had to be left for marking inside the loop itself. The traversal and analysis of the inspector loop gives us a conservative result about the existence of any cross-processor collisions (overlaps) between the references. The shadow data structures used by our **Run-time library** for reference tracing are *triplets* for 7 pointers, list of values for 3 other the pointers and hash tables for the reduction

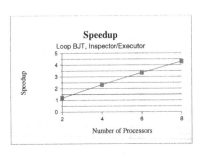 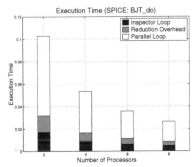

(a) Speedup - Loop BJT   (b) Breakdown of Execution Time - Loop BJT

Fig. 10. The input data is extended from a 8 bits adder. the execution time of loop BJT is about 31% of total execution time of SPICE.

operand addresses. Had our 'guess' been incorrect, then our adaptive run-time library would have automatically 'demoted' the triplets (for linked lists with constant, monotonic stride) to lists and then hash tables. The run-time library also collects range information on the fly (min/max values of specific base pointers). Then we have generated four versions of the loop that represent a combination of four situations:

1. Conservative test (inspector) is sufficient to qualify the loop as parallel
2. Speculative execution is needed in order to mark the dynamic existence of the groups (based on the actual control flow) and qualify/disqualify the loop as parallel after execution
3. The reduction parallelization needs to be verified (not described in this paper)
4. The parallelization is known to be valid because it has been proven in a previous instantiation and no modifications of addresses has been found in the outer loop.

Finally we have instrumented (with the help of the same grouping algorithms) the remainder of the loop containing BJT to flag any shared integer variable (potential address modification). Depending on the dynamic situation, simple code generated by the compiler decides which version to run.

In our experiments with two different input sets we have had to run the conservative inspector and and validate the reduction parallelization only three times: The first time and two other times when address modification outside the loop have been flagged. (For the reduction validation it was sufficient to show that the range of the reduction operand addresses did not overlap with the rest of the references.)

The experimental setup for our speedup measurement consisted of a 16 processor HP-V class system with 4Gb memory, running the HPUX11 operating system.

Figure 10(a) reports overall actual obtained speedup. The results seem to scale up to 8 processors. We have not reported numbers for larger number of processors because our input set was fairly small. (Forking overhead is 5% of the serial time - very significant). Execution time breakdown per phase is presented in this Figure 10(b).

6   Conclusion

The paper presents several techniques to increase the potential speedup and efficiency of run-time parallelized loops. Great emphasis has been put on efficiently applying the run-time parallelization for sparse codes. The detailed case study, SPICE, is one of the most difficult codes and our techniques have proven themselves to be quite useful. We believe that other sparse codes will behave similarly or better. SPICE is an interesting case study because it requires all the above methods (and more) and - more importantly - is the most similar to the problems arising in C codes: memory management, extensive use of pointers, linked structure traversals, etc. So by parallelizing SPICE we hope to gain valuable experience applicable to C programs.

References

1. Charmm: A program for macromolecular energy, minimization, and dynamics calculations. *J. of Computational Chemistry*, 4(6), 1983. 233
2. W. Blume et. al. Advanced Program Restructuring for High-Performance Computers with Polaris. *IEEE Computer*, 29(12):78–82, December 1996. 244
3. Y. Hao and L. Rauchwerger Adaptive Reduction Parallelization Techniques. Tech. Rept., Dept. of Computer Science, Texas A&M Univ., Dec. 1999. 237
4. J. Hoeflinger. *Interprocedural Parallelization Using Memory Classification Analysis*. PhD thesis, University of Illinois, Urbana-Champaign, August, 1998. 238
5. S. Leung and J. Zahorjan. Improving the performance of runtime parallelization. In *4th PPOPP*, pages 83–91, May 1993. 233
6. Z. Li. Array privatization for parallel execution of loops. In *Proc. of the 19th Int. Symposium on Computer Architecture*, pages 313–322, 1992. 234
7. M. J. Frisch et. al. *Gaussian 94, Revision B.1*. Gaussian, Inc., Pittsburgh PA, 1995. 233
8. D. E. Maydan et. al. Data dependence and data-flow analysis of arrays. In *Proc. 5th Workshop on Languages and Compilers for Parallel Computing*, Aug. 1992. 234
9. L. Nagel. *SPICE2: A Computer Program to Simulate Semiconductor Circuits*. PhD thesis, University of California, May 1975. 233
10. D. A. Padua and M. J. Wolfe. Advanced compiler optimizations for supercomputers. *Communications of the ACM*, 29:1184–1201, Dec. 1986. 233
11. Y. Paek, J. Hoeflinger, and D. Padua. Simplification of Array Access Patterns for Compiler Optimizat ions. In *Proc. of the SIGPLAN 1998 Conference on Programming Language Design and Implementation, Montreal, Canada*, June 1998. 238
12. D. Patel and L. Rauchwerger. Implementation issues of loop-level speculative run-time parallelization. In *Proc. of the 8th Int. Conference on Compiler Construction (CC'99), Amsterdam, The Netherlands*. Lecture Notes in Computer Science, Springer-Verlag, March 1999. 233

13. L. Rauchwerger, N. Amato, and D. Padua. A scalable method for run-time loop parallelization. *Int. J. Paral. Prog.*, 26(6):537–576, July 1995. 234

14. L. Rauchwerger and D. Padua. The LRPD Test: Speculative Run-Time Parallelization of Loops with Privatization and Reduction Parallelization. *IEEE Trans. on Parallel and Distributed Systems*, 10(2), 1999. 233, 234

15. L. Rauchwerger and D. Padua. Parallelizing WHILE Loops for Multiprocessor Systems. In *Proc. of 9th Int. Parallel Processing Symposium*, April 1995. 234

16. J. Saltz, R. Mirchandaney, and K. Crowley. Run-time parallelization and scheduling of loops. *IEEE Trans. Comput.*, 40(5), May 1991. 233

17. P. Tu and D. Padua. Automatic array privatization. In *Proc. 6th Workshop on Languages and Compilers for Parallel Computing*, Portland, OR, Aug. 1993. 234

18. R. G. Whirley and B. Engelmann. *DYNA3D: A Nonlinear, Explicit, Three-Dimensional Finite Element Code For Solid and Structural Mechanics*. Lawrence Livermore Labs, Nov., 1993. 233

19. M. Wolfe. *Optimizing Compilers for Supercomputers*. The MIT Press, Boston, MA, 1989. 233

20. C. Zhu and P. C. Yew. A scheme to enforce data dependence on large multiprocessor systems. *IEEE Trans. Softw. Eng.*, 13(6):726–739, June 1987. 233

MATOU: An Implementation of Mode–Automata*

Florence Maraninchi, Yann Rémond, and Yannick Raoul

VERIMAG – Joint Laboratory of Universit Joseph Fourier, CNRS and INPG
Centre Equation, 2 Av. de Vignate, F38610 GIERES
{Florence.Maraninchi,Yann.Remond}@imag.fr

Abstract. Mode-Automata have been proposed in [11]. They introduce, in the domain-specific data-flow language Lustre for reactive systems, a new construct devoted to the expression of *running modes*. The idea is to associate data-flow programs with the states of an automaton, representing modes. We define flat automata first, and then several composition operators, such as parallel composition and hierarchic composition, which give the language a state structure reminiscent from Statecharts. The semantics of this extension may be defined by describing the translation of Mode-automata into pure Lustre. However, the translation scheme is complex and it gives poor code; we study here the translation of mode-automata into the declarative format DC, used as an intermediate form in the compilers of several synchronous languages (Lustre, Esterel, ...). DC can be compiled into C, Java or Ada code. This allows to take advantage of the imperative mode-structure of a mode-automaton in order to improve the final sequential code.

1 Introduction

We are interested in *reactive* systems, which interact continuously with their environment. The *synchronous* approach [6] to the programming of reactive systems is represented by imperative languages like Esterel [2] and Argos [10], or by declarative data-flow languages like Signal [8] or Lustre [7]. In the field of reactive system programming, engineers who have to design control laws and their discrete form were used to block-diagrams. Lustre and Signal offer a structure and even a graphical syntax similar to that of block-diagrams. They have a formal semantics and can be efficiently compiled into C code, for instance. Lustre has been defined and implemented at the Verimag laboratory. Recently, the users expressed their need to specify part of a design as a state graph. Discussions about typical examples they had, led us to the following conclusion : there is a need for the expression of *running modes* in Lustre — and it would be the case for any other data-flow language. Stategraphs were used, more or less, in order to represent the mode structure of the system.

In a data-flow language for reactive systems, both the inputs and outputs of the system are described by their *flows* of values along time. Time is discrete

---

* This work has been partially supported by Esprit LTR Project SYRF 22703

A. Watt (Ed.): CC/ETAPS 2000, LNCS 1781, pp. 249–263, 2000.

and instants may be numbered by integers. If x is a flow, we will note x_n its value at the nth reaction (or nth *instant*) of the program.

A program consumes *input* flows and computes *output* flows, possibly using *local* flows which are not visible from the environment. Local and output flows are defined by *equations*. An equation "x = y + z" defines the flow x from the flows y and z in such a way that, at each instant n, $x_n = y_n + z_n$.

A set of such equations describes a network of operators. One should not write sets of equations with instantaneous loops, like : $\{x = y + z, z = x + 1, ...\}$. This is a set of fix point equations that perhaps has solutions, but it is not accepted as a data-flow program. For referencing the *past*, the operator pre is introduced : $\forall n > 0, (\text{pre}X)_n = X_{n-1}$. One typically writes T = pre(T) + i ; , where T is an output, and i is an input. It means that, at each instant, the value of the flow T is obtained by adding the value of the current input i to the previous value of T. Initialization of flows is provided by the -> operator. The equation X = 0 -> pre(X) + 1 defines the flow of integers.

In such a language, the notion of *running mode* corresponds to the fact that there may exist several equations for the same output, to be used in distinct periods of time. For instance, the coordinates of a robot arm are computed with some equations when it moves right, and as soon as it reaches an obstacle, it begins moving left and the equations of the coordinates are entirely different.

Designing a system that clearly exhibits such "independent" *running modes* is not difficult since the mode structure can be encoded explicitly with the available data-flow constructs. Typically, some Boolean flows *mode1, mode2* are used to identify the current mode, and all other variables computed by the system may have definitions of the form: $X = if\ (mode1)\ then\ ...\ else\ if\ (mode2)\ then\ ...$.

However the mode structure of the system is no longer readable in the resulting program, and modifying it is error-prone, because it is hidden in the conditionals and the code for one mode is mixed up with the code dedicated to mode changes. This is exactly the same motivation as for the *state* design pattern [5] proposed for object-oriented designs; this pattern is used for allowing an object to alter its behavior when its internal state changes.

In object-oriented designs, the motivation for modes leads to a *pattern*, i.e. a recipe for writing a structured, modifiable and readable code, using the available constructs of the language. It is not compiled in a specific way. On the contrary, in the domain of safety-critical reactive systems, we would like the code we produce to benefit from the quite imperative structure implied by modes. Encoding modes with data-flow conditionals, even if it can be done in a structured and readable way, forbids efficient compilation. We need a new language *feature*, treated in a specific way by compilers, not only a *pattern*.

Starting from these ideas, we proposed the mathematical model of *mode-automata* [11], which can be viewed as a discrete form of *hybrid automata* [1]. In [11] we gave detailed motivations and related work on the notion of mode.

The present paper investigates implementation issues. First, we augment the formalism presented in [11] with a simple notion of hierarchic composition of mode-automata. Second, we define the semantics of mode-automata and their compositions in terms of *activation conditions*, a notion available in the format DC [3] (for *"declarative code"*), used as an intermediate code in the compilers of several synchronous languages (Lustre, Esterel, Signal, Argos...).

Section 2 illustrates Lustre, flat mode-automata, DC and C for the same example. Section 3 recalls parallel composition, and defines hierarchic composition. In section 4, we show how to translate correct programs into DC, in a structural way. We give criteria for evaluating the quality of the generated code, and sketch the formal proof of the compilation scheme. Section 5 concludes, and draws some directions for further work.

2   An Example

2.1   Lustre, Mode-Automata and C

Figure 1 shows a simple Lustre program, a C program and a mode-automaton that have the same input/output behavior, illustrated by the timing diagrams. The reactive system inputs an integer i and outputs two integers X and Y. The Lustre program uses a Boolean memory M that commutes according to some conditions on X, and we can see that X and Y are updated depending on the value of M. This is a typical case where a mode-automaton can be useful.

The mode-automaton we give here has two states, and equations attached to them. The transitions are labeled by conditions on X. The important point is that X and its memory are *global* to all states. The only thing that changes when the automaton changes states is the transition function; the memory is preserved. Hence, by construction, the behavior attached to the target state starts with the value of X that had been reached applying the equations attached to the source state. This gives the timing diagram of figure 1.

The C program is an infinite loop: this is the typical form of a sequential program produced from a synchronous language. However the code inside the loop has not been obtained automatically from the Lustre program. Indeed, in the example above, it could not: the IF conditional structure is *strict* in Lustre, as in a number of data-flow languages; the C program that corresponds to the Lustre program would compute both C expressions corresponding to `pre(X)+Y+1` and `pre(X)-Y-1` *before* choosing between the two for assigning a new value to X.

On the contrary, the C program we give here is relatively close to the one we would like to obtain from the mode-automaton. We would like the assignments to x and y to be *guarded* by an imperative conditional structure. Pieces of code attached to *inactive* modes should *not* be computed.

2.2   Clocks and States

In all data-flow synchronous languages, there exists a mechanism that allows to restrict the instants in which some flows are *defined*; this mechanism is usually called *clock* [4]. Associating clocks with the flows is an indirect way of controlling the instants in which the operators are indeed *computed*. For instance, in order to avoid a dynamic error like a division by zero, one has to use clocks.

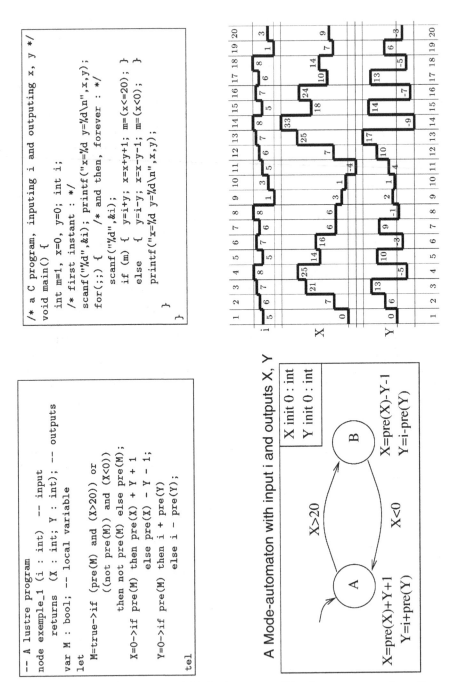

```
/* a C program, inputing i and outputing x, y */
void main() {
  int m=1, x=0, y=0; int i;
  /* first instant : */
  scanf("%d",&i); printf("x=%d y=%d\n",x,y);
  for(;;) {   /* and then, forever : */
    scanf("%d",&i);
    if (m) {  y=i+y;  x=x+y+1;  m=(x<=20); }
    else  {  y=i-y;  x=x-y-1;  m=(x<0); }
    printf("x=%d y=%d\n",x,y);
  }
}
```

```
-- A lustre program
node exemple_1 (i : int)   -- input
    returns (X : int; Y : int);  -- outputs
var M : bool; -- local variable
let
  M=true->if (pre(M) and (X>20)) or
            ((not pre(M)) and (X<0))
          then not pre(M) else pre(M);
  X=0->if pre(M) then pre(X) + Y + 1
               else pre(X) - Y - 1;
  Y=0->if pre(M) then i + pre(Y)
               else i - pre(Y);
tel
```

A Mode-automaton with input i and outputs X, Y

X init 0 : int
Y init 0 : int

A   X>20   B

X=pre(X)+Y+1   X<0   X=pre(X)-Y-1
Y=i+pre(Y)   Y=i-pre(Y)

Fig. 1. Example: Lustre, C, and Mode-Automata. The three programs have the same input/output behavior, described by the timing diagram (the horizontal axis is the discrete time; the values of the input i are chosen arbitrarily.)

The execution of the Lustre program X = if Y != 0 then U/Y else U gives a dynamic error when Y=0, because the expression U/Y is computed before the choice that depends on Y being zero or not. Using clocks, one may write: X = if Y != 0 then U/(Y when Y !=0) else U; but this is a kind of typing error: all the operands of an operator should have the same clock. One then writes: X = if Y != 0 then (U when Y !=0)/(Y when Y !=0) else U. Then the same holds for if, which can be corrected by writing: X = if Y != 0 then current ((U when Y !=0)/(Y when Y !=0)) else U ; current is the oversampling operator; in this case, it gives values to the flow X even in the instants when Y=0. The semantics of sampling (when) and oversampling (current) ensures that the expression U/Y will be computed only when Y is not zero, which guarantees that there will be no dynamic error.

We were not happy with the translation of mode-automata into pure Lustre without clocks because we would like the states of a mode-automaton to behave as *clocks*, not as *strict conditional structures*. Hence we should translate mode-automata into Lustre *with clocks*, applying transformations like the one needed for the division, systematically. However, the semantics of clocks does not guarantee that the Lustre compiler be able to produce in all cases the ideal C program of the form if (Y !=0) { X = U/Y ; } else { X = U ; }.

2.3 The Intermediate Format DC

DC [3] has a declarative style, and provides an imperative mechanism called *activation condition*. Such conditions are Boolean flows that may be associated with basic operators or sub-networks, and allow to specify *when* things are computed. The Lustre-to-DC front-end translates clocks into activation conditions, and they are used in the back-end compilers (e.g. from DC to C), where they are translated into conditionals, guarding a set of assignments.

The two following constructs define the flows X and Y, both initialized with value i and computed, at each instant, depending on the value of the activation conditions a1, ... ak, whose evaluation is sequential.

Equation defining X :　　X (init i) equcase: e1@a1, ..., ek@ak
Memorization defining Y : Y (init i) memocase: e1@a1, ..., ek@ak

For equations:

$$X_0 = \begin{cases} e1_0 \text{ if } a1_0 \\ e2_0 \text{ if } \neg a1_0 \wedge a2_0 \\ \dots \\ ek_0 \text{ if } \neg(a1_0 \vee \dots) \wedge ak_0 \\ i \text{ if } \neg(a1_0 \vee \dots \vee ak_0) \end{cases}$$

$$X_{n>0} = \begin{cases} e1_n \text{ if } a1_n \\ e2_n \text{ if } \neg a1_n \wedge a2_n \\ \dots \\ ek_n \text{ if } \neg(a1_n \vee \dots) \wedge ak_n \\ X_{n-1} \text{ if } \neg(a1_n \vee \dots \vee ak_n) \end{cases}$$

For memorizations:

$$Y_0 = i$$
$$Y_{n+1} = \begin{cases} e1_n \text{ if } a1_n \\ e2_n \text{ if } \neg a1_n \wedge a2_n \\ \dots \\ ek_n \text{ if } \neg(a1_n \vee \dots) \wedge ak_n \\ Y_n \text{ if } \neg(a1_n \vee \dots \vee ak_n) \end{cases}$$

We give below a DC program that has the same input/output behavior as the Lustre program and the mode-automaton of figure 1. Moreover, the equations attached to a state are computed only when necessary. The Boolean variable M

is used to encode the states of the mode-automaton, and serves as activation conditions. For instance, the flow X as a definition of the form:
X equcase: 0@first; (MX+Y+1)@M; (MX-Y-1)@true. Since the evaluation of activation conditions is sequential, @true means: @(not M). The C program obtained from this DC program contains the following line, in which we recognize the structure of the ideal C program presented above: if (first) {X=0;} else if(M) {X=MX+Y+1;} else {X=MX-Y-1;}. This form is guaranteed by the semantics of DC activation conditions.

```
inputs:     i     int  ;   outputs:    X     int  ;   Y      int  ;
locals:     M     bool ;   first bool ; MX    int  ;   MY     int  ;
definitions:
  first (init true) memocase: false@true;
  MX    (init 0)    memocase:   X@true;
  MY    (init 0)    memocase:   Y@true;
  M     (init true) memocase: (X<=20)@M;        (X<0)@true;
  X                 equcase:    0@first;  (MX+Y+1)@M;  (MX-Y-1)@true;
  Y                 equcase:    0@first;  (i+MY)@M;    (i-MY)@true;
```

2.4 Implementing Mode-Automata on Top of Lustre

For implementing Mode-Automata, either we translate them into Lustre with clocks, and then use the existing chain (Lustre to DC to C); or we translate them to DC (for translating them directly to C, we would have to rewrite part of the Lustre compiler, for the equations attached to states). Obtaining a Lustre program with clocks from a mode-automaton implies that the quite imperative structure of the mode-automaton be translated into the very declarative clock structure of Lustre... that has to be translated back to the imperative notion of activation condition. It is theoretically possible, but cumbersome to implement, especially when mode-automata are composed (see section 3.2 below). Moreover, keeping track of the interesting information about states along this path seems hard. We chose to translate mode-automata to DC. Producing DC code is simpler, and allows to use all the tools available for this format (formal verification, testing, debugging, etc.) without adding the Lustre intermediate form: source recovery is simpler. Moreover, DC is close to the internal formats of SCADE (the commercial version of Lustre, sold by Verilog S.A.), and the algorithms we give in this paper will be easy to reuse.

3 The Mode-Automata Language

3.1 Flat Mode-Automata: Formal Definition and Semantics

Definition 1 (Mode-automata). *Consider a set of variables $\mathcal{V}$ taking their values in a domain D, and a partial function $\mathcal{I} : \mathcal{V} \longrightarrow D$, used to define the initial value of some variables. We will note $\mathcal{V}_o = \mathrm{dom}(I)$ the set of output variables, and $\mathcal{V}_i = \mathcal{V} - \mathrm{dom}(I)$ the set of input variables. A mode-automaton on $\mathcal{V}$ is a tuple (Q, q_0, f, T) where:*

- Q is the set of states of the automaton part and $q_0 \in Q$ is the initial state
- $T \subseteq Q \times C(\mathcal{V}) \times Q$ is the set of transitions, labeled by conditions on the variables of $\mathcal{V}$
- $f : \mathcal{V} \longrightarrow (Q \longrightarrow \mathsf{EqR}(\mathcal{V}))$ is a partial function ; a variable in $\mathcal{V}$ (typically an output) may be associated with a total function from Q to the set $\mathsf{EqR}(\mathcal{V})$ of expressions that constitute right parts of the equations (not all variables are defined, but if a variable has an equation in one state, it has an equation in all states).

$\mathsf{EqR}(\mathcal{V})$ has the following syntax: $e ::= c \mid x \mid op(e, ..., e) \mid \mathbf{pre}(x)$ where c stands for constants, x stands for a name in $\mathcal{V}$, and op stands for all combinational operators. The conditions in $C(\mathcal{V})$ are Boolean expressions of the same form, but without $\mathbf{pre}$ operators. The set of mode-automata is denoted by $\mathcal{M}$.

Note that *Input* variables are intended to be used only in the right parts of the equations, or in the conditions. *Output* variables may be used everywhere. In the sequel, we use the domain $D = B \cup Z$ of Boolean and integer values, and we assume that all the expressions are typed correctly. We also assume that the equations attached to a state do not hide a cyclic dependency (like X = Y ; Y = X ;); this is the usual Lustre criterion, which is used independently for each mode here. We require that the automaton part of a mode-automaton be *deterministic*, i.e., for each state $q \in Q$, if there exist two outgoing transitions (q, c_1, q_1) and (q, c_2, q_2) and $q_1 \neq q_2$, then $c_1 \wedge c_2$ is not satisfiable. We also require that the automaton be *reactive*, i.e., for each state $q \in Q$, the formula $\bigvee_{(q,c,q') \in T} c$ is true (however we usually omit some loops in the concrete syntax of mode-automata, as we did on the example of figure 1: the mode-automaton should show the loops $(A, X \leq 20, A)$ and $(B, X \geq 0, B)$).

Finally, the Lustre programs attached to states should not make use of the following operators: initialization (the initial value of variables is given globally), sampling and oversampling (states behave as implicit clocks). The conditions that label transitions do no make use of the $\mathbf{pre}$ operator.

Definition 2 (Trace Semantics of Mode-automata). *Consider a set of variables $\mathcal{V}$ and a partial initialization function $\mathcal{I}$. A input/output/state trace of a mode-automaton $M = (Q, q_0, f, T)$ on $\mathcal{V}$ is an infinite sequence $\alpha_n, n \in [0, +\infty]$ of tuples $\alpha_n = (i_n, o_n, s_n)$.*
$\forall n, i_n$ (resp. o_n) is a valuation of the variables in $\mathcal{V} - \mathsf{dom}(I)$ (resp. $\mathsf{dom}(I)$), i.e. a total function $\mathcal{V} - \mathsf{dom}(I) \longrightarrow D$ (resp. $\mathsf{dom}(I) \longrightarrow D$) ; $s_n \in Q$. A trace σ of such tuples is indeed a trace of M if and only if:
$$s_0 = q_0 \wedge \forall x \in \mathsf{dom}(I) \quad o_0(x) = \mathcal{I}(x)$$
$(i) \wedge \ \forall(n > 0) \ \forall x \in \mathsf{dom}(I)$
$$o_n(x) = f(x)(s_n)[i_n(z)/z][i_{n-1}(z)/\mathbf{pre}(z)][o_n(y)/y][o_{n-1}(y)/\mathbf{pre}(y)]$$
$(ii) \wedge \forall(n \geq 0) \ \exists(s_n, C, s_{n+1}) \in T$ such that: $C[i_n(z)/z][o_n(y)/y] = \mathbf{true}$

In (i) and (ii) above, substitutions (denoted by [ ]) are done for all variables z in $\mathcal{V} - \mathsf{dom}(I)$, and all variables y in $\mathsf{dom}(I)$. Hence the occurrences of variable names are replaced by the current value of the variable, and the occurrences of sub-expressions of the form `pre(x)` are replaced by the previous value of the variable. For all $n > 0$, this yields a circuit-free set of equations, of which the valuation of variables at instant n is the unique solution.

3.2 Compositions

Figure 2 gives an example with parallel and hierarchic compositions. Their semantics can be given by showing how to obtain a trace-equivalent flat mode-automata from a composition of several flat automata. The compilation scheme does not follow this idea, however (see section 4).

Given two mode-automata $M1$ and $M2$ on a set $\mathcal{V}$, with the initialization function $\mathcal{I}$, and provided $\mathsf{dom}(f^1) \cap \mathsf{dom}(f^2) = \emptyset$, we denote their parallel composition by $M1 \times M2$. Its set of modes is the Cartesian product of the sets of modes of $M1$ and $M2$. The set of equations attached to a composed mode $A1A2$ (where $A1$ is a mode in $M1$ and $A2$ is a mode in $M2$) is the union of the equations attached to $A1$ in $M1$ and those attached to $A2$ in $M2$. The guard of a composed transition is the conjunction of the guards of the component transitions. The parallel composition of two mode-automata is correct if all the Lustre programs attached to the flat modes are correct: there is no instantaneous dependency loop, and each variable has exactly one equation.

The other composition is the *hierarchy* of modes. The sets of variables defined by the various mode-automata of the program are pairwise disjoint. In particular, a given variable X may not be defined at several levels (see comments in the conclusion). This composition is described by the operation $\triangleright$, applied to a mode-automaton (not necessarily reactive) used as the overall controller, and a set of refining mode-automata: $\triangleright$: $\mathcal{M} \times 2^{\mathcal{M}} \longrightarrow \mathcal{M}$.

The equations attached to the refined state are distributed on all the sub-states; the transitions sourced in a refined state also apply to all the states inside; a transition that enters a refined state should go to the initial state (among all the states inside); a transition between two states inside may happen only if no transition from the refined state is firable (the outermost transitions have priority).

3.3 A Simple Language and Its Semantics

The set $\mathcal{E}$ of mode-automata expressions is defined by the following grammar, where NIL is introduced to express that a state is not refined and M stands for a mode-automaton: $E ::= E \| E \quad | \quad \mathbf{R}_M(R_0, ..., R_n) \qquad R ::= E \mid \mathsf{NIL}$

The semantics of such a mode-automaton expression is a flat mode-automaton, obtained by applying the operations $\times$ and $\triangleright$ recursively ; since not all compositions are allowed, the semantic function may return the special error value $\bot$; if there is no composition error, the function returns a flat mode-automaton, which is both deterministic and reactive: $\mathcal{S} : \mathcal{E} \longrightarrow \mathcal{M} \cup \{\bot\}$. The recursive definition is given below (*null*, appearing below for NIL, is the function whose definition domain is empty).

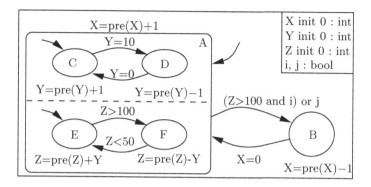

Fig. 2. A composition of mode-automata: parallel composition is denoted by a dashed line; hierarchic composition involves the main mode-automaton (with states A and B) and two refining sub-programs: the parallel composition in A, and nothing (NIL) in B. The states C, D, E and F are also "refined" by NIL. Y and Z are shared: they are computed by one of the mode-automata, and used as an input by another. The signals i and j are inputs. The corresponding expression is: $\mathbf{R}_{M_1}(\mathbf{R}_{M_2}(\text{NIL}, \text{NIL}) \| \mathbf{R}_{M_3}(\text{NIL}, \text{NIL}), \text{NIL})$, where M_1 is the mode-automaton with states A and B, M_2 is the mode-automaton with states C and D, M_3 is the mode-automaton with states D and F.

```
 1 inputs:     i,j                                        : bool ;
 2 outputs:    X, Y, Z                                    : int ;
 3 locals:     first, kA, A, B, C', D', E', F', C, D, E, F : bool ;
 4             MX, MY, MZ                                  : int ;
 5 definitions:
 6 first (init true)  memocase: false          @true;
 7 X                  equcase:  0              @first; MX+1 @A;  MX-1 @B;
 8 Y                  equcase:  0              @first; MY+1 @C;  MY-1 @D;
 9 Z                  equcase:  0              @first; MZ+Y @E;  MZ-Y @F;
10 MX (init 0)        memocase: X              @true;
11 MY (init 0)        memocase: Y              @true;
12 M  (init 0)        memocase: Z              @true;
13 kA (init false) equcase:  (((Z>100 and i) or j) or false)  @A;
14 A  (init true)  memocase: not ((Z>100 and i) or j) @A;  (X=0)@B;
15 B  (init false) memocase: not (X=0)@B;  ((Z>100 and i) or j)@A;
16 C' (init true)  memocase:true @(kA or not A);not(Y=10) @C;  (Y=0)@D;
17 D' (init false) memocase:false@(kA or not A);not(Y=0)  @D;  (Y=10)@C;
18 E' (init true)  memocase:true @(kA or not A);not(Z>100)@E;  (Z<50)@F;
19 F' (init false) memocase:false@(kA or not A);not(Z<50) @F;(Z>100)@E;
20 C                  equcase: false@not A;   C'      @true;
21 D                  equcase: false@not A;   D'      @true;
22 E                  equcase: false@not A;   E'      @true;
23 F                  equcase: false@not A;   F'      @true;
```

Fig. 3. The DC program obtained for the program of figure 2

$$\mathcal{S}(E_1\|E_2) = \begin{cases} \bot \text{ if } \mathcal{S}(E_1) = \bot \text{ or } \mathcal{S}(E_2) = \bot \text{ or } \mathsf{dom}(\mathcal{S}(E_1).f) \cap \mathsf{dom}(\mathcal{S}(E_1).f) \neq \emptyset \\ \mathcal{S}(E_1) \times \mathcal{S}(E_2) \text{ otherwise} \end{cases}$$

$$\mathcal{S}(\mathbf{R}_M(R_0, ..., R_n)) = \begin{cases} \bot \text{ if } \exists i \in [0, n] \text{ s.t. } \begin{cases} \mathcal{S}(R_i) = \bot \\ \text{ or } \mathsf{dom}(\mathcal{S}(R_i).f) \cap \mathsf{dom}(M.f) \neq \emptyset \end{cases} \\ \text{ or } \exists i, j \in [0, n].i \neq j \wedge \mathsf{dom}(\mathcal{S}(R_i).f) \cap \mathsf{dom}(\mathcal{S}(R_j).f) \neq \emptyset \\ M \triangleright (\mathcal{S}(R_1), ...\mathcal{S}(R_n)) \text{ otherwise} \end{cases}$$

$$\mathcal{S}(\mathsf{NIL}) = (\{\mathsf{NIL}\}, \mathsf{NIL}, null, \{(\mathsf{NIL}, \mathsf{true}, \mathsf{NIL})\})$$

A *Mode-automaton program* is a tuple $(\mathcal{V}, \mathcal{I}, E)$ where $\mathcal{V}$ is a set of variables, $\mathcal{I} : V \longrightarrow D$ an initialization (partial) function, and E a mode-automaton expression as defined above, composed from mode-automata on $\mathcal{V}$. $\mathcal{V}$ and $\mathcal{I}$ play the role of a set of *global variable declarations*, for all variables appearing in the mode-automata of the expression E. The set of mode-automata programs is denoted by $\mathcal{P}$. A mode-automata program $(\mathcal{V}, \mathcal{I}, E)$ is said to be *correct* if and only if $\mathcal{S}(E) \neq \bot$ and $\mathsf{dom}(\mathcal{S}(E).f) = \mathsf{dom}(I)$, i.e. there are no internal conflicts in E and the declarations are consistent with the use of the variables in E.

4   Implementation by Translation into DC

A DC program is a tuple (I, O, L, Mm, Eq) where I, O and L are the sets of input, output and local variables, Mm is the set of memorizations and Eq is the set of equations. Each memorization or equation is a tuple $< v, i, \sigma >$ where v is the name of the variable being defined, i is the initial value and σ is a *sequence* (denoted by []) of (expression@activation)s. The set of DC programs is denoted by $\mathcal{DC}$. Our translation is defined in order to guarantee the following:

Property 1 *(Form of the DC code)*
The DC code corresponding to the equations attached to a global state X, and to the conditions of the transitions sourced in X, are computed exactly when this state X is active.

For the typical programs we have in mind (a few modes, and big programs attached to modes), this is our notion of *good* code.

4.1   The Translation Algorithm

The Translation Function $\Gamma : \mathcal{P} \longrightarrow \mathcal{DC}$ is the function translating main mode-automata programs into DC programs. It is defined on top of the γ function (to be defined later). For a correct (see paragraph 3.3) program $(\mathcal{V}, \mathcal{I}, E)$:

$$\Gamma((\mathcal{V}, \mathcal{I}, E)) = \textbf{let } (L, Eq, Mm) = \gamma(\mathcal{I}, E, \texttt{false}, \texttt{true})$$
$$\textbf{in } (\mathcal{V} - \mathsf{dom}(I), \mathsf{dom}(I), L \cup \{\texttt{first}\}, Eq,$$
$$Mm \cup \{ \ < \texttt{first, true}, [\texttt{false@true}] > \ \})$$

Figure 3 gives the DC program obtained for the example of figure 2. It always contains the Boolean variable `first`, which is true at the first instant, and then false forever. It is defined by the the memorization $<$ first, true, $[$false@true$]$ $>$ (line 6). It is used as an activation condition for the encoding of other variables.

γ is the interesting function. It takes an initialization function $\mathcal{I}$, a mode-automaton expression E and two DC Boolean expressions k (for "*kill*") and a (for "*alive*"), and it gives a tuple (L, Eq, Mm), where L is a set of fresh variables needed for encoding the expression E into DC, Eq and Mm are the equations and memorizations obtained by encoding E. The variables in L are intended to become *local* variables of the DC program.

The two expressions k and a are used to encode a sub-expression depending on its context ; they are inherited parameters in the recursive definition of γ, starting from the root of the expression tree with values $k =$ false (the main program is never killed) and $a =$ true (the main program is always alive).

Since the parameter $\mathcal{I}$ of γ is transmitted unchanged through the recursive calls, we omit it as an explicit parameter, in the following definitions.

NIL and Parallel Composition There is little to do in order to encode the NIL leaves. k and a are transmitted unchanged to the operands of a parallel composition, and the global DC program is obtained by gathering the sets of fresh variables, equations and memorizations introduced for encoding the two operands:

$$\gamma(\mathsf{NIL}, k, a) = (\emptyset, \emptyset, \emptyset)$$
$$\gamma(E_1 \| E_2, k, a) = \textbf{let } (L_1, Eq_1, Mm_1) = \gamma(E_1, k, a)$$
$$(L_2, Eq_2, Mm_2) = \gamma(E_2, k, a)$$
$$\textbf{in } (L_1 \cup L_2, Eq_1 \cup Eq_2, Mm_1 \cup Mm_2)$$

Hierarchic Composition The interesting (and difficult) case is the hierarchic composition: we encode the states and transitions of the main automaton, and the *kill* and *alive* parameters transmitted to the refining mode-automata are built according to the Boolean DC variables encoding the states of this main mode-automaton.

The idea is the following: we introduce 3 fresh Boolean variables (s_i, s'_i, k_i) per state of the refined mode-automaton. ϵ is a set of equations defining the s_i variables. s_i means: "*the global program is currently in the state s_i and in all of its ancestors*" ; it is defined as being false when the context says that the automaton is not alive, otherwise it copies the value of the other state variable s'_i. s'_i is defined by a memorization in μ, which corresponds to the classical encoding of an automaton, adapted to the DC style with activation conditions. Moreover s'_i is set to its initial value whenever $k \vee \neg a$, i.e. when the automaton is being killed, or is currently not alive (see Figure 3, lines 14-23. the example is optimized a little: for the states belonging to the upper level, we do not need two state variables, and we use only one).

$$\epsilon = \{ < s_i, ?, [\text{ false@}(\neg a), s'_i@\text{true }] > \}_{i \in [0,n]}$$
$$\mu = \{ < s'_i, \Box, [\Box@(k \vee \neg a), (\neg \bigvee_{(q_i, C, q_j) \in T} C)@s_i] > \}_{i \in [0,n]}$$

("?" means any value may be chosen, because it is never used; $\square$ is "true" if $i = 0$ (initial state) and "false" otherwise).

k_i means "*the mode-automaton refining state number i has to be killed*" and is defined by an equation in χ; its definition shows two cases: either the global program is killed (k), or the state i is left because one of the outgoing transition conditions is true (see Figure 3, line 13).

$$\chi = \{< k_i, \text{ false, } [\,(k \vee \bigvee_{(q_i, C, q_j) \in T} C)@s_i\,] >\}_{i \in [0,n]}$$

Encoding the refining program R_i with s_i as the alive parameter and k_i as the kill parameter, gives the (rL_i, rEq_i, rMm_i), and encoding the equations attached to the states of the refined mode-automaton, gives the (XEq_i, XMm_i, XL_i). All the sets of fresh variables, equations and memorizations are then gathered.

$\gamma(\,\mathbf{R}_{(Q,q_0,f,T)}(R_0, ..., R_n)\,, k, a) =$
let $\Omega = \{s_0, ..., s_n, s'_0, ..., s'_n, k_0, ..., k_n\}, \quad \epsilon = ..., \chi = ..., \mu = ...$ (see above)
$\quad (rL_i, rEq_i, rMm_i) = \boxed{\gamma(R_i, s_i, k_i)}, \quad i \in [0, n] \qquad$ (refining programs)
$\quad (XEq_i, XMm_i, XL_i) = \boxed{\delta(Q, f, \text{dom}(f))} \qquad$ (refined mode-automaton)
in $(\bigcup_{i \in [0,n]} rL_i \cup \bigcup_{i \in [0,n]} XL_i \cup \Omega, \quad \bigcup_{i \in [0,n]} rEq_i \cup \bigcup_{i \in [0,n]} XEq_i \cup \epsilon \cup \chi,$
$\quad \bigcup_{i \in [0,n]} rMm_i \cup \bigcup_{i \in [0,n]} XMm_i \cup \mu)$

Encoding Lustre Equations δ takes the set Q of states of the main automaton, the function f that associates definitions of variables with the states, and the set $\text{dom}(f)$ of variables for which we need to generate DC definitions.

For each variable $v \in \text{dom}(f)$, δ gathers the DC expressions $e_i, i \in [0, n]$ obtained by translating (with the function θ given below) the Lustre equations attached to states $(f(v)(q_i), i \in [0, n])$ into a *single equation* $< v, ?, [\mathcal{I}(V)@\texttt{first}, e_0@s_0, ..., e_n@s_n] >$, adding a case for the initial instant (see Figure 3, lines 7-9). The order of the cases is irrelevant, since the s_i Boolean variables are guaranteed to be pairwise exclusive (they encode the states of the main automaton).

$\delta(Q, f, \{v\} \cup V) = $ let $(e_i, Mm_i, L_i) = \theta(f(v)(q_i)), \quad i \in [0, n]$
$\qquad\qquad\qquad\qquad (Eq', Mm', L') = \delta(Q, f, V)$
$\qquad\qquad\quad$ in $(Eq' \cup \{< v, ?, [\mathcal{I}(V)@\texttt{first}), e_0@s_0, ...e_n@s_n\,] >\},$
$\qquad\qquad\qquad Mm' \cup \bigcup_{i \in [0,n]} Mm_i, \quad L' \cup \bigcup_{i \in [0,n]} L_i)$
$\delta(Q, f, \emptyset) = (\emptyset, \emptyset, \emptyset)$

Translation of Lustre Into DC The θ function translates the Lustre expressions attached to states of the mode-automata into DC expressions, possibly creating variables and memorizations (for the **pre** sub-expressions); it returns a tuple (e, Mm, L) where e is a DC expression, Mm is a set of memorizations and L is a set of new variables, to be added to the set of local variables of the global DC program. We define θ for binary operators (expr_1 op expr_2), variables (v), constants (cst) and `pre` sub-expressions. Lustre constants and operators have a counterpart in DC.

$$\theta(\text{expr}_1 \text{ op } \text{expr}_2) = \textbf{let } (e_1, Mm_1, L_1) = \theta(\text{expr}_1), \quad (e_2, Mm_2, L_2) = \theta(\text{expr}_2)$$
$$\textbf{in} \quad (e_1 \text{ op } e_2, \ Mm_1 \cup Mm_2, \ L_1 \cup L_2)$$
$$\theta(v) = (v, \emptyset, \emptyset) \qquad \theta(\text{cst}) = (\text{cst}, \emptyset, \emptyset)$$
$$\theta(\text{pre}(v)) = \textbf{let } Mv \text{ be a fresh variable}$$
$$\textbf{in} \quad (Mv, \{< Mv, \mathcal{I}(v), [v@\text{true}] >\}, \{Mv\})$$

The last line means that `Mv` is the memory of `v`, initialized as required in the global function $\mathcal{I}$ of the program, and always computed (@true). If there are several occurrences of `pre(v)`, the variable `Mv` and its definition are created only once (see Figure 3, lines 10-12).

4.2   Correctness of the Translation Scheme

Both mode-automata and DC have a formal trace semantics, i.e. there exists a mathematically defined function f_m from mode-automata to input/output traces, and another function f_d from DC programs to input/output traces. Traces are sets of sequences of input/output tuples. We have to prove that :

$$\forall P = (\mathcal{V}, \mathcal{I}, E). \ f_m(\mathcal{S}(P)) = f_d(\gamma(\mathcal{I}, E, \text{false}, \text{true}))$$

where $P = (\mathcal{V}, \mathcal{I}, E)$ is a mode-automaton program as defined in section 3.3.

However, since the translation algorithm does not perform complex optimizations like minimizing the automaton structure, $\mathcal{S}(P)$ and $\gamma(\mathcal{I}, E, \text{false}, \text{true})$ are more than trace-equivalent: they are *isomorphic*, which is easier to prove.

We extend the semantics of mode-automata to input/output/state traces, and that of DC to input/output/local traces. We then exhibit a one-to-one function λ relating a global state of a mode-automaton program with a configuration of the local Boolean variables used for encoding states in the DC program. Then we have to prove that: first, $\mathcal{S}(P)$ and $\gamma(\mathcal{I}, E, \text{false}, \text{true})$ have the same initial state (via λ); second, if we start from a global state (of the mode-automaton program) and a configuration of the variables (of the DC program) related by λ, and take the same input into account, then the two objects produce the same output and evolve to a new global state and a new configuration of DC variables that are, again, related by λ. This is sufficient for proving that $\mathcal{S}(P)$ and $\gamma(\mathcal{I}, E, \text{false}, \text{true})$ have the same sets of input/output traces.

4.3   Quality of the Translation Scheme

We already said that the typical systems we have in mind have a few modes, and big programs attached to modes (this is not the case in our example, for sake of simplicity, but imagine that we replace `X = pre(X) − 1` by a one-page program). Our criterion for *good code* is the property 1, page 258. Our translation scheme guarantees it, due to the careful encoding of states with two variables s and s' (except at the upper level which is never killed).

We could also take the number of variables into account, for this is the main parameter that plays a role in the complexity of the static analysis algorithms that could be applied at the DC level. Reducing the number of variables was not our main aim but, yet, the encoding is not so bad: a log encoding of the states of a single mode-automaton into Boolean DC variables would make the transitions very complex for a very little gain, because the automaton components are supposed to be small. The structural encoding of composed programs ensures that *global* states are encoded in an efficient way. Since there exist optimizations techniques at the DC level, we should concentrate on the optimizations that can be performed only at the mode-automaton level. For instance, we could use the hierarchic structure of a mode-automaton program in order to *reuse* some DC variables used for the encoding of states.

5   Conclusions and Future Work

The algorithm presented in this paper has been implemented in the tool MA-TOU by Yann Rémond, on top of the DRAC set of tools for the DC format, developed at Verimag by Y. Raoul, and part of the SYRF project [12]. MATOU has been used for several case studies, among which: a simplified temperature control system for an aircraft, submitted by SAAB and already studied in the SYRF [12] project; the production cell [9] that was proposed at FZI (Karlsruhe) as a test bench for several languages and proofs tools; an operational nuclear plant controller submitted by Schneider Electric. These three examples fall in the category we are interested in: a little number of modes, and quite complex programs for each mode. The code we obtained is satisfactory, but we still need to run MATOU on a test-bench, for determining where optimizations should be applied.

Concerning the language constructs, the equations attached to states are written using a very small subset of Lustre, sufficient for demonstrating the interest of mode-automata, and for which we can perform the compilation into DC in a simple way. Our notion of hierarchic composition is also simple; in particular, we reject programs in which the same variable is defined at several levels. We are working on more permissive definitions of the hierarchic composition, inspired by some medium-size examples, in which such a situation is allowed, and treated like some special case of inheritance. However, as far as the translation into DC is concerned, the algorithm described in this paper will continue to be the basis of the implementation. For the moment, it seems that the more advanced versions of the constructs will be implemented by some transformations of the abstract tree, before generating DC code.

Further work on the definition and implementation of mode-automata includes some easy extensions (variables local to a state and its outgoing transitions; priorities between transitions sourced in the same state, importing objects from a host language like C, ...) and some extensions of the subset of Lustre we allow to label states (calling nodes with memory, using Lustre clocks, ...) that require a careful study of the interaction between the automaton structure and the Lustre constructs.

Finally, concerning the translation scheme, we managed to take the mode-structure into account fully: we avoid unnecessary computations. DC turns out to be the appropriate level for studying the introduction of an imperative construct into a data-flow language: the format is still declarative and equational, but the notion of activation condition gives a pretty good control on the final C code. Moreover, although the implementation is particular to the precise structure of DC code, we think that the ideas developed in the paper can be reused for translating modes into a wide variety of formats; for instance, we plan to study the translation of Mode-Automata into other target codes like VHDL or VERILOG. The method can also be used to introduce modes in other data-flow languages. Moreover, DC is close to SCADE and the translation of mode-automata into one of the SCADE internal formats does not bring new semantical problems.

References

1. R. Alur, C. Courcoubetis, T. A. Henzinger, and Pei-Hsin Ho. Hybrid automata: an algorithmic approach to the specification and analysis of hybrid systems. In *Workshop on Theory of Hybrid Systems*, Lyngby, Denmark, October 1993. LNCS 736, Springer Verlag. 250
2. G. Berry and G. Gonthier. The Esterel synchronous programming language: Design, semantics, implementation. *Science Of Computer Programming*, 19(2):87–152, 1992. 249
3. C2A-SYNCHRON. The common format of synchronous languages – The declarative code DC version 1.0. Technical report, SYNCHRON project, October 1995. 251, 253
4. P. Caspi. Clocks in dataflow languages. *Theoretical Computer Science*, 94:125–140, 1992. 251
5. Erich Gamma, Richard Helm, Ralph Johnson, and John Vlissides. *Design Patterns*. Addison Wesley, Reading, MA, 1995. 250
6. N. Halbwachs. *Synchronous programming of reactive systems*. Kluwer Academic Pub., 1993. 249
7. N. Halbwachs, P. Caspi, P. Raymond, and D. Pilaud. The synchronous dataflow programming language lustre. *Proceedings of the IEEE*, 79(9):1305–1320, September 1991. 249
8. P. LeGuernic, T. Gautier, M. LeBorgne, and C. LeMaire. Programming real time applications with signal. *Proceedings of the IEEE*, 79(9):1321–1336, September 1991. 249
9. Claus Lewerentz and Thomas Lindner. *Formal Development of Reactive Systems: Case Study Production Cell*. Number 891 in Lecture Notes in Computer Science. Springer Verlag, January 1995. 262
10. F. Maraninchi. Operational and compositional semantics of synchronous automaton compositions. In *CONCUR*. LNCS 630, Springer Verlag, August 1992. 249
11. F. Maraninchi and Y. Rémond. Mode-automata: About modes and states for reactive systems. In *European Symposium On Programming*, Lisbon (Portugal), March 1998. Springer Verlag, LNCS 1381. 249, 250
12. SYRF. Esprit ltr 22703, "synchronous reactive formalisms". Technical report, 1996-1999. http://www-verimag.imag.fr/SYNCHRONE/SYRF/syrf.html. 262

Compiling Adaptive Programs
by Partial Evaluation

Peter Thiemann

Institut für Informatik
Universität Freiburg, Germany
thiemann@informatik.uni-freiburg.de

Abstract. An adaptive program is an object-oriented program which
is abstracted over the particular class structure. This abstraction fosters
software reuse, because programmers can concentrate on specifying how
to process the objects which are essential to their application. The compiler of an adaptive program takes care of actually locating the objects.
The adaptive programmer merely writes a traversal specification decorated with actions. The compiler instantiates the specification with the
actual class structure and generates code that traverses a collection of
objects, performing visits and actions according to the specification.
Earlier work on adaptive programming merely stated but never verified
that compilation of adaptive programs is nothing but partial evaluation.
We employ an algebraic framework based on derivatives of traversal specifications to develop an interpretive semantics of adaptive programming.
This semantics is naturally staged in up to three stages. Compilation
can be achieved using a standard partial evaluator. Slight changes in the
binding-time properties yield several variants of the compiler, by trading
compile-time computations for run-time computations.

Keywords: object-oriented programming, semantics, compilation

1 Introduction

An adaptive program [16,18,15,19] is an object-oriented program which is abstracted over the particular class structure. Adaptive programming moves the
burden of navigating through a linked structure of objects of many different
classes from the programmer to the compiler. The key idea is to only specify the
landmarks for navigation and the actions to be taken at the landmarks, and leave
to the compiler the task of generating traversal code to locate the "landmark"
classes and to perform the actions.

This abstraction fosters software reuse in two dimensions. First, the same
adaptive program applies unchanged to many similar problems. For example,
consider the adaptive program *Average* that visits objects of class *Item* and
computes the average of the field *amount* therein. This program can be compiled
with respect to a class structure for a company, instantiating *Item* to *Employee*
and *amount* to *salary*, to compute the average salary of the employees. But the

A. Watt (Ed.): CC/ETAPS 2000, LNCS 1781, pp. 264–279, 2000.

same program can also be compiled by instantiating *Item* to *InventoryItem* and *amount* to *price*. This instance computes the average price of all items in stock.

Second, adaptive programming is attractive for programming in an evolving environment. Here, "evolving" means that classes, instance variables, and methods are added, deleted, and renamed, as customary in refactoring [17,5,8]. In this situation, many adaptive programs need merely be recompiled without change, thus alleviating the tedious work of refactoring considerably.

An adaptive program consists of two parts: a traversal specification and wrapper (action) specifications. The traversal specification mentions classes whose objects must be visited in a certain order and the instance variables that must be traversed. A wrapper specification links a class to an action that has to be performed when the traversal enters an object of that class or when it finally leaves the object.

Although a traversal specification only mentions names of classes and instance variables that are relevant for the programming task at hand, the actual class structure, for which the adaptive program is compiled, may contain intermediate classes and additional instance variables. The compiler automatically generates all the code to traverse or ignore these objects. Likewise, wrapper specifications need only be present for classes whose objects require special treatment. Hence, the programmer writes the important parts of the program and the compiler fills in the boring rest.

Contribution The starting point of this work is a notion of traversal specification (slightly extended with respect to [23]), which generalizes earlier work on adaptive programming [15,19,18]. In our framework, compiling and running an adaptive program has three stages,

1. normalization of the traversal specification and generation of the set of iterated derivatives;
2. generation of the traversal code from the set of derivatives and the class graph;
3. running the traversal code on an object graph.

Initially, we develop an interpretive semantics of adaptive programs that implements these three stages. In stage one, the compiler normalizes the traversal specification and precomputes a "state skeleton", that is, the set of states of a finite automaton which directs the traversal of an object graph. In stage two, the compiler constructs the traversal code from the class structure. In stage three, the object graph becomes available and the actual traversal takes place. These stages correspond to binding times in a multi-stage partial evaluation system [22] (for Scheme [11]). We have employed our system to obtain a staged compiler as outlined above. Thus, we have substantiated the claim of Palsberg et al [18] that "To get an executable program, an adaptive program has to be *specialized*, in the sense of partial evaluation [10], with a complete description of the actual data structures to be used."

Of course, we reap the usual benefits of partial evaluation. Once the interpretive semantics has been verified, the compiler is correct due to the correctness of the partial evaluator. Variation of the staging inside the interpreter yields either a static compiler or a dynamic compiler. Variation of the interpreter allows for experimentation with different notions of traversal specifications and so on. In any case, partial evaluation supplies compilers at the push of a button.

Overview Section 2 establishes preliminaries and defines a semantics of adaptive programs. Section 3 defines semantic functions on traversal specifications and wrapper specifications. Finally, it defines the semantics via an interpreter. Section 4 explains the steps to specialize this interpreter and how to achieve static as well as dynamic compilation. Two variants of the semantics are readily implemented by modifying the interpreter. Section 5 considers variations, extensions, and further work, Section 6 discusses related work, and Section 7 concludes.

The papers assumes some knowledge of the Scheme programming language.

2   Semantics of Adaptive Programs

This section first recalls the basic concepts of class graphs and object graphs used to define the semantics of adaptive programs. Then, we define traversal specifications and wrapper specifications and use them to define a semantics of adaptive programs.

2.1   Graphs

A *labeled directed graph* is a triple (V, E, L) where V is a set of nodes, L is a set of labels, and $E \subseteq V \times L \times V$ is the set of edges. Write $u \xrightarrow{l} v$ for the edge $(u, l, v) \in E$; then u is the source, l the label, and v the target of the edge.

Let $G = (V, E, L)$ be a labeled directed graph. A *path from v_0 to v_n* is a sequence $(v_0, l_1, v_1, l_2, \ldots, l_n, v_n)$ where $n \geq 0$, $v_0, \ldots, v_n \in V$, $l_1, \ldots, l_n \in L$, and, for all $1 \leq i \leq n$, there is an edge $v_{i-1} \xrightarrow{l_i} v_i \in E$. The set of all paths in G is $\mathsf{Paths}(G)$.

If $p = (v_0, l_1, \ldots, v_n)$ and $p' = (v'_0, l'_1, \ldots, v'_m)$ are paths with $v_n = v'_0$ then define the concatenation $p \cdot p' = (v_0, l_1, \ldots, v_n, l'_1, \ldots, v'_m)$. For sets of paths P and P' let $P \cdot P' = \{p \cdot p' \mid p \in P, p' \in P', p \cdot p' \text{ is defined}\}$.

2.2   Class Graphs and Object Graphs

Let $\mathcal{C}$ be a set of class names and $\mathcal{N}$ be a set of instance names, totally ordered by $\leq$. A *class graph* is a finite labeled directed graph $\mathcal{G}_C = (\mathcal{C}, \mathcal{E}_C, \mathcal{N} \cup \{\diamond\})$.

There are two kinds of edges in the class graph. A *construction edge* has the form $u \xrightarrow{l} v$ where $l \in \mathcal{N}$ ($l \neq \diamond$). It indicates that objects of class u have an instance variable l containing objects of class v. There is at most one construction edge with source u and label l. Each cycle in $\mathcal{G}_C$ involves at least one construction edge.

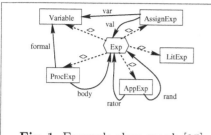
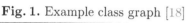

Fig. 1. Example class graph [18]

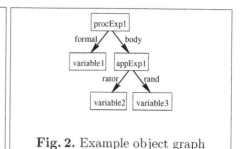

Fig. 2. Example object graph

An edge $u \xrightarrow{\diamond} v$ is a *subclass edge*, indicating that v is a subclass of u. Without lack of generality [3,19,16] we assume that class graphs are *simple*, i.e., every class is either *abstract* (all outgoing edges are subclass edges) or *concrete* (all outgoing edges are construction edges).

Figure 1 shows an example class graph with an abstract class *Exp* and five concrete classes *ProcExp*, *AssignExp*, *AppExp*, *LitExp*, and *Variable*. Dashed arrows indicate subclass edges, solid arrows indicate construction edges. Class *Exp* has the remaining classes as subclasses. Class *ProcExp* has two instance variables, `formal` of class *Variable* and `body` of class *Exp*. Class *AssignExp* also has two instance variables, `var` and `val` of class *Variable* and *Exp*, respectively. *AppExp* has two instance variables `rator` and `rand` of class *Exp*.

Let Ω be a set of objects. An *object graph* is a finite labeled graph $(\Omega, \mathcal{E}_O, \mathcal{N})$ such that there is at most one edge with source u and label l. The edge $u \xrightarrow{l} v$ means that the instance variable l in object u holds the object v.

Figure 2 shows an example object graph corresponding to the class structure in Fig. 1. The object *procExp1* has class *ProcExp*, *appExp1* has class *AppExp*, and *variable1*, *variable2*, and *variable3* all have class *Variable*.

A *class map* is a mapping $\mathsf{Class} : \Omega \to \mathcal{C}$ from objects to class names of concrete classes. The *subclass map* $\mathsf{Subclasses} : \mathcal{C} \to \mathcal{P}(\mathcal{C})$ maps a class name to the set of class names of all its subclasses, including itself. $\mathsf{Subclasses}(A)$ is the set of all $B \in \mathcal{C}$ such that there is a path $(A, \diamond, \ldots, \diamond, B)$ in the class graph.

2.3 Traversal Specifications

A traversal specification determines the continuation of a traversal of an object or class graph. Hence, a traversal specification, ρ, is either a path to an object of class B, a path leading through an instance variable l, a concatenation of specifications, or an alternative of specifications.

$$
\begin{aligned}
\rho ::= \ &B & &\text{simple path to } B \\
\mid \ &\{l\}\rho & &\text{paths via } l \\
\mid \ &\rho \cdot \rho & &\text{concatenation} \\
\mid \ &\rho + \rho & &\text{alternative}
\end{aligned}
$$

The semantics of a traversal specification, ρ, is specified relative to a starting node A. It is a set of paths in a class graph.

$$
\begin{aligned}
\mathsf{RPathSet}(A, B) &= \{(A, l_1, A_1, \ldots, l_n, A_n) \in \mathsf{Paths}(\mathcal{G}_C) \mid A_n \in \mathsf{Subclasses}(B)\} \\
\mathsf{RPathSet}(A, \{l\}\rho) &= \{(A, l_1, \ldots, l_n, A_n) \in \mathsf{RPathSet}(A, \rho) \mid l \in \{l_1, \ldots, l_n\}\} \\
\mathsf{RPathSet}(A, \rho_1 \cdot \rho_2) &= \bigcup\nolimits_{B \in \mathsf{Target}(\rho_1)} \mathsf{RPathSet}(A, \rho_1) \cdot \mathsf{RPathSet}(B, \rho_2) \\
\mathsf{RPathSet}(A, \rho_1 + \rho_2) &= \mathsf{RPathSet}(A, \rho_1) \cup \mathsf{RPathSet}(A, \rho_2)
\end{aligned}
$$

The function Target yields the set of possible target classes of a traversal.

$$
\begin{aligned}
\mathsf{Target}(B) &= \{B\} \\
\mathsf{Target}(\rho_1 \cdot \rho_2) &= \mathsf{Target}(\rho_2) \\
\mathsf{Target}(\rho_1 + \rho_2) &= \mathsf{Target}(\rho_1) \cup \mathsf{Target}(\rho_2)
\end{aligned}
$$

The definition of the semantics naturally adapts to object graphs, by replacing occurrences of class names with objects of the respective classes:

$$
\mathsf{RPathSet}_{\mathcal{G}_O}(A, B) = \{\, (o_0, l_1, o_1, \ldots, l_n, o_n) \in \mathsf{Paths}(\mathcal{G}_O) \mid \\
\mathsf{Class}(o_0) \in \mathsf{Subclasses}(A), \mathsf{Class}(o_n) \in \mathsf{Subclasses}(B)\}
$$

2.4   Declarative Semantics

An adaptive program is a pair (ρ, W) of a traversal specification ρ and a *wrapper map* W. The map W maps a class name $A \in \mathcal{C}$ to an action to be executed when visiting an object of class A. Given an object graph $\mathcal{G}_O$, the semantics of (ρ, W) with respect to some initial object o is completely determined by listing the objects in the order in which they are traversed. Formally,

$$
\begin{aligned}
\mathsf{Trav}(\rho, o) &= \mathsf{Seq}(o, \mathsf{RPathSet}_{\mathcal{G}_C}(\mathsf{Class}(o), \rho)) \\
\text{where}\quad \mathsf{Seq}(o_0, \Pi) &= o_0 \mathsf{Seq}(o_1, \Pi_1) \ldots \mathsf{Seq}(o_n, \Pi_n) \\
\text{where}\quad \{l_1, \ldots, l_n\} &= \{l \in \mathcal{N} \mid Avlw \in \Pi, v \in (\Diamond\mathcal{C})^*\} \quad l_i < l_{i+1} \\
\Pi_i &= \{w \in \mathcal{C}(\mathcal{N}\mathcal{C})^* \mid Avl_i w \in \Pi, v \in (\Diamond\mathcal{C})^*\} \\
\{o_i\} &= \{o' \mid o_0 \xrightarrow{l_i} o' \in \mathcal{E}_O\}
\end{aligned}
$$

To see that $\mathsf{Trav}(\rho, o)$ is well-defined, observe that

1. the definition of $l_1, \ldots, l_n$ works because of our restriction to simple class graphs, specifically, it is not possible that the traversal misses a construction edge in a superclass because every superclass is abstract;
2. the o_i are uniquely determined in every recursive expansion of $\mathsf{Seq}()$ because the construction edges of the object graph are deterministic.

To run the adaptive program on o means to execute the wrappers specified by W in the sequence prescribed by $\mathsf{Trav}(\rho, o)$.

The semantics is quite subtle because the properties of the class graph determine the traversal of the object graph. That is, a traversal continues in the object graph as long as there is a successful path in the class graph.

Comparison In the work of Palsberg and others [18], a primitive traversal specification has the form $D = [A, B]$ and denotes the set of all paths from class A to class B in the class graph. In order to construct a sensible semantics, their specifications must be *well-formed*, which means that a concatenation of D_1 and D_2 only makes sense if the target of D_1 is equal to the source of D_2. Likewise, for an alternative, $D_1 + D_2$, the targets of D_1 and D_2 (as well as their sources) must coincide. Their formal framework lacks via-paths, but their implementation supports them as well as ours does. It is straightforward to provide a translation from their well-formed specifications to ours and to prove that the translation preserves the semantics.

On top of that, our framework accommodates multiple sources and targets, just like the latest version of adaptive programming [16]. We believe that our approach is as powerful as that but we have not formally investigated the issue.

3   An Interpretive Semantics

The interpretive semantics of adaptive programs takes five inputs, a traversal specification, a wrapper specification, a class graph, the root of an object graph, and a list of parameters for the adaptive program. We develop representations and algorithms for each of these in the Scheme language. Finally, we discuss the implementation of the traversal.

3.1   Traversal Specification

We will use a traversal specification to denote the current state of a traversal of a class or object graph. Whenever we track an instance variable or examine the class of a node in the graph, the state of the traversal changes. This change of state is captured by two derivative functions which compute the new state.

The function, $\Phi_X(\rho)$ (pronounced "ρ is final for X"), determines if the class X is a target of ρ. For a simple path A, X must be a subclass of A to qualify as a final state. A concatenation is final for X if both components are final for X. An alternative is final for X if at least one component is final for X. A via-path is never final.

The class derivative, Δ, defined in Fig. 3 maps a traversal specification ρ and a class name X to $\rho' = \Delta_X(\rho)$. The traversal specification ρ' is the new state. In the case of a simple path A, the derivative is the class itself. For a concatenation $\rho_1 \cdot \rho_2$, if ρ_1 has become final then the new state is the derivative of ρ_2. Otherwise, the new state is the derivative of ρ_1 concatenated with ρ_2. The derivative of an alternative is the alternative of the derivatives. The class derivative of a via-l-path is simply pushed through the via-l-path.

The label derivative, $\Delta^{l'}(\rho)$, maps a traversal specification and a label to a new traversal specification. A simple path A is not affected by traversal of label l'. In a concatenation, the label can only affect the first component. In a union, the label can affect both components. In a via-l-path, the label l removes

$$
\begin{aligned}
\Phi_X(A) &= X \in \mathsf{Subclasses}(A)\\
\Phi_X(\rho_1 \cdot \rho_2) &= \Phi_X(\rho_1) \wedge \Phi_X(\rho_2)\\
\Phi_X(\rho_1 + \rho_2) &= \Phi_X(\rho_1) \vee \Phi_X(\rho_2)\\
\Phi_X(\{l\}\rho) &= \mathsf{false}
\end{aligned}
$$

$$
\begin{aligned}
\Delta_X(A) &= A\\
\Delta_X(\rho_1 \cdot \rho_2) &= \begin{cases} \Delta_X(\rho_2) & \text{if } \Phi_X(\Delta_X(\rho_1))\\ \Delta_X(\rho_1) \cdot \rho_2 & \text{otherwise} \end{cases}\\
\Delta_X(\rho_1 + \rho_2) &= \Delta_X(\rho_1) + \Delta_X(\rho_2)\\
\Delta_X(\{l\}\rho) &= \{l\}\Delta_X(\rho)
\end{aligned}
$$

$$
\begin{aligned}
\Delta^{l'}(A) &= A\\
\Delta^{l'}(\rho_1 \cdot \rho_2) &= \Delta^{l'}(\rho_1) \cdot \rho_2\\
\Delta^{l'}(\rho_1 + \rho_2) &= \Delta^{l'}(\rho_1) + \Delta^{l'}(\rho_2)\\
\Delta^{l'}(\{l\}\rho) &= \begin{cases} \Delta^{l'}(\rho) & \text{if } l = l'\\ \{l\}\Delta^{l'}(\rho) & \text{otherwise} \end{cases}
\end{aligned}
$$

Fig. 3. Derivative of a traversal specification

itself from the traversal specification, recursively. Any other via-path remains in the specification.

The relation of these three functions to the sets of paths upon which the semantics is based is easily stated and proved.

Proposition 1. *If* $(A_0, l_1, A_1, \ldots, A_n) \in \mathsf{RPathSet}(A_0, \rho)$ *then* $(A_1, \ldots, A_n) \in \mathsf{RPathSet}(A_1, \rho')$ *where* $\rho' = \Delta_{A_1}(\Delta^{l_1}(\rho))$*. Furthermore, if* $n = 1$ *then* $\Phi_{A_1}(\rho')$*.*

3.2 Wrapper Specification

Figure 4 shows an example of a concrete specification building on Figures 1 and 2 [19]. It defines an adaptive operation `print-free-vars` which traverses an object of class *Exp* and prints all the bound variables.

The line (`traverse variable`) is the traversal specification: visit all objects of class *Variable*. There are two wrapper specifications, one for class *ProcExp* and another for class *variable*. The *ProcExp* wrapper declares a `prefix` method, which must be executed whenever the traversal *enters* an object of class *ProcExp*, and a `suffix` method, to be executed whenever the traversal of an object of class *ProcExp* is finished. The *Variable* wrapper defines only a `prefix` method.

The bodies of the methods show a few particulars from our simple object system. Each method can access the current object through `this`. The parameter of the operation is visible and is updated destructively. The function `value-of-field` takes an object and the name of an instance variable and returns its current value in the object.

```
(define-operation
  (print-free-vars bound-vars)
  (traverse variable)
  (wrapper procexp
    (prefix
      (set! bound-vars
            (cons (value-of-field (value-of-field this 'formal) 'id)
                  bound-vars)))
    (suffix
      (set! bound-vars (cdr bound-vars))))
  (wrapper variable
    (prefix
      (let ((name (value-of-field this 'id)))
        (if (not (member name bound-vars))
          (display name)))))))
```

Fig. 4. An adaptive program

The wrappers of a *ProcExp* object are executed regardless whether any *Variable* object is reachable through its instances. This is exactly what the declarative semantics (see [19] and also Section 2.4) prescribes.

3.3 Traversal Code

The procedure visit in 5 implements a traversal of an object graph. It only deals with prefix wrappers, the implementation of suffix wrappers is analogous.

The visit procedure accepts three parameters, the current object, this, the current state of the traversal, state, and a list of the current values of the operation's variables, parms. It performs the traversal of the object graph below this according to state and returns the list the variables' values after completing the traversal. In addition, visit refers to the list of names of the operation's variables in the specification, formals, and to the wrapper specification to locate the code for the wrappers, (find-wrapper op-spec this-class).

To traverse an object, visit first determines the class this-class of the current object. Next, it computes the new state this-state of the traversal using the derivative function delta. From the class and the state, it computes a list, children, of names of instance variables to be tracked.

Now visit checks if there is a prefix wrapper for this-class. If so, it constructs the text of a function that takes the current object and the current values of the operation's variables as a parameter, executes the wrapper, and returns the final values of the variables. The function wrapper-semantics maps the text of the wrapper, prefix-body, and the names of the variables, formals to a corresponding function, the semantics of the wrapper. It accomplishes this mapping

```
(define (visit this state parms)
  (let* ((this-class (class-of this))
         (this-state (delta state this-class))
         (children (to-visit this-class this-state))
         (prefix-body (find-prefix-wrapper op-spec this-class))
         (parms0 (if prefix-body
                     (apply
                       ((wrapper-semantics prefix-body) this)
                      parms)
                     parms)))
    (let loop ((children children) (parms parms0))
      (if (null? children)
          parms
          (let* ((field-name (car children))
                 (edge-state (lab-delta this-state field-name)))
            (loop (cdr children)
                  (visit (value-of-field this field-name)
                         edge-state
                         parms)))))))

(define (wrapper-semantics formals body)
  (eval '(lambda (this)
           (lambda ,formals
             ,@body
             (list ,@formals)))
        (interaction-environment)))
```

Fig. 5. Naive traversal code

using a combination of Scheme's `eval` and `apply` primitives[1]. `Visit` applies the resulting function to the current object and the current values of the variables, thus computing the new values of the variables.

Finally, it visits the `children`, threading the values of the operation's variables through the computation. Whenever `visit` calls itself recursively, it adjusts the state using `lab-delta` which implements $\Delta^l(\rho)$.

Clearly, the function `to-visit` controls the traversal without using the "final" predicate. To do a proper job, the function `to-visit` checks the class graph for paths starting from the current class in the current state. Here is the specification:

$$\texttt{to-visit}(A, \rho) = \{l \in \mathcal{N} \mid (A, l, \ldots) \in \mathsf{RPathSet}_{\mathcal{G}_C}(A, \rho)\}$$

This specification is simpler than the one in Section 2.4 because A is the class of the current object and hence concrete. Clearly, `to-visit` can be computed by

---

[1] The function `interaction-environment` is predefined in R5RS Scheme and yields the current top-level variable bindings [11].

searching for paths in a graph $\mathcal{G}$ where each node is a pair of a class name and a derivative of ρ and there is an l-edge from (A, ρ) to (A', ρ') iff $A \xrightarrow{l} A' \in \mathcal{E}_C$ and $\rho' = \Delta_{A'}(\Delta^l(\rho))$. With this graph, the specification becomes

$$\texttt{to-visit}(A, \rho) = \{l \in \mathcal{N} \mid A \xrightarrow{l} A' \in \mathcal{E}_C,$$
$$\exists \text{path in } \mathcal{G} \text{ from } (A', \Delta_{A'}(\Delta^l(\rho))) \text{ to } (A'', \rho'')$$
$$\text{where } \Phi_{A''}(\rho'')\}.$$

4   Specialization

A partial evaluator for Scheme [22] transforms the interpretive semantics into a compiler for adaptive programs. The partial evaluator works *offline*, ie, it relies on a preceding binding-time analysis which propagates the binding times of the program's arguments to every expression. Thus it discovers for each expression the earliest stage at which it can be evaluated.

In the first stage, only the adaptive program (traversal specification and wrapper specification) is available and normalization of the traversal specification takes place. A companion paper [23] elaborates this normalization. It shows that a normalized traversal specification leads to a compiled program with a uniformly minimal number of specialized variants of the visit function. In addition, the first stage can precompute a table of all possible derivatives of the traversal specification. Arguably, this stage might be regarded as a preprocessing step. No interesting specialized code is generated, the specializer merely performs the normalization and reconstructs the remaining parts of the program, inserting the precomputed table.

In the second stage, the class graph becomes available. This stage constructs the graph $\mathcal{G}$ mentioned at the end of Section 3.3 and performs all the necessary path computations in advance by tabulation of to-visit. At the end, every node of $\mathcal{G}$ is marked whether or not it has a path to a final node. This requires some reorganization of the code shown, or a more powerful partial evaluator which memoizes specialization-time computations.

The second stage is the actual compilation step. It creates specialized variants of the visit procedure according to the state and the class of the visited object. The specialized code does not mention states and derivatives anymore.

In the third stage, the object graph becomes available and it remains to traverse it using a suitable entry point to the specialized code.

4.1   Binding-Time Improvements

Quite often, code subjected to specialization must be changed slightly so that the partial evaluator infers satisfactory binding-time properties. The interpretive semantics of adaptive programming is no exception.

However, the required changes are minimal and rely on a standard trick, "The Trick" [10]. The problem is with the following code fragment from Fig. 5:

```
(define (visit this class state parms)
  (let ((actual-class (class-of this)))
    (let loop ((classes (subclasses class)))
      (if (null classes)
          (error "illegal object graph")
          (let ((this-class (car classes)))
            (if (equal? actual-class this-class)
                (let ((this-state (delta state this-class)))
                  ...)
                (loop (cdr classes)))))))))
```

Fig. 6. Function visit after application of The Trick

```
(define (visit this state parms)
  (let* ((this-class (class-of this))
         (this-state (delta state this-class)))
    ...)))
```

Considering the binding times, the current object, this, and the operation's variables, parms, are available in stage 3. The current state, however, is already available in stage 2, and so should be all state information. Unfortunately, this-class depends on this, so it belongs to stage 3, and this-state depends on this-class, so it also belongs to stage 3. This results in the binding-time analysis annotating almost everything in visit as stage 3 so that no specialization can happen.

The solution is to apply "The Trick" to this-class as follows. The procedure visit gets an extra argument class which is a superclass of the class of this. This class value belongs to stage 2 because it can be easily extracted from the class graph. With this information we can replace the stage 3 value (class-of this) with a stage 2 value, as demonstrated in Figure 6. Thus, we are replacing a single stage-3-test which is known to be a member of (subclasses class) by a stage-2-loop over this set.

No further modifications are necessary. The partial evaluator even processes the function wrapper-semantics as it stands (including apply and eval [21]).

4.2 Dynamic Compilation

A later work on compiling adaptive programs [16] has introduced dynamic compilation. In this framework (but translated in the terms of this paper), the compiler need not generate different versions of visit, but rather the propagation of state information is deferred to the actual traversal. Furthermore, it is not necessary to perform the initial normalization step (it only decreases the number of variants specialized from visit), so that only the classic two stages remain.

But what is left to specialize in this situation? Considering the code fragment in Figure 6, we see that only class can be propagated before the actual traversal takes place. Therefore, in the specialized program, there will be one variant of `visit` for each class. This variant contains the prefix and suffix methods for the class (if any). It is also possible – using The Trick on `children` – to hard wire the references to the instance variables into the code. We did not pursue this last idea because its outcome did not seem worthwhile.

5 Variations

It is easy to experiment with variants of the semantics, by modifying the interpreter. Partial evaluation yields the corresponding compilers for free. This section considers two independent variants, one which restricts the execution of wrappers only to the nodes on successful paths in the object graph, and another which implements a different semantics of path expressions. Finally, we list some possible extensions.

A Variation on Wrappers It would be desirable to change the semantics of adaptive programs so that wrappers are only executed on paths that reach a final state. As it stands, a traversal continues in the object graph, executing wrappers, until there is no path in the *class graph* to a final state. While the traversal cannot be avoided, the execution of the wrappers can be avoided in our approach. The corresponding change in the semantics (Sec. 2.4) is to replace the class graph by the *object graph*, ie, to use $\mathsf{RPathSet}_{\mathcal{G}_O}(o, \rho)$ to control the traversal instead of $\mathsf{RPathSet}_{\mathcal{G}_C}(\mathsf{Class}(o), \rho)$.

The implementation defers the execution of wrappers until it is clear that the current path reaches a final state. To this end, the procedure `visit` gets one more parameter `wrapped` and it returns an indication whether or not the traversal has reached a final state, besides the new values of the operation's variables. The parameter, `wrapped`, is the composition of all prefix wrappers since the last final state encountered in the traversal. Whenever the traversal enters an object, `visit` composes the prefix wrapper (if any) with the accumulated wrappers in `wrapped`.

```
(let ((new-wrapped
       (lambda parms
         (apply ((wrapper-semantics prefix-body) this)
                (apply wrapped parms)))))
  ...)
```

The newly constructed wrapper contains a "partially applied" use of the wrapper's semantics to the current object `this`. The resulting function maps a list of the variable's old values to their new values.

If the current state is final, `visit` applies `new-wrapped` to the values of the variables. The `wrapped` parameter for traversing the children is the identity function `(lambda parms parms)`. Before returning from a final state, the suffix wrapper (if any) is executed and the result is paired with "true" because the traversal has encountered a final state.

If the current state is not final, `visit` passes the composed wrapper `new-wrapped` down to the traversal of the instances. If any of these traversals returns "true", indicating that it has found a successful path, the suffix wrapper is executed. Moreover, as soon as a traversal has returned "true", the remaining instances must be traversed with the identity function as the `wrapped` parameter. Otherwise, the prefix wrapper of the current state (and the accumulated wrappers in `wrapped`) would be executed more than once.

The actual code is more complicated since prefix and suffix wrappers are optional.

A Variation on Traversal Specifications The current semantics of traversal specifications has a few glitches. For example, the traversal specification $A \cdot A$ is satisfied by the one-element path (A). Therefore, it is not possible to specify that, eg, three instances of A are encountered before a traversal is successful. Likewise, it is not possible to specify a traversal that reaches A so that it first goes through label l and then continues through label l'. The semantics prescribes that $\{l\}\{l'\}A$ is equivalent to $\{l'\}\{l\}A$. Changing the derivative function implements such a variation.

Further Extensions Our framework is not restricted to single source and target classes. Our traversal specifications do not mention source classes and multiple target classes arise naturally (see Sec. 2.4).

A traversal specification might have further operators like negation and intersection by extending the derivative function. In the database community [1,12,2], more expressive path expressions have been considered, including l^{-1} (find an object o so that the current one is the value of instance variable $o.l$) and $\mu(l)$ (find the closest reachable object with instance variable l) [24]. These would also be interesting to investigate.

It would also be easy to admit cyclic object graphs, by introducing a suitable machinery into the traversal code and by supplying hooks to deal with back arcs. However, this has not been implemented.

6   Related Work

Due to the high-level programming style of adaptive programs, their compilation is an interesting problem. Palsberg et al [19] formalize the semantics of Lieberherr's adaptive programs [15] and identify a number of restrictions. A subsequent paper [18] removes the restrictions and simplifies the semantics, but leads to a compilation algorithm which runs in exponential time in the worst case. Both papers rely on standard results about finite automata.

Finally, Lieberherr and Patt-Shamir [16] introduce further generalizations and simplifications which lead to a polynomial-time compilation algorithm. However, whereas the earlier algorithms perform "static compilation", which processes all compile-time information at compile time, their polynomial-time algorithm performs "dynamic compilation", which means that a certain amount of compile-time information is kept until run time and hence compile-time work is spread over the code implementing the traversal. They employ a different notion of traversal specification than in their earlier work.

The algebraic approach pursued here is based on a notion of derivatives which is closely related to quotients of formal languages [9] and to derivatives of regular expressions [6,7,4]. A companion paper [23] elaborates the formal underpinnings of this approach. That paper also shows that the complexity of our approach to compilation is identical to that of Lieberherr et al's approaches.

Evaluation algorithms for attribute grammars [13,14] also rely on traversals of tree structures. These traversals are usually specified indirectly as dependences between attribute values. So the paths are inferred from the operations, not vice versa. Many have a notion of "threaded" attributes, which are implicitly passed along by the evaluator to all nodes that mention the attribute [20].

7   Conclusion

We have demonstrated that an off-the-shelf partial evaluator can perform the compilation of adaptive programs. This process is naturally staged. We have experimented with different semantics and stagings. We have found that static and dynamic compilation can be achieved essentially from the same specification by varying the binding times. Thus we have clarified the relation between the two compilation strategies.

Our compiler relies on an algebraic treatment of traversal specifications, where a notion of derivative models progress in a traversal. From this foundation we develop interpretive specifications of the semantics. These specifications are amenable to partial evaluation with almost no change.

References

1. Serge Abiteboul, Dallan Quass, Jason McHugh, Jennifer Widom, and Janet Wiener. The Lorel query language for semistructured data. *Journal of Digital Libraries*, 1(1):68–88, 1997. 276
2. Serge Abiteboul and Victor Vianu. Regular path queries with constraints. In *PODS '97. Proceedings of the Sixteenth ACM SIG-SIGMOD-SIGART Symposium on Principles of Database Systems*, pages 122–133, Tucson, Arizona, May 1997. ACM Press. 276
3. Paul L. Bergstein. Object-preserving class transformations. In *OOPSLA'91, ACM SIGPLAN Sixth Annual Conference on Object-Oriented Programming Systems, Languages, and Applications*, pages 299–313. ACM, November 1991. SIGPLAN Notices (26)11. 267
4. Gerard Berry and Ravi Sethi. From regular expressions to deterministic automata. *Theoretical Computer Science*, 48:117–126, 1986. 277
5. W. Brown, R. Malveau, H. McCormick, and T. Mowbray. *AntiPatterns: Refactoring Software, Architectures, and Projects in Crisis*. John Wiley and Sons, 1998. 265
6. Janusz A. Brzozowski. Derivatives of regular expressions. *Journal of the ACM*, 11(4):481–494, 1964. 277
7. John H. Conway. *Regular Algebra and Finite Machines*. Chapman and Hall, 1971. 277
8. Martin Fowler. *Refactoring: Improving the Design of Existing Code*. Addison-Wesley, 1999. 265

9. John E. Hopcroft and Jeffrey D. Ullman. *Introduction to automata theory, languages and computation.* Addison-Wesley, 1979. 277

10. Neil D. Jones, Carsten K. Gomard, and Peter Sestoft. *Partial Evaluation and Automatic Program Generation.* Prentice-Hall, 1993. 265, 273

11. Richard Kelsey, William Clinger, and Jonathan Rees. Revised[5] report on the algorithmic language Scheme. *Higher-Order and Symbolic Computation*, 11(1):7–105, 1998. Also appears in ACM SIGPLAN Notices 33(9), September 1998. Available electronically as http://www.neci.nj.nec.com/homepages/kelsey/r5rs.ps.gz. 265, 272

12. Michael Kifer, Wong Kim, and Yehoshua Sagiv. Querying object oriented databases. In Michael Stonebraker, editor, *Proceedings of the SIGMOD International Conference on Management of Data*, volume 21 of *SIGMOD Record*, pages 393–402, New York, NY, USA, June 1992. ACM Press. 276

13. Donald Ervin Knuth. Semantics of context-free languages. *Mathematical Systems Theory*, 2:127–145, 1968. 277, 278

14. Donald Ervin Knuth. Semantics of context-free languages. *Mathematical Systems Theory*, 5:95–96, 1971. Correction to [13]. 277

15. Karl J. Lieberherr. *Adaptive Object-Oriented Software: The Demeter Method with Propagation Patterns.* PWS Publishing Company, Boston, 1996. 264, 265, 276

16. Karl J. Lieberherr and Boaz Patt-Shamir. Traversals of object structures: Specification and efficient implementation. Technical Report NU-CCS-97-15, College of Computer Science, Northeastern University, Boston, MA, July 1997. 264, 267, 269, 274, 276

17. W. Opdyke. *Refactoring Object-Oriented Frameworks.* PhD thesis, University of Illinois at Urbana-Champain, 1992. 265

18. Jens Palsberg, Boaz Patt-Shamir, and Karl Lieberherr. A new approach to compiling adaptive programs. *Science of Computer Programming*, 29(3):303–326, September 1997. 264, 265, 267, 269, 276

19. Jens Palsberg, Cun Xiao, and Karl Lieberherr. Efficient implementation of adaptive software. *ACM Transactions on Programming Languages and Systems*, 17(2):264–292, March 1995. 264, 265, 267, 270, 271, 276

20. S. Doaitse Swierstra, P. R. Azero Alocer, and João Saraiava. Designing and implementing combinator languages. In Doaitse Swierstra, Pedro Henriques, and José Oliveira, editors, *Advanced Functional Programming, Third International School, AFP'98*, volume 1608 of *LNCS-Tutorial*, pages 150–206. Springer-Verlag, 1999. 277

21. Peter Thiemann. Towards partial evaluation of full Scheme. In Gregor Kiczales, editor, *Reflection'96*, pages 95–106, San Francisco, CA, USA, April 1996. 274

22. Peter Thiemann. *The PGG System—User Manual.* Universität Freiburg, Freiburg, Germany, February 1999. Available from ftp://ftp.informatik.uni-freiburg.de/iif/thiemann/pgg/. 265, 273

23. Peter Thiemann. An algebraic foundation for adaptive programming. In Jerzy Tiuryn, editor, *Foundations of Software Science and Computation Structures, FOSSACS 2000*, Lecture Notes in Computer Science, Berlin, Germany, March 2000. Springer-Verlag. Extended version available from http://www.informatik.uni-freiburg.de/ thiemann/papers/ adaptive-lncs.ps.gz. 265, 273, 277

24. Jan Van den Bussche and Gottfried Vossen. An extension of path expressions to simplify navigation in object-oriented queries. In *Proc. of Intl. Conf. on Deductive and Object-Oriented Databases (DOOD)*, volume 760 of *Lecture Notes in Computer Science*, pages 267–282, 1993. 276

Functional Incremental Attribute Evaluation

João Saraiva[1], Doaitse Swierstra[2], and Matthijs Kuiper[3]

[1] Depart. of Informatics
University of Minho, Portugal
jas@di.uminho.pt
[2] Depart. of Computer Science
University of Utrecht, The Netherlands
swierstra@cs.uu.nl
[3] Ordina, The Netherlands
MKuiper@factory.ordina.nl

Abstract. This paper presents a new strict, purely functional implementation of attribute grammars. Incremental evaluation is obtained via standard function memoization. Our new implementation of attribute grammars increases the incremental behaviour of the evaluators by both reducing the memoization overhead and increasing their potential incrementallity. We present also an attribute grammar transformation, which increases the incremental performance of the attribute evaluators after a change that propagates its effects to all parts of the syntax tree.
These techniques have been implemented in a purely functional attribute grammar system and the first experimental results are presented.

1 Introduction

Developments in programming languages are changing the way in which we construct programs: naive text editors are now replaced by powerful programming language *environments* which are specialized for the programming language under consideration and which help the user throughout the editing process. They use *knowledge* of the programming language to provide the users with powerful mechanisms to develop their programs. This knowledge is based on the *structure* and the *meaning* of the language. To be more precise, it is based in the syntactic and (static) semantic characteristics of the language. Having this knowledge about a language, the language-based environment is not only able to highlight keywords and beautify programs, but it can also detect features of the programs being edited that, for example, violate the properties of the underlying language. Furthermore, a language-based environment may also give information to the user about properties of the program under consideration. Finally, it may hide from the user some peculiarities included in the language that are relevant only for the programs/computers that process/execute them. All these features make a language-based environment an effective mechanism to increase the productivity of users.

After each interaction with the user a language-based environment provides immediate feedback concerning whether or not such an interaction is legal. That

A. Watt (Ed.): CC/ETAPS 2000, LNCS 1781, pp. 279–294, 2000.

is to say, the environment has to react and to provide answers in real-time. Consequently, the delay between the user interaction and the system response is an extremely important aspect in such interactive systems. Thus, one of the key features to handle such interactive environments is the ability to perform efficient re-computations. Attribute grammars, and particularly their higher-order variant, are a suitable formalism to specify such language-based environments. Furthermore, attribute grammar are executable, *i.e.*, efficient implementations are automatically obtained.

In this paper we introduce a new strict, purely functional implementation for ordered attribute grammars [Kas80]. A strict model of attribute evaluation is attractive for two main reasons: firstly, because we obtain very efficient implementations in terms of memory and time consumption. Secondly, because a rather efficient and simple incremental attribute evaluator can be derived from an attribute grammar: incremental evaluation is obtained via standard function memoization. Our new functional implementation improves the incremental behaviour of the evaluators in two ways: first, by dynamically specializing the underlying syntax tree for each of the individual traversal functions, which increases the sharing of subtrees and consequently the reuse of their shared decorations. Second, by reducing the interpretative overhead due to the memoization scheme: our technique does not induce any additional parameter/result to the evaluators functions which "glue" the different traversals. Such parameters have to be tested for equality under the memoization scheme. Consequently, fewer arguments means fewer equality tests, and as a result, lower interpretative overhead. A change that propagates its effects to all parts of the syntax tree is known to give poor performance in all models of incremental attribute evaluation. In this paper we define a simple attribute grammar transformation that *projects attributes* and that greatly improves their incremental behaviour when re-decorating the syntax tree after such a change.

In Section 2 we discuss incremental attribute evaluation, higher-order attribute grammars and the visit-function memoization scheme. In Section 3 our new functional attribute evaluator is introduced and is briefly compared with previous approaches. Section 4 presents the grammar transformation. Section 5 presents the first experimental results and Section 6 contains the conclusions.

2   Incremental Attribute Evaluation

Attribute grammars (AG) have been used with great success in the development of language-based tools since Thomas Reps first used attribute grammars to model syntax-oriented editors (in Figure 2 we will show a traditional language-based editor). In such an interactive programming environment, a user slightly modifies a *decorated tree* T into T' (to be more precise, the user changes a "pretty printed" version of such trees). After that, an *incremental attribute evaluator* uses T and its attributes instances to compute the attributes instances of T', instead of decorating T' from scratch. The underlying assumption is that the decoration of T' from scratch is more expensive (*i.e.*, more time consuming) than an incremental update of T.

Although any non-incremental attribute evaluator can be applied to completely re-decorate tree T', the goal of an *optimal incremental attribute evaluator* is to limit the amount of work to $\mathcal{O}(|\Delta|)$, where Δ is the set of *affected* and *newborn* attribute instances. The traditional approach to achieve incremental evaluation involves *propagating changes* of attribute values through the attributed tree [RTD83,RT89].

2.1   Higher-Order Attribute Grammars

Higher-Order Attribute Grammars (HAG) [VSK89] are an important extension to the attribute grammar formalism. Conventional attribute grammars are augmented with *higher-order attributes*. Higher-order attributes are attributes whose value is a tree. We may associate, once again, attributes with such a tree. Attributes of these so-called *higher-order trees*, may be higher-order attributes again. Higher-order attribute grammars have three main characteristics:

- First, when a computation can not be easily expressed in terms of the inductive structure of the underlying tree, a better suited structure can be computed before. Consider, for example, a language where the abstract grammar does not match the concrete one. Consider also that the semantic rules of such a language are easily expressed over the abstract grammar rather than over the concrete one. The mapping between both grammars can be specified within the higher-order attribute grammar formalism: the attribute equations of the concrete grammar define a higher-order attribute representing the abstract grammar. As a result, the decoration of a concrete syntax tree constructs a higher-order tree: the abstract syntax tree. The attribute equations of the abstract grammar define the semantics of the language.
- Secondly, semantic functions are redundant. In higher-order attribute grammars every computation can be modelled through attribution rules. More specifically, inductive semantic functions can be replaced by higher-order attributes. For example, a typical application of higher-order attributes is to model the (recursive) lookup function in an environment. Consequently, there is no need to have a different notation (or language) to define semantic functions in AGs.
- The third characteristic is that part of the abstract tree can be used directly as a value within a semantic equation. That is, grammar symbols can be moved from the syntactic domain to the semantic domain.

These characteristics make higher-order attribute grammars particularly suitable to model interactive language-based environments [TC90,Pen94,KS98,Sar99]. It is known that the incremental attribute evaluator for ordered attribute grammars [Kas80,RT89] can be trivially adapted for the incremental evaluation of higher-order attribute grammars. The adapted evaluator, however, decorates every instance of a higher-order attribute separately [TC90]. Note that in such traditional evaluators the usual representation for an attributed tree is an *unshared tree*. Higher-order attribute grammars define higher-order attributes, which instances are higher-order trees. Different instances of higher-order attributes may be equal trees or share common subtrees. Consequently, the most efficient representation for such high-order trees is a shared tree, *i.e.*, a *directed acyclic graph* (DAG). Consequently, there is a clash between the two representations, namely, tree and DAG. There are two ways to solve this tension: either we use specific techniques to decorate DAGs or we guarantee that the terms are, in fact, trees that are decorated by an adapted evaluator.

Let us discuss first the use of adapted evaluators. Teitelbaum [TC90] proposes a simple approach to handle DAGs: whenever a higher-order attribute has to be instantiated with a higher-order tree (*i.e.*, with a DAG), the tree sharing is broken and the attribute is actually instantiated with a tree. This tree is a "*tree-copy*" of the DAG. After that, the higher-order tree can be easily decorated by an adapted *change propagator* since attribute values can be associated with the tree nodes in the standard way. This approach, however, leads to a non-optimal incremental behaviour when higher-order attributes are affected by tree transformations, as shown in [CP96]. Note that as a result of breaking the sharing, different instantiations of higher-order attributes are, indeed, different trees. Such trees have to be decorated separately, without the possibility of reusing attribute values across the different decorations of those attributed trees. Note that instances of the same higher-order attribute are likely to be (completely or partially) decorated with the same attribute values. In order to efficiently (and incrementally) evaluate such instances, the reuse of those values should be achieved.

2.2   Visit-Function Memoization

The visit-function memoization proposed by Pennings [Pen94] is based on the following combination of ideas:

Purely functional attribute evaluators: Syntax trees are decorated by *binding-tree based attribute evaluators* [Pen94]. Such evaluators are strict, purely functional attribute evaluators. Attribute instances are not stored in the tree nodes, but, instead, they are the arguments and the results of (side-effect free) functions: the *visit-functions*. Binding-trees are used with the single purpose to "glue" the different traversal functions of the evaluator, *i.e.*, they convey information between traversals.

Data constructor memoization: Since attribute values are not stored in the syntax tree, multiple instances of the syntax tree can be shared. That is, trees are collapsed into minimal *direct acyclic graphs*. DAGs are obtained by constructing trees bottom-up and by using constructor memoization to eliminate replication of common sub-expressions. This technique, also called *hash-consing*, guarantees that two identical objects share the same records on the heap, and thus are represented by the same pointer.

The basic idea of hash-consing is very simple: whenever a new node is allocated (or *"consed"*) we check whether there exists already an identical record in the heap. If so, we avoid the allocation and simply use the existing one. Otherwise, we perform the allocation as usual. Generally, a *hash table* is used to search the heap for a duplicated record. Hash-consing can be applied to pure values only, *i.e.*, values that never change during the execution of a program: for if two updatable records have identical values now, they might not be identical later, and so merging them could lead to incorrect values. Observe that this is the case if attributes are stored in the tree nodes, because shared nodes may have to store different attribute values induced by different, but shared, attribute instances (and most probably will).

Attribute values may be large structures (*e.g.*, symbol tables, higher-order attributes, etc). Therefore, the constructors for user defined types are also shared. This technique solves the problem of expensive attribute equality test during evaluation and it also settles the problem of huge memory consumption due to multiple instances of the same attribute value in a syntax tree.

Function memoization: Due to the pure nature of the visit-functions, incremental evaluation can now be obtained by memoizing calls to visit-functions. The binding-tree based attribute evaluators are constructed as a set of strict functions. Thus, standard function memoization techniques can be used to memoize their calls. Memoization is obtained by storing in a *memo table* calls to visit-functions. Every call corresponds to a *memo entry*, in the *memo table*, that records both the arguments and the results of one call to a visit-function.

Let us describe the binding-tree attribute evaluators in more detail. Such evaluators are based on the visit-sequence paradigm [Kas80]: the visit-sequences induce a set of *visit-functions*, each of them performing the computations schedule for a particular traversal of the evaluator. The different traversal functions are "glued" by intermediate data structures: the *binding-trees*. The visit-functions and the binding-tree data types are automatically induced by a *binding analysis* of the visit-sequences [Pen94].

As a result of the binding analysis, a visit-function $\texttt{visit}_v X$ is constructed for every terminal X and every visit v such that $1 \leq v \leq n$, with n the number of visits to X. The arguments of the visit-function are the subtree labelled X, the inherited attributes of visit v and the binding-trees computed in previous visits that are destructed by visit v. The results are the binding-trees for following visits and the synthesized attributes of visit v. The first visit does not inherit any binding-tree, and the last one does not synthesize them. The introduction of binding-trees is reflected in the types of the visit-functions: they are additional arguments/results.

$$\texttt{visit}_1 \mathbf{X} :: X \rightarrow "A_{inh\_v}(X, 1)" \rightarrow (X^{1 \rightarrow 2}, \ldots, X^{1 \rightarrow n}, "A_{syn\_v}(X, 1)")$$
$$\texttt{visit}_k \mathbf{X} :: X \rightarrow "A_{inh\_v}(X, k)" \rightarrow X^{1 \rightarrow k} \rightarrow \cdots \rightarrow X^{k-1 \rightarrow k} \rightarrow$$
$$(X^{k \rightarrow k+1}, \ldots, X^{k \rightarrow n}, "A_{syn\_v}(X, k)")$$
$$\texttt{visit}_n \mathbf{X} :: X \rightarrow "A_{inh\_v}(X, n)" \rightarrow X^{1 \rightarrow n} \rightarrow \cdots \rightarrow X^{n-1 \rightarrow n} \rightarrow ("A_{syn\_v}(X, n)")$$

where $A_{inh\_v}(X, i)$ $(A_{syn\_v}(X, i))$ denotes the set of inherited (synthesized) attributes that are schedule to be used (computed) during visit i. The quotes around the set of inherited and synthesized attributes of a particular visit should be interpreted as the types of the elements of those sets. Superscripts are used to denote the origins and the targets of binding-trees. Thus, $X^{v \to w}$ denotes the constructor type of a binding-tree with origin in traversal v $(1 \le v \le n)$ and target in traversal w $(v < w \le n)$. The original syntax tree does not change during the different traversals of the evaluator. Attribute values are passed between traversals, as arguments and as results of visit-functions, or within binding-trees. Consider the following simplified visit-sequence for production named PROD : $X \to Y Z$.

> plan PROD

> | | |
> |---|---|
> | begin 1 inh($X.inh_1$) | begin 2 inh($X.inh_2$) |
> | visit $(Y, 1)$ | visit $(Z, 1)$ |
> | eval $(Y.inh_1)$ uses$(X.inh_1, Y.syn_1)$, | eval $(X.syn_2)$ |
> | visit $(Y, 2)$ | uses$(X.inh_1, Z.syn_1)$ |
> | eval $(X.syn_1)$ uses$(Y.syn_2)$, | end 2   syn$(X.syn_2)$ |
> | end 1   syn$(X.syn_1)$ | |

According to this visit-sequences, the inherited attribute $X.inh_1$ must be explicitly passed from the first visit to X (where it is defined) to the second one (where it is used). The nonterminal Y is visited twice, with both visits occurring in the first visit to X. Next, we present the memoized visit-functions (using the Haskell notation[1]) induced by this visit-sequence. Productions' name are used as constructor functions.

> visit$_1$**X** (PROD tY tZ) $\boxed{tXinh_1}$ = (PROD$^{1 \to 2}$ $\boxed{tXinh_1}, tX syn_1$)
> where $(tY^{1 \to 2}, tY syn_1) =$ **memo** visit$_1$**Y** tY^1
> $tY inh_1 = f(tXinh_1, tY syn_1)$
> $tY syn_2 =$ **memo** visit$_2$**Y** tY $tY inh_1$ $tY^{1 \to 2}$
> $tX syn_1 = tY syn_2$ $\boxed{tXinh_1}$ defined in visit$_1$**X**
>   used in   visit$_2$**X**
> visit$_2$**X** (PROD tY tZ) $tXinh_2$ (PROD$^{1 \to 2}$ $\boxed{tXinh_1}$) $= tX syn_2$
> where $tZ syn_1 =$ **memo** visit$_1$**Z** tZ $tXinh_2$
> $tX syn_2 = g(\boxed{tXinh_1}, tZ syn_1)$

The function memoization efficiently handles higher-order attribute grammars. Furthermore, the original attribute evaluator needs virtually no change: it does not need any specific purpose algorithm to keep track of which attribute values are affected by a tree change. The memoization mechanism takes care of the incremental evaluation. However, the binding-tree based function memoization has two main drawbacks. Firstly, the memoization mechanism has an interpretative overhead: aiming at improving the potential incremental behaviour of the evaluators, Pennings proposes the use of binding-trees that are *quadratic* in the number of traversals. Although this approach yields binding-tree evaluators which maximize the number of cache hits, such behaviour comes at a price:

---

[1] The **memo** annotation that we use corresponds to a primitive function of the gofer system [M.P94] that was extended with a (lazy) memoization mechanism [vD92].

first, many binding-tree constructor functions may have to be memoized, which may fill the *memo table*, and, consequently, increase the overhead of its search operation [AG93]. Second, the binding-trees induce additional arguments (and results) to the visit-functions. In our simple example, the functions $visit_2\mathbf{X}$ and $visit_2\mathbf{Y}$ get an additional argument: the binding-trees. When a large number of traversals is induced by the AG scheduling algorithm, then the visit-functions may be extended with a large number of arguments. That is to say, having more binding-trees means having more (argument) values to test for equality, when looking for a memoized call in the *memo table*. Although the equality test among "hash-consed" binging-trees per se is cheap, a large number of tests leads to a not negligible impact in searching the *memo table*.

Secondly, no total traversal of a binding-tree evaluator can be avoided after a tree transformation: the underlying syntax tree changes and, consequently, *all* the visit-functions applied to the newly created nodes (*i.e.*, the nodes in the path from the root to the modified subtrees) have to be (re)computed. The first argument of all the visit-functions that perform the different traversals has changed and, so, no previous calls can be found in the *memo table*.

3 The Visit-Tree Based Attribute Evaluators

In this section we present a new approach for purely functional implementation of attribute grammars that overcomes the two drawbacks presented by the binding-tree approach. First, it reduces the interpretative overhead due to the memoization scheme by not inducing additional "gluing" arguments to the visit-functions. Second, the syntax trees that guide our evaluators are *dynamically specialized* for each visit of the evaluator. This feature allows for entire traversals of the evaluator to be skipped: the traversal functions whose underlying specialized trees do not refer to changed subtrees can be reused.

Basically, our new approach, called visit-tree based attribute evaluator, mimics the imperative approach: attribute values defined in one traversal and used in the following ones are stored in a *new tree*, the so-called *visit-tree*. Such values have to be preserved in the (visit-)tree from the traversal that creates them until the last traversal that uses them. Each traversal builds a new visit-tree for the next traversal, with the additional values stored in its nodes. The functions that perform the subsequent traversals find the values they need, either in their arguments or in the nodes of the (visit-)tree, exactly as in the imperative approach. A set of visit-tree types is defined, one per traversal. A visit-tree for one traversal, say v, is specialized for that particular traversal of the evaluator: it contains only the attribute values which are really needed in traversal v and the following ones. The visit-trees are constructed dynamically, *i.e.*, during attribute evaluation. Consequently, the underlying data structure which guides the attribute evaluator is not fixed during evaluation. This dynamic construction/destruction of the visit-trees allows for an important optimization: subtrees that are not needed in future traversals are *discarded* from the visit-trees concerned. As result, any data no longer needed, no longer is referenced.

The formal derivation of visit-tree based attribute evaluators from higher-order attribute grammars is presented in [Sar99]. In this paper we present the visit-tree approach by informally analysing the production PROD and its visit-sequence.

Let us consider again the attribute $X.inh_1$. In the visit-tree approach, the value of attribute $X.inh_1$ is passed to the second traversal in one visit-tree. This visit-tree is one result of the first traversal of the evaluator. So, we have to define two tree data types: one for the first traversal, and another for the second one. These data types, called *visit-tree data types*, are defined next. We use superscripts to distinguish the traversal they are intended to.

> **data** X^1 = PROD^1 Y^1 Z^1
> **data** X^2 = PROD^2 "$X.inh_1$" Z^1

In the first visit to X, the nonterminal Y is visited twice. The visit-tree data type X^1 includes a reference to the first visit (the visit-tree type Y^1) only. The second visit-tree is constructed when visiting the first one (see the visit-functions below). Thus, a reference to the earliest visit suffices. Nonterminal Y is not used in the second visit to PROD. So, no reference to Y has to be included in X^2. Consequently, subtrees labelled Y are discarded from the second traversal of the evaluator. The visit-trees are arguments and results of the visit-functions. Thus, the visit-functions must explicitly destruct/construct the visit-trees.

> $\textbf{visit}_1\textbf{X}$ (PROD^1 tY^1 tZ^1) $\boxed{tXinh_1}$ = (PROD^2 $\boxed{tXinh_1}$ $tZ^1, tXsyn_1$)
> **where** $(tY^2, tYsyn_1)$ = **memo** $\textbf{visit}_1\textbf{Y}$ tY^1
> $\quad tYinh_1 = f\,(tXinh_1, tYsyn_1)$ $\boxed{tXinh_1}$ defined in $\textbf{visit}_1\textbf{X}$
> $\quad tYsyn_2$ = **memo** $\textbf{visit}_2\textbf{Y}$ tY^2 $tYinh_1$ used in $\textbf{visit}_2\textbf{X}$
> $\quad tXsyn_1 = tYsyn_2$
>
> tY^2 visit-tree constructed in
> $\textbf{visit}_2\textbf{X}$ (PROD^2 $\boxed{tXinh_1}$ tZ^1) $tXinh_2 = tXsyn_2$ the first traversal and
> **where** $tZsyn_1$ = **memo** $\textbf{visit}_1\textbf{Z}$ tZ^1 $tXinh_2$ used in the second.
> $\quad tXsyn_2 = g\,(\boxed{tXinh_1}, tZsyn_1)$

In the first traversal the attribute value $tXinh_1$ is computed, and a visit-tree node PROD^2 (which stores this value) is constructed. In the second traversal, that node is destructed and the value of $tXinh_1$ is ready to be used. The visit-function $\textbf{visit}_1\textbf{Y}$ returns the visit-tree for the next traversal (performed by $\textbf{visit}_2\textbf{Y}$). Observe that the visit-functions $\textbf{visit}_2\textbf{X}$ and $\textbf{visit}_2\textbf{Y}$ do not get any gluing arguments. The (visit-)tree and the inherited attributes are the only arguments of the functions.

In order to compare the visit-tree based evaluators with the binding-tree ones, we shall present the induced types of the visit-functions. For each traversal v, with $1 \leq v \leq n$, of a nonterminal symbol X, a visit-function $\textbf{visit}_v\textbf{X}$ is generated. Its arguments are a visit-tree of type X^v, and an additional argument for each attribute in $A_{inh\_v}(X, v)$. The result is a tuple, whose first element is the visit-tree for the next traversal and the other elements are the attributes in $A_{syn\_v}(X, v)$. The visit-function that performs the last traversal n does not construct any visit-tree. So, the visit-functions have a signature of the following form:

$$\text{visit}_v \mathbf{X} :: \mathrm{X}^v \to \text{"}A_{inh\_v}(X, v)\text{"} \to (\mathrm{X}^{v+1}, \text{"}A_{syn\_v}(X, v)\text{"})$$
$$\text{visit}_n \mathbf{X} :: \mathrm{X}^n \to \text{"}A_{inh\_v}(X, n)\text{"} \to (\text{"}A_{syn\_v}(X, n)\text{"})$$

As expected no additional arguments are included in the visit-functions of our evaluators. The visit-tree based attribute evaluators have the following properties:

- The number of visit-trees is linear in the number of traversals.
- No additional arguments/results in the visit-functions are used to explicitly pass attribute values between traversal functions.
- The visit-functions are strict in all their arguments, as a result of the order computed by the AG ordered scheduling algorithm. Thus, standard function memoization techniques can be used to achieve incremental evaluation.
- Efficient memory usage: data not needed is no longer referenced. References to grammar symbols and attribute instances can efficiently be discarded as soon as they have played their semantic role.

3.1   Combining the Binding and Visit-Tree Approaches

Although the visit-tree approach solves some of the problems of the binding-tree approach, in some situations, it can yield less efficient incremental evaluators than the binding-tree one. This situation occurs when values of attribute instances that have to be passed to following traversals are affected by tree transformations. Recall that under the visit-tree approach these attribute values remain in the tree from when they are created until their last use. Consequently, unnecessary intermediate visits may have to be performed, because the visit-tree is used to pass on such changed values.

To be more precise, let $\mathbf{T'}$ be an abstract syntax tree resulting from a tree replacement at node $\mathbf{N}$ in tree $\mathbf{T}$. Without loss of generality, consider that a strict evaluator performs three traversals to decorate $\mathbf{T'}$. Consider also that an attribute instance α is affected by the tree replacement and that α is defined in the first traversal and used in the third one only. Under the visit-tree approach no traversal of the evaluator can be skipped: *all* the visit-trees of the evaluator are affected by the tree replacement, since all the trees store the changed instance α. Although the second traversal may not be "directly" affected by the change, the visit-functions applied to the nodes in the path from the root to the node where α is stored have to be recomputed because the visit-tree for this traversal has changed. This is represented graphically in Figure 1.

Under the binding-tree approach, the binding-tree makes a "bridge" from the first (origin) to the third (destination) traversal, in order to pass the value of attribute α. As a result, the instance α does not force the re-decoration of part of the second traversal of the evaluator. Nevertheless, part of this traversal has to be decorated because the syntax tree $\mathbf{T}$ has changed.

We can also improve the potential incremental behaviour of our evaluators by combining visit-trees with binding-trees. The basic idea is that some values are

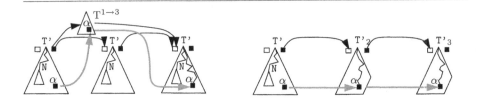

Fig. 1. Passing an attribute value between two non-consecutive traversals: the binding-trees (left) make a *"bridge"* between the origin and the destination traversal. The visit-tree (right) passes the attribute values *"through"* the intermediate traversal.

passed to the following traversals in visit-trees, and others, in binding-trees. Let us be more precise: during visit v of the evaluator, the attribute values that are alive in v and are used in $v+1$ are passed in a visit-tree. Values alive in visit v and which are used in visit w, with $w > v+1$ are passed in a binding-tree. That is, the binding-trees make the bridge for values used in non-consecutive traversals. For example, this approach will efficiently handle the situation presented in Figure 1.

3.2   Semantic Function Memoization

Pugh [PT89] proposes the memoization of the semantic function calls only. In a traditional non-functional setting Pugh's semantic function memoization has the problem of storing attributes in the tree nodes and, consequently, there is no possibility of having tree sharing. Consequently, under a traditional implementation of AGs, Pugh's approach does not handle HAGs efficiently. Besides, in a functional setting, the visit-function memoization is more efficient since the reuse of a visit-function call means that an entire visit to an arbitrarily large tree can be skipped. Such incremental behaviour is not possible under Pugh's approach because all the visits of the evaluator always have to be performed. Nevertheless, Pugh's approach can be easily implemented with the visit-function memoization if one memoizes the calls to semantic functions exactly in the same way as visit-functions.

4   Projection of Attributes

A change that propagates its effects to all parts of the tree causes inefficient behaviour in all the models of incremental atribute evaluation [Pen94,SKS97]. Nevertheless, incremental evaluation can be enhanced greatly by performing a simple transformation on the AG: *the projection of attributes*. Consider, for example, a block structured language. Typically, every inner block inherits the context of its outer block, so, any small change in that context requires the redecoration of the inner blocks, regardless of the irrelevance of the change, *i.e.*, even if the change is confined to a symbol that is not mentioned in the inner blocks. However, if every block synthesizes a list of used variables, the inherited context could be *projected* on that list, yielding better incremental behaviour.

Next we present an AG fragment defining the projection of the environment in a block structued language. We use a *standard* AG notation: productions are labelled for future references and subscripts are used to distinguish different nonterminal occurrences. Inherited (synthesized) attributes are prefixed by the down (up) arrow $\downarrow$ ($\uparrow$). The attribution rules are written as Haskell-like expressions.

$Its, It \quad <\uparrow uses : [Name] >$
$Its \quad = \text{NilIts}$
$\qquad Its.uses = \texttt{[]}$
$\qquad | \text{ConsIts } It \ Its$
$\qquad Its_1.uses = It.uses \ \texttt{++} \ Its_2.uses$
$It \quad \rightarrow \text{Decl} \quad Name$
$\qquad It.uses = [Name]$
$\qquad | \text{ Use} \quad Name$
$\qquad It.uses = [Name]$
$\qquad | \text{ Block} \quad Its$
$\qquad It.uses = Its.uses$

$It \rightarrow \text{Block } Its$
$\qquad Its.env = \boxed{project} \ Its.uses \ It.env$

$project :: [Name] \rightarrow Env \rightarrow Env$
$project \ \texttt{[]} \ \_ \qquad = \texttt{[]}$
$project \ (n\!:\!us) \ env = (getentries \ n \ env)\texttt{++}$
$\qquad\qquad\qquad\qquad (project \ us \ env)$

Fragment 1: The projection of the environment for the inner blocks.

The semantic function $\boxed{project}$ projects the environment of the outer most block on the list of identifiers synthesized for each inner block. The semantic function *getentries* is a primitive function defined on environments: given an identifier (*i.e.*, a key), it returns the entries associated with that identifier. These two inductive functions can be efficiently defined within the higher-order attribute grammar formalism. Next, we modelled both functions as a higher-order attribute using the technique of accumulating parameters. Attribute equations are given for nonterminals *Env* and *Uses* which replace the *getentries* and *project* functions. Two higher-order attributes are defined: *getentries* and *project*.

$Env \quad <\downarrow envi : Env, \uparrow envo : Env >$
$Env = \text{NilEnv}$
$\qquad Env_1.envo = Env_1.envi$
$\qquad | \text{ CEnv} \quad Name \ Env$
$\qquad Env_2.envi = \texttt{if } (Name \ \texttt{==} \ Env_1.id)$
$\qquad\qquad\qquad \texttt{then } \text{CEnv } Name \ Env_1.envi$
$\qquad\qquad\qquad \texttt{else } Env_1.envi$
$\qquad Env_1.envo = Env_2.envo$
$It \quad \rightarrow \text{Block} \qquad Its$
$\qquad \textbf{ata} \ project : Uses$
$\qquad project \qquad = Its.uses$
$\qquad project.penvi = \text{NilEnv}$
$\qquad project.env \ \ = Its.dclo$
$\qquad \boxed{Its.env} \quad = \boxed{project.penvo}$

$Uses \quad <\downarrow env : Env, \downarrow penvi : Env$
$\qquad\qquad , \uparrow penvo : Env >$
$Uses = \text{NilUses}$
$\qquad Uses_1.penvo = Uses_1.penvi$
$\qquad | \text{ ConsUses } Name \ Uses$
$\qquad \textbf{ata} \ getentries : Env$
$\qquad getentries \qquad = Uses_1.env$
$\qquad getentries.id \ \ = Name$
$\qquad getentries.lev \ = 0$
$\qquad getentries.envi = Uses_1.penvi$
$\qquad Uses_2.penvi \ = getentries.envo$
$\qquad Uses_2.env \qquad = Uses_1.env$
$\qquad Uses_1.penvo \quad = Uses_2.penvo$

Fragment 2: The environment projection modelled as higher-order attributes.

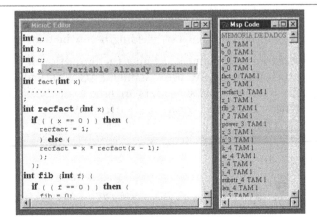

Fig. 2. A language-based environment for MICROC.

Observe that in the higher-order variant we inherit the advantages of the HAG formalism: we are no longer restricted to the implicit positional argument style that is enforced by the conventional functional languages (see the equations of production BLOCK of the previous two fragments). One key aspect of modeling inductive functions as higher-order attributes is the fact that their evaluation becomes automatically incremental. Furthermore, as a result of the ordering computed by standard AG techniques we also guarantee that the underlying inductive computation terminates, which is not ensured when functions are used.

5   Performance Results

The visit-function memoization is the model of incremental evaluation used by the LRC system [KS98]: a generator for incremental language-oriented tools. It produces purely functional C and HASKELL based attribute evaluators using the techniques described in this paper. It generates also lazy circular attribute evaluators and deforested attribute evaluators [SS99].

To benchmark the memoization scheme we consider the C based attribute evaluators and the (strict) incremental engine included in LRC. As input for the beanchmark, we use a traditional language-based editor and a block-structured language, *the* MICROC *language*. The MICROC language is a tiny C based programming language. Figure 2 shows the language-based environment of MI-CROC constructed with LRC.

The binding and the visit-tree based attribute evaluators generated by LRC for the MICROC HAG perform two traversals over the syntax tree. Two traversals are induced by the AG scheduling algorithm because a *use-before-declare* discipline is allowed in MICROC: declaration of global variables and definition of functions are not required to occur before their first use. Thus, a first traversal collects the environment and a second traversal uses such an environment to detect invalid uses of identifiers. The binding-tree approach uses a single binding-tree to glue together the two traversal functions, while the visit-tree approach uses a visit-tree. Both evaluators construct the same syntax tree in their first traversal. It is worthwhile to note that under a two traversal scheme the binding-tree and the visit-tree approach induce the same number of intermediate trees: a single binding or visit-tree. The overhead due to construct/memoing a large number of intermediate data structures used by the binding-tree approach is not reflected in such evaluators and, thus, in the next results.

Next, we present results obtained when executing the binding-tree and the visit-tree attribute evaluators. We present the number of *cache misses* (functions evaluated), *cache hits* (functions reused), the number of equality tests performed between (shared) terms and the execution time in seconds. We have clocked the execution time on a plain Silicon Graphics workstation.

Model of Evaluation	Attribute Evaluator	Hash Array	Cache Misses	Hits	Equality Tests	Runtime (sec.)
Exhaustive	Binding-tree	-	-	-	-	0.23
Evaluation	Visit-tree	-	-	-	-	0.21
Incremental	Binding-tree	10007	4323	1626	9373	0.34
Evaluation	Visit-tree	10007	3984	910	7232	0.30

The above table presents results obtained both with exhaustive evaluation, *i.e.*, without memoization of the calls to the visit-functions, and with incremental evaluation, *i.e.*, with memoization of the visit-function calls. The results of exhaustive evaluation are very similar. As we explained above, under a two traversal the binding-tree approach does not induce a large of intermediate binding-trees. It should be noticed, however, that the visit-functions that perform the second traversal of the binding-tree evaluator get an additional argument: the binding-tree gluing the traversal functions. As a result, this incremental evaluator has to compare more argument values than the visit-tree based evaluator (see the difference in the number of equality tests). Furthermore, the visit-tree induces fewer misses than the binding-tree approach. That is, fewer visit-functions have to be computed (8% fewer functions are computed). Note that the visit-trees are being specialized for each individual traversal of the evaluator and, thus, they are more likely to share subtrees and, consequently, to share their decorations.

Edit actions: To profile the incremental behaviour of our attribute evaluators we have considered two kinds of modification to the input MICROC: we consider a modification local to the body of a function and a modification that is global to the whole program. To be more precise, we modified the program in two ways: by adding a statement to a function and by adding a global variable. Next, we present the result of the incremental evaluation after the four modifications.

Edit Action	Binding-Tree				Visit-Tree			
	Misses	Hits	Tests	Time	Misses	Hits	Tests	Time
Add a statement	434	432	14376	0.03	434	429	11413	0.03
Add a global variable	3874	1949	165674	0.26	3752	1034	138507	0.24

As expected, the functional incremental evaluators handle local changes extremely well. The execution time in both evaluators is almost negligible. On the contrary, adding a global variable gives poor incremental behaviour. No gain is obtained with the incremental evaluation since almost the same visit-functions are being computed. The exhaustive evaluator achieves a better execution time, since it is not influenced by the interpretative overhead due to the memoization scheme. The incremental behaviour of the MICROC environment can be greatly improved if we consider the grammar transformation presented in Section 4. Thus, we have transformed the AG in order to project the attribute that defines the environment passed to the body of the MICROC functions. The environment is projected on the list of identifiers used by the functions.

Edit Action	Binding-Tree				Visit-Tree			
	Misses	Hits	Tests	Time	Misses	Hits	Tests	Time
Add a statement	443	441	19445	0.03	432	431	16175	0.03
Add a global variable	644	813	31444	0.11	522	509	16993	0.10

The projection of the environment drastically improved the performance of both incremental evaluators after a global modification in the input. The number of cache misses and equality tests decreased considerably. As a result, using the projection of attributes, the incremental evaluator gives a speed-up of 2 for global changes when compared to the exhaustive evaluator.

These results show that, even for a simple two traversal evaluator the visit-tree approach presents a better incremental performance. For evaluators that require a large number of traversals, we expect greater differences in performance. For example, the attribute evaluator derived from the LRC AG (LRC is a bootstrap system) performs eleven traversals over the tree. Under the binding-tree approach a single nonterminal induces thirty four binding-tree data types. Such binding-trees induce additional arguments to the visit-functions: for example, the visit-function that performs the last visit to that nonterminal symbol gets nine additional arguments. Recall that such arguments have to be tested for equality during incremental evaluation. Under the visit-tree approach, although eleven visit-tree data types still have to be defined, the visit-functions do not get any additional arguments. The LRC bootstrap grammar also shows how difficult it can be to hand-write a strict, functional attribute evaluator: the writer has to concern himself with partitioning the evaluator into different traversals and to glue the traversal functions.

6   Conclusions

This paper presented two techniques to improve the incremental behaviour of attribute grammars and their functional implementations. Firstly, we defined a new strict, functional implementation of attribute grammars, where a visit-tree is used to convey information between different traversal functions. This technique was implemented in a purely functional attribute grammar. The first experimental results show that our new approach improves the incremental performance of the evaluators by increasing the number of function calls reused, and by decreasing the interpretative overhead of the memoization scheme, when compared to previous functional implementations of AGs.

Secondly, we have defined a transformation for attribute grammars that improves their potential incremental behaviour after a global tree transformation, for all models of incremental evaluation. Our first results show that it drastically increases the performance of the AG. In our experiments we have transformed ourselves the AG. However, an attribute grammar system should apply such transformation automatically.

References

AG93.   Andrew W. Appel and Marcelo J. R. Gonçalves. Hash-consing Garbage Collection. Technical Report CS-TR-412-93, Princeton University, Dept. of Computer Science, February 1993.   285

CP96.   Alan Carle and Lori Pollock. On the Optimality of Change Propagation for Incremental Evaluation of Hierarchical Attribute Grammars. *ACM Transactions on Programming Languages and Systems*, 18(1):16–29, January 1996. 282

Kas80.   Uwe Kastens. Ordered attribute grammars. *Acta Informatica*, 13:229–256, 1980.   280, 281, 283

KS98.   Matthijs Kuiper and João Saraiva.   Lrc - A Generator for Incremental Language-Oriented Tools. In Kay Koskimies, editor, *7th International Conference on Compiler Construction*, volume 1383 of *LNCS*, pages 298–301. Springer-Verlag, April 1998.   281, 290

M.P94.   Jones M.P. The implementation of the gofer functional programming system. Technical Report Research Report YALEU/DCS/RR-1030, Yale University, Dept. of Computer Science, May 1994.   284

Pen94.   Maarten Pennings. *Generating Incremental Evaluators*. PhD thesis, Depart. of Computer Science, Utrecht University, The Netherlands, November 1994. 281, 282, 283, 288

PT89.   William Pugh and Tim Teitelbaum. Incremental computation via function caching. In *16th Annual ACM Symposium on Principles of Programming Languages*, volume 1, pages 315–328. ACM, January 1989.   288

RT89.   T. Reps and T. Teitelbaum. *The Synthesizer Generator*. Springer, 1989. 281

RTD83.   Thomas Reps, Tim Teitelbaum, and Alan Demers.   Incremental context-dependent analysis for language-based editors. *ACM Transactions on Programming Languages and Systems*, 5(3):449–477, July 1983.   281

Sar99.   João Saraiva. *Purely Functional Implementation of Attribute Grammars*. PhD thesis, Department of Computer Science, Utrecht University, The Netherlands, December 1999. 281, 286

SKS97.   João Saraiva, Matthijs Kuiper, and Doaitse Swierstra. Effective Function Cache Management for Incremental Attribute Evaluation. In Chris Clark, Tony Davie, and Kevin Hammond, editors, *9th Workshop on Implementation of Functional Languages*, pages 517–528, Scotland, September 1997. 288

SS99.   João Saraiva and Doaitse Swierstra. Data Structure Free Compilation. In Stefan Jähnichen, editor, *8th International Conference on Compiler Construction*, volume 1575 of *LNCS*, pages 1–16. Springer-Verlag, March 1999. 290

TC90.   Tim Teitelbaum and Richard Chapman. Higher-order attribute grammars and editing environments. In *ACM SIGPLAN'90 Conference on Principles of Programming Languages*, volume 25, pages 197–208. ACM, June 1990. 281, 282

vD92.   Leen van Dalen. Incremental evaluation through memoization. Master's thesis, Department of Computer Science, Utrecht University, The Netherlands, August 1992. 284

VSK89.   Harald Vogt, Doaitse Swierstra, and Matthijs Kuiper. Higher order attribute grammars. In *ACM SIGPLAN '89 Conference on Programming Language Design and Implementation*, volume 24, pages 131–145. ACM, July 1989. 281

Author Index

Lecture Notes in Computer Science

For information about Vols. 1–1707
please contact your bookseller or Springer-Verlag

Vol. 1740: R. Baumgart (Ed.): Secure Networking – CQRE [Secure] '99. Proceedings, 1999. IX, 261 pages. 1999.

Vol. 1741: A. Aggarwal, C. Pandu Rangan (Eds.), Algorithms and Computation. Proceedings, 1999. XIII, 448 pages. 1999.

Vol. 1742: P.S. Thiagarajan, R. Yap (Eds.), Advances in Computing Science – ASIAN'99. Proceedings, 1999. XI, 397 pages. 1999.

Vol. 1743: A. Moreira, S. Demeyer (Eds.), Object-Oriented Technology. Proceedings, 1999. XVII, 389 pages. 1999.

Vol. 1744: S. Staab, Extracting Degree Information from Texts. X; 187 pages. 1999. (Subseries LNAI).

Vol. 1745: P. Banerjee, V.K. Prasanna, B.P. Sinha (Eds.), High Performance Computing – HiPC'99. Proceedings, 1999. XXII, 412 pages. 1999.

Vol. 1746: M. Walker (Ed.), Cryptography and Coding. Proceedings, 1999. IX, 313 pages. 1999.

Vol. 1747: N. Foo (Ed.), Adavanced Topics in Artificial Intelligence. Proceedings, 1999. XV, 500 pages. 1999. (Subseries LNAI).

Vol. 1748: H.V. Leong, W.-C. Lee, B. Li, L. Yin (Eds.), Mobile Data Access. Proceedings, 1999. X, 245 pages. 1999.

Vol. 1749: L. C.-K. Hui, D.L. Lee (Eds.), Internet Applications. Proceedings, 1999. XX, 518 pages. 1999.

Vol. 1750: D.E. Knuth, MMIXware. VIII, 550 pages. 1999.

Vol. 1751: H. Imai, Y. Zheng (Eds.), Public Key Cryptography. Proceedings, 2000. XI, 485 pages. 2000.

Vol. 1752: S. Krakowiak, S. Shrivastava (Eds.), Advances in Distributed Systems. VIII, 509 pages. 2000.

Vol. 1753: E. Pontelli, V. Santos Costa (Eds.), Practical Aspects of Declarative Languages. Proceedings, 2000. X, 327 pages. 2000.

Vol. 1754: J. Väänänen (Ed.), Generalized Quantifiers and Computation. Proceedings, 1997. VII, 139 pages. 1999.

Vol. 1755: D. Bjørner, M. Broy, A.V. Zamulin (Eds.), Perspectives of System Informatics. Proceedings, 1999. XII, 540 pages. 2000.

Vol. 1757: N.R. Jennings, Y. Lespérance (Eds.), Intelligent Agents VI. Proceedings, 1999. XII, 380 pages. 2000. (Subseries LNAI).

Vol. 1758: H. Heys, C. Adams (Eds.), Selected Areas in Cryptography. Proceedings, 1999. VIII, 243 pages. 2000.

Vol. 1759: M.J. Zaki, C.-T. Ho (Eds.), Large-Scale Parallel Data Mining. VIII, 261 pages. 2000. (Subseries LNAI).

Vol. 1760: J.-J. Ch. Meyer, P.-Y. Schobbens (Eds.), Formal Models of Agents. Poceedings. VIII, 253 pages. 1999. (Subseries LNAI).

Vol. 1761: R. Caferra, G. Salzer (Eds.), Automated Deduction in Classical and Non-Classical Logics. Proceedings. VIII, 299 pages. 2000. (Subseries LNAI).

Vol. 1762: K.-D. Schewe, B. Thalheim (Eds.), Foundations of Information and Knowledge Systems. Proceedings, 2000. X, 305 pages. 2000.

Vol. 1763: J. Akiyama, M. Kano, M. Urabe (Eds.), Discrete and Computational Geometry. Proceedings, 1998. VIII, 333 pages. 2000.

Vol. 1764: H. Ehrig, G. Engels, H.-J. Kreowski, G. Rozenberg (Eds.), Theory and Application of Graph Transformations. Proceedings, 1998. IX, 490 pages. 2000.

Vol. 1765: T. Ishida, K. Isbister (Eds.), Digital Cities. IX, 444 pages. 2000.

Vol. 1767: G. Bongiovanni, G. Gambosi, R. Petreschi (Eds.), Algorithms and Complexity. Proceedings, 2000. VIII, 317 pages. 2000.

Vol. 1768: A. Pfitzmann (Ed.), Information Hiding. Proceedings, 1999. IX, 492 pages. 2000.

Vol. 1769: G. Haring, C. Lindemann, M. Reiser (Eds.), Performance Evaluation: Origins and Directions. X, 529 pages. 2000.

Vol. 1770: H. Reichel, S. Tison (Eds.), STACS 2000. Proceedings, 2000. XIV, 662 pages. 2000.

Vol. 1771: P. Lambrix, Part-Whole Reasoning in an Object-Centered Framework. XII, 195 pages. 2000. (Subseries LNAI).

Vol. 1772: M. Beetz, Concurrent Ractive Plans. XVI, 213 pages. 2000. (Subseries LNAI).

Vol. 1773: G. Saake, K. Schwarz, C. Türker (Eds.), Transactions and Database Dynamics. Proceedings, 1999. VIII, 247 pages. 2000.

Vol. 1774: J. Delgado, G.D. Stamoulis, A. Mullery, D. Prevedourou, K. Start (Eds.), Telecommunications and IT Convergence Towards Service E-volution. Proceedings, 2000. XIII, 350 pages. 2000.

Vol. 1776: G.H. Gonnet, D. Panario, A. Viola (Eds.), LATIN 2000: Theoretical Informatics. Proceedings, 2000. XIV, 484 pages. 2000.

Vol. 1777: C. Zaniolo, P.C. Lockemann, M.H. Scholl, T. Grust (Eds.), Advances in Database Technology – EDBT 2000. Proceedings, 2000. XII, 540 pages. 2000.

Vol. 1780: R. Conradi (Ed.), Software Process Technology. Proceedings, 2000. IX, 249 pages. 2000.

Vol. 1781: D.A. Watt (Ed.), Compiler Construction. Proceedings, 2000. X, 295 pages. 2000.

Vol. 1782: G. Smolka (Ed.), Programming Languages and Systems. Proceedings, 2000. XIII, 429 pages. 2000.

Vol. 1783: T. Maibaum (Ed.), Fundamental Approaches to Software Engineering. Proceedings, 2000. XIII, 375 pages. 2000.

Vol. 1784: J. Tiuryn (Ed.), Foundations of Software Science and Computation Structures. Proceedings, 2000. X, 391 pages. 2000.

Vol. 1785: S. Graf, M. Schwartzbach (Eds.), Tools and Algorithms for the Construction and Analysis of Systems. Proceedings, 2000. XIV, 552 pages. 2000.

Vol. 1786: B.H. Haverkort, H.C. Bohnenkamp, C.U. Smith (Eds.), Computer Performance Evaluation. Proceedings, 2000. XIV, 383 pages. 2000.

Vol. 1790: N. Lynch, B.H. Krogh (Eds.), Hybrid Systems: Computation and Control. Proceedings, 2000. XII, 465 pages. 2000.

Vol. 1794: H. Kirchner, C. Ringeissen (Eds.), Frontiers of Combining Systems. Proceedings, 2000. X, 291 pages. 2000. (Subseries LNAI).